S0-CMU-819

THE STORY OF A
RISING RACE

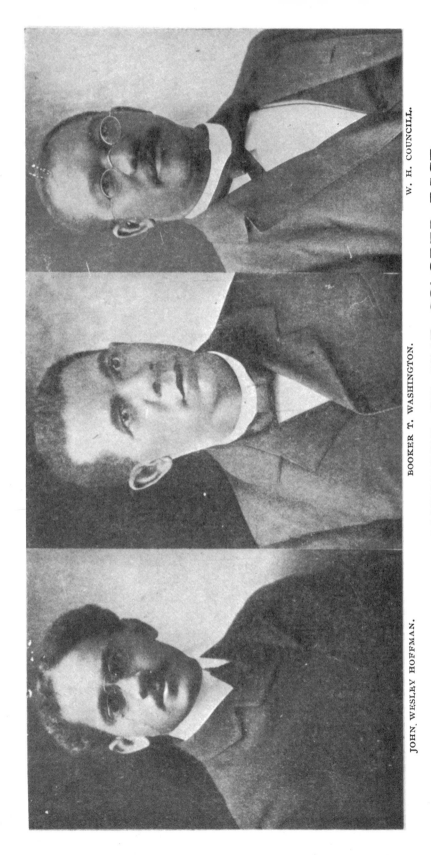

JOHN. WESLEY HOFFMAN.   BOOKER T. WASHINGTON.   W. H. COUNCILL.

SOME NOTED EDUCATORS OF THE COLORED RACE.

THE STORY OF A RISING RACE

By

J. J. Pipkin

EUGENE SHEDDEN FARLEY LIBRARY

1935

WILKES COLLEGE, WILKES

REMOVED FROM
E.S. FARLEY LIBRARY
WILKES UNIVERSITY
COLLECTION

The Black Heritage Library Collection

BOOKS FOR LIBRARIES PRESS

FREEPORT, NEW YORK

1971

E185.6
P66

First Published 1902
Reprinted 1971

Reprinted from a copy in the
Fisk University Library Negro Collection

INTERNATIONAL STANDARD BOOK NUMBER
0-8369-8901-5

LIBRARY OF CONGRESS CATALOG CARD NUMBER:
70-173609

PRINTED IN THE UNITED STATES OF AMERICA
BY
NEW WORLD BOOK MANUFACTURING CO., INC.
HALLANDALE, FLORIDA 33009

THE

STORY OF A RISING RACE

THE NEGRO IN REVELATION, IN HISTORY AND IN CITIZENSHIP

WHAT THE RACE HAS DONE AND IS DOING

IN

ARMS, ARTS, LETTERS, THE PULPIT, THE FORUM, THE SCHOOL, THE MARTS OF TRADE

AND

WITH THOSE MIGHTY WEAPONS IN THE BATTLE OF LIFE THE SHOVEL AND THE HOE

A MESSAGE TO ALL MEN THAT HE IS IN THE WAY TO SOLVE THE RACE PROBLEM FOR HIMSELF

BY

REV. J. J. PIPKIN

WITH INTRODUCTION BY

GEN. JOHN B. GORDON

Former Major-General Confederate Army, United States Senator from Georgia,
Ex-Commander United Confederate Veterans,
Author "War Reminiscences," Etc.

163617

Copyright, 1902, by N. D. Thompson Publishing Company

NOT A TERM OF REPROACH.

Supposing that this term (negro) was originally used as a phrase of contempt, is it not with us to elevate it? How often has it not happened that names originally given in reproach have been afterward adopted as a title of honor by those against whom they were used, as Methodists, Quakers, etc.? But as a proof that no unfavorable signification attached to the word when first employed, I may mention that long before the slave trade began travelers found the blacks on the coast of Africa preferring to be called Negroes. . . . And in all the pre-slave trade literature the word was spelled with a capital N. It was the slavery of the blacks that brought the term into disrepute and now that slavery is abolished, it should be restored to its original place and legitimate use.

—Dr. Edward W. Blyden.

It is not wise, to say the least, for intelligent Negroes in America to seek to drop the word "Negro." It is a good, strong and healthy word, and ought to live. It should be covered with glory: let Negroes do it.   *—George W. Williams.*

PREFACE.

IN RECENT years much has been written about the Negro —some of it fanciful, some ill-considered, some malicious, and some utterly fallacious, misleading, and dangerous.

It is a deplorable fact that notwithstanding community of interests and daily association, the white people of to-day do not fully understand the negro, and are, therefore, too ready to adopt opinions and entertain feelings that are dangerous to his peace and prejudicial to his prosperity; and we have sought to present a fund of information which will lead to a better understanding and make for the lasting good of both races. To the fair-minded white man and woman the facts set forth in this volume will be a revelation, and induce more liberal views as to the Negro's capabilities, his honorable ambition to improve, his enterprise, and his remarkable progress.

What the Negro needs is encouragement in every line of lawful endeavor, all the aid that can be extended to him by generous whites without inducing idleness, an open recognition of whatever manhood he evinces in the inevitable struggles of the poor and lowly, and the arousing of renewed determination to do his part in the uplifting of his people. If we can show him what the men and women of his race have achieved in the past, what they are achieving in the present under circumstances less favorable than those enjoyed by the dominant race, we awaken the feeling that he too ought to be up and doing, with the definite and noble aim of meeting the obligations that rest upon even the humblest citizen.

The author is a Southern man, born and bred, and he has been subjected to all the influences that are supposed to breed race prejudice; he is a Democrat of the old school; but in the name of white men North, South, East and West, he protests against everything that tends to degrade the Negro, and either rob him of self-respect or excite his animosity. We write as a follower of the Great Master who taught good-will to all men, as a minister of the gospel, as a patriotic American citizen. We endeavor to show:

That in the past the Negro has achieved much, in divers fields, to vindicate his claim to character and ability and mark him as a man;

That, considering the circumstances in which he found himself when freedom came to him, and the obstacles he has had to overcome, his progress has been remarkable;

That there are mighty agencies at work—the school, the church, and promising fields of labor—still further to promote his advancement; and

That for him also there is the possibility of a great future.

Our material has been gathered from many sources, and we are under obligations to so many who have aided and encouraged us that we forbear to mention names, lest we inadvertently omit some and so seem to do injustice. To all we tender acknowledgments and sincere thanks.

MART, TEXAS. J. J. PIPKIN.

INTRODUCTION.

IN ORDER that we may know what the Negro can do and become, it is well to consider what he has done and is doing, and what he has become and is becoming. He has been free in the Southern States now more than the third of a century. For two hundred and fifty years he worked under the limitations of slavery and became under humane white tutelage the most obedient, patient and useful servant ever known. But for forty years he has found himself outside the walls of bondage. He has been hemmed in by no barriers other than such as are placed about every man by the conditions of life. During nearly half a century he has been the master of his own fate. By a decision, fixed forever through the clash of contending armies as brave as ever met on a field of battle, his destiny was taken from the hands of his former master and placed in his own. Through a generation of the most eventful time in the history of the world, he has been under the necessity of making his own way in the presence of a strong, conquering race, which won its freedom and achieved its civilization in the struggle and conquest of thousands of years.

We are at a sufficient distance from the war to pause and take stock of the colored man's achievements. What use has he made of the liberty which came to him as an incident of the great struggle? What progress has he made in solving the problem of himself and his future? What data has he furnished, as to what he has done and learned and become, upon which a reliable opinion can be based concerning his future career? Has he moved forward or gone backward? Has he furnished grounds for hope, or reasons to despair of

him?   Where does he stand at the beginning of the Twentieth Century?

This book, to which I am asked to write the introduction,
is a record of the Negro's doings.   It is not a work of fine-
spun theories on the race question, but it is a summary of
the actual accomplishments and attainments of the colored
man.   We have a representation of what the Negro has
wrought with his hand and thought with his brain and
aspired to in his heart.   We have brought to our attention what the Negro has done as a farmer, as a mechanic,
as a doctor, as a lawyer, as a teacher, as a literary
man, as a poet, as a preacher and as a president and
organizer of great industrial colleges.   No such an all-
round survey of the Negro's work, has, according to my
knowledge, been so successfully made before.   The circulation of the book, both among the colored people and the
white people, will do good.   The doctrine here taught, by
the undoubted testimony of facts, is, that the Negro, in
common with members of every other race, must work out
his own destiny.   All that the white man can do for him is
to give him an opportunity and a fair chance.   The so-
called Negro problem has loomed so prominently in public
attention, largely because other than colored people have,
since the close of the war, been trying to work it out.   Those
who have religiously taken upon themselves the self-ap-
pointed task of working out the Negro problem, have seemingly proceeded on the assumption that the Negro had
neither head nor hands nor individual initiative.   If that
were the case, all the doctrinaires on earth could never work
out his problem.   There are thousands of Negroes all over
this country, but mostly in the South, who are neither problems to themselves, nor to their white neighbors.   They are
such as save their earnings, buy homes for their families,
and make themselves useful and upright citizens.

There are farmers whose only problem is that of seeing
how many bales of cotton they can make each acre of land

they cultivate produce. Their problem is with the weeds and the grass, which, by honest toil, they seek to keep from choking to death their young plants. Theorists have been trying to solve the colored problem at the points of their pens. This is the ink solution. The Negroes themselves have gone about solving it at the points of their scooter plows, which they are sticking deep down in their fields for bread and the comforts of life. This is the practical solution. There are blacksmiths who are helping to solve the Negro problem between the hammer and the anvil by turning iron into horseshoes so as to enable them to buy comfortable homes for their families, and besides lay up good-sized bank accounts. There are teachers who are aiding to solve the problem in the school-room by communicating knowledge to children so completely that most Negro boys and girls in the entire country can read and write. There are presidents of colleges, like Booker T. Washington, who have done so much toward the solution of the problem that the institutions over which they preside are regarded by all the people, white and black, as unmixed blessings to the country. The difficulties of the colored problem grow less and less by all the corn the Negro produces, by all the wagons he makes, by all the schools he teaches, and by every forward step he takes in becoming an industrious, productive and useful worker in the community. This book, which is a kind of cloth and paper edition of a Negro World's Exposition, comes at an opportune time. While we cannot see all that the colored man has produced brought together here in one place, as at the Columbian Dream City in Chicago in 1893, and at the great Exposition in Atlanta, we do have what he has done, described and set forth in such a way as to convince us that he has made remarkable progress since the close of the Civil War.

Between the eruption of Vesuvius, which destroyed Pompeii, and the awful fires of Mt. Pelee, which blotted the life out of St. Pierre, there are, as measured by time, 1,823 years; but, measured by the progress of the human race between the two awful events, the distance is infinitely greater. When death and silence came to Pompeii the sensation was local. It was days, perhaps weeks, before the news traveled even to Rome. But the flame that flashed thirty thousand souls into eternity in St. Pierre instantaneously lit up the world. The furious blast which in a moment consumed a city in a tropical sea was felt in every country on the planet. This illustrates the difference between the world as it is in our day and the world as it was in the beginning of the Christian era. Then the earth was large. The race was divided by mountains and seas and continents of distance, and still more widely divided by mountains of indifference and seas of ignorance and continents of indolence. Now the world is small. The race is united from St. Petersburg to Pekin and from Melbourne to Venice by a common commerce and by the invisible ties of a common sympathy. When the cry of distress is heard in the island of Martinique, shiploads of provisions and medicines start from every neighboring port to relieve it. Separate threads of peoples, not yet woven into that universal texture we call humanity, are destined, in the coming century, to be caught up by the great loom of Providence and drawn into the palpitating fabric. Africa has been called the "Dark Continent," because it is least known. Here is a country more than four thousand miles in length and four thousand in breadth, with an area of twelve million square miles and a population of nearly two hundred million, which, until 1884, when the so-called "scramble for Africa" began, has in the main been lying outside the current of human history. The work of incorporating Africa into the trend of the world's events has been slow. Da Gama doubled the Cape of Good Hope in the fifteenth century, but most of the work of exploration was done in the nineteenth century. Large areas of land in Africa are now coming under the control of the European powers. The English, the Germans, the Belgians, the Italians and the French are extending their spheres of influence, and it is only a question of a few generations when the whole continent will be covered and embraced by the general network of railroads and telegraph systems which bind into one neighborhood the other grand divisions of the globe.

It is a remarkable historical fact that Africa should become accessible to the movements of civilization just at this particular period in the march of events. The explorers have, in a general way, accomplished their work. Through their labors the wonders and wealth and area of the "Dark Continent" have been made known. Here are mountains filled with coal, and iron, and lead, and gold, and silver. Here is a soil rich and abundant enough to produce food sufficient to feed the teeming millions of the globe. Is it not wonderful that knowledge of the untold resources of Africa should come to the world just at a time when billion-dollar trusts are being formed—at a time when the captains of industry are learning to unite their uncounted millions to build railroads, bridges, electric light plants, iron foundries and cities, without *respect* to state or national boundaries—at a time when great capitalists of the West are negotiating with the governments of the East for all kinds of concessions? Is it not still more wonderful, that, just at this time, when Africa is opened up to civilization, and capital has been accumulated sufficient to develop it, there should be found in the United States 8,840,789 Negroes many of whom are already trained in the language, arts, institutions and laws of the most universally educated and enlightened country in the world? It is more like romance than cold historical truth. Africa is the natural home of the Negro. He can endure its climate and the trials incidental to changing it from a wilderness into a cultivated continent better than individuals of any other race. In America, where he has been living and advancing for two hundred and fifty years in slavery and forty years in freedom, he has acquired education and property and is acquiring self-control. Think of the call that is soon to come from Africa, not only for missionaries and preachers, but for teachers, farmers, mechanics, carpenters, civil engineers, locomotive engineers, railway conductors, merchants, doctors, lawyers and workers in every other trade useful and ornamental under heaven. Teachers, lawyers, judges and merchants are now going from the ranks of our white population to the Philippines, but the climate is hard on them and it is only by the strictest attention to the rules of health that even the robust can live there at all. But in Africa the colored man is on his native heath, and there he is destined to play an important part in the development of the country. The Negroes resent the idea of wholesale deportation to Africa, and they are right. They have helped to clear the forests and produce the wealth of this country, and they have the right won by three hundred years of service to live here. But under the leadership of such men as Bishop Turner they will migrate in constantly increasing numbers and become important factors in the redemption and development of the "Dark Continent." The men who make history are the men who become great. No one can attain to breadth and height and weight who is occupied in thought and heart with trifles. Elihu Burritt was a blacksmith, but he was at the same time a student, and while his arm wielded the hammer his mind was with Plato and Aristotle. Carey was a shoemaker, but, while he pulled thread through leather with his hands, his brain was busy with great schemes for the elevation of the Hindoos. The opening in Africa presents to the Negro a great opportunity to make history. Europe, the natural home of the Anglo-Saxons, is already made, and they have no natural new world to conquer. Africa is virgin territory. There, with few exceptions, things are as fresh as when the world was first turned over to Adam when he took up his abode in the Garden of Eden. In the process of making Africa the Negro should make himself, as the Dutch made themselves by changing Holland from a sea of water into a land of beauty. Through the conflicts of Marengo, Austerlitz, Jena and Auerstadt, a poor Corsican boy was turned into the great Napoleon. So the Negro race must find itself and its place in the world through what it accomplishes.

I. B. Gordon

ATLANTA, GA.

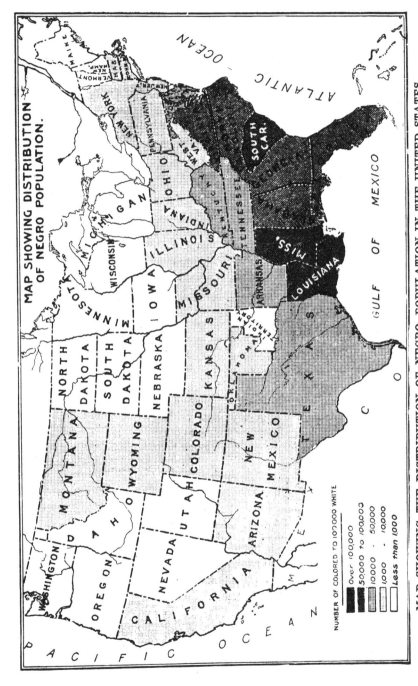

MAP SHOWING THE DISTRIBUTION OF NEGRO POPULATION IN THE UNITED STATES.

TABLE OF CONTENTS.

PAGE.

INTRODUCTION. By Gen. J. B. Gordon... vii

CHAPTER I.

The Negro in Revelation 33

CHAPTER II.

THE NEGRO AS A SOLDIER.

I. Some in Foreign Countries—II. In the United States—Capt. P. J. Bowen
—P. L. Carmouche—William Blackwell.. 39

CHAPTER III.

THE NEGRO IN POLITICS, JOURNALISM AND THE LECTURE FIELD.

The Bruces—Edmund H. Deas—Alonzo J. Rausier—James T. Rapier—Nick
Chiles—Rev. C. P. T. White—Colored Newspapers—Sojourner Truth—
Frederick Douglass.. 59

CHAPTER IV.

THE NEGRO IN LAW, MEDICINE AND DIVINITY.

Narcissa West—The African Zion Methodist Episcopal Church—Rev. John
Jasper—Bishops Francis Burns and John Wright Roberts—Rev. W. J.
Howard—John A. Whitted, D. D.—J. W. Kirby, D. D.—Henry M. Turner—
S. N. Vass, D. D.—Rev. E. P. Johnson—The African Methodist Episcopal
Church—Bishop Benjamin T. Tanner - Joseph E. Jones, D. D.—Miss Emma
B. Delaney—Bishop W. J. Gaines—Bishop Abraham Grant—The Colored
Methodist Episcopal Church—Rev. Garnett Russell Waller—A. R. Griggs,
D. D.—Rev. H. N. Bouey.. 81

CHAPTER V.

THE NEGRO IN LITERATURE AND THE FINE ARTS.

Phillis Wheatley—Paul Laurence Dunbar—James D. Corrothers—Charles W.
Chesnutt—Miss Inez C. Parker—Miss Effie Waller............................... 115

CHAPTER VI.

THE NEGRO IN BUSINESS.

I. Opening Address of the Hon. Allen D. Candler, Governor of Georgia—II.
The Meaning of Business—III. The Need of Negro Merchants—IV. Ne-
gro Business Men of Columbia, South Carolina—V. The Negro Grocer
—VI. A Negro Co-operative Foundry—Other Business Enterprises............ 133

TABLE OF CONTENTS.

CHAPTER VII.

THE NEGRO IN BUSINESS—(Continued).   PAGE.

Negro Business Men by States—Negro Business Men by Occupation—Investments in Business..163

CHAPTER VIII.

Thomas Jefferson and the Negro Julius Melbourn: A Remarkable Incident......201

CHAPTER IX.

AMONG THE SOUTHERN PEOPLE THE NEGRO FINDS HIS BEST FRIENDS.

Letter from President Cleveland—Letter from Clark Howell, Editor of the *Atlanta Constitution*, to the *New York World*—Booker T. Washington's Address at the Atlanta Exposition—Henry W. Grady on the Relations of the Southern People and the Negro—Grady Discusses the Race Problem and the Duty of North and South—Condition of the Negro, Past and Present—The Negro's Needs—The Negro and the Signs of Civilization—The Negro's Part in the South's Upbuilding—The Negro and His Relation to the South—The "Ancient Governor"..207

CHAPTER X.

INDUSTRIAL TRAINING AND NEGRO DEVELOPMENT.

I. Address by Booker T. Washington—II. Speech by Prof. W. H. Councill....265

CHAPTER XI.

TUSKEGEE NORMAL AND INDUSTRIAL INSTITUTE.

I. Character of the School and What It Seeks to Do—Summary of Work Done—Booker T. Washington Explains to a Northern Audience His Connection with the School and Notices the Relations of the Races in the South..291

CHAPTER XII.

THE COLLEGE-BRED NEGRO.

Scope of the Inquiry—Colleges by Groups—First Negro Graduate; Number of Negro Graduates, Etc.—Individual Experiences 317

CHAPTER XIII.

THE COLLEGE-BRED NEGRO—(Continued).

Occupations, Ownership of Property, Etc.—Assessed Valuation of Real Estate Some Opinions on the Higher Education of the Negro....................................349

CHAPTER XIV.

HISTORY OF SOME NEGRO UNIVERSITIES.

Shaw University—N. F. Roberts, D. D.—Albert W. Pegues, Ph. D.—Grace J. Thompson—Roger Williams University—National Baptist Publishing Board —Meharry Medical College—Charles Spencer Dinkins, D. D.——Mrs. Daisy Miller Harvey—John Hope—Joseph A. Booker, D. D.—Mrs. Maria T. Kenney—Howard University..387

TABLE OF CONTENTS.

CHAPTER XV.

PAGE.

SOME NOTABLE EDUCATORS AND THE SCHOOLS WITH WHICH THEY HAVE BEEN CONNECTED.

John Wesley Hoffman—J. D. Coleman—C. S. Brown, D. D.—Enos L. Scruggs, D. D.—Mrs. Rachel E. Reeves Robinson—Miss Judith L. Chambers— Joshua B. Simpson—John H. Jackson— Mrs. Hannah Howell Reddick— M. W. Reddick, A. M.—James R. L. Diggs —James Shelton Hathaway— Miss Mary Kimble—Charles L. Purce, D. D.—Eckstein Norton University —Edward L. Blackshear, B. A.—B. F. Allen, A. B., A. M.—W. H. Councill—William S. Scarborough—Prof. H. E. Archer....................................413

CHAPTER XVI.

MISCELLANEOUS MATTERS.

Booker T. Washington on the Negro and His Economic Value—Address of Booker T. Washington on Receiving the Honorary Degree of Master of Arts from Harvard University—Women Who Labor for the Social Advancement of the Race—Inventive Genius and Mechanical Skill—How Melbourn and Others Regarded Colonization in Liberia and What Time Has Disclosed as to That Scheme—High Tributes to the Manhood of Some Negro Slaves— Rev. Moses Dickson 447

Illustrations

PAGE.

Some Noted Educators of the Colored Race .... *Frontispiece*
Alexander Dumas 32
Toussaint L'Ouverture 40
Col. James Hunter Young 46
Capt. P. J. Bowen 53
Lieut. P. L. Carmouche 56
William Blackwell 57
Edmond H. Deas 61
Joseph E. Lee 64
Nick Chiles 67
Rev. C. P. T. White 69
Frederick Douglass 78
Dr. William T. Penn 84
McCants Stewart, A. M 85
Narcissa West 86
Rev. John Jasper 88
Rev. Joseph J. Clinton 89
Bishop Francis Burns 95
Bishop John Wright Roberts 95
Rev. W. J. Howard 96
John A. Whitted, D. D 97
J. W. Kirby, D. D 98
S. N. Vass, D. D 100
Rev. E. P. Johnson 101
Bishop Richard Allen 102
Bishop Morris Brown 102
Bishop Edward Waters 102
Bishop William Paul Quinn 102
Bishop Willis Nazery 102
Bishop D. Alexander Payne 102
Bishop Alexander W. Wayman 102
Bishop Jabez Pitt Campbell 102
Bishop James A. Shorter 102
Bishop Thomas M. D. Ward 102
Bishop John M. Brown 102

PAGE.

Bishop Henry M. Turner 102
Bishop William F. Dickerson 102
Bishop Richard H. Cain 102
Bishop Richard R. Disney 102
Bishop Wesley J. Gaines 102
Bishop B. W. Arnett 102
Bishop B. T. Tanner 102
Bishop Abraham Grant 102
J. E. Jones, D. D 105
Miss Emma B. Delaney 106
Bishop L. H. Holsey 109
Bishop Isaac Lane 109
Bishop J. A. Beebe 109
Bishop E. Cottrell 109
Bishop R. S. Williams 109
Rev. Garnett Russell Waller 111
A. R. Griggs, D. D 113
Rev. H. N. Bouey 114
Paul Laurence Dunbar 120
James D. Corrothers 121
Charles W. Chesnutt 123
Miss Inez C. Parker 125
Miss Effie Waller 131
William H. Moss 135
Capt. J. W. Warmsley 139
Theo. W. Jones 155
Prof. R. T. Greener 161
E. H. Morris 173
Prof. I. Garland Penn 181
Rev. W. W. Brown 185
Rev. E. W. Lampton 191
Mahlon Van Horn 197
E. M. Hewlett 209
J. C. Dancy 213
H. P. Cheatham 217
Bishop C. H. Phillips 221

ILLUSTRATIONS.

PAGE.

Gen. Robert Smalls 225
Mrs. Mary Church Terrell 229
Prof. Robert H. Terrell 235
John E. Bruce 251
Col. James H. Deveaux 259
John P. Green 273
John S. Durham 281
Phelps Hall, Tuskegee Institute ...290
The Faculty, Tuskegee Institute ..292
Dairy Class, Tuskegee Institute....293
Class in Chemistry, Tuskegee In-
   stitute............................... 295
Chapel, Tuskegee Institute 297
Nurse Training Class, Tuskegee
   Institute........................ 299
Booker T. Washington............... 303
Dean's Residence, Virginia Union
   University 315
Pickford Hall, Virginia Union Uni-
   versity 316
Athletic Field, Roger Williams
   University 321
Library, Roger Williams Univer-
   sity 326
Owen L. Smith 335
E. E. Cooper....................... 341
Judson W. Lyons 345
Dining Hall, Roger Williams Uni-
   versity 354
Bishop George W. Clinton...........361
Virginia Union University.............381
M. W. Gibbs........................ 386
John R. Lynch 389
N. F. Roberts, D. D................ 392
A. W. Pegues, Ph. D............... 393
Grace J. Thompson 394
President's House, Roger Williams
   University...........................396
Main Building, Roger Williams
   University 397
Hayward Hall, Roger Williams
   University 398
Mrs. Daisy Miller Harvey.............401
John Hope........................ 402
Joseph A. Booker, D. D............403

PAGE.

Mrs. Maria T. Kenney............... 404
Howard University 406
Wm. H. H. Hart 408
John Wesley Hoffman 412
C. S. Brown, D. D 418
Enos L. Scruggs, B. D........ 419
Mrs. Rachel E. R. Robinson....... 421
Miss Judith L. Chambers 421
Joshua B. Simpson 422
Mrs. Hannah Howell Reddick ...424
M. W. Reddick.................... 425
James R. L. Diggs 426
James S. Hathaway.................... 427
Miss Mary Kimble.................429
Charles L. Purce, D. D 430
Rev. C. H. Parrish................ 433
Edward L. Blackshear.... 434
Prairie View, Texas, State Normal
   and Industrial College.... 435
Prof. B. F. Allen 437
Prof. W. H. Councill 441
Prof. H. E. Archer 444
S. W. Bennett 446
Rev. N. B. Sterrett, D. D 446
W. J. Parker 446
William Ingliss 446
Thos. J. Jackson 446
Dr. Thos. E. Miller 446
Rev. J. L. Dart 446
W. D. Crum, M. D 446
E. A. Lawrence.................... 446
J. B. Parker 449
A. M. Custis, A. M. M. D 453
W. F. Powell 457
George W. Williams 461
Class in Domestic Science, Sum-
   ner High School, St. Louis, Mo..465
N. W. Cuner 469
Sumner High School, St. Louis,
   Mo 471
John M. Langston 473
H. A. Rucker..................... 477
Blanche K. Bruce 479
Rev. Moses Dickson 481

ALEXANDRE DUMAS,
The World-Famous Novelist.

CHAPTER I.

The Negro in Revelation.

TO TREAT of the Negro in revelation specifically, in a work of this kind, the inquiry concerning his origin and the part of the globe to which he was assigned in the distribution of the nations, need not extend beyond what the sacred writings teach us.

Tracing the families of man from the first pair, as noticed in Genesis, we find that before the flood they were not divided into races or separate nationalities. Even after that event, and when Noah and his sons went forth with the blessing of God to multiply and replenish the earth, the Lord said: "Behold, the people is one, and they all have one language."

Ham, one of the sons of Noah, is regarded by both Bible critics and historians as being the father of the black race— one of the three great races that peopled the earth; and we find in the 10th chapter of Genesis, verses 6 to 20, inclusive, the names of Ham's sons and some of their descendants and of the lands they occupied after "the people were scattered abroad upon the face of all the earth," as follows:

"And the sons of Ham: Cush, and Mizraim, and Phut, and Canaan; and the sons of Cush: Seba, and Havilah, and Sabtah, and Raamah, and Sabtechah; and the sons of Raamah: Sheba and Dedan. And Cush begat Nimrod; he began to be a mighty one in the earth. He was a mighty hunter before the Lord: wherefore it is said, Even as Nimrod the mighty hunter before the Lord. And the beginning of his kingdom was Babel, and Erech, and Accad, and Calneh, in the land of Shinar. Out of that land went forth Asshur, and builded Nineveh, and the city Rehoboth, and Calah, and Resen between Nineveh and Calah: the same is a great city. And Mizraim begat Ludim, and Anamim, and Lehabim, and Naphtuhim, and Pathrusim, and Casluhim (out of whom came Philistim), and Caphtorim. And Canaan begat Sidon his first-born, and Heth, and the Jebusite, and the Amorite, and the Girgasite, and the Hivite, and the Arkite, and the Sinite, and the Arvadite, and the Zemarite, and the Hamathite: and afterward were the families of the Canaanites spread abroad. And the border of the Canaanites was from Sidon, as thou comest to Gerar, unto Gaza; as thou goest, unto Sodom and Gomorrah, and Admah, and Zeboim, even unto Lasha. These are the sons of Ham, after their families, after their tongues, in their countries, and in their nations.''

Josephus' account of the distribution of the Hamitic families is as follows:

''The children of Ham possessed the land from Syria and Amanus, and the mountains of Libanus; seizing upon all that was on its sea-coasts, and as far as the ocean, and keeping it as their own. Some, indeed, of its names are utterly vanished away; others of them being changed, and another sound given them, are hardly to be discovered, yet a few there are which have kept their denominations entire. For of the four sons of Ham, time has not at all hurt the name of Chus; for the Ethiopians, over whom he reigned, are even at this day, both by themselves and by all men in Asia, called Chusites. The memory also of the Mesraites is preserved in their name; for all we who inhabit this country [of Judea] call Egypt Mestre, and the Egyptians Mestreans. Phut also was the founder of Libya, and called the inhabitants Phuthites, from himself; there is also a river in the country of the Moors which bears that name; whence it is that we may see the greatest part of the Grecian historiographers mention that river, and the adjoining country, by the appellation of Phut; but the name it has now has been by change given it from one of the sons of Mestraim, who was called Lzbzos. We will inform you presently what has been the occasion why it has been called Africa also. Canaan, the fourth son of Ham, inhabited the country now called Judea, and called from his own name Canaan. The children of these [four] were these: Sabas, who founded the Sabeans; Evilas, who founded the Evileans, who are called Getuli; Sabathes founded the Sabathens; they are now called by the Greeks Astaborans; Sabactas settled the Sabactans; and Ragmas the Ragmeans; and he had two sons, the one of which, Judadas, settled the Judadeans, a nation of the western Ethiopians, and left them his name; as did Sabas the Sabeans. But Nimrod, the son of Chus, stayed and tyrannized at Babylon. . . . Now all the children of Mesraim, being eight in number, possessed the country from Gaza to Egypt, though it retained the name of one only, the Philistim, for the Greeks called part of that country Palestine. As for the rest, Ludiem, and Enemim, and Labim, who alone inhabited in Libya, and called the country from himself; Nedim and Pethrosim, and Chesloim, and Cephthorim, we know nothing of them besides their names; for the Ethiopic war, which we shall describe hereafter, was the cause that those cities were overthrown. The sons of Canaan were these: Sidonius, who also built a city of the same name; it is called by the Greeks Sidon; Amathus inhabited in Amathine, which is even now called Amathe by the inhabitants, although the Macedonians named it Epiphamia, from one of his posterity; Arudeus possessed the island Aradus; Arucas possessed Acre which is in Libanus.''

Albert Leighton Rawson, in his Pronouncing Bible Dictionary, makes the matter of location more definite by giving the modern names of the various countries over which ''they spread abroad.'' He says: ''The sons and grandsons of Ham located in Egypt, Abyssinia, on the southwest coast of the Red Sea, in Arabia, Persia, Ethiopia, Shinar, Chaldea, West Africa, Marcotis, Libya, Memphis, Thebes, Pathros, Arabia Petræa, Damietta, Sidon and Tyre, Judea, Schechem, Arke, Sinnas, Island of Arvad, Sumrah, and Hamath.''

And again: ''Ham's descendants settled in Africa and sent many branches into Asia also. The locality of what we know specifically as the Negro race was the valleys of the Senegal, the Gambia, and the Niger, and the intermediate rivers of the coast, parts of Sudamia, and parts of Sennaar, Kordofan, and Darfur.

''There is no other ancient name so well preserved and located as that of Ham. It is identified with Jupiter Ammon, and also Zeus, because both words are derived from a root meaning hot, fervent, or sunburnt. For the last three thousand years the world has been mainly indebted for its advancement to the Semitic races; but before this period the descendants of Ham, in Egypt and Babylon, led the way as the pioneers in art, literature, and science. Mankind at the present day lies under infinite obligations to the genius and industry of those early ages, more especially for alphabetic writing, weaving cloth, architecture, astronomy, plastic art, sculpture, navigation and agriculture. The art of painting is also represented, and music indirectly, by drawings of instruments.''

It has been held by some that Ethiopia, the country extending from the neighborhood of Khartoum northward to Egypt, or perhaps the somewhat more extended region indicated by Rawson, was the original seat of the distinctively Negro race; but careful investigators conclude that he was confined to no particular locality during those ages when, as Rawson tells us, the Hamitic race was laying mankind ''under infinite obligations,'' and was to be found in East Africa, West Africa, North Africa, in the plains of India— perhaps in the whole southern portion of Asia and elsewhere on that continent and neighboring islands.

It is not our purpose to inquire minutely into this matter of the negro's location, and we notice the wide diffusion of this particular type of Ham's descendants simply to show their connection with the achievements in art, science, and literature which distinguished those countries long before modern civilization had its dawn, and incidentally to show that the Negro proved himself ages ago to be lacking in none of the qualities of mind and spirit which have characterized the great and progressive peoples. The Negro played his part in those early ages in the work of human progress; and it cannot be maintained with any show of reason that lapse of time, unfavorable conditions in the lands where they were once supreme, and hundreds of years of subjection to another race, have so enervated mind and darkened soul as to leave them without hope for the future.

Dr. Livingstone, writing of the Africans of modern days, as he saw them in their native land, says:

"In reference to the status of the Africans among the nations of the earth, we have seen nothing to justify the notion that they are of a different 'breed' or 'species' from the most civilized. The African is a man with every attribute of human kind. Centuries of barbarism have had the same deteriorating effects on Africans as Prichard describes them to have had on certain of the Irish who were driven, some generations back, to the hills of Ulster and Connaught; and these depressing influences have had such moral and physical effects on some tribes that ages probably will be required to undo what ages have done. Ethnologists reckon the African as by no means the lowest of the human family. He is nearly as strong physically as the European; and, as a race, is wonderfully persistent among the nations of the earth. Neither the diseases nor the ardent spirits which proved so fatal to North American Indians, South Sea Islanders, and Australians seem capable of annihilating the Negroes. Even when subjected to that system so destructive to human life, by which they are torn from their native soil, they spring up irrepressibly, and darken half the new continent."

Seventy years ago a writer for a popular encyclopædia wrote of the tribes in "Darkest Africa" as follows:

"The African tribes of this variety (the Negro or Ethiopic race) have in general elevated themselves so far above the simple state of nature as to have reduced the lower animals to subjection, constructed settled habitations, practiced a rude agriculture, and manufactured some articles of clothing or ornament. In political institutions they have made no advance, their governments being simple despotisms, without any regular organization. Their religion is merely the expression of the religious feeling in its lowest form of fetichism. Their languages are described as extremely rude and imperfect; almost destitute of construction, and incapable of expressing abstractions. They have no art of conveying thoughts or wants by writing, not even by the simplest symbolical characters.

"The Negro character, if inferior in intellectual vigor, is marked by a warmth of social affections, and a kindness and tenderness of feeling, which even the atrocities of foreign oppression have not been able to stifle. All travelers concur in describing the Negro as mild, amiable, simple, hospitable, unsuspecting and faithful. They are passionately fond of music, and they express their hopes and fears in extemporary effusions of song."

Compare the status of the Negroes in the United States today with that of these wild tribes, in matters of orderly society, business, learning and religion, and say whether the Negro has not the innate power to rise, under favorable conditions, to a high plane of civilization.

But the better argument for the sweeping away of false assumptions, and the refutation of specious reasoning, is the presentation of facts that directly and unequivocally contradict them. To those that follow, we could add a multitude of others, but each chapter will be found to contain enough to illustrate that feature of the general subject of which it treats. To cite all the instances that have a bearing, and name all the persons who are worthy of mention, would extend this work beyond all reasonable limits.

CHAPTER II.

The Negro as a Soldier.

I. SOME IN FOREIGN COUNTRIES.

THAT there were able and eminent military leaders among the Negroes of the earlier ages, as well as brave, disciplined and efficient soldiers, is borne out by the history of their wars of conquest and their struggles against invasion, as the race was enlarging its borders and making good its claim to the regions occupied; but it is sufficient for our purpose to notice particularly only some of whom modern history takes cognizance.

Illustrious among colored men abroad who have greatly distinguished themselves in arms is Gen. Alexandre de la Pailleterie Dumas, the Afro-French soldier. He was the son of a rich French colonist residing in Santo Domingo and a Negro woman of that country. He attained to eminence in the wars of the French Revolution and under Bonaparte, who called him "the Horatius Cocles of the Tyrol." In the Egyptian expedition he commanded Napoleon's cavalry.

A more modern example is Gen. Alfred Dodds, a mulatto, who is one of the most distinguished officers in the French army. He was recently (if he is not now) in command of the French forces in Tonquin, Farther India.

One of the most prominent of Negro slaves who have achieved distinction in spite of adverse fortune was Dominique François Toussaint L'Ouverture. He was born near Cape Français, Haiti, in 1743. Though in bondage, he won the esteem and confidence of his master by his intelligence and upright conduct, and received at the hands of this master, it is said, such instruction in reading, writing and arithmetic as fitted him for the ordinary business of life.

He was about forty-eight years old before anything occurred to bring him into prominence, but the remainder of his life (about twelve years) was crowded with remarkable incidents, during which he proved himself a general, a statesman, and a man of honor.

The space to which we are limited forbids going into details, but an abstract of events will serve to place him before the reader as a representative of high qualities which attract the attention of mankind, whether exhibited by white men or black, slave or free.

TOUSSAINT L'OUVERTURE.

When, in 1791, an insurrection against the French authorities broke out, he was asked to join the insurgents, but he refused to take any part until he had protected his master and his family in their flight and seen them safe on board a vessel bound for the United States. Afterwards, finding that the Spanish and English had combined against the French royalists, he joined the slave leader François, and the allied forces of the enemy were defeated and the French governor, Blauchelande, was reinstated in office. Toussaint and his associates now made a reasonable request of Blauchelande, that in return for the great services rendered him, he should grant them a measure of freedom; but this was spurned, and the blacks refused to disband. During the attempts to negotiate terms by which their bondage would be less galling, their general, François, had been maltreated by the French, and they became so inflamed that they fell upon the royalists, and, besides killing many, captured a large number, whom they were about to massacre, when Toussaint interfered and magnanimously saved their lives. He soon afterward became commander-in-chief, and the force which had formerly fought the French republicans was now allied with them, and during the next seven years Toussaint won numerous victories, and eventually the British general, Maitland, abandoned the island, having surrendered such posts as he held to Toussaint, whom he regarded as the real ruler, though his authority was not acknowledged till the last of the French commissioners claiming authority under Bonaparte was either driven from the island or compelled to yield. In 1799 he was undisputed master of the western part of the island; in 1801 he occupied the eastern part; and finally he threw off all pretense of allegiance to France, and promulgated a constitution which made him president for life, with power to name his successor. Bonaparte thereupon sent his brother-in-law, Leclerc, with a powerful army to subdue the island. A series of bloody conflicts ensued, in which Toussaint displayed heroic valor and generalship of a high order; but he was finally compelled to yield to the superior numbers, resources and skill of the French. He surrendered and was ostensibly pardoned (May 1, 1802), but a short time afterward he was arrested on a charge of conspiracy and sent to France. Here he was kept in prison and treated with such neglect and active cruelty as virtually made his death, which occurred next year, an assassination.

Greater than his genius as an organizer and a soldier was his magnanimous treatment of prisoners and his generous and statesmanlike exercise of the almost autocratic power that came into his hands. His treatment of his master and his family in the day when the prospect of liberty and power was opened up to him, and calamity threatened the master and his household, was worthy of the most enlightened mind of any race; and his efforts to have his soldiers return to the cultivation of their fields and devote their lives henceforth to honest industry in the pursuits of peace, mark him as having possessed some of the civic virtues of General Washington.

History has crowned L'Ouverture as one of earth's ablest soldiers and most enlightened statesmen. In concluding his sketch of Toussaint's career, Wendell Phillips used the following language:

"Now, blue-eyed Saxon, proud of your race, go back with me to the commencement of the century and select what statesman you please. Let him be either American or European, let him have a brain the result of six generations of culture, let him have the richest training of university routine, let him add to it the better education of practical life; crown his temples with the silver of seventy years, and show me the man of Saxon lineage for whom his most sanguine admirers will wreathe a laurel such as embittered foes have placed on the brow of the Negro, Toussaint L'Ouverture."

II. IN THE UNITED STATES.

George W. Williams, the colored historian, estimates that not less than three thousand Negro soldiers did service in the American army during the Revolution, including those from every northern colony enrolled in white regiments. Rhode Island first made her slaves freemen and then called on them to fight. A black regiment was raised there, of which Col. Christopher Green was made commander. Connecticut sent a black battalion into the field under command of Col. David Humphrey.

Two Virginia Negroes, Israel Titus and Samuel Jenkins, fought under Braddock and Washington in the French and Indian War.

Crispus Attucks led an attack on the British soldiers on the day of the Boston massacre, March 5, 1770, and was killed.

It has been said that one of the men killed when Maj. Pitcairn, commanding the British advance on Concord and

Lexington, April 19, 1775, ordered his troops to fire on the Americans, was a Negro bearing arms.

Peter Salem, a Negro, did service during the Revolution, and is said to have killed Maj. Pitcairn, at Bunker Hill. Other black men besides Salem fought there, of whom we have the names of Salem Poor, Titus Coburn, Alexander Ames, Barzillai Lew, and Cato Howe. After the war these men were pensioned.

Prince, a Negro soldier, was Col. Barton's chief assistant in capturing the British officer, Major-Gen. Prescott, at Newport, Rhode Island, during the Revolution.

Primus Babcock had, as late as 1818, an honorable discharge from the American army signed by Gen. Washington.

Lambo Latham and Jordan Freeman fell with Ledyard at the storming of. Fort Griswold. Freeman is said to have killed Maj. Montgomery, a British officer, who was leading an attack on Americans in a previous fight.

Hamet, one of Gen. Washington's Negroes, was drawing a pension as a Revolutionary soldier in 1839.

Oliver Cromwell served six years and nine months in Col. Israel Shreve's regiment of New Jersey troops under Washington's immediate command.

Charles Bowles became an American soldier when but sixteen years old, and served to the end of the Revolution.

Seymour Burr and Jeremy Jonah were Negro soldiers in a Connecticut regiment.

Deborah Gannett, a Negro woman, enlisted in the Fourth Massachusetts Infantry in disguise, under the name of Robert Shurtliff, 1782, and served a year and a half, for which the General Court paid her £34 in 1791–2.

Prince Richards, of East Bridgewater, Connecticut, was a pensioned Revolutionary soldier.

A Negro whose name is not known obtained the countersign by which Mad Anthony Wayne was enabled to take Stony Point, and guided and helped him to do so.

Jack Grove was a Negro steward on board an American vessel which the British captured. He insisted on retaking it, and at length prevailed upon the captain to make the attempt, which was successful.

There was in Massachusetts during those Revolutionary days one company of Negro men bearing a special designation, "The Bucks," which seems to have been a notable body of soldiers, as at the close of the war its services and standing were recognized by John Hancock presenting to it a beautiful banner.

In the settling of Kentucky some Negro men brought thither by their masters distinguished themselves as Indian fighters. The following incidents are found recorded in Thompson's "Young People's History of Kentucky:"

"Ben Stockton was a slave in the family of Major George Stockton, of Fleming county. He was a regular Negro, and though a slave, he was devoted to his master. He hated an Indian and loved to moralize over a dead one; getting into a towering rage and swearing magnificently when a horse was stolen; handled his rifle well, though somewhat foppishly, and hopped, danced, and showed his teeth when a prospect offered to chase 'the yaller varmints.' His master had confidence in his resolution and prudence, while he was a great favorite with all the hunters, and added much to their fun on dull expeditions. On one occasion, when a party of white men in pursuit of Indians who had stolen their horses called at Stockton's Station for reinforcements, Ben, among others, volunteered. They overtook the savages at Kirk's Springs, in Lewis county, and dismounted to fight; but as they advanced, they could see only eight or ten, who quickly disappeared over the mountain. Pressing on, they discovered on descending the mountain such indications as convinced them that the few they had seen were but decoys to lead them into an ambuscade at the base, and a retreat was ordered. Ben was told of it by a man near him; but he was so intent on getting a shot that he did not hear, and the order was repeated in a louder tone, whereupon he turned upon his monitor a reproving look,. grimaced and gesticulated ludicrously, and motioned to the man to be silent. He then set off rapidly down the mountain. His white comrade, unwilling to leave him, ran after him, and reached his side just as he leveled his gun at a big Indian standing tiptoe on a log and peering into the thick woods. At the crack of Ben's rifle the savage bounded into the air and fell. The others set up a fierce yell, and, as the fearless Negro said, 'skipped from tree to tree like grasshoppers.' He bawled out: 'Take dat to 'member Ben—de black white man!' and the two then beat a hasty retreat."

"In the family of Capt. James Estill, who established a station about fifteen miles south of Boonesborough, was a Negro slave, Monk, who was intelligent, bold as a lion, and as faithful to his pioneer friends as though he were a free white settler defending his own rights. About daylight, March 20, 1782, when all the men of the fort except four were absent on an Indian trail, a body of the savages came upon Miss Jennie Glass, who was outside, but near the station, milking—Monk being with her. They killed and scalped Miss Glass and captured Monk. When questioned as to the force inside the walls, the shrewd and self-possessed Negro represented it as much greater than it was and told of preparation for defense. The Indians were deceived, and after killing the cattle, they retreated across the river. When the battle of Little Mountain opened, two days afterward, Monk, who was still a prisoner with the Indians, cried out: 'Don't give way, Mas' Jim! There's only about twenty-five redskins, and you can whip 'em!' This was valuable and encouraging information to the whites. When the Indians began to advance on Lieutenant Miller, when he was sent to prevent a flank movement and guard the horse-holders, Monk called also to him to hold his ground and the white men would win. Instead of being instantly killed, as was to be apprehended, even though the savages

COL. JAMES HUNTER YOUNG.
Third North Carolina Volunteers.

might not understand his English, he made his escape before the fight closed and got back to his friends. On their return to the station, twenty-five miles, without sufficient horses for the wounded, he carried on his back, most of the way, James Berry, whose thigh was broken. He had learned to make gunpowder, and, obtaining saltpetre from Peyton's Cave, in Madison county, he frequently furnished this indispensable article to Estill's Station and Boonesborough. He has been described as being five feet five inches high and weighing two hundred pounds. He was a respected member of the Baptist Church, when whites and blacks worshiped together. He was held in high esteem by the settlers, and his young master, Wallace Estill, gave him his freedom and clothed and fed him as long as he lived thereafter—till about 1835.

"A year or two after the close of the Revolutionary War, a Mr. Woods was living near Crab Orchard, Kentucky, with his wife, one daughter (said to be ten years old), and a lame Negro man. Early one morning, her husband being away from home, Mrs. Woods, when a short distance from the house, discovered seven or eight Indians in ambush. She ran back into the house, so closely pursued that before she could fasten the door one of the savages forced his way in. The Negro instantly seized him. In the scuffle the Indian threw him, falling on top. The Negro held him in a strong grasp and called to the girl to take an axe which was in the room and kill him. This she did by two well-aimed blows; and the Negro then asked Mrs. Woods to let in another that he with the axe might dispatch him as he came, and so, one by one, kill them all. By this time, however, some men from the station near by, having discovered that the house was attacked, had come up and opened fire on the savages, by which one was killed and the others put to flight."

In the navy, especially, during the War of 1812, Negroes were engaged as fighting men. Commodore Chauncey said in 1813 that he had nearly fifty blacks on board his ship and that many of them were among his best men.   Commodore Perry spoke highly of their good conduct and of their bravery in his battles on the lakes.   The following extract from a letter written by Commodore Nathaniel Shaler, of the private armed schooner "Governor Tompkins," January 1, 1813, is of much interest.   Speaking of the result of a fight with a British frigate, he said:

"The name of one of the two of my poor fellows who was killed ought to be registered in the book of fame and remembered with reverence as long as bravery is considered a virtue. He was a black man, by the name of John Johnson. A twenty-four-pound shot struck him in the hip and tore away all the lower part of his body.   In this state the poor brave fellow lay on the deck and several times exclaimed to his shipmates: 'Fire away, my boys; no haul a color down!' The other was also a black man, by the name of John Davis, and he was struck in much the same way.   He fell near me and several times requested to be thrown overboard, saying he was only in the way of others."

General Andrew Jackson, when preparing for the defense of New Orleans, called upon the colored inhabitants of Louisiana to participate in the struggle with the British. His proclamation was dated September 21, 1814, and by the eighteenth of December a force was organized and equipped and an eloquent and commendatory address was read "To the men of color."

In the "Life and Opinions of Julius Melbourn," from which we have made copious extracts elsewhere, he has something to say in reply to an assertion that "the Negro is mild and yielding in his nature and destitute of the personal courage necessary for a soldier."   Referring to the black regiments who served during the Revolutionary War, he says: "Neither their skill, bravery, nor fidelity was ever questioned."   And then, alluding to the War of 1812, he remarks: "It will be conceded that almost the only martial glory acquired by Americans, excepting always the battle of New Orleans, was acquired by the American navy; and it will be conceded also that a great proportion of the fighting men of that navy were Negroes. The managers of the Park Theatre in New York, in testimony of the bravery of the lamented Captain Lawrence and his crew, manifested in the brilliant action with the British sloop-of-war 'Peacock,' invited him and them to a play in honor of the victory achieved on that occasion. The crew marched together into the pit, and nearly one-half of them were Negroes.''

During the Civil War about 200,000 colored soldiers were regularly enlisted for service in the Federal army and navy, and President Lincoln commissioned eight colored surgeons for duty in field and hospital. Even a cursory glance at the history of that time shows that the black troops repeatedly received from officers high in command warm commendation for their general conduct and their bearing in battle, and that a number of individuals particularly distinguished themselves. Charles E. Nash, afterward a member of Congress, had received some education in New Orleans schools. In 1863 he enlisted in the Eighty-third Regiment United States Chasseurs d' Afrique, and became acting sergeant-major of that command; at the storming of Fort Blakeley he lost a leg and was honorably discharged.

William Hannibal Thomas, the author of ''The American Negro: What he was, what he is, and what he may become,'' was a soldier during the Civil War, and lost an arm during that service. He may properly be classed among those who have borne arms for their country, though he was afterward author, teacher, lawyer and legislator. At one time he was active and efficient in promoting the building of churches and establishing schools throughout the South, laboring for the moral and intellectual as well as for the material advancement of the freedmen.

Robert Smalls was born a slave at Beaufort, South Carolina, but educated himself to some extent; having been employed

4

as a rigger of water-craft, and having led a sea-faring life for awhile, he was connected in 1861 with a transport steamer, "The Planter," and this he took over the Charleston bar and delivered to the commander of the United States blockading squadron, May, 1862; was appointed a pilot in the United States Navy, and served as such on the monitor "Keokuk" in the attack on Fort Sumter; was promoted to captain for gallant and meritorious conduct, December 1, 1863, and placed in command of "The Planter," which he held until the vessel was put out of commission, 1866. He was a member of the South Carolina Constitutional Convention, 1868; elected same year to the Legislature; to the State Senate, 1870 and 1872, and was a member of the Forty-fourth and Forty-fifth Congresses.

When the Spanish War broke out (1898), the colored men North and South were not only willing but eager to volunteer; but as there were no colored organizations they were not at first accepted. When Congress authorized the raising of ten immune colored regiments, the plan to put whites in command above the grade of second-lieutenant prevented colored men from enlisting as they would otherwise have done. But four immune regiments were organized—the Seventh, Eighth, Ninth and Tenth, and so officered.

There are four regiments of colored regulars in the United States Army, the Twenty-fourth and Twenty-fifth Infantry, and the Ninth and Tenth Cavalry. These were first mustered into the regular service in 1866, having fought during the last years of the Civil War. These regiments composed part of Shafter's force in the Santiago campaign.

The following colored volunteer troops were raised by the states named: Third Alabama Infantry; Sixth Virginia Infantry; Eighth Illinois Infantry; Companies A and B, Indiana Infantry; Thirty-third Kansas Infantry; Ninth Ohio Infantry (a battalion). The Eighth Illinois was officered by colored men throughout, J. R. Marshall commanding. This regiment did garrison duty in Santiago province for some time after the war, and Marshall was for awhile military governor of San Luis. The Ninth Ohio Battalion was commanded by Brevet-Major Charles E. Young, a graduate of West Point. Lieut. John H. Alexander, who did service in Cuba, was also a West Point graduate.

Gov. Russell, of North Carolina, called out a colored regiment, the Third Infantry, officered by colored men throughout, Col. James H. Young commanding, but it was not mustered into the service.

Company L, Sixth Massachusetts Infantry, was a colored company, the only one serving in a white regiment.

John L. Waller, a Negro man who had been United States Consul to Madagascar, was a captain in the Kansas regiment.

About one hundred Negro second-lieutenants were commissioned in the volunteer force during the Spanish-American War. There were two Negro paymasters, John R. Lynch, of Mississippi, fourth auditor of the United States Treasury, and Richard R. Wright, of Georgia, president of the State Agricultural and Mechanical College for Colored Persons. Two Negro chaplains were commissioned, the Rev. C. T. Walker, of Georgia, and the Rev. Richard Carroll, of South Carolina.

The fighting of the black troops in Cuba won the confidence of the white soldiers and their officers, and was highly commended. Col. Roosevelt said that the conduct of the Ninth and Tenth Cavalry reflected honor on the whole American people, especially on their own race. Several colored non-commissioned officers were promoted for gallant conduct in Cuba.

It will be noticed in the history of Shaw University, given elsewhere in this work, that some of the alumni of that institution became military officers.

Cuba, in her struggles for freedom, had among her own people two splendid leaders who were mulattoes, Antonio and Jose Maceo.

Five Southern States, Alabama, Georgia, North Carolina, South Carolina and Virginia, comprehend colored troops in their militia.

The following colored troops have done service in the Philippines: Twenty-fourth and Twenty-fifth Regular Infantry, parts of the Ninth and Tenth Regular Cavalry, and the Forty-eighth and Forty-ninth Volunteer Infantry—all officered by colored men.

Apropos of the conduct of the colored soldiers in Cuba, a Red Cross nurse in the hospital at Siboney, during the battle at Santiago, says, in the course of some reminiscences of that time, after speaking in detail of the work of surgeons and nurses:

"And so it went on through the long night—the patient suffering of the sick men, the heroism of the wounded—all fearing to give any trouble, desiring not to do so, and grateful for the smallest attention. The courage that faces death on the battlefield, or calmly waits for it in the hospital, is not a courage of race or color. Two of the bravest men I ever saw were here, almost side by side, on the little porch, Capt. Mills and Private Clark, one white the other black. They were wounded almost at the same time and in the same way. The patient suffering and heroism of the black soldier was fully equal to the Anglo-Saxon's. It was quite the same—the gentleness and appreciation. They were a study —these men so wide apart in life, but here so strangely close and alike on the common ground of duty and sacrifice. They received precisely the same care. Each was fed like a child, for with their bandaged eyes they were as helpless as blind men. When the ice-pads were renewed on Capt. Mills' eyes the same change was made on Private Clark's eyes. There was no difference in the food or beds. Neither ever uttered a word of complaint. . . . When told who his nearest neighbor was, Capt. Mills expressed great sympathy for Private Clark, and paid a high tribute to the bravery of the colored troops and their faithful performance of duty."

CAPT. P. J. BOWEN.

The subject of the accompanying sketch is well known among the citizens of Providence, Rhode Island, having been prominently connected there, both as a military officer and as a business man, for more than twenty years. When but a youth he engaged as an apprentice in a printing office located in the old Union Depot. He continued in his chosen

CAPT. P. J. BOWEN.
Soldier, Author, a Successful Business Man.

profession, being employed in some of the largest establishments in the city. Later he engaged in business for himself, under the style and name of the Excelsior Print Company.

In 1894, after having risen from private to lieutenant in the First Separate Company, R. I. M., he was chosen captain of the Second Separate Company, and held that office until the latter consolidated with the First Separate Company, in 1895.

Captain Bowen has also the distinction of being the author of a military drama, entitled "Fort Wagner," which was first produced in 1897.

P. L. CARMOUCHE.

Pierre Lacroix Carmouche was the first Afro-American to offer his services to President McKinley for the Spanish War, with those of two hundred and fifty other colored men whom he had induced to join him.

He went to Cuba as first lieutenant of Company L, Ninth United States Volunteer Infantry, and took an honorable part in the Santiago campaign.

He was born in the town of Donaldson, Ascension Parish, Louisiana, November 20, 1862. His father, Pierre Carmouche, was a man of marked integrity, whose word was regarded by his neighbors, black and white, as good as a bond. His mother, still living in 1902, was active and intelligent, notwithstanding advanced age.

In early boyhood, Pierre, the son, was sent to school, and it was not long before he acquired familiarity with the English tongue, which was not spoken in his father's family before he began to attend school. He learned fast, and his ambition to be well informed helped him to obtain a common school education under very adverse circumstances, for when he was just about fitted to enter a normal school, preparatory to continuing his studies in college, as has been the misfortune of many an ambitious boy before, his beloved father took sick, became an invalid, lingered for months and months, and then died, leaving four small children and their mother to care for themselves. The loss of his father caused young Carmouche to leave school. He became apprentice to a barber, learned the trade easily, worked at it for awhile, and then having an offer, accepted an apprenticeship in a dental office, where he was becoming very useful to his preceptor as an assistant, when the death of his employer put an end to the pursuit in which he was rapidly achieving proficiency.

Undaunted by these discouragements, young Carmouche, now only about seventeen years of age, sought and obtained apprenticeship in a wheelwright, blacksmith and farrier's shop. At this trade he worked faithfully, until he became master of it. He finally owned and operated the very shop in which he learned the trade, commanding the trade patronage of most of the livery stables, planters and business men of Donaldsonville and vicinity. In the municipal election of 1886, he was elected assessor for the town of Donaldsonville, and succeeded himself in 1887. About this time the Knights of Labor sentiment was spreading over the country, and he took a leading part in organizing a local branch of the order in Donaldsonville. The membership of this branch was over twelve hundred strong, and the organization in 1888 nominated him as its candidate for election as representative to the State Legislature for Ascension Parish. He has been reared a Roman Catholic, but is friendly to all denominations. He was repeatedly elected secretary of the Board of Trustees of St. Peter's Methodist-Episcopal Church at Donaldsonville, and the present beautiful edifice now replacing the old St. Peter building, in that lovely little city on the Mississippi river, eighty-two miles above New Orleans, is in part a monument to the energy and interest he displayed in assisting the Methodists of his place in their noble Christian efforts. If there was ever any doubt of the patriotism of Pierre L. Carmouche in the Parish of Ascension, Louisiana, there is certainly no such doubt there now. In a state where colored military organizations are not allowed, much less encouraged, this young man went about the parish at his own expense, after the blowing up of the Maine in the harbor of Havana on the 15th of February, 1898, and appealed to the colored people to prepare to defend the dignity of the flag of the United States. He did not rest until he was able to make to the President of the United States, through the Secretary of War, the following patriotic offer:

LIEUT. P. L. CARMOUCHE.

DONALDSONVILLE, LOUISIANA, February 26, 1898.
R. G. ALGER, Secretary of War, Washington, D. C.

Dear Sir:—After carefully considering the condition of the United States and the possibility of a declaration of war between the United States and Spain, I deem it advisable to offer my services and that of two hundred and fifty colored Americans, on short notice, in the defense of our country, at home or abroad.   Yours loyally,

P. L. CARMOUCHE.

WILLIAM BLACKWELL.

Henry W. Grady, of Georgia, and others, quoted elsewhere in this work, have alluded to the singular fidelity of the Negro

WILLIAM BLACKWELL.

during the Civil War, when fathers, sons and brothers were in the tented field and powerless to protect the women and children at home. The same spirit of devotion and loyalty was manifested in many instances by Negro men who fol-

lowed the fortunes of the Confederate Army, in the service of
their masters.   One instance may be recorded:

William, a young Negro belonging to the Blackwell family
in Union county, Kentucky, accompanied Lieut. Thomas C.
Blackwell, Company C, Fourth Kentucky Infantry, when he
entered the Confederate service in 1861, and stayed with him
and his company through all the vicissitudes of war—never
manifesting any disposition to escape northward, though
there were repeated opportunities to do so, or to become a
free man by abandoning his Confederate friends and going
over to the Federal troops.   Even after emancipation was
proclaimed he seemed to feel that it would be an act of deser-
tion if he should abandon his young master and the company of which he was in effect a member.

He enjoyed the confidence and respect of all who knew
him; and when the war closed he came back to Kentucky
with Lieutenant Blackwell and those of his men who had
survived, and in 1865 began life on his own responsibility
among the people who had known him as a slave.

The portrait accompanying this sketch was made from a
photograph taken in Uniontown soon after he got home, and
preserved by one who knew him during his four years' service in the Confederate Army.

CHAPTER III.

The Negro in Politics, Journalism, and the Lecture Field.

THE BRUCES.

AMONG the first of his race in America to hold high official position, State and National, was Blanche K. Bruce. He was born a slave in Prince Edward county, Virginia, March 1, 1841, and remained in slavery until freed by the war, though he had the unusual experience of being taught in his master's house. After the war he taught in Hannibal, Missouri; studied at Oberlin College and privately; removed to Mississippi in 1869 and became a planter; served as sheriff of Bolivar county in that State, 1871–74; was, meanwhile, 1872–73, superintendent of education for his county; was United States senator, 1875–1881, and register of the United States Treasury, 1881–85. Beginning with 1868 he was a member of every National Republican Convention that met in many years.

At Harvard University's senior class election on the 16th of December, 1901, the contestants for the position of orator were R. E. Fitzpatrick, of Boston, an Irishman, one of the brightest and most promising young speakers in Harvard, and Roscoe Conkling Bruce, son of the late Senator Bruce. The young Negro man won the oratorical honor by a vote of 269 to 100. Bruce debated against Yale in 1899 and 1901, and was one of the most popular young men of his class.

EDMUND H. DEAS.

Perhaps there is no one of his race better known or more highly respected in South Carolina than the subject of this sketch, of late resident in Washington, D. C., and in 1901 elected chairman of the Republican State Committee of his native State.

Like most men of note, he came of humble parentage, and after freedom came to his people he had a hard struggle against poverty; but this circumstance contributed no little in the way of preparing him to be the Moses of his people. We do not claim that he was born a politician; nevertheless, it is true that all the characteristics of a successful politician and statesman were found in him well developed by the time he reached his teens.   He may be called a master along this particular line, having served a regular apprenticeship in politics.   Beginning in the year 1874 as precinct chairman, in 1878 he was elected chairman of his congressional district, which position he held eight years, with credit to himself and satisfaction to his party.   Twenty-two years ago he was made a member of the State Executive Committee, and is still serving his party with signal ability in that capacity, being now (1901) its honored head.   In 1880 he was elected county chairman, which position he still holds by the unanimous suffrage of his constituents.   During all these years he has been the most active and aggressive Republican in the State.

His labors have not been confined to these honorary positions, but he has filled several offices of trust and remuneration, such as supervisor, deputy marshal, deputy treasurer of his county, examiner in pension office, Washington, D. C., and deputy collector of internal revenue, which position he has held from 1884 to the present time, with an interruption of two years during Cleveland's administration.

He has been voted for several times for presidential elector and for Congress; has been a member of five national conventions and three times a member of the notification committee.

Though he first saw the light of day in Georgetown, South Carolina, June 10, 1855, no county or State can claim him: he belongs to and lives for the the uplifting of the Negro everywhere.

EDMUND H. DEAS,

In addition to those noticed more at length under the head of Politics, Journalism, etc., we mention briefly the following persons who have distinguished themselves in some one of these lines:

The Rev. N. B. Wood is a historian, newspaper writer and lecturer, as well as a preacher.

John G. Mitchell is the editor of the *Richmond Planet*.

H. T. Keating, A. M., an educator, is editor of the *A. M. E. Review*, Philadelphia, Pennsylvania.

E. E. Cooper is the editor of *The Colored American*, Washington, D. C.

Dr. I. B. Scott is the editor of the *Southwestern Christian Advocate*, in New Orleans, Louisiana.

W. L. Martin, a graduate of Oberlin, has been a member of the Illinois Legislature.

H. A. Rucker is collector of internal revenue in one of the Georgia districts.

Mississippi has had one Negro lieutenant-governor—Alexander Davis; South Carolina, two—Alonzo J. Rausier and Richard H. Gleaves; and Louisiana, three—Oscar J. Dunn, P. B. S. Pinchback, and C. C. Antoine.

J. Milton Turner, of Missouri, John H. Smith, of North Carolina, and Henry W. Garnett, of New York, have been ministers resident and consuls-general to Liberia.

E. D. Bassett, of Pennsylvania, and John M. Langston, of the District of Columbia, have been ministers resident and consuls-general to Hayti.

Hiram R. Revels, preacher, teacher, lecturer, church officer, active in organizing colored troops during the war, was afterward United States senator from Mississippi, beginning his service in that body February 25, 1870.

Richard H. Cain was a missionary from Brooklyn to the freedmen of South Carolina; member of the South Carolina Constitutional Convention; member of the State Senate; editor of a newspaper; and member of Forty-third and Forty-fifth Congresses.

Robert C. De Large was an agent of the Freedman's Bureau in South Carolina; member of the Constitutional Convention; member of the Legislature for three terms; sinking fund commissioner; state land commissioner; and member of the Forty-second Congress.

Jere Haralson was born a slave in Georgia; when the war closed he was nineteen years old and wholly uneducated, but by industry and application he acquired the rudiments of learning; was a member of the Alabama Legislature in 1870; member of the State Senate, 1872; and member of the Forty-fourth and Forty-fifth Congresses.

John T. Walls, of Virginia, who had received a common school education, was a member of the State Constitutional Convention, 1868; member of the House of Representatives, same year; of the State Senate, 1869–1872; and was twice a member of Congress.

John R. Lynch was born a slave in Louisiana in 1847; had night-school instruction in Natchez during Federal occupation, and afterward by personal effort became a fair English scholar; was justice of the peace under Governor Ames; member of the Mississippi Legislature two terms, the last of which he was Speaker of the House; and was a member of the Forty-third and Forty-fourth Congresses.

Benjamin S. Turner was born a slave in North Carolina in 1825; was carried to Alabama in 1830; had no teaching, but became a fair scholar by diligent application to study during business hours; was elected tax-collector of Dallas county in 1867; councilman of the city of Selma, 1869; and was a member of the Forty-second Congress.

Robert B. Elliott was a graduate of Eton College, England. He studied law and became a practitioner in South Carolina; was a member of the Constitutional Convention of that State, 1868; member of the Legislature; assistant adjutant-general of South Carolina; member of the Forty-second and Forty-third Congresses; and afterward sheriff of his county.

Joseph H. Rainey was born of slave parents, but became a
fair scholar by unaided application; escaped from service in
building fortifications at Charleston and went to the West
Indies; after the war he returned and was a member of the
Constitutional Convention of South Carolina, 1868; a mem-

HON. JOSEPH E. LEE.
Collector Internal Revenue, Jacksonville, Florida.

ber of the State Senate, 1870; and a member of the Forty-
first, Forty-second, Forty-third, Forty-fourth and Forty-fifth
Congresses.

At the Cathedral in Baltimore, June 21, 1902, the Rev.
J. Harry Dorsey was ordained to the Roman Catholic priest-

hood by Cardinal Gibbons. He was the second colored man ever so ordained in this country; and to receive holy orders at his age (twenty-eight) indicates superior character, ability, and scholarship. The first one of his race ordained to the Catholic priesthood was the Rev. C. R. Uncles, a member of the Josephite Order, who received holy orders December 13, 1891. Father Totten, a colored priest who died in Chicago a few years ago, was ordained abroad.

The Hon. Judson W. Lyons, register of the United States Treasury, is a native of the State of Georgia, where he was born in Burke county about forty years ago.

He received his education in the common schools, which was supplemented and enlarged by the higher training at the Augusta Institute, now the Baptist College of Atlanta.

He taught country schools during the summers in South Carolina and Georgia, while studying at the institute.

In 1880 he was actively engaged in politics and in that year was sent as a delegate to the Republican National Convention, which met at Chicago, where he enjoyed the unique distinction of being its youngest member, being only twenty years of age. He was subsequently appointed gauger for Augusta and Savannah, and later served in the deputy collector's department.

He entered the Howard University Law School at Washington, and was graduated in the class of '84. In November of the same year he was admitted to the Augusta bar, where he continued the practice of his profession until 1898, when President McKinley appointed him register of the United States Treasury Department.

Mr. Lyons' career at the bar has been highly honorable and creditable. He has appeared before all the courts of Georgia, from the inferior to the highest courts. He has a wide and intimate knowledge of the common law of the country, and enjoys the respect and confidence of some of the leading lawyers of his State.

In 1896 he was elected national committeeman for Georgia,

and re-elected at the Philadelphia Convention in 1900. On the rostrum his quality of oratory is didactic rather than imaginative. He prefers the statement of facts to that of meaningless rhetoric, and is very effective as a public speaker.

His addresses are frequently quoted in the debates of Congress. He has administered the affairs of the great office of register of the United States Treasury which he has held for the last four years with great ability, and to the entire satisfaction of the Secretary of the Treasury and the business men of the country generally.

ALONZO J. RAUSIER.

Alonzo J. Rausier, a self-educated man, was a member of the Constitutional Convention of South Carolina, 1868; a member of the House of Representatives, 1869; was for some years chairman of the Republican Central Committee of South Carolina; elector of the Grant and Colfax ticket, 1868; elected lieutenant-governor, 1870; was president of the Southern States Convention at Columbia, 1871; was a vice-president of the National Republican Convention at Philadelphia, 1872; and was a member of the Forty-third Congress.

JAMES T. RAPIER.

James T. Rapier, born in Alabama, was educated in Canada; being a citizen of Alabama after the war, he was appointed a notary public in 1866; was a member of the first Republican convention held in Alabama, and one of the committee to draft the party platform; was a member of the Constitutional Convention of 1867; was nominated for secretary of state in 1870; was made collector of internal revenue, second Alabama district, 1871; was appointed by the governor to be state commissioner to the Vienna Exposition of 1873; and was a member of the Forty-third Congress.

NICK CHILES.

Nick Chiles, the business manager and owner of the *Topeka Plaindealer*, was born in Abbeville county, South

NICK CHILES.

Business Manager of *The Topeka Plaindealer*, who went to the relief of Mrs. Nation when deserted by the law and order people.

Carolina, of slave parents. He went to Kansas in 1886, with only five dollars in his pocket. He, however, had an abund-

ance of self-confidence and energy, with a meager education
and an inherent ability to make money; he applied himself
diligently to everything that came to hand, and has succeeded, in the face of the usual difficulties, in acquiring a reasonable amount of wealth. He is at present the owner of
three large buildings on East Seventh street in Topeka,
and also has interest in several pieces of farm land scattered over the State. He began in 1899 the publication of
the *Topeka Plaindealer*, devoted to the interest of the colored people. This paper has steadily grown in favor with
the public and now ranks as one of the strongest papers published by colored men in the United States. It has among
its readers people of both races. He gives employment to a
number of colored girls and boys, who are learning the printing and binding business at his office. In this office is
printed the official business for the colored Masons, Odd Fellows, Knights of Pythias, and several of the church minutes
are printed here. The plant of the *Plaindealer* is valued at
$2,000, and is one of the best equipped Negro offices in the
West. Mr. Chiles also owns and operates one of the best
equipped hotels in the West. In spite of intense opposition
he has successfully operated all his various business enterprises and is gradually forging to the front. When Mrs. Nation began her crusade against the joints of Topeka and the so-
called Law and Order people organized under the influence of
an aroused public sentiment, Mr. Chiles manifested a deep interest in her work. As a result of the crusade, Mrs. Nation
was arrested for destroying private property and placed in the
county jail, and there she was deserted by her so-called
friends. She called upon Nick Chiles to come forward and
furnish her bond, which he did. Mrs. Nation being a
Christian woman and desiring to promote the best interest
of the community, and also to manifest her appreciation
of the kindly interest of Mr. Chiles, invited him to associate himself with her in the publication of *The Smasher's
Mail.*

REV. C. P. T. WHITE.

In the State of South Carolina alone more than thirty colored newspapers are published. One of the strongest forces

REV. C. P. T. WHITE.
Editor of *The Messenger*, Rock Hill, South Carolina.

in this galaxy of opinion-moulders is Mr. C. P. T. White, editor of the *Rock Hill Messenger*, published at Rock Hill,

South Carolina. Mr. White is well known, not only as an editor, but as a minister of the gospel, as a politician of no mean ability, and as an orator of eloquence and power. To read his history is to read that of thousands of young men who have grown up since emancipation. He was born in Chester county, South Carolina, June 20, 1866, the fifth son of Mr. and Mrs. David White.

He received his primary training in the country school and entered Brainard Institute, Chester, South Carolina, in the fall of 1883. He received his higher training at Shaw University, Raleigh, North Carolina. Before graduation he accepted a professorship in the Friendship Institute, Rock Hill, South Carolina, in the fall of 1892, but he resigned in 1894 to accept the principalship of the Fort Mill Graded School. He began the publication of the *Messenger* January 10, 1896, which has continued ever since. In 1898 he was appointed notary public by Governor Ellerbee. He was elected secretary of the fifth congressional district of South Carolina in 1900, which position he now holds.

Fire destroyed the *Messenger* plant in April, 1898, completely, which was a total loss. He married Miss Lizzie Moore, of Charlotte, North Carolina, June 6, 1894, and one little boy has come to bring sunshine and happiness to the family.

The success of Mr. White is an example of what brain and pluck can accomplish. While still a young man, he has the respect and confidence of all who know him.

It was reported at one of the Annual Conferences held to discuss the various important questions touching the race in this country, as previously alluded to, that there are now in the United States one hundred and fifty-three periodicals, published by Negroes in the interest of their people, as follows:

MAGAZINES.—*A. M. E. Church Review*, quarterly, Philadelphia, Pennsylvania; *A. M. E. Zion Church Review*, quarterly, Charlotte, North Carolina; *Howard's American Magazine*, monthly, Harrisburgh, Pennsylvania.

DAILY PAPERS.—*The Daily Recorder*, Norfolk, Virginia; *American Citizen*, Kansas City, Missouri; *The Daily Record*, Washington, D. C.

WEEKLY PAPERS.—ALABAMA.—*Baptist Leader*, Montgomery; *Mobile Weekly Press*, Mobile; *Christian Hope*, Mobile; *National Association Notes*, Tuskegee; *Southern Watchman*, Mobile; *Christian Age*, Mobile; *Educator*, Huntsville.

CALIFORNIA.—*Western Outlook*, San Francisco.

COLORADO.— *Statesman*, Denver; *Sun*, Colorado Springs; *Western Enterprise*, Colorado Springs.

DISTRICT OF COLUMBIA.—*Bee*, Washington, *Colored American*, Washington.

FLORIDA.—*Sentinel*, Pensacola; *Evangelist*, Jackson; *East Coast Banner*, Interlaken; *Forum*, Ocala; *Recorder*, Orlando; *Samaritan Ledger*, Sanford; *Herald*, Live Oak.

GEORGIA.—*Appeal*, Atlanta; *Baptist Truth*, Savannah; *Tribune*, Savannah; *Georgia Baptist*, Augusta; *Progress*, Athens; *Dispatch*, Albany; *Southern Christian Recorder*, Atlanta; *Southern Georgia Baptist*, Waycross; *Aurora*, Atlanta; *Age*, Atlanta; *Weekly News*, Savannah; *Union*, Augusta; *Clipper*, Athens; *Herald*, Brunswick; *Enterprise*, La Grange; *Guide*, La Grange; *Voice of Missions*, Atlanta; *Iconoclast*, Albany; *Spectator*, Darien; *Sentinel*, Macon; *Monitor*, Columbus; *Investigator*, Americus; *Index*, Carpentersville.

ILLINOIS.—*Conservator*, Chicago.

INDIANA.—*World*, Indianapolis; *Freeman*, Indianapolis; *Recorder*, Indianapolis.

KANSAS.—*Plaindealer*, Topeka.

KENTUCKY.—*Lexington Standard*, Lexington; *American Baptist*, Louisville; *Bluegrass Bugle*, Frankfort; *Major*, Hopkinsville.

LOUISIANA.—*S. W. Christian Advocate*, New Orleans; *Republican Courier*, New Orleans.

MASSACHUSETTS.—*Courant*, Boston.

MARYLAND.—*Weekly Guide*, Baltimore; *Messenger*, Balti-

5

more; *Baptist Voice*, Baltimore; *Crusade*, Baltimore; *Republican Guide*, Baltimore; *Ledger*, Baltimore; *Afro-American*, Baltimore; *Signal*, Cumberland.

MICHIGAN.—*Informer*, Detroit.

MISSISSIPPI.—*New Light*, Columbus.

MISSOURI.—*American Citizen*, St. Louis.

MINNESOTA.—*Appeal*, St. Paul.

NEBRASKA.—*Enterprise*, Omaha; *Afro-American Sentinel*, Omaha; *Progress*, Omaha.

NEW JERSEY.—*Public Record*, Newark; *Union*, Orange; *W. T. Patterson's Weekly*, Asbury Park; *Public Record*, Atlantic City.

NEW YORK.—*Spectator*, Albany; *Age*, New York; *Presbyterian Herald*, New York; *Methodist Herald*, New York.

NORTH CAROLINA.—*Defender*, Raleigh; *Blade*, Raleigh; *Gazette*, Raleigh; *Baptist Sentinel*, Raleigh; *Star of Zion*, Charlotte; *Afro-American Presbyterian*, Charlotte; *Eastern Herald*, Edenton; *Neuse River Herald*, Waldron; *True Reformer*, Littleton; *Cotton Boll*, Concord.

OHIO.—*Gazette*, Cleveland; *Observer*, Xenia; *Rostrum*, Cincinnati.

OKLAHOMA TERRITORY.—*Constitution*, Oklahoma; *Guide*, Oklahoma.

PENNSYLVANIA.—*Christian Recorder*, Philadelphia; *Tribune*, Philadelphia; *Christian Banner*, Philadelphia; *Odd Fellows Journal*, Philadelphia; *Symposium*, Philadelphia.

SOUTH CAROLINA.—*Peedee Educator*, Bennettsville; *Piedmont Indicator*, Spartanburg; *People's Record*, Columbia; *Standard*, Columbia; *Christian Soldier*, Columbia; *Observer*, Charleston.

TEXAS.—*Weekly Express*, Dallas; *Rising Sun*, Rockdale; *City Times*, Galveston; *Star*, Fort Worth; *Elevator*, Wharton; *Guide*, Victoria; *Helping Hand*, Oakland; *Gazette*, Galveston; *Advance*, San Antonio; *Item*, Dallas; *Herald*, Austin; *Searchlight*, Austin; *Reporter*, Marshall; *Teacher*, Caldwell; *New Idea*, Galveston; *X-Ray*, San Antonio;

Spectator, Yoakum; *Southern Herald*, Waco; *Paul Quinn Weekly*, Waco; *Sequin*, Navasota; *Bugle*, Navasota; *Enterprise*, Bellville; *Monitor*, Marshall.

TENNESSEE.—*Ship*, Bristol; *Christian Index*, Jackson.

VIRGINIA.—*Richmond Planet*, Richmond; *Virginia Baptist*, Richmond; *Reformer*, Richmond; *National Pilot*, Petersburg; *Leader*, Alexandria; *Colored Churchman*, Bedford City.

WEST VIRGINIA.—*Pioneer Press*, Martinsburg.

SCHOOL AND COLLEGE PAPERS.—*Lane College Reporter*, Jackson, Tennessee; *Argus*, Biddle University, Charlotte, North Carolina; *Aurora*, Morris Brown College, Atlanta, Georgia; *Scroll*, Atlanta University, Atlanta, Georgia; *Tuskegee Student*, Tuskegee, Alabama; *College Arms*, Tallahassee, Florida; *College Record*, Talledega, Alabama; *Courier*, Clark University, Atlanta, Georgia; *News*, Brick Institute, Enfield, North Carolina; *Fisk Herald*, Nashville, Tennessee; *University Herald*, Howard University, Washington, D. C.

SUMMARY.—Magazines, 3; daily papers, 3; school papers, 11; weekly papers, 136. Total, 153.

The sixty-six leading newspapers were established as follows:

1839 *Christian Recorder* .... Philadelphia, Pa.
1865 *Southwestern Christian Advo-
        cate* .... New Orleans, La.
1870 *Christian Index* .... Jackson, Tenn.
1876 *Star of Zion* .... Charlotte, N. C.
1877 *Conservator* .... Chicago, Ill.
1880 *Georgia Baptist* .... Augusta, Ga.
        Leader .... Alexandria, Va.
        American Baptist .... Louisville, Ky.
1881 *New York Age* .... New York, N. Y.
1882 *Washington Bee* .... Washington, D. C.
        Pioneer Press .... Martinsburg, W. Va.
        Indianapolis World ...... Indianapolis, Ind.

1883   *Gazette* .... Cleveland, O.
       Richmond Planet .... Richmond, Va.
1884   *Philadelphia Tribune* .... Philadelphia, Pa.
       A. M. E. Church Review ..... Philadelphia, Pa.
1885   *Tribune* .... Savannah, Ga.
       Elevator .... San Francisco, Cal.
1886   *The Brotherhood* .... Natchez, Miss.
1887   *Florida Sentinel* .... Pensacola, Fla.
       National Pilot .... Petersburg, Va.
1888   *Southern Christian Recorder*..Atlanta, Ga.
1889   *Augusta Union* .... Augusta, Ga.
       American Citizen .... Kansas City, Kans.
       Statesman .... Denver, Col.
1890   *Christian Banner* .... Philadelphia, Pa.
1891   *Southern Watchman* .... Mobile, Ala.
       Raleigh Blade .... Raleigh, N. C.
       Constitution .... Guthrie, Oklahoma.
1892   *Afro-American Sentinel*...... Omaha, Neb.
       Afro-American .... Baltimore, Md.
       Lexington Standard .... Lexington, Ky.
1893   *Colored American* .... Washington, D. C.
       People's Recorder......... ...Columbia, S. C.
       Defender .... Raleigh, N. C.
       Guide .... Guthrie, Oklahoma
1894   *Weekly Express*............. Dallas, Texas.
       Western Outlook .... San Francisco, Cal.
       Weekly Press ....Mobile, Ala.
1895   *The Ship*.................... Bristol, Tenn.
       Enterprise.................. La Grange, Ga.
       Baptist Sentinel. .... Raleigh, N. C.
       Spectator................... Albany, N. Y.
       Kentucky Standard .... Louisville, Ky.
1896   *Forum*...................... Ocala, Fla.
       South Georgia Baptist........ Waycross, Ga.
       Association Notes........... Tuskegee, Ala.
       Public Record.............. Atlantic City, N. J.

1896 *Guide*......................Baltimore, Md.

  Monitor.........   ....Jacksonville, Fla.

1897 *Evangelist*.................Jacksonville, Fla.

  Informer...................Detroit, Mich.

  Herald.....................Brunswick, Ga.

  Elevator...................Wharton, Tex.

  Advance....................San Antonio, Tex.

  Helping Hand..............Oakland, Tex.

  American Eagle............St. Louis, Mo.

1898 *Atlanta Age*...............Atlanta, Ga.

  Enterprise.................Omaha, Neb.

  Appeal....................Atlanta, Ga.

  Union......................Orange, N. J.

  Symposium ....Germantown, Pa.

  Observer ....Macon, Miss.

  Republican Guide...........Baltimore, Md.

  Baptist Voice ....Baltimore, Md.

  Gazette....................Galveston, Tex.

The following papers, among others, own their own buildings:

Star of Zion, Charlotte, North Carolina, *Pioneer Press* Martinsburg, West Virginia, *Planet*, Richmond, Virginia, *Christian Recorder* and *A. M. E. Church Review*, Philadelphia, Pennsylvania, *Florida Sentinel*, Pensacola, Florida, *Forum*, Ocala, Florida, *The Ship*, Bristol, Tennessee, *Public Record*, Atlantic City, New Jersey, *Symposium*, Germantown, Pennsylvania, *Bee*, Washington, D. C., *Christian Index*, Jackson, Tennessee.

The buildings are valued as follows: $700, $900, $1,500, $1,700, $3,500, $5,500, $8,000, $10,000, $12,000, $17,500; total valuation, $61,300.

Forty-four papers own printing plants: Six less than $500, fourteen, from $500 to $1,000; twelve, from $1,000 to $2,500; nine, from $2,500 to $5,000; three, $5,000 and over. Total actual valuation, $89,450.

These papers are published by the following agencies:

Single individuals, thirty-nine; firms, eighteen; religious societies, ten; secret or other societies, three.

The Negro newspaper has not yet gained an assured footing, but it is rapidly becoming a social force. Nearly all Negro families read them, and while the papers are not yet strong enough to mould opinion, they are beginning to play a peculiar part in reflecting it.

There exists today no better means of forming, directing, and crystallizing Negro public opinion than by means of the press. A strong, fearless, national newspaper or magazine which the Negroes could feel was their own, with sane views as to work, wealth and culture, could become, in years, a vast power among Negroes. Here is a chance for a peculiar sort of philanthropic work, and one hitherto little tried—the endowed periodical. Fifty thousand dollars might, with care and foresight, launch a social force in the American world which would be of vast weight in guiding us toward the proper settlement of many vexed Negro problems.

SOJOURNER TRUTH.

An act of the legislature of New York, in 1811, liberated at once all slaves that were forty years of age, and provided that certain others should go free in 1828, while the children were to be free on reaching twenty-one. Among those entitled to freedom in 1828 was a Negro girl named Isabella, who had formerly belonged to the family of a Colonel Ardinburgh, of Hurley, Ulster county. She was subsequently twice sold. Her last master promised to set her free in 1827, a year before the time provided by law, but he refused to keep his promise, and she left him without his consent— the matter being finally settled by another man paying for the year's time.

She now took for herself the singular name of Sojourner Truth—given her, she said, by the Lord, because she was to take up the work of traveling and speaking to the people. She was wholly untaught, and had to rely upon the reading of others for such knowledge as she required from books; but having a quick mind and a retentive memory, she soon had much of the Bible and a number of hymns at her tongue's end, and became a rough but eloquent and thrilling speaker—devoting her time to public meetings and private ministrations, seeking in every way in her power to work reforms in individual lives and public policies. During the Civil War she was active in behalf of colored soldiers.

She has been described as having had a ready and pungent wit, the power of presence and movement which magnetizes and sways people, and the rare faculty of condensing an argument into a single convincing remark or question.

She conceived a plan to colonize the freedmen in the West, and traveled extensively obtaining signatures to a petition to Congress to provide for carrying out the scheme. Congress took no action, but thousands of the former slaves were influenced by her work and her representations to seek homes where they could be more independent than they could be as mere tenants of the great land-holders of the South.

A short time before her death in 1883 she claimed to be more than a hundred years old; but at that time she seemed to be renewing her youth, as some of the failing senses grew strong again, and her power as a speaker was not abated.

Regarded as somewhat of a prophetess, an oracle stirred by unaccountable impulses, she has been called the Libyan Sibyl—with what propriety we leave the reader to judge. She was, at any rate, a remarkable instance of the innate strength, profound feelings and lofty purpose that sometimes characterize individuals who have come up from the lowest depths and been denied even the rudiments of education.

FREDERICK DOUGLASS.

The name of Fred Douglass is a household word among the colored people of the United States. He was born in Tuckahoe, Maryland—date not certainly known, but he believed it to be in February, 1817. The name by which he is now known was assumed by him after his escape from slavery, which took place some time between 1836 and 1841 —probably when he was about twenty-one years old. Previously he was known to his little world as Frederick Augustus Washington Bailey.

His autobiography shows that as a slave he was for the most part treated with a brutality somewhat unusual, coming,

FREDERICK DOUGLASS.

by hire, under the control of different men, and meeting with little kindness throughout except from a daughter of his master, who was gentle and considerate, and would have taught him to read had her husband not forbidden it. The latter circumstance seems to have awakened in him a determination to learn; and with very little help from others, either in the way of instruction or the furnishing of books, he became a fair English scholar. Before he was twenty years old and while still a slave, he taught a Sunday-school and began his career as a public speaker by preaching. In 1841 he addressed a white audience for the first time, and with such effect that he was soon afterward employed by the Massachusetts Anti-Slavery Society to lecture, in which work he continued for four years, and soon came to be recognized as a great orator—a man of that true eloquence which holds an audience and makes profound and lasting impressions.

He published his autobiography in 1845, which dealt in such severe terms with those who had held him in bondage, and still claimed ownership, that it enraged them and made his stay, even in a free State, so precarious that he was glad to accept an invitation to lecture in Great Britain. While he was there a Mrs. Richardson collected money and bought his freedom, and he soon afterward returned to the United States.

In London he was not only kindly but flatteringly received, and his demeanor and his power as an orator won the admiration of even the statesmen and nobility—some of whom treated him with marked consideration.

Thenceforth he was one of the most active and aggressive of those who advocated the freedom of the slaves. As an editor, a contributor to newspapers and magazines, a public speaker—a worker in whatever line promised the success of abolition schemes, he was one of the most notable and efficient among many who gave their time and talents and means to the cause. When the war came on, he was impatient with the action of President Lincoln and Congress, and urgent to have the government adopt a line of policy which the far-seeing and prudent Lincoln regarded as dangerous to the perpetuity of the Union, if not at the time impracticable; but he had the satisfaction before the war closed of having his dearest wishes realized.

In 1871 he was appointed secretary to the Santo Domingo

Commission; in 1872 he was chosen one of the presidential electors for the State of New York; President Hayes appointed him marshal of the District of Columbia; President Garfield appointed him recorder of deeds for the District of Columbia; and President Harrison made him minister to Hayti. At the great World's Fair at Chicago he had charge of Hayti's exhibit.

He has been described as "a tall, dark mulatto, a bold, vigorous, earnest and fluent speaker, and an able debater."

His character and career vindicate the claim of the optimistic of his race and of thoughtful white men that the Negro has in him the elements from which may be evolved the orator, the statesman, the true philanthropist, and the man of honor.

He died in 1895, being then, as was believed, seventy-eight years old.

CHAPTER IV.

The Negro in Law, Medicine and Divinity.

FROM the reports of the Annual Conferences held in Atlanta, Georgia, to inquire into the condition of the colored people in the United States, and from other sources of information, we learn that many of the graduates of the great schools have entered the legal and medical professions, and that there are many able and successful practitioners, and some who have filled and are filling places of honor and public trust.

We give the names of a few as an indication that colored people are making their way in the learned professions in widely diverse localities.

About twenty years ago, Miss Charlotte E. Ray, whom a friendly lady writer described as "a dusky mulatto," a graduate of the Law College of Howard University, was admitted to practice at the bar of the Supreme Court of the District of Columbia—the first woman lawyer ever recognized in Washington City.

It is said that a Negro who was born in Georgia is one of the best lawyers in Paris, France.

Louis B. Anderson has been assistant county attorney for Cook county, Illinois.

Ferdinand L. Barnett is assistant state's attorney of Illinois.

Before the war some Negroes were prominent practitioners before the Boston bar, as Robert Morris, E. G. Walker, and others.

S. Laing Williams, a graduate of the University of Michigan and of the Columbia Law School, is a practicing lawyer in Chicago.

Miss Lutie A. Lytle is a teacher in the Law Department of the Central Tennessee College, Nashville, Tennessee.

James Derham, born a slave in Philadelphia, in 1762, belonged to a physician who had him taught to read and write, and then employed him in compounding medicine and in other work in connection with the profession. He ultimately became so skillful in medicine as to be employed as assistant to a new master (also a physician) to whom he had been sold; soon afterward he purchased his freedom, and then built up a lucrative practice; he added to his professional knowledge an acquaintance with the French and Spanish languages; and at twenty-six years of age he was one of the most eminent physicians in New Orleans. The celebrated Doctor Rush, of Philadelphia, published in *The American Museum* an account of him in which he spoke of his attainments and skill in the highest terms.

John R. Rock and John V. De Grasse were able and successful physicians in Boston, between 1850 and 1860. On the 24th of August, 1854, De Grasse was admitted to membership in the Massachusetts Medical Society.

Edward Wilson, a graduate of Williams College, is a practicing lawyer in Chicago.

J. Frank Wheaton, a lawyer, was the first colored man to be elected to the legislature in Minnesota.

Dr. J. Frank McKinley, a graduate of the Medical Department of the University of Michigan, is a noted practicing physician and surgeon.

Another graduate of the Medical Department of the University of Michigan, Dr. John R. Francis, is one of the best known physicians in Washington, D. C.

Dr. Daniel H. Williams, of Chicago, was the founder of Provident Hospital and Training School. He was appointed by President Cleveland to be surgeon-in-chief of the great Freedmen's Hospital, Washington, D. C.

Belle Garnet, a student of medicine, is a graduate nurse of Provident Hospital and Training School, Chicago.

Dentistry is so allied to medicine and surgery that we may mention in this connection Ida Gray Nelson, D. D. S., a graduate of Ann Arbor University, Michigan, who is said to be the only colored woman dentist in the United States.

As noticed in another chapter, at least eight colored men were commissioned by President Lincoln surgeons for hospital and field duty during the Civil War.

We give here portraits and brief sketches of two persons who have distinguished themselves in this field.

There was never a time in our history when the race had so many examples of substantial and permanent progress as it has to-day. In every city and hamlet there is the teacher, the artisan, the lawyer, the doctor and the business man, emphasizing in their great progress the upward movement of the Negro throughout the country.

Dr. William F. Penn, of Atlanta, Georgia, who is one of the leading colored physicians of that city, was born in Amherst county, Virginia, in 1870. His parents took him to Lynchburg early in life and there entered him in the schools. From the Lynchburg schools he went to the Hampton Normal and Agricultural Institute, and from there to the Virginia Normal and Collegiate Institute, from which he graduated in 1891. After graduating he taught in the city schools of Lynchburg, Virginia, resigning to pursue a medical course in the Leonard Medical School, at Raleigh, North Carolina, from which he went in 1893 to Yale University, New Haven, Connecticut, and graduated from the medical department of that world-famed institution in 1897, taking high rank in all of his classes until the day of graduation.

His standing in his class may be seen by the fact that he was the first Negro ever chosen in the medical school as one of the editors of the "Class Book," which goes down in history as a record of graduates, etc.

For awhile he was one of the internes at Freedmen's Hospital, Washington, D. C., under Doctor Williams, then

surgeon-in-chief, and was regarded as one of the best informed and most skillful men on the staff.

Doctor Penn went to Atlanta in 1897 to practice medicine,
and from the start took front rank among his people. Ten
days after he began practice there he was selected by the

DR. WILLIAM F. PENN, ATLANTA, GEORGIA.

city as one of the two colored physicians to vaccinate the
colored population of the city.

By official preferment he is the physician to the following
institutions of learning in Atlanta: Atlanta University,
Clark University, Gammon Theological Seminary. He has
been called from Atlanta into other sections of Georgia several times to perform difficult surgical operations, which he

has done with great success. As a physician he is regarded highly, as the steady growth of his practice attests.

The first colored person to finish any graduate course in the University of Minnesota, is McCants Stewart, son of T. McCants Stewart, now an attorney of Honolulu, Hawaii. Mr. Stewart received the Master's degree in law in 1900.

McCANTS STEWART, A. M.

He began the study of law in New York City. In 1896–7 he attended the New York University, taking special work and beginning the law course. He went to Minnesota and entered the law school in the fall of 1897, finishing with the class of '99. He was secretary of his class in his senior year, and was an active member of the Kent Literary Society, representing the society in the '98–'99 oratorical contest.

NARCISSA WEST.

Narcissa West was born in Edgefield county, South Carolina, May 15, 1867. She entered Spelman Seminary, January 1, 1886. She was graduated from the nurse training department with honor in May, 1889, but feeling the need of a more thorough general education, she continued her studies in Spelman till May, 1892, when she finished her academic course and received her diploma. Since that time she has pursued the profession of a trained nurse, in Atlanta, with marked success. She is continually in demand, and is held in high esteem, both by the physicians and the patients with whom she labors. There is always a note of satisfaction when she can be secured for a serious case. She has been

NARCISSA WEST

able, also, to demonstrate that the profession of a t r a i n e d nurse is a paying one.

The list of men and women who have attained to distinction as church officers, ministers, missionaries and other religious teachers is long and imposing. We give in the following pages portraits and biographical sketches of church people in sufficient number and variety to show how the race has asserted itself in this great department of the world's duty and endeavor. It is perhaps not irrelevant to instance here two persons whom we have not mentioned elsewhere. It is said that one of the eminent divines in London, England, is a full-blooded Negro who was born in Alabama; and in "The Triumphs of the Cross," E. P. Tenney, the author, says that "a former slave of the late Confederate President, Jefferson Davis, translated the Bible into the Sweetsa tongue, spoken by 300,000 Africans."

The Rev. Duke W. Anderson, a mulatto born in Illinois in 1812, led a busy and consecrated life as a minister of the gospel, a teacher and an anti-slavery worker. A man of commanding presence, great natural ability, profound earnestness and remarkable conciliatory as well as aggressive powers, he deserves to rank, in some respects, with Fred Douglass as a representative of the race.

Most of the colored Christians of the United States have allied themselves with the Methodists and Baptists, though there are many Presbyterians, Protestant Episcopalians, Disciples of Christ and Roman Catholics. From the "Illustrated History of Methodism" we get material which enables us to sketch briefly the rise of various separate Methodist societies in America, and an examination of the following illustrations and accompanying life-sketches, with some figures we give here, will indicate that the colored Baptists are a mighty organization. According to latest reliable statistics, there were in the United States 1,584,920 Regular (colored) Baptists, with 9,663 ministers and 14,863 churches; African Methodist Episcopal members, 641,727, with 5,245 ministers and 5,671 churches; African Union Methodist Protestant members, 3,437, with 102 ministers and 86 churches; African Methodist Episcopal Zion members, 528,461, with 2,902 ministers and 1,808 churches; Congregational Methodist members, 319, with 5 ministers and 5 churches; Colored Methodist Episcopal members, 204,317, with 2,039 ministers and 1,427 churches. There are about 40,000 Cumberland Presbyterians, with 450 ministers and 400 churches. As intimated above, these figures do not give the full strength of the colored religious bodies, as there are several organizations concerning whose membership and church holdings we have no statistics.

It is interesting to note in this connection that colored Methodists in the United States began to move for separate existence more than a hundred years ago, and that long before the Civil War there were separate organizations well administered by bishops, elders and pastors.

REV. JOHN JASPER.

THE AFRICAN ZION METHODIST EPISCOPAL CHURCH.

In 1821 a considerable secession from the Methodist Church took place in New York, led by the Rev. W. M. Stillwell, who took umbrage at c e r t a i n legislation designed for the better security of church p r o p e r t y, which he viewed as usurpation of the rights of congregations. Several hundred local preachers and members in good standing were induced to secede with him; and he also prevailed on a congregation of A f r i c a n M e t h o d i s t s to leave the Methodist Episcopal Church —which was the nucleus of the present African Zion Methodist Episcopal Church

REV. JOSEPH J. CLINTON,
Bishop of the African Zion Methodist Episcopal Church; born in Philadelphia, 1823; elected bishop in 1856.

THE REV. JOHN JASPER.

The career of this man—a full-blooded African—was extraordinary. Born a slave, never educated in the schools, toiling as slaves were required to toil until freedom came to him when he was past the noonday of life, he rose to distinction that was wide as the continent—impressing himself upon the times as only the earnest and intellectually strong man can do.

The youngest of twenty-four children, he was born in Fluvanna county, Virginia, July 4, 1812. He professed Christianity when he was twenty-seven years old, and soon afterward began to preach. By some means he had learned to read, and thenceforth the Bible seems to have been his one book. As a preacher he attracted attention almost from the start, and soon came to be **in** great demand for funeral sermons. He preached to Baptist congregations in Richmond and Petersburgh—chiefly in Richmond—for about forty years; and though devoted to his calling rather than to the accumulation of property, he acquired considerable wealth. He traveled a good deal during this time, visiting most of the leading cities in the Union, lecturing and preaching.

In the *Religious Herald*, of Richmond, Virginia, April 11, 1901, William E. Hatcher published the following sketch:

"When John Jasper passed away from the earth, he left no successor. He is the last of his race, and we shall not see his like again. He lacked a fraction of being four-score and ten, and had been a preacher for sixty-two years. The pulpit was his throne, and he and the peerless queen of England reigned in their respective spheres about the same length of time.

"Freedom did little for Jasper. It came too late to touch him with its moulding hand. It never dazzled him nor crooked him with prejudices against the white people. He clung far more to the traditions and sentiments of his bondage days than to the new things which freedom brought. He never took up with the gaudy displays which marked his race in the early days of emancipation. He held on to the old ways. He intoned in his preaching, spurned the accomplishments of the schools, sang the weird songs of his early days, and thought himself set to smash all the new-fangled notions which possessed his race.

"Personally Jasper was above all reproach. There was no whisper against his moral character. He loved justice and not only practiced it, but he demanded it at the hands of others. Those who treated him ill he would scourge with knotted whips. Not a few of the "educated fools," as he scornfully styled some who sneered at his ignorance, felt the power of his blows, as he sometimes denounced them for their criticisms of him. The fact is he was a born fighter. Fear never shook his frame. He would have attacked a regiment, if he had felt that it was his duty to do so. Much of his preaching was denunciatory. Friends would report to him ill things said of him during the week, and he would return the fire in his sermon the next Sunday afternoon. But there was a charm in his resentments. He always identified himself with the Lord, and the assaults made upon him he treated as wrongs offered to heaven. There was in him a lofty, almost sublime, contempt for opposition, and yet he rarely seemed angered by the blows struck at him. He mingled such odd hits and telling jests at the expense of his opponents that he never showed much hostility against them. His chief weapon was ridicule, and that he used with crushing skill. He may have despised his enemies, but he did not hate them.

"His speech was execrably ungrammatical, though his later reading and study probably rooted out some of the lingual excrescences of his early days. But his power to express an idea was unsurpassed, and it often occurred that, when his dictionary gave out, he could use the wrong word, and yet, by his manner and tone, make it convey his meaning. For my part, I had the impression that when he was at his happy elevations of feeling he did not need words very much; he could flash the thought out of his eye, wave it out by the sweep of his hand, or cast it forth by some queer movement of his body. Often his greatest achievements were not by word, but by long pauses or by little confidential laughs, as if no one was present except him and himself, and the two were having the jolliest time together.

"Brother Jasper was great on argument. He could not construct a perfect syllogism, but he had a way of his own, vigorous and confident, which showed that he stood ready to prove all that he said. Indeed, he had the habit of challenging all comers to answer him, and he insisted that, if what he said was not according to the Bible, those who discovered it should take the road and proclaim far and wide that John Jasper was a liar. By the way, I heard him say

one time, with affecting simplicity:- 'Bruthr'n, God Almighty never lies; he can't lie. I'm sorry to say it, but I
lies sometimes. I oughtn't to lie, an' I'm tryin' to quit it;
but God never lies.' This he said in a tone so honest and
candid that I am sure the people loved him and believed in
him more than ever. A hypocrite would never have said
such a thing.

"Many good people were out of patience with John Jasper because of his sermon on the 'Sun Do Move.' For
my own part, I deplored his mistake, as it seemed to me
to be wasting his strength in dealing with a question which
he did not understand. I heard the sermon on one occasion, without really intending to do so, and I felt that,
taken altogether, it was the weakest thing that I ever
heard from him. It presented him to the public in a light
which seemed to me most unfortunate. At the same time,
his position was exceedingly simple. It was characteristic
of the honesty and devoutness of the man. The Bible
spoke of the sun as a moving body. That was plain as
daylight to him. Here came the science men asserting that
the sun did not rise and set. Now, Jasper's general information did not enable him to reconcile the two things. To
him they were flat contradictions, and he had to choose between the two. He stood by the Bible.

"Outside of the Bible, Jasper knew very little. He did
not know books, and largely held himself aloof from people.
He did not lack very much of being a hermit in his daily
life. He had a cultivated reserve, and was busy with the
Bible. That he conned with unflagging industry. With
its historical portions he was well acquainted, especially
with those portions that were picturesque, and furnished full
play for his imagination. He was also deeply versed in the
doctrines of grace, and had had glorious experiences of
their truth in his own checkered and rugged life.

"I never asked him how he prepared his sermons; but they
bore marks of care and patience in their making. He had

special sermons—I should say a great many of them—and he did not hesitate to preach them over and over again. They did not suffer by repetition, for the occasion always imparted sufficient coloring to each delivery of a sermon to give it freshness. There were few ruts into which he ever ran, and even his old sayings would glow with the heat of his soul. Old sermons are as good as new, provided the preacher puts as much life in them as he did when they were new. He carried no paper into the pulpit, and his mind was wonderfully active when he spoke. He always swung loose, and, while he seemed restrained and almost tedious in his exordium, he never failed to climb the hills of celestial glory before he finished. If his theme was of the historic order, he would paint pictures that would burn into your soul and remain there to the end. If he was on some cardinal doctrine, like regeneration or victory over sin, his soul would catch fire, and there would invariably be a congregational conflagration. I remember more of the things that I have heard Jasper say than I could recall of all the things that I ever heard other preachers say in all my life. This may be too strongly put, but I do not really think so.

"It took a funeral to put Jasper at his best. It always brought him in sight of death and eternity, and kindled the fires of his imagination. But he was terribly conscientious in speaking of the dead. If they brought great sinners to his church and asked him to hold the funeral services, he would do it, but he would throw no mantle over the sins of his subject. If he really believed the man had died without a well-grounded Christian hope, he would unceremoniously and without apology preach him straight to the bottomless pit. I could give startling illustrations of this remark.

"I have indicated the predominant characteristic of this unique and godly minister. It was his brilliant, magnetic, courageous imagination. It covered all his defects, disarmed criticism, lifted people to the skies, and made that ill-shapen, odd-voiced, ungrammatical old preacher glow with a luster and grandeur which transfigured him. Several times, I confess, he cut all my moorings and wafted me to the gates of the spirit world. It was irresistibly affecting to hear him speak of heaven. It seemed to overmaster him, and it made him the master of others. Of course, his views of heaven were very simple. Oh, how deeply he believed in it! Rapturous visions of the Lamb on the throne and of the redeemed in their mansions possessed him, and it was an experience not to be forgotten to feel the spell of his eloquence at such a time.

"Nor did his heart sink when the final crisis came. In his own bright way, he declared that his trunk was packed and he was waiting for orders to move up. As for death, he said that the approach of death bothered him no more than the crawling of a summer fly. I think of his stern life, so marked by battle and defiance, so filled with sorrows, and recall with emotion how he used to solace himself with the assurances of coming rest, and I doubt not that he was glad when it came. Peaceful be the brave old warrior's sleep!

"I send this paper at the *Herald's* request. It has been dashed off in a day when duties new and old are striving for a place, and is unworthy, I well know, of my rare and royal theme. Few knew John Jasper as I did, none loved or believed in him more than I did, and I now lament him as a friend. He did me good while he lived, and I honor him in his death, as I did sincerely honor him in his life. This article only gives glimpses. It has no place for the story of his life, nor for the record of his ministerial labors, nor yet for that rich fund of humor, satire and illustration in which his life abounded. Many of these things, with extracts from his sermons, piquant sayings, and descriptions of his characteristic actions, I committed to paper a while ago, but I must omit them from an article already too long."

The author of a book of sketches published several years ago, referring to Jasper's theory of the sun, says: "He was always of an astronomical turn of mind, and if he had had the advantage of education, he would doubtless have made one of the foremost scientists of his time." He was married three times, and, as indicated above, seemed to prefer home life rather than that of a keeper of promiscuous company. The writer above alluded to says that "from the humblest surroundings in early life he rose to influence, and is a striking illustration of what can be accomplished by industry and perseverance."

BISHOPS FRANCIS BURNS AND JOHN WRIGHT ROBERTS.

Bishop Levi Scott, of the Methodist Episcopal Church, who was raised to the episcopate by the Seventeenth Annual Conference of that church, at Boston, Massachusetts, began his episcopal work by visiting Africa, where he presided at the Liberia Conference, founded by Americans. . . . . The report he brought back of his work and impressions in that colony formed a notable item in the address of the bishops in 1856 . . . . As a result of Bishop Scott's recommendations, permission was granted to the Liberia Conference to elect an elder in good standing to the office of bishop. This was followed in January, 1858, by the election in Liberia of Francis

1. Francis Burns, Missionary Bishop of the Methodist Episcopal Church in Western Africa, 1858-1863. 2. John Wright Roberts, Missionary Bishop for Africa, 1866-1875.

Burns, the first colored bishop in the church. Burns was a native of Albany, New York, and had early shown signs of character and ability. In 1834 he was sent to Liberia, where he did excellent work as an evangelist and as a teacher in Monrovia Seminary, and later as presiding elder. Returning to his native land to be consecrated, he was duly ordained at the Genesee Conference by Bishops Jaynes and Baker. His career as bishop in Liberia lasted for barely five years. With the view of regaining health he sailed for Baltimore in the spring of 1863, but died a few days after disembarking. His character was a high and consistent one. He was succeeded in office by John Wright Roberts, who was ordained three years afterward. Roberts vigorously carried forward the work wisely begun by his predecessor, and at his death, in 1875, the Methodist Episcopal Church in Africa numbered more than two hundred thousand members.

REV. W. J. HOWARD.

Rev. W. J. Howard, pastor of Zion Baptist Church, was born near Fredericksburg, Virginia, of slave parents, June 15, 1854. His father, a man of unusual intelligence and business capacity, died in 1858. The lad spent most of his time on the farm until 1869, when, at fifteen years of age,

he went to Washington, where for seven years he worked in barber shops and hotels, meanwhile attending night and Sunday-school. In 1877 he embarked in business for himself; but in 1881, under the influence of President G. M. P. King, he entered Wayland Seminary, graduating in May, 1886. Soon after graduation he became pastor of the Zion Baptist Church, which honorable position he has now (1902) held for fifteen

REV. W. J. HOWARD.

years. During this time more than two thousand have been added to the church, twelve hundred are enrolled in its Sunday-school, and five hundred in Endeavor Societies. His church has always stood for staunch Baptist loyalty, and for co-operation with the American Baptist Home Mission Society.

JOHN A. WHITTED, D. D.

John A. Whitted, D. D., was born near Hillsboro, North Carolina, March 10, 1860. He spent the first sixteen years of his life upon the farm. At seven years of age he began attending the Freedmen Aid Society's School at Hillsboro, four months in the year. At sixteen he began to teach in the public schools. For the next five years he spent about five months out of each year in study at Shaw University. He was converted at nineteen, and united with the Blunt Street Baptist Church, Raleigh. At twenty-one

JOHN A. WHITTED, D. D.

he entered Lincoln University, and graduated in 1885. For twelve years he held the position of principal of Shiloh Institute, and pastor of the church at Warrenton. In 1895 he became district missionary, and then general missionary, for the State of North Carolina, under the plan of co-operation. He has served as editor of the *Baptist Sentinel*, and is a member of the Executive Board of the Lott Carey Baptist Foreign Mission Convention.

J. W. KIRBY, D. D.

J. W. Kirby, D. D., was born of slave parents in Hampton, Virginia, during the Civil War. At the age of five years he was sent to a private school; a little later he entered "The Butler School," and afterward Hampton

Institute, from which he graduated in 1880. He was converted in 1881; baptized into the fellowship of the first Baptist Church, Hampton, and became at once superintendent of its Sunday-school. In 1883 he entered the Richmond Theological Seminary, graduating with honor in 1885. For six years he was p r i n c i p a l of the graded school at Bowers Hill, Virginia. He has served as pastor at Piney Grove and at P o r t s-

J. W. KIRBY, D. D.

mouth, where he built a beautiful and substantial church edifice.

For seven years he served as corresponding secretary of the Virginia Baptist State Convention; about the same length of time as trustee of Virginia Seminary. In 1896 he accepted the position of educational secretary, and assisted in securing funds from the Negro Baptists of Virginia for Virginia Union University. He is now pastor at Farmville, Virginia.

HENRY M. TURNER.

Henry McNeal Turner, son of Hardy and Sarah (Greer) Turner, was born at Newberry Court-house, South Carolina, February 1, 1834. He learned to read and write without

teachers; when fifteen years of age he was employed in a law
office at Abbeville Court-house, where the young lawyers assisted him with his studies, and he continued to apply himself till he had learned geography, arithmetic, history, astronomy, physiology and hygiene. In 1848 he united with
the Methodist Episcopal Church, South, and in 1853 he was
licensed to preach among the colored people in South Carolina, Georgia, Alabama and other Southern States. In
1858 he transferred his membership to the A. M. E. Church;
joined the Missouri Annual Conference soon afterward, and
became an itinerant minister; was afterward transferred by
Bishop D. A. Payne to the Baltimore Annual Conference,
where he remained four years, meanwhile studying Latin,
Greek, Hebrew and divinity at Trinity College, University
of Pennsylvania, receiving from that institution the degree
of LL.D., and from Wilberforce University that of D. D.
He was pastor of Israel Church, in Washington, D. C., 1863;
was commissioned chaplain of the United States colored
troops by President Lincoln (first colored chaplain ever commissioned); was mustered out in September, 1865; was commissioned chaplain in the regular army by President Johnson; was detailed as officer of Freedman's Bureau in Georgia;
resigned commission and resumed his ministry; organized
schools for colored children; was elected member of the
Georgia Constitutional Convention in 1867; member of the
Georgia Legislature, 1868 and 1870; was afterward postmaster at Macon, Georgia; inspector of customs, and afterward detective in the United States Secret Service. In
1876 he was elected by the General Conference of the A. M. E.
Church manager of its publications at Philadelphia; was
elected bishop by the General Conference at St. Louis, Missouri, in 1880. He has been one of the principal agitators
of the return of his race to Africa, and has organized four
Annual Conferences in Africa—one in Sierra Leone, one in
Liberia, one in Pretoria, and one in Queenstown. He is the
author of "Methodist Polity," of a catechism, various pub-

lished sermons and lectures, and has compiled a hymn-book for the A. M. E. Church. He married, in Baltimore, August 16, 1900, Mrs. Harriet E. Wayman, widow of the late Bishop A. W. Wayman.

S. N. VASS, D. D.

S. N. Vass, D. D., district secretary of the American Baptist Publication Society, was born at Raleigh, North Carolina, May 22, 1866. After having attended primary

S. N. VASS, D. D.

schools, he entered St. Augustine's Normal and Collegiate Institute, at ten years of age. Having graduated, he became a teacher in the public schools. At eighteen years of age he became a teacher at Shaw University, where he remained for nine years. He received from the university the degrees of B. A. in 1885, A. M. in 1888, and D. D. in 1901. He resigned his position in the university to enter the service of the American Baptist Publication Society, first as local missionary and then (1896) district secretary for the South. In this position he has the general oversight of the work of the society among the colored people. He served for one year as president of Howe Biblical Institute, at Memphis, Tennessee. He was licensed to preach at nineteen years of age, ordained at twenty-one, has been solicited by a number of churches to become pastor, but has served in that capacity only one year, while teaching in Shaw University.

REV. E. P. JOHNSON.

Rev. E. P. Johnson was born of slave parents at Columbus, Georgia, where he spent the first sixteen years of his life in slavery. After spending some time at the carpenter trade, he found employment on a farm, where, after working during the day, he walked a mile and a half to attend night school. Having saved out of his scanty wages $150, he entered Atlanta University in 1873, and graduated in 1879. With some help from Northern friends, he supported himself during his period of study by doing odd jobs and by teaching during vacation. After a valuable experience as pastor, teacher and missionary, he became the general educational missionary of Georgia in 1899, under the plan of co-operation, and still holds that important office.

REV. E. P. JOHNSON.

As early as 1787 the colored people of the Methodist Society in Philadelphia, feeling no longer comfortable in immediate religious association with white folks, organized themselves into a separate congregation and began building a church of their own. This secession met with great opposition from the Methodist elder; but they persisted in carrying out their plans. The result was expulsion from the society. Happily some large-minded citizens helped them out in their monetary difficulties, and Bishop White, of the Protestant

163617

BISHOPS OF THE AFRICAN METHODIST EPISCOPAL CHURCH.

THE AFRICAN METHODIST EPISCOPAL CHURCH.

TABULATED FACTS AS TO ITS BISHOPS.

	NAME	BORN	PLACE OF BIRTH	ELECTED BISHOP	WHERE ELECTED	DIED
1	Richard Allen	1760	Philadelphia, Pa.	1818	Philadelphia, Pa.	1831
2	Morris Brown	1770	Charleston, S. C.	1828	Philadelphia, Pa.	1849
3	Edward Waters		West River, Md.	1832	Philadelphia, Pa.	1847
4	William Paul Quinn	1795	Calcutta, India	1844		1873
5	Willis Nazery	1803	Isle of Wight Co., Va.	1852	New York City	1875
6	D. Alexander Payne	1811	Charleston, S. C.	1852	New York City	
7	Alexander W. Wayman	1821	Caroline Co., Md.	1864	Philadelphia, Pa.	
8	Jabez Pitt Campbell	1815	State o Delaware	1864	Philadelphia, Pa.	
9	James A. Shorter	1817	Washington, D. C.	1868	Washington, D. C.	
10	Thomas M. D. Ward	1823	Hanover, Pa.	1868	Washington, D. C.	
11	John M. Brown	1817	Odessa, Del.	1868	Washington, D. C.	
12	Henry M. Turner	1833	Newberry, S. C.	1880	St. Louis, Mo.	
13	William F. Dickerson	1845	Woodbury, N. J.	1880	St. Louis, Mo.	1884
14	Richard H. Cain	1825	Greenbrier Co., W. Va.	1880	St. Louis, Mo.	
15	Richard R. Disney	1833	North East, Md.		Chatham, Ont.	
16	Wesley J. Gaines	1840	Wilkes Co., Ga.	1888	Indianapolis, Ind.	
17	B. W. Arnett	1838	Brownsville, Pa.	1888	Indianapolis, Ind.	
18	B. T. Tanner	1835	Pittsburgh, Pa.	1888	Indianapolis, Ind.	
19	Abraham Grant	1848	Lake City, Fla.	1888	Indianapolis, Ind.	

Episcopal Church, consented to ordain one of their number as pastor. The holding of the church property led to considerable legal difficulties; and many meanwhile became Episcopalians. Four years later Richard Allen, who had been a Southern slave, and later became a bishop, converted a blacksmith-shop in his yard into a meeting-house, and this was dedicated in June, 1794, by Bishop Asbury. The church was named Bethel, and was placed under the control of the Methodist Episcopal Church, but not according to the prescribed form. Richard Allen, when he received ordination as pastor in 1799, was the first colored preacher in the United States. Sixteen years later difficulties arose with those in control of the Methodist Episcopal Church in Philadelphia. A contribution of $600 to the central fund was demanded in return for a regular preaching supply; but the price was deemed too dear, considering the quality of the preaching, and finally the Bethel people refused to contribute more than $100. This sum was declined, as inadequate, and the people were declared contumacious. The resident elder, Robert R. Roberts, afterward bishop, entering the church on an ensuing Sabbath, to take possession of the pulpit, was not

7

allowed to proceed more than half way, and had to retire. A law-suit which grew out of the dispute ended in favor of the Bethel people.

In April, 1816, a convention, invitations to attend which had been sent to colored people in various districts throughout the Republic, met in Philadelphia. There were seventeen delegates—five from Philadelphia, seven from Baltimore, three from Attleborough, Massachusetts; one from Salem, New Jersey; and one from Wilmington, Delaware. Daniel Coker, having been elected bishop, resigned in favor of Richard Allen, who was consecrated bishop by the Rev. Absalom Jones, a priest of the Protestant Episcopal Church. The name chosen for the organization was the African Methodist Episcopal Church, and it adopted the Book of Discipline of the Methodist Church, with its Articles of Religion and its General Rules, as drafted by the two Wesleys, entire and complete with the sole omission of the presiding elder. Probably 3,000 persons joined the organization at its inception; and ten years later the membership had more than doubled. Bishop Allen served as bishop for fifteen years, dying in 1831. A man of but little education, he yet possessed remarkable judgment and energy and won general respect. A monument to his memory stands in Philadelphia Park.

BISHOP BENJAMIN T. TANNER.

Benj. Tucker Tanner was born in Pittsburgh, Pennsylvania, December 25, 1835. He was educated in the schools of Pittsburgh, in Avery College, Allegheny, and in the Western Theological Seminary. Avery conferred on him in 1870 the degree of A. M., and Wilberforce subsequently those of D. D. and LL.D. He was married August 19, 1858, to Sarah E. Miller.

He was for sixteen years editor of the *Christian Recorder,* the organ of the A. M. E. Church; was the founder and for four years the editor of the *A. M. E. Church Review.* He was elected bishop in 1888. He is a member of the Negro-

American Academy, and is the author of a number of books, of which we may name, "Is the Negro Accursed?" "Apology for African Methodism;" "Outlines of A. M. E. Church History;" "The Dispensations in the History of the Church;" "The Negro in Holy Writ;" "A Hint to Ministers, Especially of the A. M. E. Church;" and "The Color of Solomon—What?"

JOSEPH E. JONES, D.D.

Doctor Jones was born of slave parents at Lynchburg, Virginia, October, 1852. At six years of age he began work in a tobacco factory. By the indefatigable efforts of his mother he had educational advantages while the war was in progress, and at its close was put into school, where he remained three years. After spending three years in the Richmond Theological Institute, he entered the preparatory department of Colgate University, 1871, and graduated in 1876. After graduation he was appointed instructor in the Richmond Theological Seminary, and for twenty-five years has discharged

JOSEPH E. JONES, D. D.

his duties with marked fidelity. He served as corresponding secretary of the Baptist Foreign Mission Convention for twelve years; president of the State Sunday-school Convention for six years; and has been a member of the Educational Board for about eighteen years. He is editor of the *Virginia Baptist.*

MISS EMMA B. DELANEY.

Miss Emma B. Delaney, missionary to Africa, was born January 18, 1871, at Fernandina, Florida. Her father,

MISS EMMA B. DELANEY.

Daniel S. Delaney, was for thirty years in government service as pilot on the revenue cutter, "Boutwell" being the only colored pilot in the service. Her mother, Annie L. Delaney, is an influential Christian. When eight years old Emma was sent to the Convent School of Fernandina. Having finished the course there, she entered Spelman Seminary in 1889. In 1892 she was graduated from the Nurse Training Department, receiving a gold medal for proficiency. In 1894 she finished the academic course, and in 1896 the missionary training course. During the summer months, while pursuing the missionary course, she labored successfully in Gainesville, Macon and Athens, Georgia. For two terms she was matron at Florida Institute, Live Oak. Wherever she has been she has done faithful, efficient mission work. For years she felt herself called to the foreign field, and has anxiously awaited the word to go forward.

BISHOP W. J. GAINES.

Wesley J. Gaines, sixteenth bishop of the A. M. E. Church, was born a slave, in Wilkes county, Georgia, October 4, 1840. He received theological instruction from a Protestant Episcopal clergyman at Athens, Georgia; became a minister of the Methodist Episcopal Church, South, in 1860; was married to Miss Julia A. Camper, August 20, 1863; united with the African Methodist Episcopal Church in 1865; was consecutively pastor, presiding elder, mission secretary and bishop.

Through his exertions and influence Bethel Church, in Atlanta, the largest colored church in the South, was built; he founded Morris Brown College, in Atlanta; is a trustee of Wilberforce University, in Ohio; is vice-president of Payne Theological Seminary; is president of the Board of Trustees of Waters College, Jacksonville, Florida; president of the Financial Board of the African Methodist Church; author of "African Methodism in the South," and of "The Negro and the White Man." He has strenuously opposed all schemes for the removal of the Negro from the United States.

BISHOP ABRAHAM GRANT.

The subject of this sketch was born a slave in Lake City, Florida, August 25, 1848. During the Civil War he was sold at Columbus, Georgia, for $6,000 in Confederate money. After the close of the war he returned to Florida and clerked in a grocery store for his former owner—taking lessons meanwhile for a short time daily in a missionary school. Subsequently he was steward in hotels at Lake City and Jacksonville, Florida, and for a short time attended night school at Cookman Institute. In October, 1868, he was converted at a camp-meeting and joined the A. M. E. Church in Jacksonville, Florida; served as class-leader and steward till April 7, 1873, when he was licensed to preach; was ordained deacon in December, 1873; elder, March 4, 1876. While in Jacksonville he was inspector of customs, and was also appointed county commissioner of Duvall county. In 1878 he was transferred to Texas; was pastor at San Antonio and Austin; became presiding elder and vice-president of Paul Quinn College, at Waco; was elected bishop May 24, 1888; was bishop of the Ninth district, subsequently of the Sixth district, then of Florida, Georgia and Alabama; afterward in charge of Fourth Episcopal District, and president of the Board of Trustees of Wilberforce University. Was for four years president of Board of Publication of the A. M. E. Church, at Philadelphia; and for eight years president of the Church Extension Board, A. M. E. Church. Was member of the Ecumenical Methodist Conference at Washington, D. C., 1891; has traveled in Europe; presided over conferences in Liberia; and was a member of the Ecumenical Missionary Conference at New York, April, 1900; and of the Ecumenical Methodist Conference in London, England, September, 1900.

THE COLORED METHODIST EPISCOPAL CHURCH.

Between the years 1866 and 1870 the bishops of the Methodist Episcopal Church, South, formed several Annual Conferences composed of colored ministers. The preachers of these colored conferences requested the General Conference of 1870 to appoint a commission of five to consider, in connection with delegates of their own, the propriety of organizing the colored members into a distinct ecclesiastical body. The General Conference of 1866 had directed the bishops to organize the colored members into an independent body if the time should come "when, in their godly judgment, it would be better for them." So in December, 1870, a conventional General Conference, composed of representatives of eight Annual Conferences of colored preachers, was held in Jackson, Tennessee. Bishops Payne and McTyeire presided, and the colored conferences were organized into a separate ecclesiastical body. Two colored ministers were ordained bishops—the Rev. W. H. Miles and the Rev. R. H. Vanderhorst. The name chosen for the church was "The Colored Methodist Episcopal Church." All property held by the Methodist Episcopal Church, South, for the use of their colored members, was turned over to the new church. The value of this property was estimated at between a million and a million and a half of dollars. Two schools were established by the southern church for the education of teachers and preachers of the colored church. One, known as Paine Institute, named in honor of Moses U. Paine, who gave to the endowment $25,000, is located at Augusta,

BISHOPS OF THE COLORED METHODIST EPISCOPAL CHURCH.

Georgia. The other, known by the name of the Normal and Theological Institute of the Colored Methodist Episcopal Church, is located at Jackson, Tennessee. An assessment is every year placed upon each of the Annual Conferences of the Methodist Episcopal Church, South, for the support of these schools.

J. H. HOKE, D. D.

J. H. Hoke, D. D., was born of slave parents in the State of Alabama. His mistress taught him to read and write, and predicted that he would become an Episcopalian preacher. In 1867 he united with the Baptist Church in Jacksonville, Alabama. After spending three years as a student in Talladega College, Alabama, he taught in the public schools of the State for ten years. In 1875 he moved to Arkansas, serving as pastor in Augusta, Searcy and Hot Springs, meanwhile teaching in the public schools. In 1888 he was chosen general missionary for the State of Arkansas, and has filled that position to the present time. He has been president of the State Convention two years and secretary five years; also president of the State Educational Association. He was one of the founders, and has always been an ardent supporter of the Arkansas Baptist College at Little Rock. Few men have wielded a larger influence or have done a more desirable work than Doctor Hoke.

REV. GARNETT RUSSELL WALLER.

The subject of this sketch was born at Eastville, Northampton county, Virginia, in 1858—the second of seven sons of Ellen and John Waller. The latter died, leaving the mother the burden of eight small children. In 1872 she moved to Baltimore, Maryland, where each boy was given a common school training, and a trade; after which she encouraged them to follow the bent of their minds as to their life's work. One took up the law, three followed their trades, one took up medicine, and Garnett R. Waller was one of the two who felt called to the gospel ministry.

After spending three years in successful business, as a first-class shoe-maker, he entered the Lincoln University, Pennsylvania, and graduated in 1884. He graduated from the Newton (Massachusetts) Theological Institution with high honors in Hebrew and cognate studies, in 1887. During his course at Newton, Mr. Waller engaged extensively in evan-

REV. GARNETT RUSSELL WALLER.

gelistic work in Boston, New Bedford, and Syracuse, New York, founding in the last named city the First Baptist Church, which has had a prosperous history.

After graduation he accepted a call to the State of Maryland as general evangelist of the Southern Baptist Convention.

His work was a marked success from the beginning. His present charge is one of the many churches, Sunday-schools, and missions organized by him during his evangelistic labors in the State, over twelve years ago, in a small building on Aisquith street, with eleven members. In 1892 the property on Aisquith street was sold, and the congregation erected an edifice on Oak street, in a more advantageous section. Owing, however, to an ever-increasing membership, it was soon deemed necessary to purchase the present dignified and commodious structure, known as the Trinity Baptist Temple, seating seven hundred in the main auditorium, with sixteen other apartments for institutional work, such as a fitting school for young men in preparation for college and professional work. One hundred and twenty-five have received instruction in this department, the majority of whom are now successful in their respective callings. The church maintains three mission stations, all doing good work. Mothers' meetings and sewing schools, training school for kindergarten teachers, music and missionary training schools, social science association, composed of leading rare thinkers—these are some of the agencies for good employed by this progressive church.

Mr. Waller is an instructive and forceful preacher, an indefatigable worker, and an uncompromising advocate of temperance. He is a man of almost ascetic habits, having never used tobacco in any form.

As president of the Maryland Baptist Orphanage, president of the North Baltimore Stock and Loan Association for four years, secretary and treasurer of the Ministers' Conference (composed of thirty white and ten colored ministers), and corresponding secretary of General State Association, Mr. Waller has wielded an influence and power for good in his State that will prove a lasting benefit to his race.

He has high ideals as to church work, and so persistent has he been to develop them, that he has uniformly refused any inducement to leave his present charge.

His paper before the Hampton Negro Conference, on the "Relation of the Pastor to the Community," received the highest praise.

A. R. GRIGGS, D. D.

Allan Ralph Griggs was born of slave parents in Hancock county, Georgia, about 1850. His father's name was Sutton; his mother, Brazilia, belonged to a family by the name of Griggs. He remembers seeing his mother but twice, the last time after he had been sold at auction. He was taken to Grimes county, Texas, where he labored on a farm till 1867. He was converted in 1869, licensed and ordained in 1874. In 1875 he became pastor of the Baptist church in Dallas; while here he attended Ministers' Institutes, under the auspices of the Home Mission Society. In 1881 he aided in the founding

A. R. GRIGGS, D. D.

of Bishop College, and became one of its trustees. In 1886 he entered Richmond Theological Seminary, where he remained two sessions. He has been president of the National Baptist Convention, and is now superintendent of missions and educational agent in Texas. He is editor and publisher of the *National Baptist Bulletin.*

REV. H. N. BOUEY.

Rev. H. N. Bouey was born of slave parents, August 4, 1849, near Augusta, Columbia county, Georgia. At twenty-one he entered the Home Mission School at Augusta, where he remained two years. In 1875 and 1876 he served as probate judge in Edgefield county, South Carolina. Having labored as a missionary in South Carolina for one year, he went as a missionary to Liberia, Africa. In 1882–6 he served as Sunday School missionary in Alabama. In

REV. H. N. BOUEY.

1887–8 was pastor in Columbia, South Carolina; in 1889 he became general missionary for Missouri, a position which he has recently resigned to return as a missionary to Liberia. During the twelve years that he has been general missionary in Missouri, the Baptist cause among the Negroes has been unified and strengthened, the college has been founded, and the most harmonious relationship has been established and maintained between the white and Negro Baptists.

CHAPTER V.

THE NEGRO IN LITERATURE AND THE FINE ARTS.

UNDER the heads of "The College-Bred Negro," "Law, Medicine and Divinity," and "Politics, Journalism and the Lecture Field," may be found the names of some who are well-known as authors; but we include in this chapter a few prominent names of those only whose chief distinction is that of art or authorship.

In the world of art, in this and other countries, the colored race has furnished eminent names, among whom we may mention Guillaume Guillon Lethierre, a famous French artist of the classical school, who was once president of the School of Fine Arts at Rome, and some of whose paintings now adorn the walls of the Louvre Museum in Paris.

Edmonia Lewis began her career as a sculptress before the war, and persevered under the discouragements of poverty and the lack of liberal education, until she became famous. She finally had a studio in Rome, and while there, and before taking up her residence there, she produced a number of admirable works.

Henry Ossawa Tanner, though a comparatively young man, has taken high rank as an artist. He is a son of Bishop B. T. Tanner, noticed elsewhere, and was born in Pittsburgh, Pennsylvania, June 21, 1859. Having taken his ordinary school course, he studied in the Pennsylvania Academy of Fine Arts under Thomas Eakins, and was afterward a pupil of Jean Paul Laurens and Benjamin Constant, in Paris, France. Had honorable mention in 1896; took third-class medal in 1897; was awarded the Walter Lippincott prize in Philadelphia, in 1900; took second medal at the Paris Exposition in 1900; and is represented in the Luxemburg, the Wilstach Collection, Carnegie Institute, and in the Pennsylva-

115

nia Academy of Fine Arts. He was married in London December 14, 1899, to Jessie Macaulay Olsson.

Samuel Coleridge Taylor, an English mulatto married to an American woman of color, has become famous as a composer of classical music—his compositions being exceedingly popular in England as well as in the United States.

Blind Tom, a Negro and the slave of General Bethune, of Columbus, Georgia, gathering his first inspiration from listening to his young mistress play the piano, was one of the most remarkable musical prodigies of the nineteenth century.

Of authors whom, for lack of material, we have not been able to notice at greater length, we may mention:

John Stephen Durham, of Philadelphia, a former United States minister to Santo Domingo, is an author of note, as well as a politician, and has published in *Lippincott's Magazine* a novel dealing with life in Hayti.

Mrs. Fannie Barrier Williams, a prominent member of the Chicago Woman's Club, is distinguished as an authoress and a newspaper correspondent.

Alexander Poushkin, who belonged to an ancient family of Coyars, was the most celebrated Russian poet produced in the nineteenth century. He was of the Negro race, having the curly hair of that people and a darker complexion than ordinary Russians. He has been called "the Russian Byron." A strange ancestor, his maternal great-grandfather, was so great a favorite with Peter the Great that he conferred upon him a title of nobility. Poushkin was a man of varied talents, being a writer of prose fiction and history as well as of poetry, and having an ambition to figure in public affairs. He was exiled for some years, 1820–1824, for revolutionary sentiments; but in 1829 he was in the administrative service of the government in the Caucasus. He died in his thirty-eighth year from a wound received in a duel.

Jose Maria Heredia, regarded by some as the greatest of Spanish-American poets, is said to have been a mulatto; and the poet Placidio was a quadroon.

Paul Granier de Cassagnac, of France, editor, author, Bonapartist in French politics, is of mixed blood—is, in the language of one, "quite palpably colored."

Alexandre Davy de la Pailleterie Dumas, known as Dumas pere, son of the famous French General Dumas, noticed elsewhere, was, of course, the grandson of the St. Domingo Negro woman spoken of in connection with General Dumas. He was a noted. dramatic author and novelist. He was for awhile in the government service at Paris (1823 and subsequently), and took an active part in the revolution of 1830. He was a voluminous writer, of somewhat varied powers, his plays, novels and historical studies numbering many volumes, his literary labors extending over forty-three years. Alexandre Dumas, known as Dumas fils, son of the preceding, was also a most prolific and popular author, his writings embracing poems, plays, novels and essays. He began the publication of his productions when he was but eighteen years old. He was elected a member of the French Academy, January 30, 1874.

Notable among the writers who have shown the power of the men and women of the race to "wreak themselves upon expression," is George W. Williams, of New York, the author of a "History of the Negro Race in America from 1619 to 1880"—an exhaustive work (in two volumes of about eleven hundred pages). It is ably written, and gives evidence of not only a capable mind, but of conscientious and painstaking investigation and a will not to yield to discouragements and be thwarted from a worthy purpose by the obstacles that present themselves to the inquirer in a new historic field. He was the first colored man ever elected to the Ohio Legislature, and was at one time judge advocate of the G. A. R. of Ohio.

In the report of the Fifth Annual Conference in Atlanta, much of which is printed in another part of this work, will be found a list of more than thirty authors not mentioned above,

besides an astonishing number of college-bred Negroes who
have entered other fields of intellectual activity.

PHILLIS WHEATLEY.

In 1761 a Negro girl was brought on a slave ship to Boston,
and sold to Mrs. John Wheatley. Her mistress gave her
the name Phillis, and she was afterward known as Phillis
Wheatley. She was eight years old at the time she was sold
into slavery, but her appearance, after being properly dressed
and set to household work, and her evident sprightliness, so
impressed her mistress that she concluded to teach her to
read. This once begun eventuated in her becoming a good
English scholar and so proficient in Latin that she translated
Ovid's "Metamorphoses"—doing it so well that after it was
published in Boston, it was republished in England and
favorably received by the literary critics of that day.

At the age of sixteen she embraced the Christian religion
and took membership at the "Old South Meeting House." At
the age of twenty she was set free. Her health now began
to fail, and her former mistress sent her on a voyage to England. She had already published a small volume of poems,
and the fame of the "African poetess" had preceded her to
England. These poems, with probably some additions, were
republished in London, 1773. Her talents, her modest demeanor, and conversational powers that were held to be exceptional, made her a favorite with people of rank as well as
with those of letters.

Mrs. Wheatley, her former mistress, was so attached to
her that she shortened her stay in London by an earnest request that she return home, which she did only to find the
affectionate lady ill unto death. Not long after the death of
Mrs. Wheatley her husband and daughter died, leaving of
the family one son, who went to live in England, and Phillis,
left alone, shortly afterward married a colored man named
John Peters. The husband proved to be utterly incapable of appreciating so fine a nature, and her married life was

unhappy. She died in 1784, before she was thirty-one years old.

Brought, an almost naked savage child, from the wilds of Africa, a slave for about twelve years, meanwhile becoming a scholar and a poetess of distinction, as a freedwoman the associate of people of culture and refinement in Boston and London,—her case is a remarkable one. It is rare, certainly; but it ought to serve as an incentive to the young men and women of the race to improve their talents, refine their manners, live uprightly and achieve the very best of which they are capable.

PAUL LAURENCE DUNBAR.

Paul Laurence Dunbar, poet, novelist and newspaper writer, was born in Dayton, Ohio, June 27, 1872, son of Joshua and Matilda (Burton) Dunbar. His father had been a slave in Kentucky, but fled to Canada by underground railroad before the war. After the war ended he came back and made his home in Ohio.

Paul was educated in the common and high schools of his town. After graduating from the high school be began business to support his mother, then widowed. At this early age he contributed to newspapers, and was encouraged by Doctor Tobey, of Toledo, to continue his literary efforts. He wrote, for some time, for eastern magazines before the editors knew him to be a Negro.

In 1893 (at twenty-one years of age) he published his first book, "Oak and Ivy." His second one, "Majors and Minors," was reviewed by William Dean Howells in so kindly and discriminating a manner as to attract to the young author greatly increased attention. Howells pronounced Dunbar "the first black man to feel the life of the Negro æsthetically and express it lyrically."

In 1896 two volumes were republished as one, entitled "Lyrics of Lowly Life." This was followed by "Folks from Dixie" (1898); "Lyrics of the Hearthstone" appeared in

8

1899, as did also "Poems of Cabin and Field." "The Un-called," a story which first appeared in *Lippincott's Maga-zine*, has been described as "strong in motive and delineation, a story of the soul's struggle against environment—the story of a waif forced into the ministerial life by an adopted mother. The intensity is relieved by many humorous episodes and not a little quaint philosophy." One reviewer says: "The evolution of the hero in 'Uncalled' is a strong character study, and

PAUL LAURENCE DUNBAR.

the action of the minor characters and the construction of the story generally, prove that Dunbar is master of the difficult art of writing a long novel of sustained interest. He demonstrates three things: first, the Negro's gift of telling a story, illustrated in the humorous and dialect pieces; second, the Negro's serious revelation of his passion of love; and third, of far greater importance just now, the Negro's sense of verbal melody. Of the last, the entire collection of his poems is a triumphant and well-nigh unerring demonstration."

JAMES D. CORROTHERS.

This man, who has for some years been known as a poet and prose writer, has recently achieved unusual distinction by the publication of "The Black Cat Club," a collection of humorous stories and folk-lore. Of this work the *Literary Digest* says: "The date of publication of 'The Black Cat Club' should be commemorated by cultivated people of color as a second 'Emancipation Day.'

"Small and unpretentious as the book is, it marks the beginning of the independence of the literature pertaining to the American Negro. The humor of the black race has, in particular, been too much under the domination of white men. The early 'Jim Crow' idea of Negro fun held sway for many years in this country, and is still supreme in England. And the later 'Uncle Remus' conception, while it takes a true and somewhat typical specimen for subject, nevertheless views him through an atmosphere of kindly, yet obscuring, sentimentality. In short, it is unconsciously patronizing.

JAMES D. CORROTHERS.

"Even writers with colored blood in their veins have had the white man's view imposed upon them. The Negro is by nature imitative.

. . . "The Negro does not plot. His humor is 'touch-and-go.' His stories are pointless in form, though so insinuating in quality that they can never after be crowded out of the mind. Certain phrases, such as 'Ole Massa's Gone to Phillimoyo'k' (the title of a folk-tale in the present book), are overflowing with such natural, spontaneous humor that any number of varying stories could be built around each. In fact, 'protean' is the adjective that exactly applies to Negro folk-lore—so elusive is the secret of its informing principle.

"There is no logic, and only the semblance of literary

'form,' about Mr. Corrothers's book. The club, whose proceedings it records, is an organization with an utterly fantastic purpose, the worship of The Black Cat. The place selected is Chicago, where every type of Negro and Negro dialect is to be found. These types are presented as they are, without exaggeration or extenuation. As the author says, 'a window is let into Negro life so that the reader may see for himself.' Negro expressions, sayings and peculiar by-words are, to continue quotation from the author, 'set down at just such times and places as a Negro would naturally make use of them.'

"The original verse of the book is of all sorts, simple doggerel and pure lyric, yet equally filled with Negro humor and sentiment. ''Way in de Woods, an' Nobody Dah,' is a gem of flawless verse, with a depth of awe and mystery that is more than primitive; it is elemental. In one instance Mr. Corrothers has taken a genial revenge on behalf of his race. Negroes have borne the jokes as well as the burdens of the white men from the days of Homer. It is now the turn of the 'blameless Ethiopian.' The Rev. Dark Loud-mouth recounts to the Black Cat Club the way in which James Whitcomb Riley really received the bump on the head which the papers reported was the result of an attempted robbery. There is an air of realism about the narrative of this watermelon raid which would convince Mr. Riley him-self that it had actually happened, though 'I 'speck you's lied on 'at white man,' is the judgment of a less susceptible Negro auditor."

CHARLES W. CHESNUTT.

Charles W. Chesnutt was born in Cleveland, Ohio, in 1858, of free-born colored parents who had emigrated to Ohio from North Carolina several years before his birth. When he was eight or nine years old his parents returned to North Carolina, where he was reared. He began to teach in the public schools of that State at sixteen, and early in the

CHARLES W. CHESNUTT.

eighties became first assistant teacher, and afterwards principal, of the State Colored Normal School at Fayetteville, North
Carolina, the town which, under the name of "Patesville," is
the scene of many of his stories.   In 1883 he left the South,
and after a short sojourn in New York, during which he was
engaged in newspaper work, returned to Cleveland, where he
has since resided.   He was for a while employed as a stenographer in the law department of the New York, Chicago and
St. Louis Railway Company.   He was admitted to practice
at the Ohio bar in 1887.

Mr. Chesnutt's literary work began early, but was entirely desultory until within recent years.   He contributed
short stories and essays to the periodical press at various
times, and in 1887 began to publish in the *Atlantic Monthly*
the series of dialect stories of North Carolina folk-lore and
superstition subsequently published under the title, "The
Conjure Woman."   In August, 1888, his story, "The Wife
of His Youth," appeared in the *Atlantic Monthly*, and attracted wide attention.   This was followed, early in 1899,
by "The Conjure Woman," and later in the same year by
a "Life of Frederick Douglass," in the Beacon Series of
American Biographies, and "The Wife of His Youth and
Other Stories of the Color Line," "The House Behind
the Cedars," a novel, published in 1900, and "The Marrow
of Tradition," 1901, a novel on the race problem in the South.

The favorable reception with which his publications met,
North and South, shows that almost from the beginning of
his serious and sustained literary labors he took high rank
as an author.   Of "The House Behind the Cedars" the
Boston Herald said: "One of the most vitally interesting
books touching upon racial distinctions in the South that we
have ever read.   As a story it is a brilliant performance—
clear, to the point, keen in its interest, penetrating in its
presentation of character."

And the *Cleveland Plain Dealer:* "It cannot fail to win
for Mr. Chesnutt an honorable place among those novelists

whose works are read for their absorbing interest and remem-bered because they have a deeper purpose than the mere amusement of an idle hour.''

The Living Church (Milwaukee): "It has delicacy of manner, strength, and imagination, is full of robust English, and is possessed of unusual literary merit."

The *Richmond* (Va.) *Times:* ''The author's treatment of the difficult subject is strong, delicate, artistic, and gives his novel a unique place in American literature.''

MISS INEZ C. PARKER.

There is now living in Rolla, Missouri, a young woman who is a remarkable instance of the fact that even in the higher realms of thought and feeling which are regarded as peculiar to the most gifted of all races—the poets—the Negro may be at home.

MISS INEZ C. PARKER.

Miss Inez C. Parker, the person alluded to, is less notable in one particular t h a n Phillis Wheatley—and only a little less, even in that. Miss Wheatley was born a savage, in the wilds of Africa; brought a captive to American shores, utterly ignorant of the language which she was afterward to employ to make her famous; but she fell in the hands of generous and humane people who taught her carefully, instilled refined and ennobling principles, and inspired her to write her message—the first given out by a Negro woman—to assure the English-speaking world, in its own tongue, that the Muses company with

her lowly race. Miss Parker, it is true, was born free, and
in the land of light and liberty and ambitious endeavor; but
she was born of parents who were once slaves, and are still
poor and humble workers for their daily bread—the father a
native Georgian, the mother a native Missourian. They
were without the means to give her enlarged opportunities
for education; but she attended the public schools, afterward
having the advantage of some instruction by private teachers, and at length graduated from the high school department
of the public school of her native town. She had instruction
in music, but is disposed to place but a too light estimate on
her proficiency; and one authority* says that unaided she
learned French so as to both speak and write it, and that she
is a fair Latin scholar, and has such skill as an artist that
some paintings of hers have received favorable notice from
capable critics. She is said to be an omnivorous reader, and
in this way has acquired large information, liberal views,
and a lively interest in all that concerns mankind, especially
the people of her own race.

It will be noted that the beginnings of her career, though
not specially auspicious, were somewhat more so than those
of Miss Wheatley. She has widened the contrast between
them by the superiority of her work. Miss Parker's attainments as a scholar are probably not so considerable, but she
is the finer genius and is more distinctly the true poetess.
Those who know her personally speak of her in the highest
terms, declaring that she is modest and amiable, and that
her character is above reproach. This is confirmed by the
fact that the former slave-holding families now residing in
Rolla have her interests at heart and show her marked
kindness—some of them employing her to teach elocution
and music in their families.

Living with her parents in the house in which she was
born, she devotes her time to study, literary work, and
occasional teaching. The simplicity of her life evidently

* Dr. J. W. McClure, of Sedalia.

has its influence in giving that tone to her poetical productions which appeals to the human heart and challenges admiration by its fidelity to nature.

She has written a great deal for one of her age, and much of this has appeared from time to time in prominent journals and magazines. Of the three poems that follow this sketch, two of them dialect, it may be remarked that the lines on "Hope" won the prize offered by a Chicago magazine in which it was afterward published, and that of from thirty to forty contestants all but her were white. The "Honey Chile" was published in a St. Louis paper and created a stir in literary circles. A cultured gentleman was so struck with it that he wrote and published a kind of answer or companion piece. "When Daddy Plays de Banjo" was published in the *St. Louis Post-Dispatch*, and it was noticed editorially in a most complimentary manner.

Having space for only these, they are submitted to the candid judgment of the reader. The writer of this sketch is informed that Miss Parker has taken several prizes for poems and short stories.

If she has the good fortune to be able to make the most of her powers, she is destined to attain to rare distinction in the literary world.

HOPE.

The morn was dreary and gray with mist,
By faintest glimmer of gold unkissed;
But Hope looked forth with a vision bright,
And whispered low, with a smile of light:
"Oh, heart, dear heart, be of good cheer;
The noon will be fairer—never fear!"

Wind-swept the noon came, wet with rain,
All sighs and shadows, all tears and pain;
But Hope looked forth with a steadfast eye,
And whispered low as the wind shrieked by:
"Oh, heart, faint heart, be of good cheer;
At eve 'twill be fairer—never fear!"

The shrouded sun found a cloudy tomb,
And without a star came a night of gloom;
But Hope looked forth with a vision bright,
And whispered low, with a smile of light:
"Oh, heart, sad heart, be of good cheer;
The morn will be fairer—never fear!"

HONEY CHILE.

Passin' 'long you's prob'ly seed 'im—
      He wa'n't very big;
But wuz jes as smaht as howdy 'n'
      Fatteh dan a pig!
He'd sof' brown cheeks wid two big dimples
      In 'em when 'e'd smile,
An' big black eyes as bright as dollahs--
      Dat wuz Honey Chile.

Spect you's seed 'im lots o' times
      A-settin' in de do',
Wid 'is playthings all around 'im
      Scattehed on de flo'—
He'd toys o' mos' all soht an' 'scription.
      Foh I spent a pile
Gittin ev'ything I could to
      'Muse my Honey Chile.

Use to have to go an' leave 'im
      Soon as it wuz dawn,
An' when he'd wake 'e'd fin' 'is mammy'd
      Done got up an' gone;
I did n' know my wuhk wuz hahd
      An' heavy all de while;
I jes made it light by thinkin'
      'Bout my Honey Chile.

In de evenin's when de sun wuz
      Sinkin' in de wes',
I'd come back—ole mammy-bird---
      Back to de li'l' home-nest;
Lis'nin' to dat baby chirp
      My haht wid joy 'u'd bile,
An' I'd sing an' be so happy
      Rockin' Honey Chile.

Wukkin in de white folks' kitchen
   I 'u'd plot an' plan,
How I'd raise dat boy to be
   De fines' kind uv man;
Lots o' times about de fewchah
   I'd jes have to smile,
Think'n' how I wuz goin to 'range it
   Foh my Honey Chile.

But a day come when my hopes
   Dey vanish lak de snow—
Honey Chile he went to sleep
   To neveh wake no mo'!
While his mammy's haht wuz broke
   He jes lay still 'an' smile—
Looked jes lak a li'l' glad angel—
   Oh, my Honey Chile!

Jes peahs lak I couldn't stay heah
   'Cept I wants to save
'Nough to buy a pretty mon'ment
   Foh dat baby's grave;
An' I wants to have dis on it,
   Writ in propeh style:
"Tell we meets beyon' de riveh,
   Good-bye, Honey Chile."

WHEN DADDY PLAYS DE BANJO.

When daddy plays de banjo
   'E smiles jes kinder gay,
An' 'is foot jes taps de flo' right sof'
   An' 'is eyes look fah away;
An' up an' down an' 'cross de strings
   'Is han' behgins to walk,
An' us chillen lis'en stiller'n mice
   To hear dat banjo talk.

'E don' have time to play it much
   Except'n' in de night,
Afteh suppeh when de dishes
   Am all washed an' out o' sight;

Den daddy goes right to de wall
    An' lif's dat banjo down,
An' behgins to choon it up an' make
    Hit make a funny soun'.

But when he do behgin to play
    Jes lis'en an' be still!
Kaze you's goin' to hear de mockin'-bird
    Behgin to chirp an' trill,
An' de sky'll be blue and sunny,
    An' you'll hear de hum uv bees,
An' you'll feel de souf win' blowin'
    Thoo de blossoms on de trees.

You'll hear de brook a-tinkle-tinklin'
    'Cross de pebbles white,
An' a-dimplin' an' a-dancin'
    In de shaddeh an' de light;
Den you'll hear de bell a-ringin',
    An' de folks a-singin' choons,
At de chu'ch what we all goes to
    Uv a Sunday aftehnoons.

Den daddy stracks anudder choon
    An' you behgins to think
About de "swing yo' pardners all,"
    An' Lizy dresst in pink,
Wid roses in 'er hair, an' slim
    White slippers on her feet,
An' how, when she am goin' to dance,
    She look so mighty neat.

A-lis'nin' to de music den
    Peahs lak de sun shine clare,
Den suddent, 'fo' you knows it,
    Dah am twilight in de air,
An' great big twinkly stars come out,
    All hazy, soft an' slow,
An' 'mongs' de pines a night-bird sings
    Right trembly-lak an' low.

An' den you jis kin shet yo' eyes
    An' see de purply sky
Wid de new moon hangin' in it
    Lak a sickle 'way up high,

An' den you thinks about dat star—
    Hit's bigger dan de rest—
Dat shines right 'bove li'l' buddy's grave
    Out yander in de west.

You feels de dew a-fallin'
    An' hears mammy sorter sigh,
An' you jes keeps on a-grinnin,
    Yet you'd somehow lak to cry;
An' you's stiller dan befo' to hear
    Dem tones so sof' an' deep,
When all to oncet de music stops
    An' daddy am asleep!

MISS EFFIE WALLER.

MISS EFFIE WALLER.

Pike, the extreme eastern part of Kentucky, in a mountainous region, where the colored population has always been so small as to make it difficult for the State to maintain schools into which the scattered children could be gathered, is to be credited with a poetess, the daughter of parents who before the war were Negro slaves.

Effie Waller was born in Pikeville—the youngest of the four children of Frank and Sibbie Waller. During her earlier school years her parents lived at a distance of more than four miles from the nearest school. They were

unable to provide for private tuition, and as she was of delicate
health she was able to attend school very little; but by dint
of personal application she attained to such scholarship by
the time she was eighteen that she secured a certificate of
proficiency to teach in the common schools of the State,
since which time she has had fair success in that way when
not attending the State Normal School at Frankfort, which
she did during the years 1900 and 1901.

She began to practice "the rhyming art" at a very early
age, contributing poems to the newspapers of Pikeville,
Kentucky, and Williamson, West Virginia. Lately she has
made a collection of her productions, to be brought out in
book form, entitled "Songs of the Months and Other Poems."

CHAPTER VI.

The Negro in Business.

THE following seven papers are among those submitted to the Fourth Annual Conference held in Atlanta, Georgia, to consider various questions as to the condition, prospects and needs of the Negroes, as planned by the Atlanta University, some years ago. All except the address of Governor Candler were written by Negroes who have special knowledge of their subjects. Prof. John Hope is a teacher in one of the Atlanta institutions and a graduate of Brown University. Miss Hattie G. Escridge is a graduate of Atlanta University, and is book-keeper in her father's grocery store. Mr. H. E. Lindsay is a very successful Negro merchant, and Mr. W. O. Murphy, also a graduate of Atlanta University, is junior partner in one of the oldest Negro firms in that city. Mr. C. W. Fearn is the manager of a very interesting co-operative venture among Negro mechanics of Chattanooga. Messrs. Porter and Seabrooke, from whose thesis paper No. VII. is compiled, were seniors in Atlanta University in 1899. The latter has, since graduation, gone into the shoe business in Charleston, South Carolina.

I. OPENING ADDRESS OF THE HON. ALLAN D. CANDLER, GOVERNOR OF GEORGIA.

Mr. President, Ladies and Gentlemen of the Conference:—
I have come before you tonight with no prepared oration or speech. My duties are so exacting, that I have no time really to prepare such an address as this occasion merits. I have come because I am a friend to this old institution, and because I want you to know that the State of Georgia, through its chief executive, recognizes the usefulness of this institu-

tion to the State. (Applause.) And first, I want to endorse as my sentiments, and the sentiments of all good men in this commonwealth, the remarks which have been made by your distinguished president. All good men, fair men, philanthropic men, in this State endorse every one of those remarks. "The Negro in Business:" It is a theme worthy of the attention of every patriot in this and every other State in the greatest Republic of all the ages.

Unfortunately, in our portion of the great Republic, there have been too few avenues to successful effort open even to the white race, and much fewer avenues to successful effort open to the colored race. A generation ago we emerged from one of the most cruel, and I would be pardoned to say, that in my judgment, one of the most unnecessary wars that ever devastated the face of the earth. The result of this war was the freeing of the colored race; and like the young child which has not long had an opportunity to be taught, a new world was opened to this race. The position that they occupied prior to that time was entirely changed. They became in the eyes of the law the equals of the other races that inhabit this Republic. They were clothed not only with all the privileges, but all the responsibilities of citizenship. The scenes that surrounded them were new scenes; they had never been accustomed to them. They were like a child that is transported in a day from the scenes of his birth to other scenes, entirely different, if you please, on another continent. Necessarily, those things which attracted their attention at that time being novel, not only attracted, but riveted their attention. Yet the things which they saw, the conditions that existed were abnormal conditions. The people of the entire South were in a state of turmoil, in an abnormal state. In other words, everybody talked about the war, and about the results of the war, and especially did everybody talk about politics.

The young men of my own race at that time saw things that I had never seen; saw things that the men who had controlled the destinies of this State prior to that time, had never seen. They saw a riot at the polls, they saw methods employed by political parties, and I exempt none—all were guilty—they saw methods employed by political parties, in party elections, which were perfectly abhorrent to the men who had controlled the destinies of this State prior to that

WILLIAM H. MOSS.
An enterprising Afro-American of Boston, Massachusetts,

time; and these young men of my race, and the colored men, seeing these things, concluded that that was politics, legitimate politics, and hearing nobody talk about anything but politics, they concluded that politics was the chief end of life; but in this conference to-day, in the discussion of the problems, we are realizing the fact that there are other things

9

besides politics. Those men, as a rule, no matter in what class or race they belong, who regard politics as the chief end of life, are always unsatisfactory citizens of the country, no matter to what race they belong.

. . . .

But it is not astonishing that the young men of thirty years ago — the young men of both races, who had aspirations, who desired to make for themselves a name in the world — concluded' and looked upon politics as the only avenue to distinction, because that is all they discussed. Nobody talked anything else. Upon the farms you would hear the old colored men and the white men talk about their cotton crops; you would hear that, but there was no distinction in that. Those that desired to make for themselves a name, saw no avenue except'through politics. Now other avenues are open, and in the future still other avenues will be opened. It is more honorable to be a successful merchant, or to be a useful, intelligent mechanic, than it is to be a third-rate member of the American Congress. A man serves his God better, because congressmen, when I was in Congress, didn't serve God much; they served the other fellow. He can serve his fellow-citizens better, and he will serve his God better than any man who stands in the arena of partisan politics.

Now it has been demonstrated in this old institution. Thirty years ago I was a teacher. I took an interest in educational matters. I came here when they were founding the Atlanta University for the training of the youth of the Negro race for usefulness and good citizenship, because I had an interest in it. From that time to this I have not been on this ground. During that thirty years I know that this institution has done more (and I do not desire to disparage other institutions; I do not intend to disparage them), so far as my information has gone, to elevate the colored race than any other institution in the bounds of this State. (Applause.) You have done a good work; you have been a conservative people; and there is a great work ahead of you yet — a great work especially for all the teachers of this country, of both races.

I do believe that education properly so called, training in arts and science and literature, and morality, and especially in morality, is the most potent, indeed the only, education that can make us citizens worthy of the great Republic in which we live; and thus believing, I came here tonight to lend whatever encouragement I can to this institution which, I repeat, is doing more, in my judgment, and has done more, for the elevation of the race for which it is intended than any other institution in Georgia.

I want you to know that I am in full sympathy with you. I want you to know that I represent ninety per cent of the people of my race in this State. I want you to know that while there are men in Georgia who do not feel as I do about this matter — who do not feel that institutions like this, intended for the colored race, should receive the encouragement of every white man in Georgia — the percentage of those is very small.

I want to say tonight, in all sincerity, that the only consoling feature and reflection in connection with some of the horrid scenes that have been enacted in this State in the past — the only consoling reflection is, that those men who have engaged in these things constitute a very small percentage of both races. The man who would denounce the entire colored race for the act of one member of that race, or a few members of that race, is unjust. The man who would denounce the entire white race of this State because of the lawless acts of a few, is unjust. The people of Georgia are made of the same flesh and bones as their brethren in New England. Georgia was one of the old Thirteen. Massachusetts was one, and so was Connecticut, and so was New York. We were one people, with one common cause, and established the greatest Republic that has ever existed in the annals of the world; and we are now one people, and if crimes are

committed here in Georgia now by my race, don't blame me.
Don't blame the teachers, and the law-abiding people of this
State; they are not responsible for them.   If crimes are committed by the colored race, don't blame the entire colored
race for it, for I tell you before God tonight that I believe
that ninety per cent of the colored race of Georgia desire to
be law-abiding citizens.   They are as patriotic as I am, and
there is a very small proportion of the races that are responsible for these troubles.   I was reared among the colored
race.   I have lived with them all my life, and I know that
there are good white people, and I know that there are good
colored people, and I know that there are bad white people,
and I know that there are bad colored people.   I would advise
all of my fellow-citizens of both races to draw a line, separating the virtuous and intelligent on the one side, from the
vicious and ignorant on the other; and when we have drawn
that line, and arrayed ourselves on both sides of it, let those
who love order, and who love justice, and who love equity,
fair play, let's be careful that those who are allied on one
side, on the side of ignorance and vice, let's be careful that
they do not pull us over on their side.   We will reach our
hands to them, good white men and colored men — we will
stretch out our hands to those fellows on the other side, and
pull them over to us, if we can; but let's not allow them to
pull us over on their side.

I know that the colored man is as loyal to his friends as
I am.   I know that he loves law and order.   I know this,
that it has taken my race six hundred years to get up to the
point where we are.   I know it is unreasonable to suppose
that a race emerging from a state of servitude should accomplish in one generation what it has taken our race six hundred years to accomplish.   But at the same time I know that
these same colored men and women in Georgia are just as loyal
to their convictions, and to their duties, and as God-serving,
and as God-loving as my race are; and we want to teach one
thing, not the law of hate, but the law of love.   Hate never

CAPT. J. W. WARMSLEY.
Now in the Philippine Islands.

benefited anybody; love benefits everybody. Because, I repeat, I believe the only real happiness ever enjoyed in this world is in an effort to make other people happy.

But I have spoken to you longer than I intended. I would not have gone anywhere else tonight but to the Atlanta University. I have some visitors at my house that I have not seen for forty years, and I excused myself, telling them that I felt it my duty to come over to Atlanta University and lend my assistance in the effort to elevate and benefit the race among whom I have been born and reared, and for whom I have nothing but the kindest feeling and regard, and for whose elevation I have the most earnest desire; and besides, one of my guests told me to come, and I have come. I have delivered my little message. I have spoken sincerely, and I wish you God-speed in this work, and I believe that useful as the Atlanta University has been in the past, that on the line of this discussion, that the colored race will be crowned with abundant success. God grant that it may be. (Applause.)

II. THE MEANING OF BUSINESS.

(Paper submitted by Professor John Hope, of the Atlanta Baptist College.)

The Negro status has changed considerably since the Civil War, but he is today to a great extent what he has always been in this country—the laborer, the day hand, the man who works for wages. The great hiring class is the white people. The Negro develops the resources, the white man pays him for his services. To be sure, some few Negroes have accumulated a little capital. But the rule has been as I have stated: the white man has converted and reconverted the Negro's labor and the Negro's money into capital until we find an immense section of developed country owned by whites and worked by colored.

However, the Negroes multiply, and the succeeding generations, though wiser, show no alarming signs of physical weakness. Therefore, if we still have a demand for our services as laborer, the wolf can be kept from the door. We can still eat, drink and be merry, with no thought of tomorrow's death. But in that contingency we perceive a portent. To say "if we still have a demand for our services" implies a doubt. Already the Negro has no monopoly of the labor market. The white man is his competitor in many fields; and in some of the humbler walks, here in the South where honest toil has been held in reproach, white men are crowding Negroes out of places which in my childhood belonged to the Negro by right of his birth. For in the matter of inheriting work the Negro has been a prince. But we are already opening our eyes to the fact that we are not employed South because we are loved, but because we are a necessity, and that as soon as white capital can secure competent white labor for the same money with which it secures Negro labor, white capital is seized with a violent attack of race sympathy, and refuses to hire Negroes where white men are obtainable. To say nothing of high-grade artisans like brickmasons and carpenters, who are crowding Negroes, you see white porters, ditchers, newsboys, elevator boys, and the like, getting positions once the exclusive property of our people.

Let me say here, that while ignorance and incompetency may in some sense explain the mysterious departure of the Negro whitewasher, carpenter, newsboy and washer-woman in many quarters, I have seen too many competent Negroes superseded by whites—at times incompetent whites—to lay much stress on ignorance and incompetency as a total explanation. This change of affairs in the labor market South is due to competition between the races in new fields. The labor prince finds himself losing some of his old estate. Industrial education and labor unions for Negroes will not change his condition. They may modify it, but the condition will not be very materially changed. The white man will meet the Negro on the same ground and work for the same wages. That much we may as well take for granted, calculate the consequences of it, and strive by every means to overcome this falling off in our old-time advantages.

We must take in some, if not all, of the wages, turn it into capital, hold it, increase it. This must be done as a means of employment for the thousands who cannot get work from old sources. Employment must be had, and this employment will have to come to Negroes from Negro sources.

This phase of the Negro's condition is so easily seen that it needs no further consideration. *Negro* capital will have to give an opportunity to Negro workmen who will be crowded out by white competition; and when I say Negro workmen I would include both sexes. Twenty-five years from today it will be a less marvelous phenomenon for colored girls and women to see white girls and women pushing baby carriages and carrying clothes-baskets than it is today for white women to see colored women performing on the piano. Employment for colored men and women, colored boys and girls, must be supplied by colored people.

But supposing there should remain our old-time monopoly of labor; suppose we should do all the tearing down and building up and draw our wages, man by man, and there should be no press for bread, no fear of the winter's blast, from the winter's poverty; could we as a race afford to remain the great labor class, subject to the great capitalist class? The wage-earner, the man on a salary, may, by rigid self-denial, secure for himself a home, he may besides husband his earnings so carefully as to have a small income, but the wage-earner and man of salary seldom save a competence. It is exceedingly rare that they can retire from labor and spend an old age of leisure with dignity. It is usually the case that their last and feeblest days mark their most desperate struggle for sustenance. At that time of life when men ought to be most able to provide for themselves and others, these men are least able. There is little or no independence in the wage-earner, because there is no practical security. Bread is a great arbiter in this world. Say what you will of liberty and religion, back of the shrillest, most heart-rending cries this hard old world has ever heard has been the need of bread. The name of the cry may have been liberty, it may have been taxation without representation, it may have been vested rights, but much of the truth is that men have wanted the bread conditions to be easier. Millions of empty stomachs made the French Revolution possible. There is not much race independence for the race that cannot speak its mind through men whose capital can help or harm those who would bring oppression. We need capital to dictate terms. This notion is old enough but bears repetition.

However, suppose the wolf is kept from the door, and suppose the Negro has such independence as the law now grants white men. Suppose he can go and come as other men do; suppose he is molested in no political or civil rights, and suppose he gets a fair trial under the most unfavorable circumstances, is all this the *summum bonum*, is this the end of life—that it brings man to the point where he has his bread and his rights? It seems to me that the highest privilege, the greatest blessing, and the highest point of development which any man could seek, is that of being an interested and controlling member in the foremost matters of his own country, and through this interest and control becoming a partner in the world's activity. We are taught in Holy Writ that we cannot live by bread alone, and that life is more than raiment. Nor has man gained all that appeals to him as worth possession when he has his rights. Rights every man ought to have equal with every other man. But we are infinitely better off when we not only have the rights but comprehend their significance, the cause and the use of them. To attain to this position of dignity and manhood we must get into the world current. We cannot stem it by standing on the shore, nor can we ever know its power until we have leaped into the rushing stream.

This partnership in the world's business, to be sure, is fostered by the guarantee of fair enforcement of equal laws.

But the desire for partnership, and the ability to be partner, must be in the man himself. The law and public sentiment may protect a business man, but they cannot make him. The making is largely with the man himself. Now the age in which we are living is an economic one; manufacturing and merchandising claim the world's attention. No doubt this remark in a modified form has been made time and time again, ever since Jacob of old carried on his little business transactions. But as we scan history, it does appear that, through combinations and inventions, we are now under the immediate sway of business more than humanity has ever been before. Life and progress are most perceptible today in business activities. To be sure there are religious, moral and educational movements, glorious, noble and far-reaching. But the greatest, at least in its immediate consequences on the world, is the business movement; and nobody can tell to what extent even the moral, religious and educational efforts are influenced by business motives. Education and philanthropy often find their explanation in terms of business. Whenever an enterprise is proposed, the question arises, not is it right, is it best, but does it pay, how much will it bring? Empires have their reason for being, not through abstract formulæ of political principles, not through religious creeds, but through their value to the world's business. It is not thirst for christianity that is joining Russia with the Chinese sea, and the historic shores of northern Africa, with the diamond fields of the south. The struggle for business, buying and selling and owning are actually to-day the most daring and gigantic undertakings that have marred and made this world. I am not here to defend these motives, but to point out their existence, and to say, that our temporal, I say nothing of spiritual, salvation depends on our aptitude for conceiving the significance of present-day movements, and becoming a conscious, positive, aggressive party to them.

This idea of business is a *large* one, I admit. And many

a man accumulates thousands of dollars without realizing his relations to the rest of the world, his dependence on the world, and his independence of it as a result of his accumulations. But it is this idea that ought to be promoted among us in order that men of education and power may know that outside of the learned professions there is a vast field for personal honor and emolument, and for doing a great public good. In fact, we can have very few really learned professional men until we do have some capital, for a professional man must have time and facilities for increasing his knowledge. These cannot be obtained without money. This money must come from Negroes. Wage-earners alone cannot supply enough money. I therefore regard it as a menace to the progress and utility of professional men that business enterprise among us increases so slowly. We have not enough of teachers, preachers and physicians. In fact, there is still room, even under present conditions, for a few more lawyers. But none of these make sufficient money to supply them advantages necessary to their highest development and usefulness. More money diffused among the masses through Negro capital will alter this unfavorable state of things. No field calls for trained minds and creative genius to a greater extent than does business. To calculate prices months hence, to see what will be the result with such and such a factor removed or introduced, calls for men of large parts and superior knowledge, no matter where gained. I know of no men who as a class go so far for the good of others as do Negro men for the good of the race. There is a big lump of public spirit among us. All we need is to be shown how to use this public spirit. From now on, for many years, it must be employed in business channels, if it would do most and immediate service.

I do not believe that the ultimate contribution of the Negro to the world will be his development of natural forces. It is to be more than that. There are in him emotional, spiritual elements that presage gifts from the Negro more en-

10

nobling and enduring than factories and railroads and banks.
But without these factories, railroads and banks he cannot
accomplish his highest aim.   We are living among the so-
called Anglo-Saxons and dealing with them.   They are a
conquering people who turn their conquests into their pockets.   The vanquished may not always recognize this as true,
but the fact remains.   Now our end as a race most likely
will not be of the same nature as that of the Anglo-Saxon.
In the long run each will play a very different part; but, for
the present, for the sake of self-preservation and for the sake
of grasping the meaning of the civilization in which we live,
we must to a large extent adopt the life and use the methods
of this people with whom we are associated.   Business seems
to be not simply the raw material of Anglo-Saxon civilization—and by business I mean those efforts directly or indirectly concerned with a purposive tendency to material
development and progress, with the point in view of the
effort bringing material profit or advantage to the one making the effort; and I would include all such efforts, whether
made in peace or war.   I was saying, business seems to be
not simply the raw material of the Anglo-Saxon civilization,
but almost the civilization itself.   It is at least its main-
spring to action.   Living among such a people is it not
obvious that we cannot escape its most powerful motive and
survive?   To the finite vision, to say the least, the policy
of avoiding entrance in the world's *business* would be suicide
to the Negro.   Yet as a matter of great account, we ought
to note that as good a showing as we have made, that showing is but as pebbles on the shore of business enterprise.

Ladies and gentlemen, I have talked on for some minutes
without giving you the name of the talk.   I once heard a
scholarly Massachusetts congressman lecture, and he said
the subject of his lecture was "Whence and Whither," but
that the subject had nothing to do with the lecture.   In
refusing to christen my remarks I may escape the charge of
irrelevance.   Yet, if you force me to a confession, I dare say

I had in mind "The business man's contribution to the development of our race."

All of us know that material wealth is not the test of highest development and manhood. Yet, inasmuch as this highest development is dependent on the material foundation, the man who lays that foundation is as great a benefactor to the race as that man or generation that will in the end present that final gift, which shall yield the rich, ripe fruit of the emotions and the soul—the consummation of those aspirations that look beyond material things to the things that are abiding and eternal. In some such noble form as this the vocation of the business man presents itself to me; and were I a vender of peanuts or an owner of a mill, I should feel that I, along with preachers and teachers and the rest of the saints, was doing God's service in the cause of the elevation of my people.

III. THE NEED OF NEGRO MERCHANTS.

(Abstract of paper submitted by Miss Hattie G. Escridge, N, '98.)

One way, I think, toward the solution of the much-talked-of Negro problem is for us to enter into business. Let us keep our money among ourselves. Let us spend our money with each other. Let us protect each other as the other races do.

Every Negro who successfully carries on a business of his own, helps the race as well as himself, for no Negro can rise without reflecting honor upon other Negroes. By Negroes sticking together and spending whatever they have to spend with their own race, soon they would be able to unite and open large, up-to-date, dry goods, millinery, hardware and all other establishments as run by their white brothers, thereby giving employment to hundreds who otherwise have nothing to do. *All the young people who are graduating from our schools to-day, cannot be school teachers and preachers.*

Of course, education is used in all avocations of life, but it looks like a loss of time to spend a number of years in

school, to do just what any common laborer has to do. The
Negro has helped to make rich every race on earth but his
own. They will walk three blocks or more to trade with a
white man, when there is a Negro store next to their door.
They say the Negro does not have as good material as the
white man. In all cases that is not true, for they have both
bought from the same wholesale grocer and have the same
material. If there is any difference, give the advantage to
the Negro, for he is doing no more than the white merchant
has done before. If there are weak points in the race, we
should help to make them strong. It will be only by our
coming together that we shall ever succeed. The different
commodities that are brought into market by the Negro could
be disposed of with the Negro merchants and by bartering as
they do with the white merchants, benefit themselves and
aid the Negro merchant, and thereby the farmer and the
grocer would be building each other up and giving strength
financially to both.

IV. NEGRO BUSINESS MEN OF COLUMBIA, SOUTH CAROLINA.

(Paper submitted by Mr. H. E. Lindsay.)

Columbia has a population of over twenty thousand people,
half of these being colored. The Negroes here, as in most
Southern cities and towns, are well represented in the various mechanical trades. As to what they are doing in business can best be understood from the following:

We have about twenty-five grocery, dry goods and clothing stores in the city, varying in size from the little subur-
ban shop, with its assortment of wood and shelf goods, to the
well-stocked and neatly kept store, whose only difference
from other stores is the color of its clerks.

Possibly the business that represents the largest outlay of
capital is conducted by Mr. I. J. Miller, the clothier. His
store is located in the heart of the business center of the city.
Besides giving his business his strict personal attention, he
is aided by three clerks.

During last fall his estimated stock was $10,000 at one time. Mr. Miller, about fifteen years ago, commenced this enterprise with scarcely a shelf of goods; through toil and perseverance he has succeeded in establishing a business that not only reflects credit upon himself and the race, but stands comparison with the most favored enterprise of its kind in the city.

The next I shall mention is the well-known merchant tailor, Mr. R. J. Palmer. Mr. Palmer, on account of his thorough knowledge of his business, has for many years been the recognized leader in his line. He occupies his own building, valued at eight thousand dollars; it is located in one of the best business blocks in the city.

He carries in connection with his tailoring business a complete line of clothing and gents' furnishings—his stock representing some thousands of dollars. He visits the northern markets as often as twice a year to select his stock.

The enterprise of which I have the honor to be head is younger than the two mentioned above, and much the junior of many other enterprises of the race here, and we feel indeed gratified at occupying even third place.

Our enterprise is a grocery and provision store, with one branch business at its old stand, near the western suburbs. I was placed in charge of the business before reaching my maturity, and since completing a normal course at Allen University in 1892, I have devoted my entire attention to its management.

Our beginning was certainly humble. We opened up with a few dozen canned goods, wood, etc.; our stock valued at about forty dollars. In five years' time we made three additions to our building, and out of a little shop had grown a general merchandise store, where we sold from a paper of pins to a suit of clothes, from a pound of bacon to a barrel of flour. We conduct our business with five clerks and a delivery with each store.

Some of the other enterprises worthy of mention are Mr.

J. P. Evans, grocer, Mrs. Caroline Alston, dry goods, Mr. Richard Bell, grocer.

Mr. Evans has been conducting his business at the same old stand for over twenty years. His patrons are about equally divided between the two races.

Mrs. Caroline Alston, a lady who conducts a dry goods store, has met with much success in her more than twenty years' experience in business, and enjoys the esteem and confidence of the white race as well as her own.

Mr. Richard Bell, a comparatively young man, has succeeded well in his business; and in point of neatness and cleanliness his store is a model after which any one might pattern.

We have one drug store, Dr. James J. Leggett, a graduate of Howard University, in charge; two harness and saddlery shops; five confectioners; no saloons; seventeen boot and shoe repair shops; six blacksmith and wheelwright shops; two butchers; three newspapers, with two job printing offices.

The *People's Recorder*, a paper published and edited by Holmes and Nix, has a creditable circulation throughout the State, and is the most influential paper of the three. They have a creditable job department, in which are employed several printers.

The next is the *South Carolina Standard*. J. R. Wilson is one of its editors. The *Standard* is a neatly printed paper; their job department is second to none in the city, as their work will testify.

The *Christian Soldier* is a bright little paper edited by Rev. Richard Carrol, founder of the new orphan home.

We have twenty barber shops; the leading shops are all colored. We have three lawyers and three physicians: Dr. C. C. Johnson, Dr. C. L. Walton, and Dr. Matilda Evans.

Doctor Evans is an example to all women of our race who are standing aside and allowing the men to monopolize all the professions. She has won many friends since her coming to our city, less than two years ago, and has met with constant success.

We have two undertaking establishments, two mattress manufactories, three tailoring establishments.   Among the carpenters and brickmasons we have fully a dozen contractors, many of whom are worthy of mention, being honest and reliable, and have accumulated wealth.   Ninety per cent. of the carpenters and brickmasons are colored.

Rev. M. G. Johnson represents a building association that does a majority of the business among colored people.   The above is but a partial list of the many enterprises among the Negroes of Columbia.

V. THE NEGRO GROCER.

(Paper submitted by W. O. Murphy, '91.)

Were the questions asked, What is at this moment the strongest power in operation for controlling, regulating and inciting the actions of men?   What has most at its disposal the conditions and destinies of the world? we must answer at once, BUSINESS, in its various ranks and departments, of which commerce, foreign and domestic, is the most appropriate representation.   In all prosperous and advancing communities—advancing in arts, knowledge, literature and social refinement—BUSINESS IS KING.

Other influences in society may be equally indispensable, and some may think far more dignified, but, nevertheless, BUSINESS IS KING.

The statesman and the scholar, the nobleman and the prince, equally with the manufacturer, the mechanic and the laborer, pursue their several objects only by leave granted and means furnished by this potentate.

These facts were true a hundred years ago, and they are true to-day; and we as progressive, up-to-date citizens must push our way in and share the fruits of commercial effort.

Well has it been said that "man is the only animal that buys and sells or exchanges commodities with his fellows.

10

Other animals make an attempt, at least, to do every other thing that men can do except trade; and among them are types of every profession except the merchant. The beaver, the bee and the bird can build as well as some of our mechanics; the fox surpasses some lawyers in cunning; musicians are content to be called nightingales of song; the tiger is an uneducated warrior; lions are the lords of the forest—but the merchant who buys from one people to sell to another has no representative in the animal creation.''

Civilization depends upon the activity of the merchant, who by his zeal and acumen not only supplies the wants of the trade, but seeks out new products of other climes and furnishes a new market for commodities more or less unmarketable in regions where they are indigenous.

So we see that a business man is at once a leader, a servant, and a benefactor to the community, if he is a thorough business man.

This brings me to my subject, ''The Negro Grocer.'' I do not know that I can be considered as authority on this subject, as I am only twenty-eight years old, yet twenty-seven of these years have I spent in this business; so when I look backward in the dim past it seems, sometimes, that I now know less about ''The Negro Grocer'' in particular, and business in general, than when I was born a Negro in business.

There are in the city of Atlanta about six hundred licensed grocers, of whom forty-nine are Negroes. It has been estimated that the grocery trade of Atlanta amounts to approximately $1,000,000 per month, or $250,000 per week.

The population of Atlanta is placed at one hundred thousand, of whom forty thousand are Negroes; allowing five persons to each family gives us eight thousand Negro families. If each family expends three dollars per week for groceries, and I think such is a fair estimate, we have twenty-four thousand dollars spent each week by Negroes for Negro consumption.

If the forty-nine Negro grocers of Atlanta furnished the forty thousand Negroes this $24,000 worth of groceries each week, every one of these faithful forty-nine would have the pleasure of receiving over his counters nearly five hundred dollars each week.

You need not ask me, Are they doing it?

In addition to the $24,000 spent each week by Negroes for Negro consumption, a large sum is spent daily by servants who in a great measure are able to carry this trade whither they will. You need not inquire, Do they take it to the Negro grocer?

So much for the reality. We all know that the Negro eats, and eats, not always sumptuously, but certainly, at times, to his utmost capacity.

We know that these goods are paid for—*i. e.*, most of them; we also know that these forty-nine Negro grocers do not sell one-half of the goods purchased and consumed by Negroes in Atlanta.

Now for "the why."

That is the problem that confronts the Negro grocers of Atlanta, some of whom, years ago, embarked in business with no capital save a few dollars, their honest hearts and their necessities; no established credit; ignorant of most of the ordinary rules of business—many of them at the start would not have known an invoice from a bill of lading; with nothing to guide them but their native shrewdness, and nothing to save them from disaster save what they might accumulate by the strictest economy.

Yet in spite of all these drawbacks some of the forty-nine have managed to establish a fair credit and accumulate a few dollars and a little property.

The need is not so much for more grocers, but for younger and more intelligent ones; and we are looking to our schools for suitable material, so as to at least capture the $24,000 spent weekly by Negroes for groceries in Atlanta.

It was this idea that induced me to accept the invitation

to speak to you on this occasion. I thought I might drop a word which would be the means of inducing some young man to make an earnest attempt to engage in some kind of business in Atlanta and help these poor, struggling, hopeful forty-nine Negro grocers capture that $24,000 spent here each week by Negroes.

With the same ambition that sustained you in scholastic efforts; with the same energy and push that prompted you in your athletic contests; with the same pride that makes you prize your degree; with the same love that makes you boast of your *alma mater;* with the same economy and fidelity that actuated your forefathers, and with the same persistence that controls the forty-nine now struggling in the grocery business in Atlanta, we can capture our share, not only of the $24,000 spent by Negroes, but we can have a fighting chance for the $250,000 spent by Atlanta citizens, regardless of their race.

VI. A NEGRO CO-OPERATIVE FOUNDRY.

(Paper submitted by Mr. C. H. Fearn, Manager.)

The Southern Stove, Hollow-ware and Foundry Company was temporarily organized on the 15th day of February, 1897, and was permanently organized and incorporated at Chattanooga, under the laws of the State of Tennessee, on August 15, 1897. Our charter provides for a capital stock of five thousand dollars, to be divided into shares of twenty-five dollars each, which are sold only to colored people, either for cash or upon monthly payments, but in no case is a certificate of stock issued until fully paid for.

The foundry was built and began operations on a small scale on or about October 27, 1897, and has now increased and been perfected, until we manufacture stoves, hollow-ware of all kinds, fire grates complete, boiler grate bars, refrigerator cups, shoe lasts and stands, and other kinds of castings generally made in foundries. We also do a repair business

HON. THEO. W. JONES.

Ex-Member of Illinois Legislature. Successful Business Man, Chicago, Illinois.

which has now grown until it has become a business that pays well and is one of our chief sources of revenue.

The land, buildings, machinery, and all patterns are fully paid for except part of the stove patterns, and these we are paying for in products of our foundry; and we can say that we are virtually free from debt. Of the capital stock authorized we have sold $1,466 worth, and this has all been used strictly in equipping the plant; but this sum does not represent now the worth of our plant, as all our profits have been allowed to accumulate and have been used in the business.

By a unanimous vote at the various meetings of the directors of the company, it has been decided to draw no dividends until we shall have a fully perfected plant, and one upon a paying basis.

Our stockholders, or the majority of them, are active members of the company, and are men who are masters of different trades which are needed to successfully operate a foundry. We have men who have in the past been the mainstays of other foundries—men who for years have followed the business of pattern makers, moulders, cupola tenders, engineers, repair workers, stove mounters and blacksmiths. And we boast that to-day we are fully able to do work that any other men can do.

The objects in forming and operating the Southern Stove, Hollow-ware and Foundry Company are many. First, we believe if we can now invest our capital, together with our labor, that we will build up a business that will in years to come furnish us our means of support—a business that we can increase and build up until we shall look on it with pride and have the satisfaction to know that we are the owners and masters of the same.

We believe that to solve the great problems that confront us there is no better way for our race to attain the position it deserves than to become masters of the art of manufacturing. If we as colored men are able to run and operate the foundries that are built with the white man's capital, why

can't we do the same with ours?   When other races see that
we are able to become the masters of the different trades and
to employ our own capital, direct and control our own industries, then the time will come that we will cease to be the
serfs, but we will be the brother laborers in the great struggle of life.

We believe that by establishing foundries and work-shops
by the older men of our race, and the successful operation of
the same, that it will be to the betterment of the young men
of our race.   They will follow our example, and, being able
to have a place to learn the higher trades and to invest the
savings of their labor, it will stop the roving disposition of
our race and make them better citizens.   It is our duty to
watch, protect and guide our young men.   It is our duty to
establish places where they can learn to be masters of all
trades.

We believe it is our duty to our race to produce as well as
to buy.   No race or people can be prosperous who always
buy and never produce.   We must make if we expect to own,
and what we make must be for ourselves instead of for
others.

There is no doubt but what the South will be the work-
shop of the world; and as the South is the home of the
colored man, why can't he own and control the shops?
Gentlemen, I tell you the Southern Stove, Hollow-ware and
Foundry Company is a young plant, but I say it is a success.   It today stands out to the world as an evidence that
the colored man can manufacture.   Today we are offered
orders that will take us months to complete.   We need more
capital, we need more men, and we can say to you that if we
had the necessary capital to operate our plant as it should
be, that we could do the rest and we would show to the world
that the Southern Stove, Hollow-ware and Foundry Company
was an industry that is not only a pride to our race, but an
honor to the people of the country in which we operate.

We would be pleased to have any one come and inspect

our plant. It is a worthy enterprise and deserves support. We believe the time is not far distant when the name of the Southern Stove, Hollow-ware and Foundry Company will adorn the lists of the best and most prosperous manufacturing plants of the United States of America, and then, and not until then, will the object of this institution be attained.

VII. NEGRO BUSINESS VENTURES IN ATLANTA, GEORGIA.

According to the United States census of 1890 there were in Atlanta, Georgia, 28,117 Negroes. At present there are probably from thirty-five to forty thousand. Among this population the class in sociology of Atlanta University counted sixty-one business enterprises of sufficient size to be noticed. These were as follows:

Grocery stores	22	Undertakers	2
General merchandise stores	5	Saloons	2
Wood yards	6	Tailor, with stock	1
Barber shops, with hired employes and over $300 invested	6	Drug store	1
		Creamery	1
Meat markets	7	Pool and billiard parlor	1
Restaurants	2	Loan and investment company	1
Blacksmiths and wheelwrights, with stock	2	Carriage and wagon builder	1
		Real estate dealer	1

Total...61

There are some of the above that combine several businesses—*e. g.*, one of the grocery stores has a meat market, in connection; two others have wood yards; one a coal and wood yard; and one combines a grocery, restaurant, wood and coal yard and a meat market. In one of the above mentioned wood yards, coal is also sold; in another there is a restaurant.

The capital invested in these enterprises is as follows:

GROCERY STORES.

CAPITAL.	NUMBER OF STORES.	CAPITAL.	NUMBER OF STORES.
$100	1	$ 500	6
150	1	600	1
200	2	800	4
250	2	1,000	2
300	1	1,275	1
400	1		
		Total	22

Total capital invested.............................$11,925

`OTHER ENTERPRISES.

BUSINESS.	AMOUNTS INVESTED.							TOTAL.
General merchandise	$3,800	$2,000	$1,000	$ 500	$ 500	$	$	$ 7,800
Wood yard	500	500	400	200	150	50		1,800
Barber shop	3,000	2,500	2,000	1,800	400	300		10,000
Meat market	500	200	150	80	75	75	30	1,110
Restaurant	500	125						625
Undertaker	7,000	6,000						13,000
Blacksmith	800	600						1,400
Saloon	1,500	1,200						2,700
Tailor	200							200
Drug store	1,900							1,900
Creamery	300							300
Pool room	1,600							1,600
Investment company	4,000							4,000
Carriage builder	900							900
Real estate	5,000							5,000
Total								$52,335

This makes a total investment of $64,260 in all businesses.

At present three firms have an investment of $5,000 and over; four between $2,500 and $5,000; eleven from $1,000 to $2,500; twenty from $500 to $1,000; and twenty-three under $500.

The number of years in business is as follows:

YEARS IN BUSINESS.

BUSINESS.	UNDER 1 YR.	1-3 YRS.	3-5 YRS.	5-7 YRS.	7-10 YRS.	10-12 YRS.	12-15 YRS.	15-18 YRS.	20-25 YRS.	25-30 YRS.
Grocery,	1	1	2	3	2	5	3		2	1
Gen'l md'se,		2					1	1		1
Wood yard,		2		1	1				1	
Barber shop,			1		1	2		1	1	
Meat market,		1	1	1	2		2			
Restaurant,		1	1							
Undertaker,						1	1			
Blacksmith,			1		1					
Saloon	1					1				
Tailor,							1			
Drug store,			1							
Creamery,				1						
Pool room,		1								
Inves'nt co.,				1						
Car'ge bldr.,			1							
Real estate,						1				
Total,	2	8	8	7	7	10	8	2	4	2

The oldest business is a general merchandise establishment, twenty-nine years old; next comes a grocery, twenty-five years old, and two groceries and a barber shop, each twenty years old.

A comparison of the years in business and the invested capital is of interest:

	UNDER $500.	$500-1,000.	$1,000-2,500.	$2,500-5,000.	$5,000-OVER.
UNDER 3 Years.	6	2	2	....	....
3-5	3	4	2	....	....
5-10	5	8	....	1	....
10-15	3	5	5	....	3
15-20	1	....	....	2	....
20-30	2	1	2	1	....

The general merchandise store, which is twenty-nine years old, has $1,000 invested; the grocery store, which is twenty-five years old, has the same amount invested; contrasting with these is a grocery with the same investment, three years old. The two twenty-year-old groceries have, respectively, $400 and $500 invested; the general merchandise store, which has the largest investment, $3,800, is fifteen years old. The undertaking firm, with $7,000 invested, has been in operation fourteen years, while the $6,000 firm has been running ten years. Thus we can see that in the main there has been a growth in capital, due to the saving of profits; at the same time there are a number of old shops which show no growth, but continue to live, and there is also evidence of ability to begin new businesses with some considerable capital.

Nearly all these investments have grown from very small beginnings, as, for instance:

	CAPITAL AT START.	CAPITAL AT PRESENT.
Drug store,	$900	$1,900
Restaurant,	50	500
Grocer,	150	600
Tailor,	75	200
Undertaker,	0	7,000

PROF. R. T. GREENER.
Consul to Vladivostok, Russia.

The next question is as to the manner in which these establishments are conducted, and their special advantages and disadvantages. Most of them must, of course, depend primarily on Negro patronage. Of twenty-five firms especially studied in 1898, none depended wholly on white trade; nine had considerable white patronage, and two some white trade; the rest depended wholly on Negro trade. Much depends naturally on the character of the business; a drug store would get white trade only by chance or in an emergency; a grocery store might get a little transient white patronage now and then; wood yard might get trade of both races; restaurants and barber shops must draw the color-line without exception and either serve all whites or all Negroes; undertakers can serve Negroes only. All these considerations make, of course, a vast difference between white and Negro business men. A Negro undertaker in Atlanta is in a city of 35,000 people, chiefly of the laboring class; a white undertaker has a constituency of, perhaps, 80,000, largely well-to-do merchants and artisans. The white grocer has not only the advantage of training and capital, but also of a constituency three times as large and ten times as rich as his Negro competitor. Moreover, seventy-five per cent of the Negro firms are compelled by custom to do business largely on a credit basis, and, too, have fewer means of compelling payment. Finally, the Negro merchants, as a class, are poorly trained for the work. The twenty-five studied in 1898 were educated as follows:

College training 1
Common school education 9
Read and write only 12
No education 3

CHAPTER VII.

The Negro in Business.

(CONTINUED.)

IT IS hardly possible to place too great stress on the deep significance of business ventures among American Negroes. Physical emancipation came in 1863, but economic emancipation is still a long way off. The great majority of Negroes are still serfs bound to the soil, or house-servants. Emancipation, in striking off their shackles, set them adrift penniless. It would not have been wonderful or unprecedented if the Freedman had sunk into sluggish laziness, ignorance and crime after the war. That he did not wholly, is due to his own vigor and ambition and the crusade of education from the North. What have these efforts, seconded by the common school and, to a limited extent, the college, been able to accomplish in the line of making the Freedman a factor in the economic re-birth of the South?

Of the various answers that might be made to this question, none is more interesting than that which shows the extent to which the Negro is engaging in the various branches of business. Naturally business, of all vocations, was furthest removed from slavery. Even the ante-bellum plantation owner was hardly a good business man, and his slaves were at best careless sharers in a monarchical communism, and, at worst, dumb-driven cattle.

For a Negro then to go into business means a great deal. It is, indeed, a step in social progress worth measuring. It means hard labor, thrift in saving, a comprehension of social movements and ability to learn a new vocation—all this taking place, not by concerted guided action, but spontaneously here and there, in hamlet and city, North and South. To measure such a movement is difficult, and yet worth the trial. We need to know accurately the different kinds of business ventures that appear, the order of their appearance, their measure of success and the capital invested in them. We need to know what sort of men go into business, how long they have been engaged, and how they managed to get a start. Finally, we should know where this economic advance is being most strongly felt, and what the present tendencies are.

In the census of 1890, the following Negro business men are returned:*

Hotel keepers	420	Grocers	1,829
Saloon keepers	932	Retail merchants unspecified	4,490
Livery stable keepers	390	Publishers	20
Druggists	135		
Total			8,216

There are many obvious errors in these returns; the first three items are greatly exaggerated, without doubt, containing many lodging houses misnamed "hotels;" employes in saloons erroneously returned as "saloon keepers;" and hostlers returned as "livery stable keepers." The unspecified retail merchants also probably include some clerks, hucksters and restaurant keepers. With some allowances for these errors, it is probable that there are in the United States at least 5,000 Negro business men. Of these the following study has returns from something less than one-half, living in thirty different States and Territories, as follows:

TABLE No. 1.   NEGRO BUSINESS MEN BY STATES.

Alabama	136	Illinois	23
Arkansas	94	Kansas	30
California	43	Kentucky	72
Colorado	8	Louisiana	11
Delaware	16	Massachusetts	14
District of Columbia	50	Maryland	49
Florida	78	Mississippi	78
Georgia	324	Missouri	49
Indiana	4	New Jersey	36
Indian Territory	7	New York	80

* Eleventh Census, Population, Vol. II, pp. 355, ff.

TABLE No. 1. NEGRO BUSINESS MEN BY STATES—CONTINUED.

North Carolina	98	Tennessee	131
Ohio	14	Texas	159
Oklahoma	7	Virginia	105
Pennsylvania	47	Washington	10
South Carolina	123	West Virginia	9
Total			1,906

Condensing this table we have reported from

The North, east of the Mississippi	218	West of the Mississippi	407
The South, east of the Mississippi	1,281		
	Total		1,906

The value of this comparison is somewhat spoiled by the fact that the Negroes in the States of Georgia and Alabama and the middle South were more thoroughly canvassed than those in other parts of the country, since the Conference had more correspondents there. Nevertheless, it is clear that it is density of Negro population in the main that gives the Negro business man his best chance.

There were, of course, wide gaps and large omissions in such an inquiry. Small towns in considerable numbers, and country stores, were not returned, and many minor enterprises in larger towns. Of the large cities, the most important omission was the city of New Orleans. With the latter exception it would seem, after careful inquiry, that the returns represent fully seventy-five per cent. of the more important business enterprises among Negroes, and consequently give a fair picture of their economic advance in this line.

The term "business man" in this study has been interpreted to include all with stocks of goods to sell, and also all other persons who have at least $500 of capital invested; for instance, while the ordinary barber should be classed as an artisan, a man with $500 or more invested in a shop, with several hired assistants, is a capitalist rather than an artisan, and one hundred and sixty-two such men have been classed as business men. So, too, it seemed best to include thirty-one blacksmiths and wheelwrights who had considerable capital invested and kept stocks of wagons or other goods on sale. In several other cases there was some difficulty in drawing a line between artisans and business men, and the decision had to be more or less arbitrary, although the investment of considerable capital directly in the business was the usual criterion.

The different kinds of business reported were as follows:

TABLE No. 2. NEGRO BUSINESS MEN, ACCORDING TO OCCUPATION.

Grocers	432	Cigar manufacturers	8
General merchandise dealers	166	Photographers	8
Barbers with $500 or more invested	162	Brokers and money lenders	8
		Dealers in feed	7
Publishers and job printers	89	Dealers in fruit	6
Undertakers	80	Milliners	5
Saloon keepers	68	Banks	4
Druggists	64	Second-hand stores	4
Restaurant keepers	61	Harness shops	4
Hackmen and expressmen, owning outfits	53	Employment agencies	4
		Florists	4
Builders and contractors	48	Crockery stores	4
Dealers in meat	47	Carpet cleaning works	4
Merchant tailors	40	Upholstering shops	3
Dealers in fuel	27	Hair goods stores	3
Dealers in real estate	36	Lumber mills	3
Wagon makers and blacksmiths	32	Cleaning and dyeing shops	3
Hotels	30	Brick contractors	3
Green grocers, dairymen, etc	30	Dealers in cotton	3
Livery stable keepers	26	Ice-cream depots	2
Confectioners	25	Wire goods manufacturers	2
Caterers	24	Dressmaking shops	2
Plumbing, tinware and hardware shops	17	Private cemeteries	2
		Bicycle stores	2
Shoe dealers and repairers	17	Mechanics with shops	2
Fish dealers	15	Shirt factory	1
Furniture dealers	13	Toilet supply shop	1
Building and loan associations	13	Broom manufactory	1
Jewelers	11	Cotton mill	1
Market gardeners and planters	11	Assembly hall	1
Clothing dealers	10	Naval stores dealer	1
Wall paper and paint shops	10	School of music	1
Bakers, with shops	10	Fan manufactory	1
Dry goods dealers	9	Carpet manufactory	1
Cotton gin proprietors	9	Handle factory	1
Steam laundries	8	Rubber goods shop	1
Proprietors of machine shops	8	Book store	1
Miscellaneous, undesignated			82

Total..1,906

It must be remembered in scanning these figures, that on most lines of business here reported, only establishments of considerable size and success have been reported. There are, for instance, large numbers of ice-cream dealers, pool rooms, cleaning and dyeing shops, employment agencies, and the like among Negroes; most of these, however, are small and short-lived, and only a few well-established businesses in these lines have been reported. Again, under the method employed in gathering these facts, it is hardly possible that the real proportion between the different kinds of business is correctly pictured, and there are doubtless large omissions here and there.

Perhaps the most instructive way of studying these businesses would be in the light of their historic evolution from the past economic condition of the Negro. For example, it is easy to see how the barber, the caterer and the restaurant keeper were the direct economic progeny of the house-servant, just as the market gardener, the saw-mill proprietor and the florist were descended from the field-hand. We may, indeed, divide the business men in the above table as follows:

(*a*) HOUSE-SERVANT CLASS.—Barbers, restaurant keepers, expressmen, butchers, caterers, liverymen, bakers, milliners, etc.—462.

(*b*) FIELD-HAND CLASS.—Market gardeners, green grocers, dairymen, cotton-gin owners, florists, lumber-mill owners, etc.—61.

(*c*) PLANTATION MECHANIC CLASS.—Builders and contractors, blacksmiths, brickmakers, jewelers, shoe dealers and repairers, machinists, cigar manufacturers, tinners, paper hangers and painters, harness dealers, upholsterers, etc.—176.

(*d*) THE TRADERS.—Grocers, general merchants and dealers in fuel, fish, clothing, furniture, feed, dry goods, second-hand dealers—695.

(*e*) THE CAPITALISTS.—Bankers, real estate dealers, money lenders, building and loan associations, etc.—67.

11

(*f*) THE MANUFACTURERS.—Makers of shirts, brooms, fans, carpets, handles, rubber goods and the cotton mill—9.

(*g*) CO-OPERATIVE EFFORTS.—Undertakers, druggists, publishers, cemeteries, printers, etc.—189.

(*h*) EFFORTS FOR AMUSEMENT.—Saloons, pool rooms, photographers, bicycle dealers, etc.—101.

No economic development is altogether accidental—previous occupation, enforced co-operation, the natural instinct to barter, and the efforts for recreation, explain among American Negroes, as among other people, their present occupations. Let us take up the classes in order as indicated above.

It is a well-known fact that the aristocracy of the plantation slaves were the house-servants—those who, for appearance, ability and intelligence, were selected from the mass of the slaves to perform household duties at the master's house. Often such servants were educated and skillful, and at all times they were the class which, when emancipation came, made the first steps toward independent livelihood. The master's valet set up his barber shop in town, and soon had a lucrative trade; the cook became proprietor of a small eating stand or restaurant, or, if he was exceptionally efficient and noted for certain dishes, he became a caterer. It was in this way that the famous guild of black caterers arose in Philadelphia. In similar ways, but more slowly, a little saving of capital transformed the driver into the expressman, the coachman into the livery stable keeper, the laundress into the proprietress of a public laundry. The most successful of these ventures hitherto have been those of the barber, the restaurant-keeper, the caterer and the expressman. There were in 1890 some 17,480 Negro barbers reported. Most of these were journeymen working for wages; the rest were largely proprietors of small shops, either entirely without assistants, or with one helper on Saturday nights. Neither of these classes would come under consideration here. There are, however, a number of barbers, one hundred and sixty-two of whom are reported here, and whose actual number may be three hundred or more, who are really business men. They own large, elegant shops with costly furniture, hire from three to eight assistants and do a lucrative business. The one hundred and sixty-two reported have nearly $200,000 capital invested, as follows:

Having investment of $ 500 to $1,000 60
     "   "   1,000 to   2,500 63
     "   "   2,500 to   5,000 12
     "   "   5,000 to 10,000 3
Others, over $500 24

Of the restaurant keepers nineteen had from $1,000 to $2,500 invested, and twelve from $2,500 to $5,000; fourteen had from $500 to $1,000. The caterers, as a class, are well-to-do men of intelligence. It is difficult to discriminate in these cases between their capital and their accumulated wealth. Their reported capital is:

Having investment of $ 100 to $ 500 1
     "   "   500 to   1,000 1
     "   "   1,000 to   2,500 5
     "   "   2,500 to   5,000 5
     "   "   5,000 to 10,000 4
     "   "   10,000 to 50,000 2
Unknown 6

The expressmen and hackmen have considerable business in several southern cities. The fifty reported had capital as follows:

Having investment of $ 500 to $ 1,000 8
     "   "   1,000 to   2,500 16
     "   "   2,500 to   5,000 20
     "   "   5,000 to 10,000 9

This whole class represented directly after the war, and up to about ten or fifteen years ago, the most prosperous class of Negroes. The caterers, barbers and stewards were leaders in all social movements among Negroes, and held the major part of the accumulated wealth. Lately, however, the class has lost ground. The palatial hotel and large restaurant have displaced the individual caterer in business, both white and black; the cab and transfer lines are crowding the single hackmen, and in many other lines of work the influence of aggregated capital has proven disastrous to the emancipated house-servant. The barbering business has fallen into dislike among Negroes, partly because it had so long the stigma of race attached and nearly all barbers were Negroes, and especially because the Negro barber was compelled to draw the color-line.

The great mass of the slaves were field-hands driven to the most unskilled kinds of agriculture. This, today, forms the great unrisen horde of freedmen who swarm in the country districts of the South, and whose social development and economic emancipation has scarcely begun. In a few cases some of them own large plantations and have money invested in cotton gins, plantation stores, market gardening and shipping to northern markets. Possibly they might be called business men. Eleven such are so denominated in this study, and have capital invested as follows:

Having investment of $	500 to $	1,000	1
"	"	1,000 to	2,500	2
"	"	2,500 to	5,000	2
"	"	5,000 to	10,000	4
"	"	50,000 and over	1
Unknown			1

Of course this does not take account of those who are simply large land owners and farmers. These eleven, and scores of others like them, not reported in this query, represent a sort of border class—the first turning of the field-hand from pure agriculture to something like merchandising. The green grocers, dairymen, and the like, have gone a step further and established market stalls or stores for the sale of the products of their farms. Thirty of these are reported, which does not include the numerous small hucksters:

Having investment of $	100 to $	500	7
"	"	500 to	1,000	6
"	"	1,000 to	2,500	12
"	"	2,500 to	5,000	3
"	"	5,000 to	10,000	2

The other callings which have developed logically from this class are few in number, and of importance chiefly as indicating tendencies. The three lumber mills have an aggregate capital of $10,000, and the four florists, $6,200. Much future interest attaches to the economic development of the former field-hand and present metayer. There is, as yet, no trace of house industries or domestic manufactures of any sort, although it would seem that, theoretically, the economic hope of the black South lies there.

The *elite* of the field-hands were the slave mechanics—a class which, in some respects, rivaled the house-servants in importance. During slavery they were the artisans of the South, and although emancipation brought the severe competition of better trained mechanics, and complicated the situation by drawing the color-line, still Negro mechanics continue to do a large amount of work in the South. Moreover, some, by saving money, have become capitalists on a considerable scale; especially is this true of carpenters and builders. It is difficult to estimate the invested capital of a contractor, as it varies so from job to job and from season to season. Forty-one contractors are reported, as follows:

Having investment	of $	500 to $ 1,000	10
"	"	1,000 to 2,500	14
"	"	2,500 to 5,000	4
"	"	5,000 to 10,000	8
"	"	10,000 to 50,000	5

One large brickmaker has $10,000 invested. The tin shops usually have small investments, under $2,500. Three have over $5,000. The eleven jewelers are watch and clock repairers with small stocks of goods. They have sums varying from $100 to $5,000 invested. Nearly all the other vocations mentioned as belonging to this class have small capital, and are but a step removed from the journeyman mechanic. The shoemaking business some years ago had a considerable number of large enterprises making shoes to order. The ready-made machine shoe has driven all but a few of these shops out of business, leaving only the small repair shops. A few of the older shops, of which six are reported, still do a large custom business, and to these are now being added regular shoe stores, of which eleven are here reported. The great industrial schools are trying to make these enterprises, and the mechanical industries whence they sprung, their especial field of work and, eventually, their efforts will undoubtedly bear fruit. As yet there is, however, little trace of this movement.

So far we have considered three great classes of business venture, the logical origin of which is plainly seen in the house-servant, the field-hand and the slave mechanic. Of course this does not say that every individual green grocer was a field-hand before the war, or every barber a house-servant. It merely serves as a rough indication of a social evolution, and is true when applied to the great mass of the Negroes.

We now come to the traders—the merchants proper. The African Negro is a born trader, and despite the communism of the slave plantation, considerable barter went on among the slaves, and between them and the whites. The Negroes, under the better class of masters, enjoyed a *peculium* earned by working overtime, and expended as they wished. In some cases they owned quite a little property and were able to buy their freedom. In most cases they merely kept themselves in a little pocket money.

While trade and property were not unknown to slaves, yet the Negro merchant is distinctly a *post-bellum* institution. The Negro grocery and general merchandise store is the direct descendant of the "store-house" on the old plantation, where the "rations" were distributed every Saturday to the assembled slaves. After emancipation these "rations" became "supplies" advanced to the black tenant, and the "store-house" developed into a store with a variety of goods. Finally, merchants outside the plantations began to furnish supplies for the various plantations round about. In this development the Negro who had saved a little capital was

HON. E. H. MORRIS.

Grand Master Colored Odd Fellows in United States. Richest Colored Man
in Chicago, Illinois.

easily attracted into the grocery and general merchandise business; if he had tenants on his own farm, he set up a little store to "furnish" them. If not, he set up a little store in town and caught the transient trade of farmers and laborers. In this way the business has spread until there is scarcely a town or hamlet in the South which has not its Negro grocer. The five hundred and ninety-eight grocers and general merchants reported here form, therefore, only a small part of the total merchants thus engaged. The census of 1890, reporting six thousand three hundred and nineteen retail merchants, perhaps approximates the truth.

Combining the grocers and general merchants, we find that those reported represent a total investment of $1,828,-243, in sums as follows:

Investment under $		500	174	32 per cent.
"	of	500 to 1,000	164	30 per cent.
"		1,000 to 2,500	171	31 per cent.
"		2,500 to 5,000	23 }	7 per cent.
"		5,000 and over	15 }	

A little less than a third of these stores are small shops with a few hundred dollars worth of shelf goods bought on credit. Another third are stores worth $1,000 to $2,500, invested in a considerable variety of goods. They have Negro clerks and usually make a good appearance. Seven per cent. are large ventures. It is a question as to what, under present conditions, is to be the future of such stores. Certainly it would seem that they may form a very important field of enterprise in the future, especially when the black peasant becomes emancipated, and the present cry of "Negro money for Negro merchants" continues to grow louder.

The other merchants deal principally in wood and coal, fish, new and second-hand furniture and clothing, dry goods, feed and fruit. Taking the dealers in these eight articles, we find they have $251,994 invested, as follows:

Investment under $		500	15
"	of	500 to 1,000	17
"		1,000 to 2,500	32
"		2,500 to 5,000	13
"		5,000 and over	14
"		unknown	8

It would seem probable that we might expect a considerable increase in these minor businesses among Negroes in the future. The great drawback is the little knowledge of business methods among Negroes. Their whole training, their idealistic temperament, is against them. Moreover, it is difficult to overcome these defects, because it is so hard to get openings for Negro youth to learn business methods. Even in the North how many firms stand ready to allow a bright black boy to come into their counting rooms and learn the difficult technique of modern commercial life?

It is a difficult thing for those unused to the notion of property to learn to save. Moreover, the national crime perpetrated in the mismanagement of the Freedman's Bank had wide-spread influence in discouraging the saving habit. As it is today, there is not among all these millions any far-reaching movement to encourage or facilitate saving except such local efforts as have arisen among themselves. While their extravagance and carelessness in the expenditure of their incomes is characteristic of the race, and will be for some time, yet there is some considerable saving even now, and much money is invested. Land and houses are naturally favorite investments, and there are a number of real estate agents. It is difficult to separate capital from accumulated wealth in the case of many who live on the income from rents or buy and sell real estate for a profit. Thirty-six such capitalists have been reported, with about $750,000 invested. There are four banks—in Washington, D. C.; Richmond, Virginia; and Birmingham, Alabama; and several large insurance companies which insure against sickness and death, and collect weekly premiums. There are a number of brokers and money lenders springing up here and there, especially in cities like Washington, where there is a large salaried class.

The most gratifying phenomenon is the spread of building and loan associations, of which there are thirteen reported:

Philadelphia, Pennsylvania.. 3
Washington, D. C.. 1
Hampton, Virginia... 1
Ocala, Florida.. 1
Sacramento, California.. 1
Wilmington, North Carolina.. 2
Augusta, Georgia... 1
Little Rock, Arkansas.. 1
Portsmouth, Virginia... 1
Anderson, South Carolina... 1

There are probably several more of these associations not reported. The crying need of the future is more agencies to encourage saving among Negroes. Penny savings banks with branches in the country districts, building and loan associations and the like would form a promising field for philanthropic effort. The Negroes, themselves, have as yet too few persons trained in handling and investing money. They would, however, co-operate with others, and such movements well-started would spread.

If the general training of the Negro was unfavorable to general business enterprise, it was even more ill-suited to imparting the technical knowledge which the manufacturer needs. It will, therefore, be many years before the Negro will enter this field. Still, there are even now some interesting ventures which must be regarded as experiments. There is the Coleman Cotton Mill, spoken of in the Atlanta University Publications, No. 4. During the past year machinery has been installed, but the mill has not yet started. The foundry described among the contributed papers is small but successful, and looks as though it might survive. There are several broom factories, one of which is reported here, and a number of minor manufactures which partake something of the nature of handicrafts. As yet there is little or no trace of house industries. Here is another field for philanthropic effort. If, throughout the South, the Negro peasant proprietor could eke out the scanty earnings of the farm by home manufactures, it would solve many vexed problems: it would establish the country home, elevate the Negro womanhood from the rough work of the field, lessen the temptation to migrate to cities and decrease idleness and crime. Lack of profitable congenial occupation for the rising middle class of Negroes is the central economic problem of the South to-day, and house industries would, in a measure, solve it.

Under co-operative effort have been grouped a number of business ventures whose existence is due primarily to the peculiar environment of the Negro in this land. Segregated as a social group, there are many semi-social functions in which the prevailing prejudice makes it pleasanter that he should serve himself if posssble. Undertakers, for instance, must come in close and sympathetic relations with the family. This has led to Negroes taking up this branch of business, and in no line have they had greater success. Twenty-three of those reported had over $5,000 capital invested, and there are, in fact, many more than this. Probably $500,000 is invested by Negroes in this business. Then, too, the demand for pomp and display at funerals has compelled these undertakers to equip their establishments unusually well. In Philadelphia, Baltimore, Atlanta and other cities there are Negro undertaking establishments equal in most of their appointments to the best white establishments. The advent of the Negro physician and undertaker naturally called for the drug store. Sixty-four drug stores are reported; forty-seven of which have over $1,000 invested. They are especially popular in the South for the social feature of the soda fountain and for their business partnership with sick benefit societies. They are usually neat and well conducted, and are a favorite venture for young Negro physicians. There are many private cemeteries owned by companies and societies, only two of which are reported here. They arose from the color-line in burial and the poor condition of the public burial grounds for colored people. Finally, a demand for news and books among themselves has led to the establishment of many hundred newspapers, of which over a hundred still survive, and to three or four publishing houses. The more successful publishing houses are connected with the large Negro church organizations, as the African Methodist at Philadelphia and Nashville; the Methodist Zion at Charlotte, North Carolina; and the Baptist at Nashville. These publish denominational literature, papers and books. They own four buildings in all, and the largest has a plant valued at $45,000. There are some other small publishing establishments of no great importance. The newspapers are dealt with in another place.

These enterprises are peculiar instances of the "advantage of the disadvantage"—of the way in which a hostile environment has forced the Negro to do for himself. On the whole he has begun to supply well some of the needs thus created.

Efforts to supply the large social demand for recreation and amusement are a large part of the co-operative efforts noted above. The Negro church has, until recently, been the chief purveyor of amusement to the mass of Negroes, and even now it supplies by far the larger part of social intercourse and entertainment for the masses. At the same time there is a large unsatisfied demand for recreation natural to a light-hearted people who work hard. The saloon and the pool room supply a part of this demand, and of the sixty-eight saloons reported, fifty-four have over $1,000 invested. The abuse of alcoholic liquors is not one of the especial offenses of the Negro, and yet he spends considerable in this way, especially during the Christmas holidays. The saloon among these people, even more than among the Irish and other city groups, is a distinct social center. In the country towns of the black belt, the field-hands gather there to gossip, loaf and joke. In the cities a crowd of jolly fellows can be met there and in the adjacent pool rooms. Consequently, the business has attracted Negroes with capital, in spite of the fact that the Negro church distinctly frowns on the vocation, which means some social ostracism for the

liquor dealer. Next to saloons in importance come the
traveling Negro vaudeville shows. None of these are reported here, for having no permanent headquarters they
were difficult to reach; but there are known to be some three
or four successful companies of this sort traveling about the
country. Most of them are compelled to have white managers in order to get entree into the theaters, but they are
largely under Negro control, and represent a considerable
investment of Negro capital. Other caterers to amusements
are the bicycle dealers, photographers and the like.

There is a large field for development here, and for considerable education and social uplifting. Few people, for
instance, have stronger dramatic instincts than Negroes,
and yet the theater is almost unknown among them. Much
could be done to elevate and enlighten the masses by a
judicious catering to their unsatisfied demand for amusement. Here is a chance for philanthropy and five per cent.
for black and white capitalists.

Compared with the immense sums of money invested in
American business enterprises, the showing of the Negro
race seems very meager; but when one considers that Negro
business has all grown up since emancipation, and the
poverty and lack of training of the freedmen—they had
nothing when they received their freedom—the saving and
investment by Negroes of six or eight millions in business
enterprises, managed by themselves, is a very creditable
accomplishment. Seventy-nine per cent. of this investment
is in sums less than $2,500, which shows the popular char-
acter of the business movement. It is a significant fact that
of the twelve enterprises having an investment of $50,000
or over, more than half are in the South.

The figures here given deal with those enterprises only
that are managed wholly by Negroes. Wealthy Negroes,
North and South, invest largely in enterprises conducted by
whites, as of course, Negro business ventures have not yet
reached a point where they attract the capitalist.

The next question of interest is how long the different enterprises reported have been in existence, and what the average age of each business venture is.

Of all the businesses reported, 32 per cent. have been established one year or less; 16 per cent. from one to three years; 14.7 per cent. from three to five years; 24.9 per cent. from five to ten years; 25.9 per cent. from ten to twenty years; 11.8 per cent. from twenty to thirty years; 3.5 per cent. for thirty years or more.

Those enterprises that show the longest average establishment (over fifteen years) are those kinds of business toward which the freedmen most naturally turned, viz., barbers, caterers, building contractors, market gardeners and florists.

Next comes those established more than ten and less than fifteen years: Real estate dealers, grocers, undertakers, building and loan associations, fuel dealers, expressmen, hardware, green grocers, butchers, clothiers, bakers, jewelers and dealers in hair goods.

These represent most of the successful businesses which are enterprises of the freedmen's sons rather than the ex-slaves themselves. Those businesses toward which capital has but recently turned are, among others: General merchandise, saloons, banks and insurance societies, publishing houses, newspapers, drug stores, hotels, dry goods stores, shoe stores, confectionery stores, photograph galleries, etc.

Businesses like the grocery business, conducting restaurants, fish dealing, tailoring, second-hand stores and the like, have a large number of both old and new ventures. On the whole, then, it may be said that the tendency is to venture more and more boldly into the purely commercial lines where capital and experience are the determining factors, and where a severe test of the Negro's ability to enter modern competitive business life will be made.

A closer study of the geographical distribution of Negro business is instructive.

PROF. I. GARLAND PENN.

Cities having twenty or more Negro merchants are as follows:

Birmingham, Alabama, thirty-two; Mobile, Alabama, twenty-five; Montgomery, Alabama, twenty; Little Rock, Arkansas, forty-two; Washington, District of Columbia, forty-nine; Atlanta, Georgia, fifty; Savannah, Georgia, thirty; Macon, Georgia, twenty-seven; Louisville, Kentucky, thirty-five; Baltimore, Maryland, thirty-one; Vicksburg, Mississippi, twenty-one; New York City, New York, sixty-three; Wilmington, North Carolina, twenty; Philadelphia, Pennsylvania, forty-five; Charleston, South Carolina, fifty-eight; Nashville, Tennessee, forty-five; San Antonio, Texas, twenty-four; Houston, Texas, thirty-seven; Richmond, Virginia, twenty-eight.

Washington, District of Columbia, is the capital of Negro population of America, even more than of the whites, and here in most directions one can see the Negro's best development. At the same time, sharp competition and lack of capital have made development in business enterprise here slow. The forty-nine business houses have an investment of $146,200. There are two having $15,000 each invested, four having $10,000 each and ten having $5,000 or over.

An eleven-year-old confectionery store is a large and complete establishment. A book store makes a specialty of rare editions and bindings. One newspaper has fifteen persons on its pay-roll, and the largest hotel has eighteen well-furnished bed-rooms, dining and reception-rooms and steam heat.

With this one may compare the situation in Houston, Texas, in the far Southwest, where there are thirty-seven merchants, with an invested capital of $309,250. Here one business, a real estate broker, has a capital of $75,000, another real estate dealer, $50,000 and a third, $40,000. One business has a capital of $15,000, one with $14,000, one with $12,000, two with $10,000 and ten with from $5,000 to $8,000.

In Richmond, Virginia, there are two insurance and banking houses, one having a capital of $135,000; the other, $75,000.

In Kansas City, Kansas, the coal and wood dealers do a business of $2,000 a month, and the drug store of $500 a month. A hall rents for $50 a month, and there is a daily paper.

At Griffin, Georgia, a barber has $2,700 of assessed property; a liveryman, $18,000 and a dairy, $6,000. The last business is co-operative, and is managed by a society. It has been very successful so far.

From a border state comes this report for one of the smaller cities:

At Lexington, Kentucky, there is a well-conducted drug store which keeps the proprietor and one clerk busy. A contractor employs thirty or forty men, and has handled some large contracts, among others, the new county courthouse, which cost $20,000. An agricultural society holds annual fairs, which are largely attended. One of the undertakers is very successful and does a large business.

The following report has especial interest, as the town is composed entirely of Negroes, and is governed by them from the mayor down:

NEGRO MERCHANTS OF MOUND BAYOU, MISSISSIPPI.

KINDS OF BUSINESS.	Years in Business.	Capital Invested.	Assessed Real Estate.
General merchandise	10	$5,000	$ 3,000
Merchandise and ginning	8	1,000	2000
General merchandise	2	300	500
General merchandise	8	150	800
General merchandise	3	750	
Merchandise and blacksmith	7	150	800
Merchandise and saw mill	10	1,000	10,000

It has been said that the southern Negro has made little or no progress since the war. The following facts contradict this statement:

At Wilmington, North Carolina, Negroes hold $500,000 in real and personal property; own fifteen churches, five of

12

which are worth $90,000; own two public halls worth $20,000, and have four physicians and four lawyers.

The Negro merchants of Mobile, Alabama, have a capital invested of $49,500.

Charleston, the metropolis of South Carolina, has more Negro business men than any other city, and the capital invested is $203,500, including one $100,000 truck farm, and several other establishments with more than $20,000 capital.

For a small place, Americus, Georgia, has a good representation of business men.

At Montgomery, the capital of Alabama, are a number of merchants with large investments. A dry goods store, with a capital of $8,000, did a business of $35,000 last year—"a fine store."

Jacksonville, Florida, has a dry goods store that did a business of $15,000 last year. It employs five women clerks. The commission merchants do $25,000 worth of business annually and employ fifteen clerks. The capacity of the lumber mill is 20,000 feet a day; it sells to northern and southern markets.

The few Negro merchants who live in the far West make an unusually good showing. At San Francisco there are three well-established newspapers. One real estate dealer has $100,000 invested. There is a fine hair-dressing establishment, an expert electrician and a restaurant employing fifteen persons. The total capital invested is $140,000.

The colored merchants of Seattle, Washington, have $25,000 invested; Cleveland, Ohio, $35,000; Norfolk, Virginia, $30,000; Portsmouth, Virginia, $35,000; Athens, Georgia, only $2,500 invested, which, however, brings an average daily income of $100.

The extreme Northeast has its quota of business enterprises. In New Bedford, Massachusetts, which was a center for fugitive slaves and refugees, the negro tailor employs eleven men and women. He does the largest business in the city in refitting men's and women's garments, and makes ladies'

REV. W. W. BROWN.
Founder of G. U. O. of T. R.

tailoring a specialty. The majority of lady patrons are of the best class of people. The largest Negro drug store is one of the best appointed in the city, and is patronized largely by the wealthy. It is prominently located. The photographer commenced as errand boy, and eventually bought out the leading photographer in southeastern Massachusetts. The shoe dealer sell shoes and does a large repair business. The hair store is the largest in the city. The proprietor of the second largest drug store is also a large real estate holder. Beside these merchants there are several conducting business on a small scale: grocers, newsdealers, restaurant keepers, clothes cleaners, tailors, expressmen, ice-cream dealers, etc.

This section can best close with one of the curious coincidences which the rise of the Negro often involves. Not far from Jamestown, where, in 1619, the first slaves were landed, is Williamsburg, the quaint old capital of Virginia, one of the most picturesque of the older American towns. In this place the largest and in every way the chief general store is a Negro's, situated on the main broad thoroughfare—the Duke of Gloucester street—and it commands the patronage of white and black for miles around. The capital invested in this store is $40,000.

A few typical cases selected from a list of some two hundred business men will illustrate the success and difficulties of this class of merchants. Says one:

"I was born a slave at Petersburg, Virginia, in the year 1845. My early surroundings were the same that nearly all the race at the South in those days had to face.

.   .   .   .

After the outbreak of the Civil War the old home lost its attraction for me. During part of '64 and '65 I was employed along with the Thirteenth Ohio Cavalry. In '68 I came to Baltimore. For eighteen years I was engaged in the furniture moving business, in which I had some success. My next venture was to open an upholstering establishment in the fall of '84. Desiring a permanent location I purchased property, which, with the improvements since added, is now worth five thousand dollars. Besides my shop, I operate a storage warehouse in the rear of my premises. I was married in '74. Have one son, who is working at the trade with me. I regret to say that I am not an educated man. All the time spent at school would not exceed a week. The small learning obtained was picked up here and there at odd times and ways. I learned my trade by first watching mechanics hired to work for me. I have made it a rule to profit by observation.

"I had but little capital to begin with. I thought it expedient to proceed cautiously. I had some appreciation of the importance of building up a reputation, which requires time as well as work. I made it my aim not simply to get a customer, but to hold him as long as possible. I employed competent workmen and gave strict attention to all the details. I planned to deal on a cash basis. Work was paid for promptly and bills were not allowed to go beyond the time. I have adhered to this course ever since.

"Considering everything, I think I have had fair success. I have been able to save some money, and, besides, I can boast of having obtained creditable footing among men of business. My shop is never idle. I do not regard quick and large profits as always indicative of success in business. The gain that has not integrity and merit to justify it may be looked upon with suspicion. I have received considerate treatment at the hands of the white people. The larger part of my patronage comes from that source. They confide in my skill and honesty. They visit my store and I am frequently called to their houses. The contact is friendly, both parties understanding that it is of a business and not of a social character.

"Negro business men are situated pretty much as are business men of the other race. What helps or hinders in the one case has like effect in the other case. We must study the laws of business. We must demonstrate that we can be trusted for integrity of conduct and efficiency of service. Absolute trustworthiness will go farther than color. Instead of making our shops and stores a rendezvous for loafers, it must be understood that business only is in order during business hours. We must not make the mistake of trying to give attention to business one-half the day and spending the remainder in looking after political matters. Negro business men must have one aim."

A colored jeweler writes as follows:

"I was born on the island of Barbadoes, British West Indies, in the town of Bridgetown. My father was a man in fair circumstances and was enabled to give his children some education and provide well for them. Most West Indian parents have their boys learn some trade after leaving school, even though in some cases they take a profession afterwards, the object being to provide them with a means of earning a living with their hands if they fail to succeed otherwise. So to follow the bent of my mind—mechanics—I was put apprentice to a watchmaker, where I spent five years at the bench, until I had a fair knowledge of the trade. I then came to this country in the spring of '85, where I have remained since.

"The popular system of education in the West Indies in my time was private tuition, especially for primary instruction. And so I went to several pay schools, and last to a public school, receiving what would be called here a good grammar course. Some reading in later life has been of much benefit to me.

"My first venture was in Kansas City. About four months after my arrival in this country I applied for work at some of the leading jewelry stores of the above city and found out for the first time that the roads to success in this country for the black man were not so free and open as those of his brother in white. So I worked as porter for two years, and then encouraged by the success of pleasing my friends with private work done for them during my leisure hours at my room, I bought a small frame building, opened a watch repairing shop and became Kansas City's first Negro jeweler.

"With close attention to business, by observing frugality, and by manifesting a disposition to please my patrons with courteous treatment and efficient work, I have succeeded, so my critics say, 'well.' I had the misfortune to lose $500 in a bank failure, and the good fortune to have saved encugh to be notated in four figures. The white people I deal with treat me well. Those whom I do not deal with do not molest me. I don't know how they regard me.

"Negro business men are helped by competing with inferior white businesses and by the prejudice which some white businesses have to Negro patronage. The average Negro business man is hindered by his neglect to keep his business in such a manner as to invite the patronage of the better class of white and black patrons, and the inability to find efficient and trustworthy partners in a good business. In fine, the envy, distrust and lack of patronage of his own race greatly hinders the progress and success of the Negro business man."

One member of a firm of merchant tailors writes:

"I was born in Huntsville, Alabama, in 1876. My parents were in comfortable circumstances, and I led a typical village boy's life. My father was a brick contractor. In 1894 I left Huntsville, Alabama, and came to this city and was employed by Mr. Rotholz (white), of the People's Tailoring Company, and remained in his employ until I went in business for myself. My partner was born in Huntsville, Alabama, in 1877. His father was a mattress maker, and being quite successful was then, and now is, in comfortable circumstances. He came to Birmingham one year later than I did and was employed by the same firm, but resigned to go into business with me.

"I was educated at the city school and the A. and M. College, from which I graduated, at Normal, Alabama. My partner also attended the same school.

"Having received excellent training from my employer, I determined to go in business for myself, and after a consultation with my partner we started our business September 1, 1897. We estimate our business to be worth $3,500.

"Our success is shown by the steady increase of our business. Our motto: Never to promise that which we cannot fulfill, has made itself felt, and by sticking to it we have won hundreds of customers. While we have competition in the form of two more colored and fourteen white establishments I think we have no cause to complain. Competition notwithstanding, we have a fair share of the white patronage. We are regarded by the whites as respectable, law abiding citizens and first-class tailors, having been called into court as expert witnesses on cloth.

"The helps and hindrances of Negro business men are two extremes; while we have little or no help we have hindrances ten-fold. The business tact and integrity of a Negro in business is doubted to such an extent that from his creditors he gets little or no consideration on his bills, while the white competitors have their own time. I find there is *no* outside help for the Negro in business; it is only his untiring energy and push, together with the class of work which he turns out, that speaks for him."

A florist writes:

"I was born in Anne Arundel county, Maryland, ten miles from Annapolis. I was raised on a farm; my grandfather and grandmother served as father and mother. When I was twenty-one years old I came to Annapolis and was employed by a doctor to drive for him and to serve as waiter-boy. I married when I became twenty-two years old. I left the doctor when I was about twenty-four years old and went to work on the railroad. I soon stopped working there and went to work at gardening. Soon after I went to work at flowering.

REV. E. W. LAMPTON.
Financial Secretary A. M. E. Church.

"I went a little while to night school, but on account of not being able to hear well and speak plainly, I stopped without securing an education.

"I was working for a white woman pruning trees and looking after the garden. One day I picked up a bouquet of flowers that had been thrown out on an ash-pile. I untied the seemingly dead flowers and found a rose-geranium which seemed to have a little life in it by its smell, and I carried it home and planted it. It lived and I have been growing flowers ever since. I have had good success notwithstanding I have had many drawbacks. I am living off my flowers. The whites visit my place, buy flowers from me and speak kindly of me."

A co-operative grocery store gives the following account:

"Four men were the prime movers in the organization of our company. Only two of these men could be called educated. One was educated at Selma University, the other in a northern college. They were helped some by their parents, but depended mostly on themselves for their education.

"We started with about one hundred dollars in a grocery business. We were moved to organize the company, which is chartered, by talking over the duty of the fathers to open business for their children as well as to educate them.

"We have good success. The whites regard us as a worthy business organization. The wholesale men honor our orders right along.

"The idea is now becoming general that the Negro must unite and rise, or remain down. This is a great help to Negro business. The crop lien system is a great hindrance to Negro business. Exclusion from the commercial clubs is another; imperfection in the knowledge of keeping a first-class set of books is also a great hindrance. The lack of confidence in each other is the greatest hindrance."

A dry goods merchant writes:

"I was born in Lowndes county, Alabama, June 15, 1867. I left there in 1880 and have been a citizen of Montgomery ever since. I have worked on a farm, in a saw mill and on a railroad previous to engaging in my present business.

"I was educated in the common schools of Lowndes and at a private night school since settling in Montgomery.

"After working for several years in the dry goods business I felt that there was a good opening for colored men along that line; so I left my employer and rented a small store on one of the principal streets. After paying the first month's rent in advance and giving notes for the balance I found that I had spent one-third of my capital. The balance went for goods.

"My success has been all that could be expected. The whites regard me just as they do any other business man, as far as I am able to judge.

"The Negro business man having once gained the confidence of the people will obtain patronage in direct proportion to his business ability."

A successful lumber merchant writes:

"I was born in Monmouth county, New Jersey, in 1862, of parents in extremely humble circumstances. I attended public school about twelve months of my life. I could read and write when I left school, in 1874. I had to work for a livelihood and not attend school. My father was a white man and died in the Civil War a few months before I was born. I was reared on a farm. I came to Florida thirteen years ago. I did not have three dollars in cash when I arrived here. I did not have a friend or acquaintance in this state. I hewed cross-ties for ten cents apiece. I have laid up no money. I have spent all I have made in my business. I own a saw mill and planing mill, grist mill and novelty works, cost about $6,000 (I have added $1,000 this year). I own over one thousand acres of land, some improved. I own eight mules and three horses. The gross earnings of my business are about $25,000 per year. I had $125 in cash and had no experience when I began.

"I do not consider myself educated, only practically; I am my own shipping clerk, chief engineer, blacksmith, book-

13

keeper, solicitor of work and collector. I do all the best sort
of work. I learned all this in Florida.

"I had $125 in cash and mortgaged my home for $850,
which I paid before it was due. I worked for another company as foreman in the woods and hired my work done; at
night I repaired anything that was broken during the day.

"I have more friends among the whites than the colored.
I sell most of my products to whites. They treat me well in
business. I attend strictly to my business. I am plain and
straightforward in my manners and treat all alike, both white
and colored. In my mill both white and colored are employed.

"The lack of capital has been my greatest trouble. There
is no discrimination in my business. I aim to equal and
excel in quality of work and material; I furnish good material, well manufactured. I have a splendid trade—at present
I am building two miles of iron track."

An undertaker writes:

"I was born in the city of Galveston, Texas, in 1862.
I followed various occupations. I came to New York at the
age of twenty years and married when I was twenty-two
years old. I now have a large family. I worked in club
houses for many years in New York.

"I had only a common school education. I would advise
every young man to seek for knowledge, as I find that very
essential in any or every vocation of life.

"I accumulated a little money with the intention of being
my own master. I was somewhat puzzled as to what business I should select, but finally made up my mind to become
an undertaker. I went to an embalming school and learned
the art of embalming. I am now a licensed undertaker of
New York City.

"I have been pretty successful. I do very little white work.
I depend entirely on the Negro support. I am the official
undertaker for seven societies. I have been in business one
year and seven months.

"I have gained the confidence and respect of the majority of the Negroes in New York City. Therefore they and self-respect are the most helpful to me as a business man. The hindrances are lack of capital and education."

A publisher writes that he was born in Maybinton, South Carolina, in 1859, and was a slave. At a very early age he worked his mother's farm, and being the oldest boy he was obliged to help support her.

In 1870 his family moved to Columbia, South Carolina, where he entered the public school. He occupied his time when not in school by doing jobs of work; his uncle being a member of the South Carolina Legislature, in 1871-2, succeeded in getting him the position of page in the legislature. Afterward he worked for a while in a dry goods store as porter and in the Columbia Central National Bank as messenger.

His opportunities for education were few and meager, he did not enter school until he was eleven years old. Through many difficulties he pursued with zeal the school training which he received. He had a great desire to obtain a thorough education, but was not able.

His intense convictions led him to support all movements designed to elevate or ameliorate the condition of his people; so he decided in 1894 to go to work with pen and tongue and arouse the people to action. With a partner therefore he started the paper known as *The People's Recorder*. He is also proprietor of a large grocery store known as "Our Store," which filled a long-felt want in the City of Columbia. This store was open for three years when it was moved to Orangeburg, South Carolina.

The firm is doing a great work in the newspaper business. The paper is strictly a race paper. It is received in the homes of the people as a welcome visitor, and there are many white families who are subscribers.

The Negro in business has many disadvantages to contend against, especially from the intelligent class of people who regard themselves as the "best class" of Negroes. Experience teaches that the poorer class, or what is commonly called the "common people," are more inclined to support race enterprises and professional men than the first class named. The Negro business man scarcely receives any help outside of his race.

The education of 185 Negro business men was obtained as follows:

From institutions of higher training	41
From public schools in towns or cities	35
From public schools in the country	32
From grammar schools.	15
From normal schools	14
From night schools	13
From private instruction	9
From instruction at home	3
With little or no education	23
Total	185

This would seem to be a fair sample of the training these merchants received.

It is of interest to know at what sort of work these merchants were engaged when they saved enough to enter business, or how else their capital was obtained. To questions on these points men answered as follows:

Borrowed their capital, 30.

Saved money from work as follows:

Keeping boarders 4	Drayman 2	Barber 2	Steward 3
Railroad hand 1	Messenger 1	Miner 1	Teacher 5
Lunch counter 2	Blacksmith 1	Bartender 1	Farmer 5
Working at a trade 11	Seamstress 1	Laborer 6	Clerk 4
Government service 2	Fruit stand 1	Porter 5	Peddlers, etc... 6

The following sketch of Col. John McKee shows what an intelligent and determined Negro can do if he makes the most of himself and his opportunities.

Col. John McKee was one of the richest colored men in the United States. He was a Virginia Negro, born free, we believe, but without even a wooden spoon in his mouth. He was apprenticed to a brickmaker, ran away to work in a

MAHLON VAN HORN.
U. S. Consul in Danish West Indies.

Baltimore confectioner's, a job much more attractive to a boy, but was caught by the sheriff and sent back to the brick-yard. When he came of age he emigrated to Philadelphia, and worked in a livery stable, whence he graduated into the employ of a restaurant keeper. As became an industrious apprentice, he married his employer's daughter, and carried on the business after his father-in-law retired. He began to dabble in real estate when still a young man, and made the bulk of his fortune out of it after giving up the restaurant business in 1866.

It is said that Colonel McKee owned more than 1,000,000 acres of land at one time. At the time of his death he owned from three hundred to four hundred Philadelphia houses, free and clear, and the value of his estate is estimated at between $1,500,000 and $2,000,000. He was the founder and owner of McKee City in New Jersey. He owned coal and oil territory in West Virginia and Kentucky and a great tract of land, more than 20,000 acres, in Steuben county, New York. In short, he was a real estate operator of wide interests and striking success. He started with nothing and died a millionaire, a lesson to colored men.

The number of well-to-do Negroes is increasing visibly. When a colored man once gets a start and saves enough to get interested in the game, he is likely to succeed. In spite of many exclusions and prohibitions there is field enough for him. It cannot be expected, however, that many men, white or black, will have the shrewdness and business judgment that Col. McKee had.

Another colored man who was successful and achieved distinction in the line of industrial effort was Alexander Miles, who was one of the founders of the city of Duluth, and was afterward at the head of that great fraternal organization The United Brotherhood.

Before the Civil War there were several Negro men in northern cities who were prominent because of enterprise and success in business, of whom we may cite in the single city of Cincinnati, Henry Boyd, builder and manufacturer; Samuel T. Wilcox, grocer; and A. S. Thomas and J. P. Ball, daguerreotype artists.

The most advanced thinkers and workers among the Negroes have been giving much thought to the problems confronting the race.

The following resolutions were adopted by a recent conference:

1. Negroes ought to enter into business life in increasing numbers. The present disproportion in the distribution of Negroes in the various occupations is unfortunate. It gives the race a one-sided development, unnecessarily increases competition in certain lines of industry, and puts the mass of the negro people out of sympathy and touch with the industrial and mercantile spirit of the age. Moreover the growth of a class of merchants among us would be a far-sighted measure of self-defense, and would make for wealth and mutual co-operation.

2. We need as merchants the best trained young men we can find. A college training ought to be one of the best preparations for a broad business life; and thorough English and high school training is indispensable.

3. Negroes going into business should remember that their customers demand courtesy, honesty and careful methods, and they should not expect patronage when their manner of conducting business does not justify it.

4. The mass of the Negroes must learn to patronize business enterprises conducted by their own race when it is possible to do so. We *must* co-operate or we are lost. Ten million people who join in intelligent self-help can never be long ignored or mistreated.

5. The business men reported to the conference are to be congratulated. They are pioneers in a great movement, and some of them have made a creditable record. We earnestly ask Negroes—and especially the better class of thinking Negroes—to patronize these establishments and encourage them in every way.

13

6. The most advisable work for the immediate future would seem to be:

(*a*) Continued agitation in churches, schools and newspapers, and by all other avenues, of the necessity of business careers for young people.

(*b*) Increased effort to encourage saving and habits of thrift among the young that we may have more capital at our disposal.

(*c*) The organization in every town and hamlet where colored people dwell, of Negro Business Men's Leagues, and the gradual federation from these to state and national organizations.

CHAPTER VIII.

Thomas Jefferson and the Negro Julius Melbourn: A Remarkable Incident.

IT IS well known that the great Father of Democracy was opposed to having African slavery perpetuated in the United States, and that he was hopeful of its early extinction, even after it was recognized by the constitution of 1787. We get a more particular view of his position in this matter, however, and of his opinion of the Negro, from Julius Melbourn's account of a conversation among several eminent gentlemen whom he met at Jefferson's table in the summer of 1815—and of a private talk he had with Mr. Jefferson a few days before.

The following statements are taken from a work published fifty-five years ago, entitled "Life and Opinions of Julius Melbourn, with Sketches of the Lives and Characters of Thomas Jefferson, John Quincy Adams, John Randolph and several other Eminent Statesmen." The work was edited and prepared for the press by a member of congress— Melbourn and his family being then resident in England, where they had been for about twelve years.

This man Julius was born a slave in North Carolina, July 4, 1790, and was owned by a Major Johnson until he was five years old, when he was bought by Mrs. Melbourn, a widow living in Raleigh, who educated him, meanwhile (in 1806), giving him his freedom. After leaving the Johnson family he came to be known as Julius Melbourn.

Describing his appearance he says: "My hair is curly,

or rather woolly, and my nose is more flattened than is generally the case with pure-blooded Europeans.'' In another place he said that indeed ''his hair was kinky.''

In July, 1815, he set out on a tour northward, meaning to visit Mr. Jefferson on the way, and having a letter of introduction to him from a lawyer friend, a Mr. Pendleton. ''I had heard Mr. Jefferson so much talked of,'' he says, ''had read so much about him in the newspapers and so much of his own writings, of which I was a great admirer, that my curiosity to see that great man and converse with him was intense.''

When he arrived at Monticello, he was conducted to Jefferson's study, where he found him sitting at a table covered with books and papers. ''He rose,'' says Melbourn, ''when I entered and received me with great politeness and apparent cordiality. I instantly found myself at perfect ease in his presence. Though he was not, and I presume never had been, a handsome man, there was such strong evidence of great intellectual power in his high forehead and the form of his face and head that I could not fail of admiring him. A philosophical calmness and a glow of benevolence were so visibly expressed in his countenance and so distinctly marked every feature that while he was reading Mr. Pendleton's letter, and before he had uttered a word, I was charmed with him and loved him as an old and familiar friend. I suppose that part of the letter which stated that I was born a slave and was of African descent excited his curiosity, for he immediately began a conversation, evidently with a view to ascertain the strength of my mind and to what degree it had been cultivated. He inquired whether I had seen the building then lately erected for the University of Virginia, and said he intended it should be free for the instruction of all. He expressed his deep anxiety for the improvement of the minds and the elevation of the characters of 'our colored brethren,' as he was pleased to call them.''

A long conversation then ensued, in which they touched

upon English and American literature, and discussed Hume, Montesquieu and John Adams, in connection with government and human rights, in which Jefferson expressed the opinion that Hume "finally settled down in the professed belief that the fitness of things required that an immense majority of men should be slaves to a pitiable minority of their brethren."

Continuing the narrative, Melbourn says: "I remained in the neighborhood of Monticello nearly a week, and spent a portion of every day in Mr. Jefferson's library, at his pressing invitation. On Tuesday before I left those quiet and philosophical shades I received a card from Mr. Jefferson, inviting me to dine with him in company with a few friends the next day at 4 o'clock. I went to his house and found there Chief-Justice Marshall, William Wirt, Samuel Dexter, of Boston, and Dr. Samuel L. Mitchell, of New York. There was also there another remarkable man from the North. It was Elder John Leland, who sent Mr. Jefferson the great cheese. He was a Baptist minister, who then lived in the western part of Massachusetts. He was very zealous, both as a politician and a sectarian. . . . The Chief-Justice had come into the neighborhood on some business pertaining to the university, Mr. Wirt was on his annual visit to Mr. Jefferson, and Mr. Dexter and Doctor Mitchell, being on a tour to South Carolina, had so arranged their journey as on their way to call on the old sage at Monticello. I was announced as a young gentleman from North Carolina who had been introduced by Mr. Pendleton, well-known to most of the persons present."

The author then occupies several pages in describing the gentlemen present and giving the substance of their remarks on the appointment of Judge Story to the Supreme Bench, on law in general, on the conduct of the New England States during the war then recently ended, and on the relative powers of the State and Federal governments, at length touching upon the danger of disunion. When this point was reached, Melbourn says that "Mr. Dexter remarked that he did not apprehend any danger of a separation of the States because of any difference of opinion as to the ordinary measures of government. The people of every State are strongly attached to the Union, and to prevent a division both parties will always yield a little. Public opinion will force leading politicians into a compromise. But there is one evil from which I apprehend that dreadful result—I mean slavery in the Southern States and the slave representation."

"Oh!" said Mr. Jefferson, "dismiss your fears on that subject. Slavery will soon be abolished in all the States."

"Never," said Judge Marshall; "never by the voluntary consent of the slave-holding States."

"I regret," replied Mr. Jefferson, "that so attentive an observer as you are, Chief-Justice, should entertain such an opinion. I well know that at the time American independence was declared no member, either North or South, expected that slavery would continue as long as it has."

"I can well believe that," said Mr. Wirt, "for they must have felt that the continuance of slavery was directly adverse to their declaration that all men are born free and equal," etc.

"But," said Doctor Mitchell, "I very much doubt whether, according to the laws of nature, the Africans are not formed to be subject to the Caucasian race. From my own observations I am satisfied that nature has formed an essential difference between the two races, and much to the disadvantage of the Negro race."

Mitchell then described the brain and nervous system, and pointed out differences in development, size and quality in the brains of Negroes and whites, and intimated that intellectual inferiority unfitted the Negro for freedom.

"As regards personal rights," said Mr. Jefferson, "it seems to me palpably absurd that the individual rights of volition and motion should depend on the degree of intellectual power possessed by the individual. I should hardly be willing to subscribe to the doctrine that, because the

Chief-Justice has a stronger mind or a more capacious and better-formed brain than I, he has a right to make me his slave." He then suggested that different diet, exercise, climate, occupation and other circumstances might result in making an immense difference between even two white brothers, and more marked difference between the offspring of the two. Then Judge Marshall spoke again. "I do not mean to advocate slavery," he said. "I wish, from my soul I wish it was abolished; but when we count on political results we must look at society *as it is*. I do not found my opinion on the perpetuity of slavery upon the natural inferiority of the Negro." He then adverted to the fact that nearly every man at the South who had any influence in the elections was a slave-holder, and argued that our legislators would be slave-holders or under the influence of slave-holders, and insisted that the pecuniary influence which would have to be contended with in an effort to free the slaves could not be overcome except by force. After arguing on this proposition for awhile he remarked to Mr. Jefferson:

"You, Mr. President, ascribe too much virtue and benevolence to our people if you suppose the disposition to emancipate the Negroes is increasing. You must recollect that at the beginning of the Revolution, Chancellor Wythe and yourself were deterred from introducing a bill in the legislature for the abolition of slavery because you became satisfied that the time had not then come when the public mind was prepared for the adoption of that measure; but you then anticipated that it would soon be viewed more favorably by the community. Your expectations, however, have not been realized. At this moment I venture to affirm that a bill for Negro emancipation would meet with prompt and indignant condemnation. I repeat that interest, pecuniary interest, will forever prevent the emancipation of the slave at the South. I do not say that the slave ought not to be emancipated—I say he will not be emancipated."

"And I," said Mr. Leland, "say he ought not to be emancipated. I do not predicate my opinion on the anatomical discoveries of Doctor Mitchell; but I think the Negroes are the children of Ham, and, according to the Bible, they are doomed to be the servants of servants.'' He then spoke of his observations, from which he drew extreme conclusions as to their inferiority and evil propensities. Thereupon Mr. Jefferson said to him: ''I am happy to have it in my power at this moment to prove to you and Doctor Mitchell, by ocular demonstration, that the experience of one of you and the theory of the other have led you to erroneous conclusions. Look at the young gentleman who sits opposite to you. Mr. Melbourn was born a slave and is of African descent. He was emancipated by a pious and benevolent lady, and is now a man of wealth. He has by his own efforts and industry cultivated and well-improved his mind—a mind which I religiously believe, your missionary observations, friend Leland, and Doctor Mitchell's dissections to the contrary notwithstanding, is of the first order of human intellects.''

I was much embarrassed, says Melbourn, at this compliment from so great a man as Mr. Jefferson, and I presume I appeared quite awkward. The whole company gazed on me with astonishment. The piercing eye of the Chief-Justice in particular was fixed most intently upon me. Mr. Jefferson then related some part of my history (for I had previously told him my story), and he animadverted with great severity on the treatment I had received at Natchez and upon the laws which legalized that treatment. While he was talking I perceived Mr. Wirt's countenance several times redden with apparent indignation. It was now late and I took my leave; but as I was retiring Mr. Wirt followed me into the hall, and, taking me by the hand, expressed a desire to continue his acquaintance with me.

CHAPTER IX.

AMONG THE SOUTHERN PEOPLE THE NEGRO FINDS HIS BEST FRIENDS.

WITHOUT entering into argument to show that the South is the home of the Negro, and that among those who understand him best he will find the best field in which to work out his destiny, we present the series of papers which constitute this chapter. They are submitted as corroborative of the remark of Hon. Clark Howell, in his comment on the character of Booker T. Washington's speech before the Atlanta Exposition: "It is to the South that the Negro must turn for his best friends," etc.

In recognition of the American Negro as a factor in the industrial progress of the South, the Board of Directors of the great Atlanta Exposition of 1895 invited Washington to participate in the opening exercises, which he did in an address that received the warmest commendation of thoughtful men, North and South. As an indication of this we introduce the address with two letters—one written to the speaker, the other to a leading New York paper.

I. LETTER FROM EX-PRESIDENT CLEVELAND.

GRAY GABLES, BUZZARD'S BAY, MASS , October 6, 1895.
BOOKER T. WASHINGTON, ESQ.

My Dear Sir:—I thank you for sending me a copy of your address, delivered at the Atlanta Exposition, September 18, 1895.

I thank you with much enthusiasm for making the address. I have read it with intense interest, and I think the exposition would be fully justified if it did not do more than furnish the opportunity for its delivery. Your words cannot fail to delight and encourage all who wish well for your race; and if our colored fellow-citizens do not from your utterances gather new hope and form new determinations to gain every valuable advantage offered them by their citizenship, it will be strange indeed.   Yours very truly,

GROVER CLEVELAND.

II. HON. CLARK HOWELL, EDITOR OF THE "ATLANTA CONSTITUTION," TO THE "NEW YORK WORLD."

ATLANTA, GEORGIA, September 19, 1895.

To the Editor of the World:—I do not exaggerate when I say that Prof. Booker T. Washington's address yesterday was one of the most notable speeches, both as to character and the warmth of its reception, ever delivered to a Southern audience.   It was an epoch-making talk, and marks distinctly a turning point in the progress of the Negro race, and its effect in bringing about a perfect understanding between the whites and blacks of the South will be immediate.   The address was a revelation.   It was the first time that a Negro orator had appeared on a similar occasion before a Southern audience.

The propriety of inviting a representative of the Negro race to participate in the opening exercises was fully discussed a month ago, when the opening program was being arranged.   Some opposition was manifested on account of the fear that public sentiment was not prepared for such an advanced step.   The invitation, however, was extended by a vote of the Board of Directors, and the cordial greeting which the audience gave Washington's address shows that the board made no mistake.   There was not a line in the address which would have been changed even by the most sensitive of those who thought the invitation to be imprudent.   The whole speech is a platform on which the whites and blacks can stand with full justice to each race.

The speech is a full vindication from the mouth of a representative Negro of the doctrine so eloquently advanced by Grady and those who have agreed with him, that it is to the South that the Negro must turn for his best friends, and that his welfare is so closely identified with the progress of the white people of the South that each race is mutually dependent upon the other, and that the so-called "race-problem" must be solved in the development of the natural relations growing out of the association between the whites and blacks of the South.

The question of social equality is eliminated as a factor in the development of the problem, and the situation is aptly expressed by Washington in the statement that "in all things that are purely social we can be as separate as fingers, yet one as the hand in all things essential to mutual progress."

The speech will do good, and the unanimous approval with which it has been received demonstrates the fact that it has already done good.

CLARK HOWELL.

E. M. HEWLETT.
Harvard Graduate. U. S. Magistrate D. C.

III. MR. WASHINGTON'S ADDRESS.

Mr. President and Gentlemen of the Board of Directors and Citizens:

One-third of the population of the South is of the Negro race. No enterprise seeking the material, civil or moral welfare of this section can disregard this element of our population and reach the highest success. I but convey to you, Mr. President and Directors, the sentiment of the masses of my race when I say that in no way have the value and manhood of the American Negro been more fittingly and generously recognized than by the managers of this magnificent exposition at every stage of its progress. It is a recognition that will do more to cement the friendship of the two races than any occurrence since the dawn of our freedom.

Not only this, but the opportunity here afforded will awaken among us a new era of industrial progress. Ignorant and inexperienced, it is not strange that in the first years of our new life we began at the top instead of at the bottom; that a seat in Congress or the State Legislature was sought more than real estate or industrial skill; that the political convention or stump speaking had more attraction than starting a dairy farm or truck garden.

A ship lost at sea for many days suddenly sighted a friendly vessel. From the mast of the unfortunate vessel was seen a signal: "Water, water; we die of thirst!" The answer from the friendly vessel at once came back: "Cast down your bucket where you are." A second time the signal, "Water, water; send us water!" ran up from the distressed vessel, and was answered: "Cast down your bucket where you are." And a third and fourth signal for water was answered: "Cast down your bucket where you are." The captain of the distressed vessel, at last heeding the injunction, cast down his bucket, and it came up full of fresh, sparkling water from the mouth of the Amazon river. To those of my race who depend on bettering their condition in a foreign land, or who underestimate the importance of cultivating friendly relations with the Southern white man, who is their next-door neighbor, I would say: "Cast down your bucket where you are"—cast it down in making friends in every manly way of the people of all races by whom we are surrounded.

Cast it down in agriculture, mechanics, in commerce, in domestic service, and in the professions. And in this connection it is well to bear in mind that whatever other sins the South may be called to bear, when it comes to business, pure and simple, it is in the South that the Negro is given a man's chance in the commercial world, and in nothing is this exposition more eloquent than in emphasizing this chance. Our greatest danger is, that in the great leap from slavery to freedom we may overlook the fact that the masses of us are to live by the productions of our hands, and fail to keep in mind that we shall prosper in proportion as we learn to dignify and glorify common labor, and put brains and skill into the common occupations of life; shall prosper in proportion as we learn to draw the line between the superficial and the substantial, the ornamental gewgaws of life and the useful. No race can prosper until it learns that there is as much dignity in tilling a field as in writing a poem. It is at the bottom of life we must begin, and not at the top. Nor should we permit our grievances to overshadow our opportunities.

To those of the white race who look to the incoming of those of foreign birth and strange tongue and habits for the prosperity of the South, were I permitted, I would repeat what I say to my own race, "Cast down your bucket where you are." Cast it down among the eight million Negroes whose habits you know, whose fidelity and love you have tested in days when to have proved treacherous meant the ruin of your firesides. Cast down your bucket among these people who have, without strikes and labor wars, tilled your fields, cleared your forests, builded your railroads and cities, and brought forth treasures from the bowels of the earth, and helped make possible this magnificent representation of the progress of the South. Casting down your bucket among my people, helping and encouraging them as you are doing on these grounds, and to education of head, hand and heart, you will find that they will buy your surplus land, make blossom the waste places in your fields, and run your factories. While doing this, you can be sure in the future, as in the past, that you and your families will be surrounded by the most patient, faithful, law-abiding and unresentful people that the world has seen. As we have proved our loyalty to you in the past, in nursing your children, watching by the sick bed of your mothers and fathers, and often following them with tear-dimmed eyes to their graves, so in the future, in our humble way, we shall stand by you with a devotion that no foreigner can approach, ready to lay down our lives, if need be, in defense of yours, interlacing our industrial, commercial, civil and religious life with yours in a way that shall make the interests of both races one.   In all things that are purely social we can be as separate as the fingers, yet one as the hand in all things essential to mutual progress.

There is no defense or security for any of us except in the highest intelligence and development of all. If anywhere there are efforts tending to curtail the fullest growth of the Negro, let these efforts be turned into stimulating, encouraging and making him a most useful and intelligent citizen. Efforts or means so invested will pay a thousand per cent. interest. These efforts will be twice blessed—"blessing him that gives and him that takes."

There is no escape through law of God or man from the inevitable:

> "The laws of changeless justice bind
>   Oppressor with oppressed;
> And close as sin and suffering joined,
>   We march to fate abreast."

Nearly sixteen millions of hands will aid you in pulling the load upwards, or they will pull against you the load

J. C. DANCY, OF NORTH CAROLINA.
Recorder of Deeds, D. C.

downwards.   We shall constitute one-third and more of the ignorance and crime of the South, or one-third its intelligence and progress; we shall contribute one-third to the business and industrial prosperity of the South, or we shall prove a veritable body of death, stagnating, depressing, retarding every effort to advance the body politic.

Gentlemen of the exposition, as we present to you our humble effort as an exhibition of our progress, you must not expect overmuch.   Starting thirty years ago with ownership here and there in a few quilts and pumpkins and chickens, remember the path that has led from these to the invention and production of agricultural implements, buggies, steam engines, newspapers, books, statuary, carving, painting, the management of drug stores and banks, has not been trodden without contact with thorns and thistles.

.   .   .   .

The wisest among my race understand that the agitation of questions of social equality is the extremest folly, and that progress in the enjoyment of all the privileges that will come to us must be the result of severe and constant struggle, rather than of artificial forcing.   No race that has anything to contribute to the markets of the world is long in any degree ostracized.   It is important and right that all privileges of the law be ours, but it is vastly more important that we be prepared for the exercise of these privileges.   The opportunity to earn a dollar in a factory just now is worth infinitely more than the opportunity to spend a dollar in an opera house.

In conclusion, ... I pledge that in your effort to work out the great and intricate problem which God has laid at the doors of the South, you shall have at all times the patient, sympathetic help of my race; only let this be constantly in mind, that, while from representations in these buildings of the product of field, of forest, of mine, of factory, letters and art, much good will come, yet far above and beyond material benefits will be that higher good that, let us pray

God, will come in a blotting out of sectional differences and racial animosities and suspicions, in a determination to administer absolute justice, and in a willing obedience among all classes to the mandates of law. This, coupled with our material prosperity, will bring into our blessed South a new heaven and a new earth.

IV. HENRY W. GRADY ON THE RELATIONS OF THE SOUTHERN PEOPLE AND THE NEGRO.

In New York City, on the night of December 22, 1886, that brilliant and broad-minded young Georgian, Henry W. Grady, spoke before the New England Society, at its annual banquet, as follows:

"The relations of the Southern people with the Negro are close and cordial. We remember with what fidelity for four years he guarded our defenseless women and children, whose husbands and fathers were fighting against his freedom. To his credit be it said that whenever he struck a blow for his own liberty, he fought in open battle, and when at last he raised his black and humble hands that the shackles might be struck off, those hands were innocent of wrong against his helpless charges, and worthy to be taken in loving grasp by every man who honors loyalty and devotion.

"Ruffians have maltreated him, rascals have misled him, philanthropists established a bank for him; but the South with the North protests against injustice to this simple and sincere people. To liberty and enfranchisement is as far as law can carry the Negro. The rest may be left to conscience and common sense. It should be left to those among whom his lot is cast; with whom he is indissolubly connected and whose prosperity depends upon their possessing his intelligent sympathy and confidence. Faith has been kept with him in spite of calumnious assertions to the contrary by those who assume to speak for us, or by frank opponents. Faith will be kept with him in future if the South holds her reason and integrity. . . . The South found her jewel in the

14

toad's head of defeat [in the Civil War]. The shackles that held her in narrow limitations fell forever when the shackles of the Negro slave were broken.

"Under the old regime the Negroes were slaves of the South, the South was a slave to the system. The old plantation, with its simple police regulation and its feudal habit, was the only type possible under slavery. Thus was gathered in the hands of a splendid and chivalric oligarchy the substance that should have been diffused among the people. . . . The old South rested everything on slavery and agriculture, unconscious that these could neither give nor maintain healthy growth. The new South presents a perfect Democracy, the oligarchs leading in the popular movement—a social system compact and close-knitted, less splendid on the surface, but stronger at the core; a hundred farms for every plantation, fifty homes for every palace, and a diversified industry that meets the complex needs of this complex age."

V. GRADY DISCUSSES THE RACE PROBLEM AND THE DUTY OF NORTH AND SOUTH.

A short time before he died Henry W. Grady was invited by the Merchants' Association of Boston to join them in a banquet and discuss the race problem. He delivered on that occasion a speech so remarkable that it attracted the attention of the whole country, and was published in full by nearly every high-class daily newspaper. When he came in the course of his address, to notice specifically the race question, he said:

"In 1880 the South had fewer Northern-born citizens than she had in 1870—fewer in 1870 than in 1860. Why is this? Why is it, though the sectional line be now but a mist that the breath may dispel, fewer men of the North have crossed it over to the South than when it was crimson with the best blood of the republic, or even when the slave-holder stood guard every inch of its way?

H. P. CHEATHAM.

"There can be but one answer. It is the very problem we are now to consider. The key that opens that problem will unlock to the world the fairest half of this republic, and free the halted feet of thousands whose eyes are already kindling with its beauty. Better than this, it will open the hearts of brothers for thirty years estranged, and clasp in lasting comradeship a million hands now withheld in doubt. Nothing but this problem and the suspicions it breeds hinders a clear understanding and a perfect union. Nothing else stands between us and such love as bound Georgia and Massachusetts at Valley Forge and Yorktown, chastened by the sacrifices at Manassas and Gettysburgh, and illumined with the coming of better work and a nobler destiny than was ever wrought with the sword or sought at the cannon's mouth.

"If this does not invite your patient hearing tonight—hear one thing more. My people, your brothers in the South—brothers in blood, in destiny, in all that is best in our past and future—are so beset with this problem that their very existence depends on its right solution. Nor are they wholly to blame for its presence. The slave-ships of the republic sailed from your ports—the slaves worked in our fields. You will not defend the traffic nor I the institution. But I do hereby declare that in its wise and humane administration, in lifting the slave to heights of which he had not dreamed in his savage home, and giving him a happiness he has not found in freedom—our fathers left their sons a saving and excellent heritage. In the storm of war this institution was lost. I thank God as heartily as you do that human slavery is gone forever from American soil. But the freedman remains. With him a problem without precedent or parallel. Note its complicated conditions. Two utterly dissimilar races on the same soil—with equal political and civil rights—almost equal in numbers but terribly unequal in intelligence and responsibility—the experiment sought by neither but approached by both with doubt—these are the conditions.

Under these, adverse at every point, we are required to carry these two races in peace and honor to the end.

. . . .

"I bespeak your patience while, with vigorous plainness of speech, seeking your judgment rather than your applause, I proceed step by step. We give to the world this year a crop of 7,500,000 bales of cotton, worth $450,000,000, and its cash equivalent in grain, grasses and fruits. This enormous crop could not have come from the hands of sullen and discontented labor. It comes from peaceful fields, in which laughter and gossip rise above the hum of industry, and contentment runs with the singing plow.

"It is claimed that this ignorant labor is defrauded of its just hire. I present the tax-books of Georgia, which show that the Negro, twenty-five years ago a slave, has in Georgia alone $10,000,000 of assessed property, worth twice that much. Does not that record honor him and vindicate his neighbors? What people, penniless, illiterate, has done so well? For every Afro-American agitator, stirring the strife in which alone he prospers, I can show you a thousand Negroes, happy in their cabin homes, tilling their own land by day, and at night taking from the lips of their children the helpful message their State sends them from the school-house door. And the school-house itself bears testimony. In Georgia we added last year $250,000 to the school fund, making a total of more than $1,000,000; and this in the face of a prejudice not yet conquered, of the facts that the whites are assessed for $368,000,000, the blacks for $10,000,000, and yet 49 per cent of the beneficiaries are black children; and in the doubt of many wise men whether education helps, or can help, our problem. Charleston, with her taxes cut half in two since 1860, pays more in proportion for public schools than Boston. Although it is easier to give much out of much than little out of little, the South, with one-seventh of the taxable property of the country, with relatively larger debt, having received only one-twelfth as much of public land, and having back of its tax-books none of the half billion of bonds that enrich the North, and though it pays annually $26,000,000 to your section as pensions, yet gives nearly one-sixth of the public school fund. The South, since 1865, has spent $122,000,000 in education, and this year is pledged to $37,000,000 for state and city schools, although the blacks, paying but one-thirtieth of the taxes, get nearly one-half of the fund.

"Go into our fields and see whites and blacks working side by side; on our buildings in the same squad; in our shops at the same forge. Often the blacks crowd the whites from work, or lower wages by the greater need or the simpler habits, and yet are permitted because we want to bar them from no avenue in which their feet are permitted to tread. They could not there be elected orators of the white universities, as they have been here; but they do enter there a hundred useful trades that are closed to them here. We hold it better and wiser to tend the vegetables in the garden than to water the exotics in the window. In the South there are Negro lawyers, teachers, editors, dentists, doctors, preachers, multiplying with the increasing ability of their race to support them. In villages and towns they have their military companies equipped from the armories of the State, their churches and societies, built and supported largely by their neighbors. What is the testimony of the courts? In penal legislation we have steadily reduced felonies to misdemeanors, and have led the world in mitigating punishment for crime, that we might save, as far as possible, this dependent race from its own weakness. In our penitentiary record sixty per cent. of the prosecutors are Negroes, and in every court the Negro criminal strikes the colored juror, that white men may judge his case. . . . In the North the percentage of Negro prisoners is six times as great as of native whites; in the South only four times as great. If prejudice wrongs him in Southern courts, the record shows it to be deeper in Northern courts.

RT. REV. C. H. PHILLIPS.
New Bishop in C. M. C.

"I assert here, and a bar as intelligent and upright as the bar of Massachusetts will solemnly indorse my assertion, that in the Southern courts, from highest to lowest, pleading for life, liberty, or property, the Negro has distinct advantages, because he *is* a Negro, apt to be overreached, oppressed—and that this advantage reaches from the juror in making his verdict to the judge in measuring his sentence. Now, can it be seriously maintained that we are terrorizing the people from whose willing hands come every year $1,000,000,000 of farm crops? Or have robbed a people who twenty-five years from unrewarded slavery have amassed in one State alone $20,000,000 of property? Or that we intend to oppress the people we are arming every day? Or deceive them when we are educating them to the utmost limit of our ability? Or outlaw them when we work side by side with them? Or re-enslave them under legal forms, when for their benefit we have even imprudently narrowed the limit of felonies and mitigated the severity of law? My fellow-countryman, as you yourself may sometimes have to appeal to the bar of human judgment for justice and for right, give to my people tonight the fair and unanswerable conclusion of these incontestable facts.

"But it is claimed that under this fair seeming there is disorder and violence. This I admit. And there will be until there is one ideal community on earth after which we may pattern. But how widely it is misjudged! It is hard to measure with exactness whatever touches the Negro. His helplessness, his isolation, his centuries of servitude—these dispose us to emphasize and magnify his wrongs. This disposition, inflamed by prejudice and partisanry, has led to injustice and delusion. Lawless men may ravage a county in Iowa and it is accepted as an incident—in the South a drunken row is declared to be the fixed habit of the community.

"Regulators may whip vagabonds in Indiana by platoons and it scarcely arrests attention—a chance collision in the

South among relatively the same classes is accepted as evidence that one race is destroying the other. We might as well claim that the Union was ungrateful to the colored soldiers who followed its flag because a Grand Army post in Connecticut closed its doors to a Negro veteran, as for you to give racial significance to every incident in the South, or to accept exceptional grounds as the rule of our society. I am not of those who becloud American honor with the parade of outrages of either section, and belie American character by declaring them to be significant and representative. I prefer to maintain that they are neither and stand for nothing but the passion and the sin of our poor fallen humanity. If society, like a machine, were no stronger than its weakest part, I should despair of both sections. But, knowing that society, sentient and responsible in every fiber, can mend and repair until the whole has the strength of the best, I despair of neither. The gentlemen who come with me here, knit into Georgia's busy life as they are, never saw, I dare assert, an outrage committed on a Negro! And if they did, not one of you would be swifter to prevent or punish. It is through them, and the men who think with them—making nine-tenths of every Southern community—that these two races have been carried thus far with less of violence than would have been possible anywhere else on earth. And in their fairness and courage and steadfastness—more than in all the laws that can be passed or all the bayonets that can be mustered—is the hope of our future.

"When will the black cast a free ballot? When ignorance anywhere is not dominated by the will of the intelligent. When the laborer anywhere casts a vote unhindered by his boss. When the vote of the poor anywhere is not influenced by the power of the rich. When the strong and the steadfast do not everywhere control the suffrage of the weak and shiftless—then and not till then will the ballot of the Negro be free. The white people of the South are banded, not in prejudice against the blacks, not in sectional estrangement, not in the hope of political dominion, but in a deep and abiding necessity. Here is this vast, ignorant and purchasable vote, clannish, credulous, impulsive and passionate, tempting every art of the demagogue, but insensible to the appeal of the statesman. Wrongly started in that it was led into alienation from its neighbor and taught to rely on the protection of an outside force, it cannot be merged and lost in the two great parties through logical currents for it lacks political conviction and even that information on which conviction is based. It must remain a faction, strong enough in every community to control on the slightest division of the whites. Under that division it becomes the prey of the cunning and unscrupulous of both parties. Its credulity is imposed on, its patience inflamed, its cupidity tempted, its impulses misdirected, and its superstition made to play its part in a campaign in which every interest of society is jeopardized and every approach to the ballot-box debauched. It is against such campaigns as this, the folly and the bitterness and the danger of which every Southern community has drunk deeply, that the white people of the South are banded together.

.   .   .   .

"We are challenged with the smallness of our vote. This has long been charged flippantly to be evidence, and has now been solemnly and officially declared to be proof of political turpitude and baseness on our part.

.   .   .   .

"It is deplorable that in both sections a larger percentage of the vote is not regularly cast, but more inexplicable that this should be so in New England than in the South. What invites the Negro to the ballot-box? He knows that of all men it has promised him most and yielded him least. His first appeal to suffrage was the promise of forty acres and a mule. His second, the threat that Democratic success meant his re-enslavement. Both have been proved false in his experience. He looked for a home and he got the Freedman's

GENERAL ROBT. SMALLS, BEAUFORT, SOUTH CAROLINA.
Collector of Customs. A Noted Record.

Bank.   He fought under the promise of the loaf and in victory was denied the crumbs.   Discouraged and deceived, he
has realized at last that his best friends are his neighbors
with whom his lot is cast, and whose prosperity is bound up
in his; and that he has gained nothing in politics to com-
pensate the loss of their confidence and sympathy that is at
last his best and his enduring hope.   And so, without leaders or organization—and lacking the resolute heroism of my
party friends in Vermont that makes their hopeless march
over the hills a high and inspiring pilgrimage—he shrewdly
measures the occasional agitator, balances his little account
with politics, touches up his mule, and jogs down the fur-
row, letting the mad world wag as it will!

.   .   .   .

"If the problem be solved at all—and I firmly believe it
will, though nowhere else has it been—it will be solved
by the people most deeply bound in interest, most deeply
pledged in honor to its solution.   I would rather see my
people render back this question rightly solved than to see
them gather all the spoils over which faction has contended
since Cataline conspired and Cæsar fought.   Meantime we treat
the Negro fairly, measuring to him justice in the fullness
the strong should give to the weak, and leading him in the
steadfast ways of citizenship that he may no longer be the
prey of the unscrupulous and the sport of the thoughtless.
We open to him every pursuit in which he can prosper and
seek to broaden his training and capacity.   We seek to hold
his confidence and friendship, and to pin him to the soil with
ownership, that he may catch in the fire of his own hearthstone that sense of responsibility the shiftless can never
know.   And we gather him into that alliance of intelligence and responsibility that, though it now runs close to
racial lines, welcomes the responsible and intelligent of any
race.   By this course, confirmed in our judgment and justified in the progress already made, we hope to progress
slowly but surely to the end.

"The love we feel for that race you cannot measure nor comprehend. As I attest it here, the spirit of my old black mammy from her home up there looks down to bless, and through the tumult of this night steals the sweet music of her croonings as thirty years ago she held me in her black arms and led me smiling into sleep. This scene vanishes as I speak and I catch a vision of an old Southern home, with its lofty pillars, and its white pigeons fluttering down through the golden air. I see white women with strained and anxious faces and children alert, yet helpless. I see night come down with its dangers and its apprehensions, and in a big, homely room I feel on my tired head the touch of whtie white hands—now worn and wrinkled, but fairer to me yet than the hands of any other mortal woman, and stronger yet to lead me than the hands of mortal man—as they lay my mother's blessing there while at her knees—the truest altar I have yet found—I thank God that she is safe in her sanctuary, because her slaves, sentinel in the silent cabin or guard at her chamber door, put a black man's loyalty between her and danger.

"I catch another vision. The crisis of battle—a soldier struck, staggering, fallen. I see a slave, scuffling through the smoke, winding his black arms about the fallen form, reckless of the hurtling death, bending his trusty face to catch the words that tremble on the stricken lips, so wrestling meantime with agony that he would lay down his life in his master's stead. I see him by the weary bedside, ministering with uncomplaining patience, praying with all his humble heart that God will lift his master up, until death comes in mercy and in honor to still the soldier's agony and seal the soldier's life. I see him by the open grave, mute, motionless, uncovered, suffering for the death of him who in life fought against his freedom. I see him when the mound is heaped and the great drama of his life is closed, turn away with downcast eyes and with uncertain step start out into new and strange fields, faltering, struggling, but moving on, until his shambling figure is lost in the light of this better and brighter day. And from the grave comes a voice saying: 'Follow him! Put your arms about him in his need, even as he put his arms about me. Be his friend, as he was mine.' And out into this new world—strange to me as to him, dazzling, bewildering both—I follow! And may God forget my people when they forget these!

"Whatever the future may hold for them—whether they plod along in the servitude from which they have never been lifted since the Cyrenian was laid hold upon by the Roman soldiers and made to bear the cross of the fainting Christ—whether they find homes again in Africa, and thus hasten the prophecy of the psalmist, who said, 'And suddenly Ethiopia shall hold out her hands unto God'—whether forever dislocated and separated they remain a weak people beset by stronger, and exist, as the Turk, who lives in the jealousy rather than in the conscience of Europe—or whether, in this miraculous republic, they break through the caste of twenty centuries, and, belying universal history, reach the full stature of citizenship, and in peace maintain it—we shall give them the uttermost justice and abiding friendship. And whatever we do, into whatever seeming estrangement we may be driven, nothing shall disturb the love we bear this republic, or mitigate our consecration to its service. When General Lee, whose heart was the temple of our hopes and whose arm was clothed with our strength, renewed his allegiance to this government at Appomattox, he spoke from a heart too great to be false, and he spoke for every honest man from Maryland to Texas. From that day to this, Hamilcar has nowhere in the South sworn young Hannibal to hatred and vengeance—but everywhere to loyalty and love.

VI. CONDITION OF THE NEGRO, PAST AND PRESENT.

At a meeting of the "Current Topics Club" of Pilgrim Congregational Church in St. Louis, on the night of December 5, 1901, Dr. James W. Lee, pastor of St. John's Methodist

MRS. MARY CHURCH TERRELL.

Graduate of Oberlin College.   Eloquent Speaker and Linguist of Note.

Episcopal Church, South, and formerly a presiding elder of
the St. Louis Conference, a humane and thoughtful man and
a thorough Southerner, made a frank statement of the status
of the Negro race as seen during life in the South, as follows:

"There are at this time in the United States 8,840,789 of
the best fed, best clothed, best housed and best educated
Negroes to be found on the face of the earth. They have
reached the place they occupy to-day, so high above that of
the race to which they belong in Africa, through two hundred and forty years of discipline gained in slavery, and
through thirty-seven years of experience gained in freedom.
The slavery into which the Negroes were sold in America
was the most glorious freedom, however, in comparison with
the slavery from which they were bought, or stolen, in Africa.
It is well that American slavery ended when it did. But
that it did last until the Negro could learn the first lessons
in civilization is the best thing that has happened to him in
his long and awful existence. The African slave trade, which
John Wesley called 'the sum of all villainies,' and David Livingstone, 'the open sore of the world,' was, in so far as it concerned the Negroes sold into slavery in America, providential;
and the institution of slavery in this country was providential, and yet a merciful God does not sanction either the
traffic or the institution. But we are taught in the scriptures that God often makes the wrath of man to praise Him.
Joseph was sold by his own brethren to traveling merchants,
and carried as a slave into Egypt. When these same brethren returned from the burial of their father, Joseph said to
them: 'As for you, ye thought evil against me, but God
meant it unto good, to bring to pass, as it is this day, to
save much people alive.'

"So far as the slave-traders were concerned, they thought
evil against the Negro. They thought only of the money they
could make, through buying him and selling him, but God
meant it unto good, to save to civilization millions of human
beings, and through them carry civilization to a continent of

savage human beings in Africa. Nevertheless, Jacob's sons were guilty of a great sin for selling their brother Joseph, and the people of this country were guilty of a great sin for buying the Negro and for enslaving him. For the wrongs of slavery the northern and southern sections of the Union are alike responsible. The North mainly for the traffic, and the South mainly for the institution. But both sections have atoned for their wrong-doing. The South civilized the Negro and the North set him free.

"More attention has been devoted to the people of African descent since 1865 than to those among us of any other nationality. They have, in themselves, given us, and are giving us, our great national problem. The Negro problem is everybody's problem, and will not down, or suffer itself, as yet, to be solved. This question is up in one form or another in all our conventions, political, commercial and religious. It divided the Methodist Church, separated the States into warring armies, and continues to produce division in all kinds of meetings, from labor unions to women's clubs. The poor Indians have been here from the beginning, and were here, perhaps, a thousand years before the Pilgrim Fathers landed on the coast of Cape Cod, but no one seems to think the red man of sufficient importance to make a problem of. He has been outrageously treated, robbed of his land, driven from his valleys and his rivers, but no one seems to take his sorrows to heart. By tacit but universal consent the black man is our national problem.

"Pharaoh in the government of Egypt was never more perplexed at the presence of the Israelite in his country than we, as a people, are to-day at the presence of the Negro among us. We may comfort ourselves, however, with the thought that the American people are accustomed to succeed in whatever they undertake with all their hearts and strength to do. And it does seem as though every serious-minded man and woman in these United States was at this time set and determined on finding some rational,

15

humane and Christian way to settle the Negro question; his place, his capacity and his future. One thing we all know beyond any doubt, the Negro is here; and another, it is time for us all to know that he is here to stay. We cannot deport him and work his problem out in Africa; we cannot concentrate him into some single State or group of States, and work it out there. We must take him just where he is and scattered as he is, mainly over the States which once united to form the Southern Confederacy, and work it out there.

"The South is a better place for the Negro than Africa itself. The Negro finds under the soft skies and in the warm sunshine of the South the very conditions he needs to grow in and to come to the best he finds within himself. Then the Southern people are the best friends he has ever found. They understand his weaknesses and the points of strength in his character. They civilized him and have given to him all the practical knowledge he possesses. They have received the rewards of his labor. They know better how to work out his future than any other people. It is evident to all who have studied the history of the Negro that his development and progress is only possible in relation with a superior race. Not only is it necessary that he be in connection with the white people in order to reach a higher state of civilization, but he can only maintain civilization in relation with them.

"In despair of seeing any solution to the Negro problem certain colored leaders, and not a few white people, have proposed the scheme of wholesale deportation to Africa. This is impossible, but were it feasible, it is wrong. It is a short-cut and wholesale method of ridding the country of a great duty and a great responsibility. If the Negroes have not maintained civilization in Hayti, as is well known they have not, after having been trained and taught in the principles of orderly life, how can we expect they would maintain it in wild and lawless and barbarous Africa? The forests there have never been cleared—it is a wilderness in which the Negroes would lapse into barbarism in less than a hundred years.

"The Hebrews were in training in Egypt four hundred and thirty years before they were ready to go up to the promised land. There, because of the traditional hatred the Egyptians had for shepherds, and because of the Egyptian caste prejudice for all foreigners, the races were kept apart, so that the Hebrews gradually grew into a homogeneous and unmixed people. If there had been free intermarriage and social equality, the Hebrew race would have been absorbed, and there would have been no Moses to write the world's moral law; and no David to sing away the world's doubt and sorrow. Our own Anglo-Saxon race has become capable of self-government only after more than a thousand years of civil and spiritual authority.

"Had there been any free intermarriage and social equality between the Hebrews and the Egyptians, if there had been such a man as Moses at all, he never would have refused to be called the son of Pharaoh's daughter, he never would have chosen the reproach of Christ rather than the pleasures of Egypt, he never would have fled into Midian to be in training with God for forty years, he would never have had any respect for the recompense of reward stored up for him in the future of the human race, he would have remained an Egyptian prince to the end of his life, and after death he would have been embalmed and placed in a royal tomb, as was old Rameses II., his king, and now, perhaps, after three thousand three hundred years he would have been found, as old Rameses II. has been found, as dry and parched and brown as more than three thousand years of silence in mummied confinement could make him. He would be lying among the other curiosities beside his ugly old king in the Gizeh museum at Cairo, or else he would have been bought for $250 by some tourists from England or America to lend interest to a museum in London or New York. Instead of a miserable parched and powdered and $250 end like this, he has come to the recompense of the reward for which he had respect. He is the world's acknowledged leader in the kingdom of moral law. His ethics furnish underpinning for civilized government and protection for civilized life. The instinctive and constitutional and fundamental race antipathy the white man feels for the black man is notice served by the Almighty in the very structure of the white man's being that He intends for the colored man to come to himself and to his estate as a separate, distinct and homogeneous race; that there may go from this people law-givers, prophets, leaders and preachers to redeem the Negro race in Africa. What God seems to write in the fiber of subjective mind and spirit can be changed by no objective act of parliament, or objective amendments to constitutions. When an instinct is found flowing into the blood of a people, it may be accepted as coming from heaven. The caste feeling, therefore, which so many decry and seek to eradicate, is not wrong, but right, because structural. To spend our time and money in battling against this is waste. The thing to do is to recognize it and give sympathy and support in line with it. The reason why we have not made greater headway since the war in lifting up the Negro than we have is because we have expended so much of our energy in tearing down fences which God built, and which He puts up again as soon as we think they are down. Had there been no caste feeling in Egypt against the children of Israel there would have been no chosen people and no Holy Scriptures. Caste does not mean hate and enmity. Between peoples of different caste there may be and there should be mutual respect and trust and love and sympathy.

"The Negro must remain in training with the white race here steadily until his natural tendencies are superseded by a higher nature, that when the days of his probation are ended he may go forth as teacher, as preacher, as mechanic, and as a capable and God-fearing man to do the work in

PROF. ROBT. H. TERRELL.

Graduate of Harvard. U. S. Magistrate, D. C.

Africa for which God has seemingly so marvelously raised him up and so strangely kept him and trained him.

"The people of the North and the people of the South must learn to be patient with one another, and especially must both learn to be patient with the Negro. We have all gained much knowledge since 1865, but if we are patient and sweet and tender and kind, God will teach us a great deal more. That the South is the place where the Negro's future is to be worked out, is coming to be more and more the conviction of all who have his interests at heart. The people of the South are more kindly disposed toward him than the people of other sections of the country. There has been talk in regions where the Negroes are few in numbers about social equality. Equality of this sort is not the kind the Negro needs. What the Negro needs is industrial equality, and he finds more of that in the South than anywhere else on earth. There are those who think the Negro should be admitted to the same railway coaches, the same hotels, the same schools and to the same churches as the white people. Those who live in the South do not think so, but they believe he should be permitted to work upon the same building, to plow in the same field, to hammer iron in the same shop, to spin cotton in the same factory, and to make syrup at the same sugar-cane mill along with the white people. It is clear to those who know the facts that the Negro enjoys more equality in the realm of carpentry, and mechanics, and engineering, and agriculture, and milling in the South than he is permitted to enjoy in the North. While a pastor in Rome, Georgia, I built a church. The foreman in its construction was a Negro, and he had many white men at work under him. I am building a church in St. Louis now, a semi-Southern city, but Northern sentiment is so strong here against Negro industrial equality, that if I were to go out to the corner of King's highway and Washington avenue, where the church is going up, to-morrow, and tell the workmen there that I had concluded to put a Negro foreman in charge, there is not a stone-mason, or carpenter, or hod-carrier connected with the building but would lay down his tools. I could employ a Negro foreman to build a church in Rome, Georgia, but I cannot do it in St. Louis, Missouri.

"I read in the *Globe-Democrat* last spring an account of a scene at the Liggett & Meyers tobacco factory that would have been impossible in the South. It seems that the managers needed about one hundred and fifty additional children, from ten to fifteen years of age, to stem tobacco. As they had already about all the white children they could find, they employed young Negroes to do the work; but these little darkies had no sooner appeared in the factory to take up their task than they were caught bodily by the white children and pitched out of the windows. This would have happened, perhaps, in almost any tobacco factory in the Northern States, but it would never have happened in the Southern States. And yet the same children who pitch young Negroes out of the windows when they come to work with them would not object to sitting down in the school, or in the railway car, or in the church with them. What is the use to offer the Negro equality in the church, or theater, or school, or railway coach, if he has no equality in the shop or the factory? The South offers him equality where his rations are involved. They do believe in feeding him or giving him a chance to feed himself. The equality the doctrinaires offer the Negro would do him no good. It is not the side of himself upon which he needs equality. The equality he needs touches him in the regions of his practical life, and not in the realms of the drama or the upholstered railway palace.

"During the time when the civil rights bill was being agitated, one Negro down South met another on the street and undertook to explain to his sable brother the provisions of the bill. 'Why,' said the first speaker, 'by the provisions of this bill you can go to the first-class theater, just the same as the white folks. You can go to the four-dollar-a-day hotels and sit down at the first table along with them; you can pay your two dollars and get your sleeping car and sleep under the white sheets just the same as the white folks, and then, when you die, you can be buried in a metallic coffin, just like the white folks. Why, sir, by the provisions of this bill——'

" 'Look here, nigger, stop rite dar,' interposed the son of Ham addressed. 'Did you say there was provisions in that bill? If dey is, den I want 'em. I don't care anything about your four-dollar-a-day hotel or your Pullman palace car, or sleeping under white sheets, or getting buried in an italic coffin; but if dere is provisions in de bill I am tor dem. I want a ham and a sack of flour jist as quick as I can git 'em.'

"This story illustrates the difference between the Northern and Southern attitude in regard to the Negro. Our friends in the North have been anxious about his civil rights, while the Southern people have been concerned about his right to work for bread and meat. One section does not seem to care whether he eats or not, just so he votes; the other section is not exceedingly anxious as to whether he votes or not, just so he eats. As it is necessary for him to eat 1,095 times a year and to vote only once, it seems to me that those who are mainly concerned about giving him the right to eat, with no emphasis on voting, are better friends to him than those concerned mainly about giving him the right to vote, with no emphasis on eating.

"The future of the Negro is not to be worked out along political lines, but along the lines of industry, morality and religion. The side of his nature upon which he is richest is the religious. He is born, seemingly, with more religion than human beings of any other race. Those who are to help him work out his future must take knowledge of this fact. If we are to lift him up we must take hold of him on his tropical, fertile side. Naturally he is endowed with the most lively sense of the unseen. Because of this, he is in danger of being led into all sorts of extravagance. Religion with him is a luxury, in which he revels. If ever the divine and rational and perfect life of Jesus Christ is thoroughly reproduced in the religious side of the Negro race, that people will rise up as a strong man armed and go forth to redeem the continent of Africa. I believe it would be wise if all our people would concentrate their efforts for awhile now upon cultivating the religious side of our brother in black. Let his political side alone. There is more religious raw material in him than material of any other sort.

"In this way the learning and morality and Christian character of our noblest and best people would touch and influence and build up those colored young men and women looking for their life-work in preaching the gospel to their people, or instructing them in the common schools. The Southern Methodist Church has a negro college in Augusta, Georgia, presided over by one of our most cultivated ministers, who is himself a member of one of the old aristocratic South Carolina families. This institution is devoted to preparing colored young men for the ministry among their own people, and to preparing teachers for work in the common colored schools. It is doing more good than any institution of the same grade in the whole Southern States. The teachers in it are consecrated Southern white people. There is a perfect understanding between the professors and the students—the professors know their place, and the colored students know their place. There is no friction, but mutual respect and trust, as was felt before the war between the Christian master and the faithful servant.

"Another leading line along which the Negro's future is to be worked out is industrial. He should be helped, as many are helping him, in this direction. Everybody rejoices in the success of Booker T. Washington with his industrial school at Tuskegee, Alabama. Booker T. Washington himself is the greatest thing the Negro race has produced in this generation. Prof. Huxley was at dinner with a company of gentlemen some years ago in London, when France and the French were being discussed. The party, being English, were almost united in the opinion that the French were a light, shallow, unpromising people. 'Yes,' said Mr. Huxley, 'but there is one thing we must all remember, France has Pasteur.' So, while many people today are ready to think there is no hopeful future for the Negro race, we should all remember that it has Booker T. Washington. In the opinion of Prof. Huxley, Pasteur was, himself, reason sufficient for the existence of the French people; and Booker T. Washington is, himself, sufficient reason to give us hope for the future of the Negro. He has been raised up to show what the Negro can do with his hands, and to illustrate, in himself, what the Negro can become, as a man.

"If all who want to help the Negro work out his future will turn their attention toward helping him along industrial, moral and religious lines for the next generation, and for the time being let his political fortunes take care of themselves, we will find in thirty years that he is not such a difficult proposition as the whole country seems united in agreeing that he is today."

VII. THE NEGRO'S NEEDS.

Doctor Lee's address before the "Current Topics Club" was followed by one at a meeting of the St. Louis Evangelical Alliance, December 30, 1901, in which he discussed the Negro's needs, after giving a succinct history of the introduction of African slavery into this country. His remarks were as follows:

"As a general thing the relation of the slave to his owner was one of sympathy and good-will. Some of the most attractive and saintly and beautiful characters who have ever lived in the world, grew up among the Negroes in the South under the institution of slavery. From among those old

Negro saints, loving their cabins, their kinsfolk and the scenes in the midst of which they grew up, artists have found about the only types of character among us who have any promise of living in the popular songs of the people. There is a charm and a winsomeness about the character of 'Old Black Joe' that takes hold of the imagination completely. I knew 'Old Black Joe,'. and there are others here, if they ever lived in the South, who knew him. Stephen Collins Foster has given us his portrait without exaggeration. There he sits, back yonder in the days before 1860, in front of his cabin, under the shade of a peach tree, too old to work, talking to himself and saying substantially:

"Gone are the days when my heart was young and gay,
Gone are my friends from the cotton fields away,
Gone from this earth to a better land I know,
I hear their gentle voices calling, 'Old Black Joe.'

"Where are the hearts once so happy and so free?
The children so dear that I held upon my knee?
Gone to the shore where my soul has longed to go,
I hear their gentle voices calling, 'Old Black Joe.'

"I'm coming, I'm coming,
For my head is bending low,
I hear those gentle voices calling, 'Old Black Joe.'"

" 'Old Black Joe' grew up and grew old at home, loving his master and his missus, holding in the evening of his life their children or their grandchildren upon his knee, giving them quaint and interesting information about Br'er Rabbit and Br'er Fox. One who never knew him can never know what a lovely and tender-hearted old man he was. Such a specimen of generous, fragrant, responsive, confiding and simple manhood never could have been produced in the midst of a cruel and hard and harsh environment. Among many other types which have been given immortality in music, there is the Negro brought up on a plantation in the far South. He was sold to a master in another State.

16

Still, with change of master and change of location, he re-
tains his simplicity of character, his love for the old place
and the old people.   He has wandered far, but has never left
the native and genuine and beautiful instincts of the human
soul.   Now in his old age, he sits down and gives himself
up to memories of the past.   He is thinking of the old plantation of his younger days, and to himself he meditates.
and says:

> 'All 'round the little farm I wandered,
>   when I was young,
> Den many happy days I squandered,
>   many de songs I sung.
> When I was playing with my brudder,
>   happy was I,
> Oh take me to my kind old mudder,
>   dere let me live and die.
>
> 'One little hut among the bushes,
>   one dat I love,
> Still sadly to my mem'ry rushes,
>   no matter where I rove,
> When will I see the bees a'humming,
>   all round de comb?
> When will I hear the banjo tumming,
>   down in my good old home?
>
> 'All de world am sad and dreary,
>   ebrywhere I roam,
> Oh darkies how my heart grows weary,
>   far from the old folks at home.'

"This old Suwanee Negro has gone into all the world. He
has been idealized and made immortal in the most popular
song, perhaps, ever written in this country. The great
singers always strike chords in the common heart, not only
in New York, but also in St. Petersburg and Vienna and
Paris and London, when they respond to encores from the
great audiences with 'Old Folks at Home.' It is well
worth considering. Just why should others have been passed
by—revolutionary heroes, early settlers, lonely Indians,

hunters on the plains, exiles of Erin, and this good humble, simple, pure-hearted, old Suwanee Negro selected to live forever in America's most universal and popular song? The main reason, I believe, is found in the element of homesickness, which makes up one of the permanent and essential qualities of the true Negro's life. There is a far away look on his face, and a longing deep in his nature, for things beyond him and above him. By this sigh for the distant, by this yearning for the years of youth and the time of gladness with which he somehow feels himself in correspondence through love for his God, the source of all spring-time and youth, he is transfigured. His nature glows; his face becomes luminous with an inner light; his heart swells with unutterable hopes. Having no intellectual entanglements with doubt and unbelief, he receives the impressions made by the impact of the unseen upon the surface of his religious nature as literal truth. He is so perfectly unsophisticated, so genuine and thoroughly himself, so completely artless and guileless, that all artists, as well as everybody else, falls in love with him. The poor exile of Erin who has been standing on the beach, with the dew on his thin robe so long, is rather a touching figure. He makes a very good theme for poetry, as he stands looking from his sad foreign shore across the waters to the sweetest sea-beaten isle of the ocean, but one cannot resist the impression that he knows too well how to take care of himself in an election, to be really as deeply sad and lonely as he looks. Hence the world does not take him seriously enough to sing with any enthusiasm about his short-lived loneliness and grief. The old Suwanee Negro, on the other hand, has no opportunity to mend his earthly fortunes. His homesickness is permanent and organic. Nothing is left him but his loved ones and his home in heaven. To these he turns with all the ardor and strength of a renewed, radiant nature. He has not a single earthly hope. Hence the artist passes by the Irishman and the successful American and enshrines in everlasting song this heavenly-minded old darky, and the world gladly gives him the homage due to perfect simplicity and beauty of character. The barriers imposed upon the Negro by the institution of slavery he did not resent, but accepted in obedience and good-will. He gave his nights to innocent and refreshing sleep, and not to intrigues and conspiracies. Slavery as a barrier served as a controller and generator of religious energy. When the river which has been spreading itself over a shallow expanse is shut within narrow rock walls, or when an expanded body of steam is confined in a cylinder, the limitation in each case is a direct creator of power. Because of the limitation placed about the Negro by the institution of slavery, there was but one side of himself through which he had untrammeled opportunity to flower, and that was his religious side, which covers about three-fourths of the surface of the Negro's life. Because of this the Negro was contented and happy in slavery, and because he did, through large expression of himself on the side of his religious nature, become obedient, polite, humble and tender-hearted, his master loved him with great tenderness. The Southern people therefore like the Negroes. They have seen them at their best estate. They know when they grow up under the nurture and admonition of the Lord, genuinely pious and true, that they are charming and attractive human beings. Hence we find under the institution of slavery imitations of the highest types of character that we are to find among them under the conditions of freedom. While the barrier of slavery has been taken away, still the Negro is under limitations just as great, and these are in reality the conditions of his advancement. It is now the barriers of poverty, of meager attainment, which he is to force, and which he must learn will yield only to the steady push of industry and unrelaxed training. These barriers are the provisions of providence for keeping him at his topmost level and for getting out of him all there is in him. Goethe well says: 'Everything that frees our spirit without giving us the mastery of our spirit is pernicious.' The fact that the Negro is about four thousand years behind the white man in the career of civilization, is a limitation he must recognize about him. But this should be a source of inspiration. All the accumulations of history which have been made through the battles and strife of the ages he finds himself in touch with without a fight. That these vast stores of accumulated human gain are above him, and have been stored up without his aid or co-operation, furnishes him an altitude up which he has the pleasure of climbing. A poor man rescued from slow death should not, upon coming to consciousness and life, be unhappy because he finds himself poor in comparison with those who rescued him. He should be delighted at the opportunity of breathing and acting. The Negro just rescued from slavery worse than death in Africa, and from slavery better for him, while it lasted, than freedom in America, should not sympathize with himself and commiserate himself because of the respects in which he is not equal to those who have been wrestling with the problems of civilized existence for thousands of years before he was born to civilization. He should rejoice at the privilege of just living and breathing and having his being in an enlightened Christian country. The Negro has not made quite enough of the fact that he is alive in the midst of the greatest government the world ever saw. He has been looking at himself too much from the standpoint of the white man in America and not enough from the standpoint of the black man in Africa. There is not a poor white man among us, measuring all things from the purely worldly standpoint, but can work himself to the boiling point of misery by looking at himself from the standpoint of privilege enjoyed by an Astor with his millions, his yachts and his mansions.

"The Negroes have been too much inclined to gird at their limitations of position and gifts, and have placed too much hope in outside amendments to the constitution and civil rights bills to redress their inequalities. The stoic Epictetus, though a slave, did not cry out against his limitations, but

got even with his master and everybody else by writing his
discourses, and afterwards had emperors for his disciples.
'Against the superiority of another,' says Goethe, 'there is no
remedy but love.' Against the superiority of the white man
under slavery, the Negro found a remedy in loving him. This
gave him a simplicity and beauty of character; and now under freedom, he will find the only remedy against any superiority with which he meets, to be love; this will insure simplicity and beauty of character again. While the Negro is to
work out his own destiny, it is the solemn duty of the white
man who brought him by force to this country, to help him.
And first of all he must have the sympathy and love of the
white man. These are not to be exhausted in words and theories. There have been enough theories, kindly and Christian,
about the Negro since the war, had they been practical, not
only to have given to every one of them in the South, forty
acres of land and a mule, but a life of the most rosy com-
pleteness. It has taken the colored man a third of a century
to learn that fine theories do not help him. What the Negro
needs more than anything else today is fair treatment by the
great industrial classes of the country.

"There are forty thousand Negroes in St. Louis, and among
them many first-class carpenters and brick-masons, yet because of their color, they are excluded from work on all the
great buildings, in all the great machine shops, and from all
the main trunk lines of legitimate industry. They are still
permitted to break rock in the streets, to dig ditches, to clean
out sewers, to drive drays, hacks and coal wagons, but from
all higher grades of work, which call for skill, and which
command better wages, they are as absolutely shut out as
though they were not human beings. Laboring men have a
perfect right to organize themselves into brotherhoods and
unions for their protection, and for the advancement of their
interests. There is not any doubt but that they have lifted
themselves and their labor to a higher plane through organization. But it is not right to exclude men from the unions

on account of color. The right of the Negro to live is certainly inalienable, but how can he live and support his family if he is not given a fair opportunity along with other men, to work anywhere and in any line of industry for which he qualifies himself? The Negro is entitled to absolute industrial equality. It must be remembered that he did not just arrive on the shores of America yesterday, and were he a new-comer, the right to work anywhere would still be his. But the Negro has been here ever since 1620—two hundred and eighty-one years. He cleared most of the forests in the Southern States. He produced the cotton by the sale and manufacture of which has come much of the wealth of this country. He produced the cane from which the laboring men have been sweetening their coffee for two hundred years. He produced the syrup which has been doubling and quadrupling the value of waffles and pan-cakes which the laboring men have been enjoying at breakfast for a couple of centuries. He should not be treated as an alien and a foreigner by labor unions, for he is less a foreigner than almost any other class of people. If anybody is native and to the manor born, he is. We owe it not only to the Negro, but to ourselves to give him the same opportunity to work that is enjoyed by the white man. I am a Southerner, and have all the feelings common to Southern people with reference to Negro social equality. But Southern people have no opposition to Negro industrial equality. They believe in it. After an address delivered at the 'Current Topics Club' of the Pilgrim Congregational Church, some weeks ago, on the subject of the Negro's future, a committee of Negroes representing the leading colored interests of the city called at my house to express the thanks of the colored people of St. Louis to me for the address I delivered. As they were intelligent Negroes, I embraced the opportunity to get all the information I could about the present conditions of the Negro in this city. I was simply amazed at what I learned. No one who has not paid attention to the question, can have any proper

16

conception of the difficulties with which Negroes right here in our midst are confronted today. The most pathetic aspect of the whole Negro problem is found in the gradual closing against him of all the leading industries. This takes from him the stimulus of qualifying himself for work. He is thrown back into a life of idleness, or else is shut up for the means of subsistence to odd jobs, or such small tasks here and there as he may find to do. He has no way of bringing his wrongs to the consideration of the public. We can hardly bring ourselves to realize how pitiable his condition is, in view of the industrial inequalities which have been gathering against him during the last quarter of a century. He is the nation's ward. The most bloody war ever waged between civilized States was continued for four long years to give him his freedom. Billions of dollars were spent in his behalf. Billions more have been spent since the war in paying pensions to old soldiers who fought to give him his freedom. The Grand Army of the Republic holds its great annual reunion every year, and the most thrilling and inspiring thought that comes to them on these great occasions is that they knocked the shackles from the limbs of four millions of slaves. And yet this man who has cost the country more lives and more money than any other man ever cost any country in all history, stands among us in the pitiable plight of being debarred from every great line of handicraft. There is not a Pole or Scandinavian just landed in America yesterday, however full his head may be of anarchy, and his heart of enmity to the government, but enjoys opportunities we deny to our Negroes, who naturally love the government, and who have been here nearly three hundred years, and who have never produced an anarchist in all history. The glory of freeing the slaves will depart from the Grand Army of the Republic, and from the States which remained true to the Union if they permit them, because of want of fair opportunities to work enjoyed by others, to enslave themselves again by vices cradled in idleness into which they have been unjustly driven.

"One other interesting fact about the Negro needs to be carefully weighed and considered by those who desire to assist him in working out his destiny, and that is the vast stores of religious raw material that are lying in the depths of his nature. There are deposits here which run back over thousands of years, covering much of his lonely, fear-beset life in the midst of the deep, dark, lion-and-tiger-haunted forests of Africa. This is the most wonderful and immense asset of the Negro's life. Through this side of himself he is to find his power and his mission in the world. He as little understands himself here as others understand him. But all who have seen the Negroes in their great meetings have recognized the religious element as the deepest and most important in their nature. It is mysterious and impenetrable and beyond analysis, but its weird presence no one can doubt. Great congregations come under its spell and are held as one palpitating mass as if clasped together by an unseen power. The music through which they seek to give expression to their religious feelings is the most wonderful ever heard and touches the soul. There are intimations of vast storms, of wide-spreading plains, of mountains of the moon, of struggles with wild beasts in the dark woods, long rivers like the Nile, of the gold coast with its awful idolatry. The influence of this music is felt as much by the cultivated as the uncultivated. Rev. Dr. Henry M. Field telephoned me one morning in Atlanta to meet him at the hotel and accompany him to Spellman's Seminary. This is a school built by John D. Rockefeller for the education of colored girls. There were eight hundred students in the institution at the time. Announcing ourselves, the principal brought the whole school into the chapel. Doctor Field wanted to hear them sing. They began with regulation Sunday-school songs, and Doctor Field was not much impressed, though they sang as well as others. I asked the principal to have them give us some regular Negro music. They did not like this, for it has been the effort of the educated Negroes to get as far from what is native and peculiar to themselves as possible. But some one in the audience moaned or intoned all alone a line of 'Swing low, sweet chariot.' She was joined by another, then they fell in by fours and eights, until the whole eight hundred were giving us the most weird and affecting music to which one ever listened. 'I looked up the road and what did I see a-coming for to carry me home; a band of angels a-coming after me, coming for to carry me home; swing low, sweet chariot, coming for to carry me home.' The great organist at Luzerne, Switzerland, never had more success in seemingly pulling down out of the clouds, through his instrument, real storms with thunder and lightning and hail and wind and rain than these singers, with their voices, had in seeming to fill the air with real chariots—swinging low, down from the sky, and with real hands of angels coming down every road leading to the chapel.

"The effect on the distinguished traveler and editor, Doctor Field, was remarkable. The fountains of the great deep of his emotions were broken up, and he was weeping like a child. In a short address after the service of song, he told the students that they made a great mistake in seeking, through vain and shallow imitation of the white folks, to get themselves educated away from the real sources of power which belonged to them as a race.

"Through the explorations of Livingstone and Stanley a map of the vast objective continent of Africa has been made approximately correct. Its rivers, lakes, mountains and plains have been partially surveyed and named. Now a Livingstone is needed to explore and give to the world a map of the immense subjective continent of religious and emotional Africa. In this interior, and as yet untraveled, unknown of himself, the Negro is to find the wealth and glory of his nature, and the reason of his existence in the world.

Noted Newspaper Correspondent.

When the explorer returns to civilization from the long and difficult journey into the interior continent of religious and emotional Africa, he will be able to give to the Negro a geography of himself, from which he can see his place and his mission in the world. From this he will doubtless learn that he has been in training for nearly three hundred years in America, in order that he may be ready at the call of God to go forth to redeem his race from barbarism, worse than death, in Africa."

VIII. THE NEGRO AND THE SIGNS OF CIVILIZATION.

BY BOOKER T. WASHINGTON.

There are certain visible signs of civilization and strength which the world demands that each individual or race exhibit before it is taken seriously into consideration in the affairs of the world. Unless these visible evidences of ability and strength are forthcoming, mere abstract talking and mere claiming of "rights" amount to little. This is a principle that is as broad and old as the world and is not confined to the conditions that exist between the white man and the black man in the South. We may be inclined to exalt intellectual acquirements over the material, but all will acknowledge that the possession of the material has an influence that is lasting and unmistakable. As one goes through our western States and sees the Scandinavians in Minnesota, for example, owning and operating nearly one-third of the farms in the State, and then as he goes through one of the cities of Minnesota and sees block after block of brick stores owned by these Scandinavians, as he sees factories and street railways owned and operated by these same people, and as he notes that as a rule these people live in neat, well-kept cottages, that have been paid for, where there is refinement and culture, on nice streets, he can't help but have confidence in and respect for such people, no matter how he has been educated to feel regarding them. The material, visible and tangible elements in this case teach a lesson that almost nothing else can. It may be said in opposition to this view that this is exalting too high the material side of life. I do not take this view. Let us see what is back of this material possession. In the first place, the possession of property is an evidence of mental discipline, mental grasp and control. It is an evidence of self-sacrifice. It is an evidence of economy. It is an evidence of thrift and industry. It is an evidence of fixedness of character and purpose. It is an evidence of interest in pure and intelligent government, for no man can possess property without having the deepest interest in all that pertains to local and national government. The black man who owns $50,000 worth of property in a town is going to think a good many times before he votes for the officer who will have the liberty of taxing his property. If he thinks that a colored law-maker will use his taxing power wrongfully, he is not likely to vote for him merely for the sentimental reason that he is a black man. The black man who owns $50,000 worth of property in a town is not likely to continue to vote for a republican law-maker if he knows that a democratic one will bring lower taxes and better protection to his property. Say or think what we will there is but one way for the Negro to get up, and that is for him to pay the cost, and when he has paid the cost—paid the price of his freedom—it will appear in the beautiful, well-kept home, in the increasing bank account, in the farm and crops that are free from debt, in the ownership of railroad and municipal stocks and bonds, in the well-kept store, in the well-fitted laundry, in the absence of mere superficial display. These are a few of the universal and indisputable signs of the highest civilization, and the Negro must possess them or be debarred. All mere abstract talk about the possibility of possessing them or his intention to possess them counts for little. He must actually possess them, and the only way to possess them is to possess them. From every standpoint of interest it is the duty of the Negro himself, and the duty of the Southern white man as well as the white man in the

North, to see that the Negro be helped forward as fast as possible towards the possession of these evidences of civilization. How can it best be done? Where is the beginning to be made? It can be done by the Negro beginning right now and where he finds himself. What I am anxious for is for the Negro to be in actual possession of all the elements of the highest civilization, and when he is so possessed the burden of his future treatment by the white man must rest upon the white man.

I repeat, let the Negro begin right where he is, by putting the greatest amount of intelligence in skill and dignity into the occupations by which he is surrounded. Let him learn to do common things in an uncommon manner. Whenever in the South, for example, the Negro is the carpenter, let him realize that he cannot remain the carpenter unless people are sure that no one can excel him as a carpenter. This black carpenter should strive in every way possible to keep himself abreast of the best woodwork done in the world. He should be constantly studying the best journals and books bearing on carpentry. He should watch for every improvement in his line. When this carpenter's son is educated in college or elsewhere, he should see that his son studies mechanical and architectural drawing. He should not only have his son taught practical carpentry, but should see that in addition to his literary education, he is a first-class architect as well—that, if possible, he has an idea of landscape gardening and house furnishing. In a word, he should see that his son knows so much about woodwork, house construction, and everything that pertains to making a house all that it should be, that his services are in constant demand. One such Negro in each community will give character to a hundred other Negroes. It is the kind of effort that will put the Negro on his feet. What I have said of carpentry is equally true of dozens of occupations now within the Negro's hands. The second or third generation of this black man need not be carpenters, but can aspire successfully to something higher because the foundation has been laid.

It is not only the duty of the Negro to thus put himself in possession of the signs of civilization, but it is also the plainest duty of the white man, North and South, to help the Negro to do so in a more generous manner than ever before. One-third of the population of the South is colored. Ignorance in any country or among any people is the sign of poverty, crime and incompetency. No State can have the highest civilization and prosperity with one-third of its population down. This one-third will prove a constant millstone about the neck of the other two-thirds. Every one-room Negro cabin in the South, where there is ignorance, poverty and stupidity, is an adverse advertisement of the State, the bad effects of which no white man in the next generation can escape.

IX. THE NEGRO'S PART IN THE SOUTH'S UPBUILDING.

I have read a little pamphlet, written by a well-educated colored man, Mr. George W. Carver, giving the result of some of his experiments in raising sweet potatoes this year. In this pamphlet, this colored man has shown in plain, simple language, based on scientific principles, how he has raised two hundred and sixty-six bushels of sweet potatoes on a single acre of common land, and made a net profit of $121. The average yield of sweet potatoes in the South, where this experiment was tried, is thirty-seven bushels per acre. This same colored man is now preparing to make the same land produce five hundred bushels of potatoes. I have watched this experiment with a good deal of interest. The thing that has interested me most regarding this experiment has been the deep interest which the neighboring white farmers took in it. I do not believe that a single one of the dozens of white farmers who visited the field to see the unusual yield of potatoes ever thought of having any prejudice or feeling against this colored man because his education had enabled him to make an unusual success in the raising of potatoes. On the other hand, there were many evidences of the deepest respect for this colored man and gratitude for the information which he had furnished.

If I were to write a volume, I do not think I could state the case of the Negro more strongly than this illustration puts it.

I am fully aware of all the disadvantages to which the Negro is subjected. Notwithstanding all this, I believe I do not overestimate matters when I say that it seldom ever happens in history that a race has such an opportunity to make itself felt in the upbuilding of a country as is now true of the Negro race, especially in the South. I feel equally confident in saying that no individual or race that makes itself permanently felt in the building of a country is long left without proper reward and recognition.

The most important problem that is now confronting the Negro and the Negro's friends, is the turning of the force of the Negro's education in that direction that will contribute most effectually toward the betterment of the condition of the country and the Negro himself.

Recurring again to the instance of the colored man who made his education felt in the production of sweet potatoes, I would say that if we had a hundred such men in each county in the South there would be no race problem to discuss. But how are we to get such men? In the first place, those interested in the education of the Negro must begin to look facts and conditions in the face. Too great a gap has been left between the Negro's real condition and the position which we have tried to fit him for through the medium of our text-books. We overlook in many cases the long years of schooling in experience and discipline that any race must have before it can get the greatest amount of good out of the text-book matter that has been given the black man Much that the Negro has studied presupposes conditions that do not as yet exist in his case. I do not want to be misunderstood. I favor the highest and most thorough development of the Negro's mind. No race can accomplish anything till its mind is awakened. But the weak point has been in the past, in too many cases, between the Negro's educated brains and his opportunity or manner of earning his daily living. There has been almost no thought of connecting the educated brain with the educated hand. The education of the Negro, in too many cases, has presumed that he had years of wealth, culture and even luxury behind him, just as is true of New England. Even Mr. Cornelius Vanderbilt, with his millions behind him, finds it necessary to put his son into a machine shop, and thus connect his brain-training with something that is vital and practical. If this is true of the Vanderbilts, should it not be a thousandfold more true of the Negro in his present condition? Education of the head increases wants. Unless the hands are educated at the same time, so as to supply these increased wants, in too many cases you will have an individual who is of little benefit to society.

But, to return more directly to my subject, I would say without hesitation that, judging by what I have experienced and observed, the best way for the Negro to contribute toward the building up of the South and his own welfare, is for him to turn the force of his education, during the next fifty years, very largely in the direction of scientific and industrial training, in connection with moral and religious training. It is almost a crime, in many cases, to take young men from the farm, or from a farming district, and educate them, as is often done, in every other subject except agriculture—the one subject that they should know the most about. The result is that the young man, instead of being educated to love agriculture, is educated out of sympathy with it; and instead of returning to his old father's farm, after leaving college, and showing him how to raise more produce with less labor, the young man is often tempted to go into the city or town to live by his wits.

In most parts of the South the Negro has the labor in his possession, but he will not hold it unless he is taught to put brains and skill into the common occupations that are about him, and at the same time to dignify common labor.

In most of the cities of the South the Negro can be an architect, a contractor, a builder and a brickmaker; and what is true of these callings is true of any number of other occupations—for women as well as men.

Whenever a black man makes himself of real service to a community or State, that service will not remain unrecognized, as is the case of the man who raised the sweet potatoes. If our people enter heartily, in a whole-souled manner, into all the industrial walks of life, by preparing to do some conscientious work, by doing something better than some one else can do it, they will not only make a great contribution to the wealth of the South, but they will earn the gratitude of the white citizens to the extent that every black man will find a secure place in the hearts of the white people of the section.

Not only this, but it is only through industrial development that the Negro can promote his own development. I know how strong the temptation is to say that what the Negro wants to have emphasized is the languages, fine arts and the various professions. These are very well for a few, but for the great mass of our people this is not what we want in this generation. The best way to promote what is called "higher education" for the black man is for us in this generation to throw aside all nonsense, all non-essentials, and begin at the bottom and work up through agriculture, the trades, domestic science and household economy. In this way we lay a material foundation for our children and grandchildren to get the greatest benefit out of abstract education.

COL. JAS. H. DEVEAUX.

Collector of Customs, Savannah, Georgia.

X. THE NEGRO AND HIS RELATION TO THE SOUTH.

[Booker T. Washington's Address Before the Southern Industrial Convention at Huntsville, Alabama, October 12, 1899.]

"In all discussion and legislation bearing upon the presence of the Negro in America, it should be borne in mind that we are dealing with a people who were forced to come here without their consent and in the face of a most earnest protest. This gives the Negro a claim upon your sympathy and generosity that no other race can possess. Besides, though forced from his native land into residence in a country that was not of his choosing, he has earned his right to the title of American citizen by obedience to the law, by patriotism and fidelity, and by the millions which his brawny arms and willing hands have added to the wealth of this country.

.   .   .   .

"In saying what I have today, although a Negro and an ex-slave myself, there is no white man whose heart is more wrapped up in every interest of the South and loves it more dearly than is true of myself. She can have no sorrow that I do not share; she can have no prosperity that I do not rejoice in; she can commit no error that I do not deplore; she can take no step forward that I do not approve.

"Different in race, in color, in history, we can teach the world that, although thus differing, it is possible for us to dwell side by side in love, in peace and in material prosperity. We can be one, as I believe we will be in a larger degree in the future, in sympathy, purpose, forbearance and mutual helpfulness. Let him who would embitter, who would bring strife between your race and mine, 'be accursed in his basket and his store, accursed in the fruit of his body and in the fruit of his land.' No man can plan the degradation of another race without being himself degraded. The highest test of the civilization of any race is its willingness to extend a helping hand to the less fortunate.

"The South extends a protecting arm and a welcome voice to the foreigner, all nationalities, languages and conditions;

but in this I pray that you will not forget the black man at your door, whose habits you know, whose fidelity you have tested. You may make of others larger gatherers of wealth, but you cannot make of them more law-abiding, useful and God-fearing people than the Negroes, who have been by your side for three centuries, and whose toil in forest, field and mine has helped to make the South the land of promise and glorious possibility.

. . . .

"If the South is to go forward and not stand still, if she is to reach the highest reward from her wonderful resources and keep abreast of the progress of the world, she must reach that point, without needless delay, where she will not be continually advertising to the world that she has a race question to settle. We must reach that point where at every election, from the choice of a magistrate to that of a governor, the decision will not hinge upon a discussion or a revival of the race question. We must arrive at the period where the great fundamental questions of good roads, education of farmers, agricultural and mineral development, manufacturing and industrial and public school education will be, in a large degree, the absorbing topics in our political campaigns. But that we may get this question from among us, the white man has a duty to perform; the black man has a duty to perform. No question is ever permanently settled until it is settled in the principles of highest justice. Capital and lawlessness will not dwell together. The white man who learns to disregard the law when a Negro is concerned, will soon disregard it when a white man is concerned.

. . . .

"For years all acknowledge that the South has suffered from the low price of cotton because of over-production. The economic history of the world teaches that an ignorant farming class means a single crop, and that a single crop means, too often, low prices from over-production or famine from under-production. The Negro constitutes the principal farming class of the South. So long as the Negro is ignorant in head, unskilled in hand, unacquainted with labor-saving machinery, so long will he confine himself to a single crop, and over-production of cotton will result. So long as this is true you will be bound in economic fetters; you will be hugging the bear while crying for some one to help you let go. Every man, black and white, in the South, with his crop mortgaged, in debt at the end of the year, buying his meat from Iowa, his corn from Illinois, his shoes from New York, his clothing from Pennsylvania, his wagon from Indiana, his plow from Massachusetts, his mule from Missouri, his coffin from Ohio, every one who is thus situated is a citizen who is not producing the highest results for his State. It is argued that the South is too poor to educate such an individual so as to make him an intelligent producer. I reply that the South is too poor not to educate such an individual.

"Ignorance is manyfold more costly to tax-payers than intelligence. Every black youth that is given this training of hand and strength of mind, so that he is able to grasp the full meaning and responsibility of the meaning of life, so that he can go into some forest and turn the raw material into wagons and buggies, becomes a citizen who is able to add to the wealth of the State and to bear his share of the expenses of educational government. Do you suggest that this cannot be done? I answer that it is being done every day at Tuskegee, and should be duplicated in a hundred places in every Southern State. This I take to be the 'White Man's Burden' just now—no, no, not his burden, but his privilege, his opportunity to give the black man sight, to give him strength, skill of hand, light of mind and honesty of heart. Do this, my white friends, and I will paint you a picture that shall represent the future, partly as the outcome of this industrial convention, and will represent the land where your race and mine must dwell.

"Fourteen slaves brought into the South a few centuries

ago, in ignorance, superstition and weakness, are now a free
people, multiplied into eight millions. They are surrounded,
protected, encouraged, educated in hand, heart and head,
given the full protection of the law, the highest justice meted
out to them through courts and legislative enactments. They
are stimulated and not oppressed, made citizens and not
aliens, made to understand by word and act that, in proportion as they show themselves worthy to bear responsibilities,
the greater opportunities will be given them. I see them
loving you, trusting you, adding to the wealth, the intelligence, the renown of each Southern Commonwealth. In
turn, I see you confiding in them, ennobling them, beckoning
them on to the highest success, and we have all been made
to appreciate in full that—

> 'The slave's chain and the master's alike are broken,
> The one curse of the race held both in tether;
> They are rising, all are rising,
> The black and white together.' "

XI. "THE ANCIENT GOVERNOR."

An illustration of the respect and consideration with which
worthy Negroes are treated by Kentuckians is furnished by
the story of Daniel Clark, as related in Thompson's "Young
People's History of Kentucky." When Gov. James Clark
came to Frankfort (1836) to assume the duties of his office
he had with him as a body-servant a Negro man, Daniel,
who, many years before, had been brought by slave-dealers
from Africa to Charleston, South Carolina, and afterward
came into the possession of the Clark family in Kentucky.
He was old enough when bought or captured in his native
country to note the incidents of the ocean voyage, which he
remembered distinctly during his long life. On coming to
Frankfort he was employed about the governor's mansion
and the executive office, and for thirty-six years, through all
the changes of administration, he continued in this service,
and came to be known as the "Ancient Governor." On the

17

27th of January, 1872, the Senate of Kentucky passed a bill by a majority of thirty out of thirty-four votes cast, giving him a pension of $12.50 per month for life, on the ground that he was then, in the language of the bill, "a very old and infirm man, not able to work or to perform the full duties of said office any longer, and as an evidence of the appreciation in which Kentucky holds his faithfulness and honesty, and of her unwillingness that he shall want for a support." Pending the consideration of the bill by the House he died; and the legislature passed a joint resolution, February 17th, commending him as "a notable example to all men, white or black, of industry, sobriety, courtesy according to his station, and integrity in office."

CHAPTER X.

INDUSTRIAL TRAINING AND NEGRO DEVELOPMENT.

I. ADDRESS BY BOOKER T. WASHINGTON.

"SINCE the war no one subject has been more misunderstood than that of the object and value of industrial educationfor the Negro. To begin with, it must be borne in mind that the condition that existed in the South immediately after the war, and that now exists, is a peculiar one, without a parallel in history. This being true, it seems to me that the wise and honest thing is to make a study of the actual condition and environment of the Negro, and do that which is best for him, regardless of whether the same thing has been done for another race in exactly the same way. There are those among our friends of the white race, and those among my own race, who assert with a good deal of earnestness, that there is no difference between the white man and the black man in this country. This sounds very pleasant and tickles the fancy, but when we apply the test of hard, cold logic to it, we must acknowledge that there is a difference; not an inherent one, not a racial one, but a difference growing out of unequal opportunities in the past.

"If I might be permitted to even seem to criticise some of the educational work that has been done in the South, I would say that the weak point has been in a failure to recognize this difference.

"Negro education, immediately after the war, in most cases, was begun too nearly at the point where New England education had ended. Let me illustrate: One of the saddest sights I ever saw was the placing of a $300 rosewood piano in a country school in the South that was located in the midst of the 'Black Belt.' Am I arguing against the teaching of instrumental music to the Negroes in that community? Not at all; only I should have deferred those music lessons about twenty-five years. There are such pianos in thousands of New England homes, but behind the piano in the New England home there were one hundred years of toil, sacrifice and economy; there was the small manufacturing industry, started several years ago by hand-power, now grown into a great business; there was the ownership in land, a comfortable home free from debt, a bank account. In this 'Black Belt' community where this piano went, four-fifths of the people owned no land, many lived in rented one-room cabins, many were in debt for food supplies, many mortgaged their crops for the food on which to live and not one had a bank account. In this case how much wiser it would have been to have taught the girls in this community how to do their own sewing, how to cook intelligently and economically, housekeeping, something of dairying and horticulture; the boys something of farming in connection with their common school education, instead of awakening in these people a desire for a musical instrument, which resulted in their parents going in debt for a third-rate piano or organ before a home was purchased. These industrial lessons would have awakened in this community a desire for homes and would have given the people the ability to free themselves from industrial slavery, to the extent that most of them would have soon purchased homes. After the home and the necessaries of life were supplied, could come the piano; one piano lesson in a home is worth twenty in a rented log cabin.

"Only a few days ago I saw a colored minister preparing his Sunday sermon just as the New England minister prepares his sermon. But this colored minister was in a broken-down, leaky, rented log cabin, with weeds in the yard, surrounded by evidences of poverty, filth and want of thrift. This minister had spent some time in school studying theology. How much better would it have been to have had this minister taught the dignity of labor, theoretical and practical farming in connection with his theology, so that he could have added to his meager salary and set an example to his people in the matter of living in a decent house and correct farming—in a word, this minister should have been taught that his condition, and that of his people, was not that of a New England community, and he should have been so trained as to meet the actual needs and conditions of the colored people in this community.

"God, for two hundred and fifty years, was preparing the way for the redemption of the Negro through industrial development. First, He made the Southern white man do business with the Negro for two hundred and fifty years in a way that no one else has done business with him. If a Southern white man wanted a house or a bridge built, he consulted a Negro mechanic about the plan, about the building of the house or the bridge. If he wanted a suit of clothes or a pair of shoes made, it was the Negro tailor or shoemaker that he talked to. Secondly, every large slave plantation in the South was, in a limited sense, an industrial school. On these plantations there were scores of young colored men and women who were constantly being trained, not alone as common farmers, but as carpenters, blacksmiths, wheelwrights, plasterers, brick-masons, engineers, bridge-builders, cooks, dressmakers, housekeepers, etc. I would be the last to apologize for the curse of slavery, but I am simply stating facts. This training was crude and was given for selfish purposes and did not answer the highest purpose, because there was an absence of literary training in connection with that of the hand. Nevertheless, this business contact with the Southern white man and the industrial training received on these plantations, put us at the close of the war into possession of all the common and skilled labor in the South. For nearly twenty years after the war, except in one or two cases, the value of the industrial training given by the Negroes' former masters on the plantations and elsewhere was overlooked. Negro men and women were educated in literature, mathematics and the sciences, with no thought of what had taken place on these plantations for two and a half centuries. After twenty years, those who were trained as mechanics, etc., during slavery, began to disappear by death, and gradually we awoke to the fact that we had no one to take their places. We had trained scores of young men in Greek, but few in carpentry, or mechanical or architectural drawing; we had trained many in Latin, but almost none as engineers, bridge-builders and machinists. Numbers were taken from the farm and educated, but were educated in everything except agriculture; hence they had no sympathy with farm life and did not return to it.

"The place made vacant by old Uncle Jim, who was trained as a carpenter during slavery, and who, since the war, had been the leading contractor and builder in the Southern town, had to be filled. No young colored carpenter capable of filling Uncle Jim's place could be found. The result was that his place was filled by a white mechanic from the North, or from Europe or from elsewhere. What is true of carpentry and house building in this case is true, in a degree, of every line of skilled labor, and is becoming true of common labor. I do not mean to say that all of the skilled labor has been taken out of the Negro's hands, but I do mean to say that in no part of the South is he so strong in the matter of skilled labor as he was twenty years ago, except, possibly, in the country districts and the smaller towns. In the more Northern of Southern cities, such as Richmond and Baltimore, the change is most apparent, and it is being felt in every Southern city. Wherever the Negro has lost ground industrially in the South, it is not because there is a prejudice against him as a skilled laborer on the part of the native Southern white man, for the Southern white man generally prefers to do business with the Negro mechanic, rather than with the white one; for he is accustomed to doing business with the Negro in this respect. There is almost no prejudice against the Negro in the South in matters of business, so far as the native whites are concerned, and here is the entering wedge for the solution of the race problem. Where the white mechanic or factory operative gets a hold, the trades union soon follows and the Negro is crowded to the wall.

"But what is the remedy for this condition? First, it is most important that the Negro and our white friends honestly face the facts as they are, otherwise the time will not be far distant when the Negro in the South will be crowded to the ragged edge of industrial life, as he is in the North. There is still time to repair the damage and to reclaim what we have lost.

"I stated in the beginning that the industrial education for the Negro has been misunderstood. This has been chiefly because some have gotten the idea that industrial development was opposed to the Negro's higher mental development. This has little or nothing to do with the subject under discussion; and we should no longer permit such an idea to aid in depriving the Negro of the legacy in the form of skilled labor, that was purchased by his forefathers at the price of two hundred and fifty years in slavery. I would say to the black boy what I would say to the white boy: get all the mental development that your time and pocket-book will afford—the more the better, but the time has come when a larger proportion, not all (for we need professional men and women), of the educated colored men and women, should give themselves to industrial or business life. The professional class will be helped in proportion as the rank and file have an industrial foundation so that they can pay for professional services. Whether they receive the training of the hand while pursuing their academic training or after their academic training is finished, or whether they will get their literary training in an industrial school or college, is a question which each individual must decide for himself; but, no matter how or where educated, the educated men and women must come to the rescue of the race in the effort to get and hold its industrial footing.   I would not have the standard of mental development lowered one whit, for with the Negro, as with all races, mental strength is the basis of all progress; but I would have a larger proportion of this mental strength reach the Negro's actual needs through the medium of the hand. Just now the need is not so much for common carpenters, brick-masons, farmers and laundry-women as for industrial leaders; men who, in addition to their practical knowledge, can draw plans, make estimates, take contracts; those who understand the latest methods of truck gardening and the science underlying practical agriculture; those who understand machinery to the extent that they can operate steam and electric laundries, so that our women can hold onto the laundry work in the South that is so fast drifting into the hands of others in the large cities and towns.

"It is possible for a race or an individual to have mental development and yet be so handicapped by custom, prejudice and lack of employment as to dwarf and discourage the whole life, and this is the condition that prevails among my race in most of the large cities of the North, and it is to prevent this same condition in the South that I plead with all the earnestness of my heart.   Mental development alone will not give us what we want; but mental development, tied to hand and heart training, will be the salvation of the Negro.

"In many respects the next twenty years are going to be the most serious in the history of the race.   Within this period it will be largely decided whether the Negro is going to be able to retain the hold which he now has upon the industries of the South, or whether his place will be filled by white people from a distance.   The only way that we can prevent the industries slipping from the Negro in all parts of the South, as they have already in certain parts of the South, is for all the educators, ministers and friends of the Negro to unite to push forward, in a whole-souled manner, the industrial or business development of the Negro, either in school or out of school, or both. Four times as many young men and women of my race should be receiving industrial training. Just now the Negro is in a position to feel and appreciate the need of this in a way that no one else can. No one can fully appreciate what I am saying who has not walked the streets of a Northern city day after day, seeking employment, only to find every door closed against him on account of his color, except along certain lines of menial service. It is to prevent the same thing taking place in the South that I plead. We may argue that mental development will take care of all this. Mental development is a good thing. Gold is also a good thing; but gold is worthless without opportunity to make it touch the world of trade. Education increases an individual's wants many fold. It is cruel in many cases to increase the wants of the black youth by mental development alone, without at the same time increasing his ability to supply these increased wants along the lines at which he can find employment.

"I repeat that the value and object of industrial education has been misunderstood by many. Many have had the thought that industrial training was meant to make the Negro work much as he worked during the days of slavery. This is far from my idea of it. If this training has any value for the Negro, as it has for the white man, it consists in teaching the Negro how rather not to work, but how to make the forces of nature—air, water, horse power, steam and electric power—work for him; how to lift labor up out of toil and drudgery into that which is dignified and beautiful. The Negro in the South works, and he works ·hard; but his lack of skill, coupled with ignorance, causes him to do his work in the most costly and shiftless manner, and this keeps him near the bottom of the ladder in the business world. I repeat that industrial education teaches the Negro how not to work. Let him who doubts this contrast the Negro in the South, toiling through a field of oats with an old-fashioned reaper, with a white man on a modern farm in the West, sitting upon a modern 'harvester,' behind two spirited horses, with an umbrella over him, using a machine that cuts and binds the oats at the same time—doing four times as much work as the black man with one-half the labor.   Let us give the black man so much skill and brains that he can cut oats like the white man; then he can compete with him.   The Negro works in cotton, and has no trouble so long as his labor is confined to the lower forms of work—the planting, the picking and the ginning.   But when the Negro attempts to follow the bale of cotton up through the higher stages, through the mill where it is made into the finer fabrics, where the larger profit appears, he is told that he is not wanted.   The Negro can work in wood and iron, and no one objects so long as he confines his work to the felling of trees and the sawing of boards, to the digging of iron ore and the making of pig iron; but when the Negro attempts to follow his tree into the factory, where it is made into chairs and desks and railway coaches, or when he attempts to follow the pig iron into the factory, where it is made into knife-blades and watch-springs, the Negro's trouble begins.   And what is the objection? Simply that the Negro lacks skill, coupled with brains, to the extent that he can compete with the white man, or that when white men refuse to work with colored men, enough skilled and educated colored men cannot be found able to superintend and man every part of any large industry, and hence, for these reasons, we are constantly being barred out.   The Negro must become in a larger measure an intelligent producer as well as consumer.   There should be more vital connection between the Negro's educated brain and his opportunity of earning his daily living.   Without more attention being given to industrial development, we are likely to have an over-production of educated politicians—men who are bent on living by their wits.   As we get farther away from the war period, the Negro will not find himself held to the Republican party by feelings of gratitude.   He will feel himself free to vote for any party, and we are in danger of

JOHN P. GREEN.

Ex-Member Ohio Senate, now U. S. Stamp Agent, D. C.

having the vote or 'influence' of a large proportion of the educated black men in the market for the highest bidder, unless attention is given to the education of the hand, or to industrial development.

"A very weak argument often used against pushing industrial training for the Negro is that the Southern white man favors it, and, therefore, it is not best for the Negro. Although I was born a slave, I am thankful that I am able to so far rid myself of prejudice as to be able to accept a good thing, whether it comes from a black man or from a white man, a Southern man or a Northern man. Industrial education will not only help the Negro directly in the matter of industrial development, but it will help in bringing about more satisfactory relations between him and the Southern white man. For the sake of the Negro and the Southern white man, there are many things in the relations of the two races that must soon be changed. We cannot depend wholly upon abuse or condemnation of the Southern white man to bring about these changes. Each race must be educated to see matters in a broad, high, generous, Christian spirit; we must bring the two races together, not estrange them. The Negro must live for all time by the side of the Southern white man. The man is unwise who does not cultivate in every manly way the friendship and good-will of his next-door neighbor, whether he is black or white. I repeat that industrial training will help cement the friendship of the two races. The history of the world proves that trade, commerce, is the forerunner of peace and civilization as between races and nations. We are interested in the political welfare of Cuba and the Sandwich Islands because we have business interests with these islands. The Jew that was once in about the same position that the Negro is today, has now complete recognition, because he has entwined himself about America in a business or industrial sense. Say or think what we will, it is the tangible or visible element that is going to tell largely during the next twenty years in the solution of the race problem. Every white man will respect the Negro who owns a two-story brick business block in the center of town and has $5,000 in the bank.

. . . .

"I know that what I have said will likely suggest the idea that I have put stress upon the lower things of life—the material; that I have overlooked the higher side—the ethical and religious. I do not overlook or undervalue the higher. All that I advocate in this article is not as an end, but as a means. I know as a race we have got to be patient in the laying of a firm foundation, that our tendency is too often to get the shadow instead of the substance, the appearance rather than the reality. I believe further that in a large measure he who would make the statesmen, the men of letters, the men for the professions for the Negro race of the future, must today, in a large measure, make the intelligent artisans, the manufacturers, the contractors, the real estate dealers, the land-owners, the successful farmers, the merchants, those skilled in domestic economy. Further, I know that it is not an easy thing to make a good Christian of a hungry man. I mean that just in proportion as the race gets a proper industrial foundation—gets habits of industry, thrift, economy, land, homes, profitable work—in the same proportion will its moral and religious life be improved. I have written with a heart full of gratitude to all religious organizations and individuals for what they have done for us as a race, and I speak as plainly as I do because I feel that I have had opportunity in a measure to come face to face with the enormous amount of work that must still be done by the generous men and women of this country before there will be in reality, as well as in name, high Christian civilization among both races in the South.

"To accomplish this, every agency now at work in the South needs reinforcement."

II. SPEECH BY PROF. W. H. COUNCILL.

The following address on Negro development and the importance of training, good conduct and the use of opportunities, was delivered by Professor Councill at the Southern Industrial Convention in Philadelphia, June 13, 1901:

"Forty years ago North and South crossed swords over the prostate form of the Negro slave. Today North and South, singing songs of peace and union, welcome the free Negro to participate in the industrial, commercial and educational development of our country. Forty years ago I was a slave boy responsible to my master. Today I am a free man, responsible to my country and to my God for what I do with my freedom. Forty years ago I could have brought to you only the prayers of a few Negroes who could read, scattered here and there over the nation; but today I bring to you the greetings of thousands of educated, refined, cultured Negroes, engaged in all the professions and callings of life, and three millions who can read and write. Forty years ago I could have brought to you only a few thousands of dollars owned by my race in the entire country. Today, I thank God, I bring to you in the name of my people 270,000 homes and farms, which, together with other property, reach in value a billion dollars. Forty years ago I could have brought to you not a single Negro school in the entire South. Today I bring you 20,000 Negro schoolhouses, 30,000 Negro teachers and 3,000,000 Negro pupils treading beneath the Stars and Stripes, singing freedom's song, while the earth quakes beneath their industrious tread and the heavens answer back in showers of blessings.

"Whom shall I thank for my redemption from the blackness of savage night—an hour as dark as the brow of midnight, as black as the hinges of hell? By the ordering of some mysterious power, the South poured into 4,000,000 savages industry and Christianity and prepared them for the blessed day of freedom. Then, by the ordering of a still more mysterious Providence, both North and South were called upon to sacrifice their best blood and spend billions of treasure for the freedom of those 4,000,000 Christians brought up from barbarism through the school of slavery. God does not pay a great price for small things, and in His own good time He will make it plain. I thank the entire Anglo-Saxon race for my contact with it. If at some points it was cruel and hard, at many more points it has been helpful and uplifting to my people. I have no bitterness in my heart toward your race. I have only blessings for you and yours. I turn back only a few years to view the resting-place of two noble men. Under yon wide-spreading elm rest the bones of my father, and by his side rest the bones of your father. The ivy creeps around and clings to the little marble slabs which mark their graves. The violet and will rose fill the air with the aroma of peace, while the birds sing in subdued and mellow notes. Peace reigns there. Cursed be the man who would disturb the quietness of their sacred abode by rattling the bones of hatred and contention: cursed be the man who would scatter the seeds of malice and strife among the descendants of those peaceful slumberers. I have nothing but blessings for North and South. Tread softly, speak gently, whisper love, for a kind Confederate master slumbers here; tread lightly, murmur gently, whisper peace, for a noble Union soldier sleeps there. Wake them not. Let them dream on—dream away their differences; dream out strife; dream in peace and joy; dream in union; dream in a united land dedicated to freedom.

"I came through the Richmond slave pen to this platform upon which I stand. I do not regret the hard struggles of my life and the bitter experiences necessary to my growth, for, after all, adversity tests and develops man. It should sweeten his nature and make him sympathize with his fellow-men. God sometimes heaves men up from the bottom of the unfortunate masses as gold is thrown up and diamonds brought forth by volcanic eruptions. Let us all who toil and struggle take heart and labor on. Be concerned about only one thing, and that is how to be a useful and helpful man in the world. When hungry and weary, darkness all around me, naked and bare, in the midst of these trials, when a small boy, I walked forth one night, my eyes turned toward the stars in heaven, my only witnesses. With tears flowing down my black cheeks, my little hand upraised, I promised God that if He would help me to be a man I would try to make conditions more favorable for all other little boys and girls and young people in the world. It was a great promise, but I have tried to keep it without regard to race or color. I know no better way to show my love to God than to render this service to my fellow-man.

"No ten millions of people have ever enjoyed better chances for material progress than the ten millions of Negroes in the South today. Every avenue in which we are capable of walking is open to us. Now and then there are exceptions, but every Negro of the ten millions in the South can get work, can make money, and can save it. The three great civilizing, refining agencies—the work-shop, the school-room, and the church—are open to us. Ten millions of people in the childhood of development never before in all the history of the world stood face to face with so great opportunities and possibilities and so few oppositions as confront us in the South today. Our few troubles are only the pressures which have been found among all people necessary in all ages to crystallize racial tendencies into sturdy character.

"The statement that the Negro is not a tax-payer is generally accepted as truth, without a challenge from his best friends; but is it a fact? The Negro pays taxes, both directly and indirectly. To say that people who do such a large per cent. of the agricultural labor of a country, paying rent on the lands, do not pay taxes, must be proven by some system of mathematics not yet invented.

"In the whole country (census of 1890) the Negro occupied 1,500,000 farms and homes. He owns 270,000 of them. It will be a bold man who will assert that the renters of 1,230,000 homes and farms do not only pay the tax, but the insurance and all other charges upon such property. The Negro pays without a murmur his proportion of the pension tax for ex-Confederates—those grand men who, leaving their footprints in blood on the snow-covered hills of Virginia, followed Lee's tattered banners down to Appomattox. It is not only unjust but cruel to try to take from this young race those honors which have been so grandly achieved by honest toil. The Negro asks the races in superior condition not to stand in his sunshine, not to misrepresent him, but give him a chance to use his good right arm in striking for higher civilization—only a chance to stand or fall like other men.

"It is charged that the nearly two hundred colleges, academies, seminaries, normal and industrial schools scattered over the South since the war have not made the Negro better. If that is so, it is unwise to dedicate another building to the education of the Negro; but the charge is not true. Crime is not committed because of education, but because of the lack of the proper kind of education. Negro criminals are of the most illiterate, stupid and besotted element. They come from among that class which has not yet been reached by the process of education and true civilization. The white South has acted admirably, the North has given grandly, the Negro has done well for himself; yet there still hovers over us a black cloud of ignorance which cannot be removed by disfranchising the Negro nor by any injustice or oppression. This nation must soon or late adopt measures to lift up its ignorant masses.

"I am now collecting statistics by which it is shown that the larger per cent. of the 270,000 farms and homes owned by Negroes are the property of Negroes who can read and write.

"Let us examine Negro crime as shown by the eleventh census:

18

	Whites.	Negroes.
In all prisons in the United States	57,310	24,272
Rate per cent. neither read nor write	70.68	54.13
Rate of literacy, read and write	86.58	39.11
Per cent. with trades	14.70	2.50
Per cent. without trades	67.65	90.41

"It will be observed that the Negro criminal element is about thirty-three to 10,000 of the Negro population, or 24,272 for the whole race in the United States. It is admitted by all that 40 per cent. of Negro illiteracy has been wiped out since freedom, or 2,800,000 Negroes out of 7,000,000 have learned to read and write. Of the 24,272 Negro criminals, 54.13 per cent., or 13,138, can neither read nor write; so in 2,800,000 Negroes who can read and write there are 11,134 criminals, according to government statistics, kept by the men who make, construe and execute all laws in this country. Do these statistics justify the assertion, born of ignorance, that education is injuring the Negro and ruining the South?

"The compiler of the eleventh census says: 'Of juvenile criminals, the smallest ratio is found among Negroes under twenty years of age.' He further says that from twenty to twenty-nine years of age the smallest ratio is among Negroes.

"I am indebted to Hon. Judson W. Lyons, register of the United States Treasury, for the following statistics, showing the wonderful influence of Negro labor in the commercial industries of the world: More cotton is exported from the United States than any other one article. In the last ten years 30,000,000,000 pounds of cotton, valued at $2,250,-000,000, have been exported. The United States produces more cotton than all the balance of the world. The cotton manufacturers of Great Britain, Germany, France, Belgium and Italy depend upon our cotton exports. Ten years ago $254,000,000 were invested in cotton manufactories, employing 221,585 operatives, who received for wages $67,489,000 per annum. The South produced from 1880 to 1890 620,-

JNO. S. DURHAM.
Ex-Minister to Port-au-Prince, Hayti.

000,000 bushels of corn, 73,000,000 bushels of wheat and 97,000,000 bushels of oats. Negroes perform four-fifths of the labor of the South. Therefore their share of the average annual production of corn, wheat, oats and cotton was $431,320,000 per annum. The entire cotton acreage of the South would form an area of 40,000 square miles. Negro labor cultivates 32,000 square miles of this space.

"Gentlemen, is it wise for the American nation to under-value this great wealth-producing element of its population? Should not the law-making powers of the country encourage and seek to settle and make contented this vast wealth-producing people of our land?

"The few disturbances and outbreaks in the South show the wonderful organic forces in the South. We have here 10,000,000 of Negroes and 15,000,000 whites, and yet we have probably in the whole South only one Negro and white man in 10,000 who clash. The other 9,999 rub against one another every hour of the day, in every walk of life, transact their business and go on their way in perfect friendship. These peaceful relations of the 9,999 give a bolder prominence to the one exception which is held up by enemies as a general rule. The love and attachment between the races of the South are more than wonderful, when we consider the untiring efforts of busy and meddlesome enemies seeking to scatter seeds of discord and break up our peace. We 9,999 will stand firmly for good-will and happiness of both races in the South. No enemy shall take that one sinner in 10,000 and disrupt and tear us asunder. We have labored side by side for centuries, and have never harmed each other. The Negro is too often badly misrepresented. It often seems hard for another people to do him justice. Each race must write its own history; each race must interpret its own aspirations.

"It is a weak and mistaken policy which advocates meager provisions and facilities for the training and education of the Negro. It is the educated mind and the trained hand which must make valuable our natural resources—mind and muscle to the river, mind and muscle to the soil, mind and muscle to raw materials, mind and muscle to the forest, mind and muscle to the waste places. Mind alone gives life to all, gives value to all, makes all blossom into fruitage. The nation must treat the Negro fairly, must educate his head, heart and hand, or buy Gatling guns and drive him into the Gulf of Mexico, as the Indian is being driven into his grave toward the setting sun. Since the Negro is a recognized part of the productive element of this nation, it will be well for the nation to remember that no government can rise higher or run faster than the weakest element in it. It would be a sin for the strong white man, in whose hands we are as Lilliputians in the hands of Brobdingnags, to do one thing or say one thing or insinuate one thing to cripple Negro education. Let the South be proud of what the North has done for Negro education. If it were in my power I would select the highest place in the blackest South, and there I would erect a monument of the most imperishable marble, with its head far in the azure depths above, to the sacred memory of the teachers from the North, who, forsaking the comforts and civilization of their homes, have sacrificed all for the redemption of the South from its long night of ignorance and industrial stagnation. Let the South be proud of what its fathers did to raise four millions of savages to ten millions of Christians. What we are we owe it all to the South. Our ambition, our inspiration, the directing energies of our destiny, are all Southern, breathed into us by Southern men.

"There can be no doubt that the South has the most loyal and docile labor in the world. Nowhere on the globe is such loyalty to employer to be found. The Negro is true to his master under all circumstances. His obligation is more sacred than racial ties. Would Irish waiters serve all the world except Irishmen? Would a German barber shave every man except a German? Would the American Indian discriminate against himself? Do you say it is cowardice in the Negro? It is not so. It is Negro religion which rises above every worldly consideration to the purely ideal, spiritual world, where there are no races, parties or clans. This element in Negro nature, so much slandered by his white brother, is the noblest quality in mankind.

"We teach every Negro boy and girl to work; we ask nothing but a chance to work and to be paid for our work; we envy no man; take nothing from any man. We teach that every honest Negro drayman, servant-girl, washer-woman, mechanic, hotel-boy, barber who does his duty in an intelligent, competent and trustworthy manner is a queen or a prince among men; no honest labor is dishonorable. It is more blessed to serve than to be served in any walk of life. The servant-girl's hood and apron above an honest heart and educated brain are as honorable as the college cap and gown. Let the Negro race carry the pick in one hand and the olive branch of peace in the other.

"The Negro leaders must go forth as saviors of the masses of our people, to pour into them hope, industry, true Christianity, enlightenment of mind and conscience, and, above all, contentment. I regret that there is an element of white men in this country who continually nag the Negro; they will do no real harm, but render the uneducated Negro unhappy, discontented, suspicious, and interfere with his efficiency as a laborer. It unsettles Negro labor, and produces a kind of stagnation in the community. Gentlemen of the convention, you can stop this unwise and unjust treatment of your laboring class. We all regret this condition of affairs and we must labor with the good element of white men, which has constantly increased, both North and South, for the elevation of the Negro and the true happiness of all the people of our American republic.

"Any coward can oppress a people—can be unfair—but it takes a brave man to treat all men, of whatever race and condition, fairly and justly. Any other ideal, any other treatment of men, transmits to posterity a race of moral weaklings and cowards. Teach every Negro boy and girl that the salvation of life, the salvation of everything in the world, is the glorious end of education and duty. Then there could be no race conflict. I would rather see every Negro of the ten millions in this country driven into the Gulf of Mexico and sink beneath its waters with spotless souls, than to live with the blood of human beings, with the blood of another race, dripping from victorious daggers in Negro hands.

"It is no exaggeration to say that not one white man in a hundred has studied the better side of Negro life. Ninety-nine out of every hundred notices that appear in the public press deal with the evil side of Negro life. The American white man has little conception of the real progress made by the Negro in the last forty years. He sees the shiftless dudes and criminal Negro, but rarely stops to note that intelligent, industrious, sober, earnest, law-abiding and God-fearing army of Negroes, 3,000,000 strong, who are forging their way, step by step, onward, in the face of slander and attempted detraction, to respectable citizenship and recognition in the world. The men who know the Negro and who have studied him from contact with his better life are the solid, substantial business men of the country, who are always willing to testify to the worth of my people. The politician, whose stock in trade is in proportion to his loud and bitter abuse of the Negro, is ignorant of the true character and progress of the race. There would be no Negro problem were it not for these politicians, who cry aloud to arouse the ignorant masses and thereby ride into power on popular prejudice. Notwithstanding all this, there is a large class of white men throughout the South and throughout the nation, who, in public and private life, by word and deed, are laboring to hold in check baneful influences and generate healthful energies for the betterment of the Negro and the peace and salvation of the government. They are not ashamed to put their strong arms around their black brother, help him to his feet, and fight back the mob to give him a chance to stand. To these men, in the humble and business walk of life, the Negro must look for help and the nation for salvation.

"Whatever views we may hold in regard to the civilization and development of Africa, however fondly we may wish the repatriation of the Negro element in our population, it still remains a fact that the Negro is a permanent fixture in the American body politic. He will not go out. He cannot be killed out. Ten millions of people can neither be removed nor destroyed in a day by the snap of a finger, nor the belching forth of deadly guns. We are down to hard work, trying to make the best of ourselves that we can. The masses of the Negro race are working hard, accumulating property and character, enriching the nation by their industrious arms, obeying the laws, fighting for the Stars and Stripes, and serving God, and that God will shape for them a grand and noble destiny. God has always taken care of these questions, and I believe He will continue to do so.

'Truth forever on the scaffold, wrong forever on the throne,
Yet that scaffold sways the future, and behind the dim unknown
Standeth God within the shadow, keeping watch above His own.'

"Violence is the argument of cowards and unwise people. Shotguns correct nothing; swords conquer nothing. Those who use the sword must perish by it. The Negro has the most powerful weapon known to men. It is the only convincing argument; it is the only weapon which brings lasting conquest; it is the sword of the spirit; it is faith in God. The Negro cannot hope to succeed with carnal weapons, but with spirit forces there is no ocean which he cannot cross; no Alps which he cannot scale. Persecutions in time turn on the persecutor with a thousandfold more destructive malignity than was visited upon the persecuted. Wrongs are like the boomerang, and return to those who hurl them with more deadly results than they inflict upon the intended victim. No people were ever persecuted down; they were always persecuted up. If we have been persecuted in this country, such persecution has more than doubled our population in thirty-eight years and has increased our material wealth by $1,000,000,000 in the same time.

> 'Let us call tyrants *tyrants*, and maintain
> That only freedom comes by the grace of God,
> And all that comes not by His grace must fail.'

"Discarding politics and considering the relations of the two races in the South, their mutual helpfulness in all the essential elements of civilization, the results are marvelous beyond anything in history. The contribution to Negro education and religion in proportion to the ability of the South exceeds that of any other section of our country. The North and West, with limitless resources, have had a hundred years of unbroken prosperity. The South has been the scene of conflicts. Vast armies have thundered over her and wasted her life; her whole social and commercial fabric has been destroyed. Yet out of this wreck she has crawled, and with the new order of things promises more excellent development. In my lifetime I have seen in this change of Southern affairs a grander miracle than was enacted when Christ called Lazarus from the grave. Old slave plantations have been turned into industrial schools for the old slaves; masters' old mansions turned into colleges for the slaves, and old slaves now presidents of these colleges. Normal, which I have the honor to represent, was once a famous inn and racetrack. There stood the distillery; there stood the grog-shop; there stood the auction-block whereon the Negro was sold. Today it is one of the largest Negro collegiate and industrial schools in the world, and every man on its board of trustees was a commissioned officer in the Confederate army.

"The prophet has said: 'The people that walked in darkness have seen a great light. They that dwell in the land of the shadow of death, upon them hath the light shined.' All this has taken place in my day in the South.

"Whatever lifts up the white race in the South must lift up the Negro race. Breathe into the white boys and girls of the South intelligence, justice, truth, mercy and industry and the Negro will be benefited. Nothing has ever been in my way but ignorance, either on my own part or the part of the other man. There is but one superiority, and that is the superiority of virtue. That man is superior who does the superior thing to lift mankind to superior conditions. The *Atlanta News*, in combating a proposition to divide the school fund between the races in proportion to the taxes paid by each, exclaims: 'What an attitude would we occupy before the world if we should disfranchise the illiterate and abolish their schools!' The *Nashville American*, commenting on the position taken by the supporters of the movement, says: 'A very indefensible attitude. The caring for the Negro rests with the Southern white people. They must school them and give them employment.

"When by persecution Galileo was forced to deny his doctrine of the movement of the heavenly bodies, he followed his recantation with these remarkable words: 'It moves, for all that.' So, notwithstanding the unfair discussion of the Negro question, notwithstanding the foundationless charges of criminality among the educated Negro, the race moves just the same. Notwithstanding the doctrine of the inferiority of race, instead of inferiority of condition, the Negro race moves onward. The aggregate Negro is viewed, while the individual Negro is ignored, in making up the popular verdict against the race. Let our critics view the units of the race, and they will have a better opinion of us. Let every white man judge the Negro by his best experience with him, and not by the worst which he hears of him. Let the question of inferiority and superiority rest. If we do good work and show ourselves worthy, no amount of injustice or detraction can keep us down in the end.

"The solution of the race problem does not depend upon whether the Negro votes or not. Colleges cannot solve it;

houses and lands cannot solve it; wealth and all the power, ease and comfort which it brings may aggravate it. If the Negro remains in this country, the race question can be settled only by each race understanding its relation to the other and each knowing its place and each keeping its place. The solution of the race problem does not mean social equality between the races, but it does mean that the American public must do justice to the Negro of merit. The solution of the race problem does not mean the triumph of one race over another. It does not necessarily mean the measuring of industrial and literary capacities. It does not mean comparison of racial endurance and racial possibilities, but it does mean peace and mutual helpfulness between the races. If this is not to be the result of discussion and present educational effort, then our civilization is a failure and our Christianity a farce. If every white man in the land would say all the good things he can about every black man in the land and do all the good things he can for every black man in the land, and every black man in the land would say all the good things he can about every white man in the land and do all the good things he can for every white man in the land, the race question with all its concomitant evils would disappear before God's sunshine of peace, good-will and prosperity forever.''

PHELPS HALL, BIBLE AND TRAINING SCHOOL, TUSKEGEE INSTITUTE.

CHAPTER XI.

TUSKEGEE NORMAL AND INDUSTRIAL INSTITUTE.

I. CHARACTER OF THE SCHOOL AND WHAT IT SEEKS TO DO.

This institution for the instruction and training of colored youth has become famous among the great schools of the United States. The influence that emanates from it is wide-spread, and it is beneficent in its effects not only upon the colored population, but upon the whites in that great degree in which the interests of the two races are common. This is true alike of the public teachings of the distinguished principal, Booker T. Washington, and of the attainments and conduct of the little army of students who annually go from its recitation rooms, its laboratories, its shops and its fields, to carry into their life work the principles and purposes with which they have been imbued, and the intellectual strength and manual skill that fit them for usefulness and for rising to positions of honor and independence.

A succinct statement of the general character of the school and what it seeks to accomplish and is accomplishing may very appropriately find a place in this book, and we here present extracts from the nineteenth annual report of the principal, that for the year ended May 31, 1900, as embodying such statement:

"There has not been a year since freedom came to the Negro that has witnessed such wide-spread discussion, both North and South, of all phases of his condition, as the present one. I cannot rid myself of the feeling that much, if not all, of this discussion is going to prove most helpful to the Negro's education and general development.

"I am of the opinion that there is more thoughtful interest in the Negro at the present time than has ever before existed.

The mere spasmodic and sentimental interest in him has been, in a large degree, replaced by the more substantial, thoughtful kind, based upon a comprehension of the facts.

"One is often surp.ised at the misleading and unfounded statements made regarding the progress of the Negro, but these very exaggerations serve a good purpose in causing individuals to seek facts for themselves.

"For example, I have recently seen a statement going the rounds of the press, to the effect that, out of 1,200 students

THE FACULTY, TUSKEGEE INSTITUTE.

educated at industrial schools only twelve were farming, and three working at the trades for which they were educated. Whether the Tuskegee Institute was included in this list, I do not know.

"It is to be regretted that those who presume to speak with authority on the advancement of the Negro do not in more cases actually visit him, where they can see his better life. Few of the people who make discouraging statements regarding him have ever taken the trouble to inspect his home life,

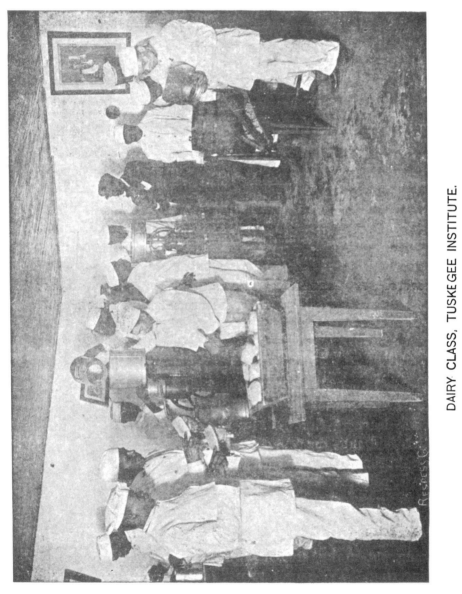

DAIRY CLASS, TUSKEGEE INSTITUTE.

his school life, his church life, or his business or industrial life. It is always misleading to judge any race or community by its worst. The Negro race should, like other races, be judged by its best types rather than by its worst.

"Any one who judges of the value of industrial education by the mere number who actually follow the industry or trade learned at a school makes a mistake. One might as well judge of the value of arithmetic by the number of people who spend their time after leaving school in working out problems in arithmetic.

"The chief value of industrial education is to give to the students habits of industry, thrift, economy, and an idea of the dignity of labor. But, in addition to this, in the present economic condition of the colored people, it is most important that a very large proportion of those trained in such institutions as this actually spend their time at industrial occupations. Let us value the work of Tuskegee by this test: On January 10th of this school year we dedicated the Slater-Armstrong Memorial Trades' Building. This building is in the form of a double Greek cross, and in its main dimensions is 283 x 315 feet, and is two stories high. The plans of this building were drawn by our instructor in mechanical drawing, a colored man. 800,000 bricks were required to construct it, and every one of them was manufactured by our students while learning the trade of brickmaking. All the bricks were laid into the building by students who were being taught the trade of brickmasonry. The plastering, carpentry work, painting and tin-roofing were done by students while learning those trades. The whole number of students who received training on this building alone was about 196. It is to be lighted by electricity, and all the electric fixtures are being put in by students who are learning electrical engineering. The power to operate the machinery in this building comes from a 125 horse-power engine and a 75 horse-power boiler. All this machinery is not only operated by students who are learning the trade of steam engineering,

CLASS IN CHEMISTRY, TUSKEGEE INSTITUTE.

but was installed by students under the guidance of their instructor.

"Let us take another example, that of agriculture. Our students actually cultivate every day 700 acres of land while studying agriculture. The students studying dairying actually milk and care for 75 milch cows daily. Besides, they of course take care of the dairy products. All of this is done while learning the industry of dairying. The whole number of students receiving instruction in the divisions of agriculture and dairying the past year is 142.

"The students who are receiving training in farming have cared for 619 head of hogs this year; and so I could go on and give not theory, nor hearsay, but actual facts, gleaned from all the departments of the school.

"It does not look reasonable that, of all the large number of students engaged upon the farms and in the dairy, that only about one per cent. should make any practical use of their knowledge after leaving Tuskegee. But this is not the fact. The best place to get a true estimate of an individual is at his home. The same is true of an institution. Let us take, for example, Macon county, Alabama, in which the Tuskegee Institute is located. By a careful investigation it is found that there are not less than 35 graduates and former students in Macon county and the town of Tuskegee alone who are working at trades or industries which they learned at this institution. At the present time a large two-story brick building is going up in the town of Tuskegee that is to be used as a store. In the first place, the store is owned by a graduate of this institution. From the making of the brick to the completion of all the details of this building, the work is being done by graduates or former students of this school; and so the examples could be multiplied. Following the graduates and former students into the outer world, the record is as follows: A careful examination shows that at least three-fourths of them are actually using during the whole time, or a part of the time, the industrial knowledge which they gained here. Even those who do not use this knowledge in making a living use it as housekeepers in their private homes; and those who teach in the public schools, either directly or indirectly, use it in helping their pupils.

"Aside from all that I have said, it must be kept in mind that the whole subject of industrial training on any large and systematic scale is new, and besides is confined to a very few institutions in the South. Industrial training could not be expected to revolutionize the progress of a race within ten or

CHAPEL, TUSKEGEE INSTITUTE.

fifteen years. At the present time the call for graduates from this institution to take positions as instructors of industries in other smaller institutions, as well as in city schools, is so urgent and constant that many of our graduates who would work independently at their trades are not permitted to do so. In fact, one of the most regrettable things in connection with our whole work is that the calls for our graduates are so many more than we can supply. As the demand for instructors in industrial branches of various schools becomes supplied, a still larger precentage of graduates will use their knowledge of the trades in independent occupations.

"The average attendance for the school year has been 1,083—321 young women and 762 young men. The total enrollment has been 1,231—359 young women and 872 young men. Nine-tenths of the number have boarded and slept on the school grounds. In all the departments, including officers, clerks and instructors, 103 persons are in the employ of the school. Counting students, officers and teachers, together with their families, the total number of persons constantly upon the school grounds is about 1,200. Students have come to us from twenty-seven States and Territories, from Africa, Porto Rico, Cuba, Jamaica and Barbadoes. There are twelve students from Cuba alone.

"During the present school year students have been trained in the following twenty-eight industries, in addition to the religious and academic training: Agriculture, dairying, horticulture, stock-raising, blacksmithing, brick-masonry, carpentry, carriage trimming, cooking, architectural, free-hand and mechanical drawing, plain sewing, plastering, plumbing, printing, saw-milling, foundrying, housekeeping, harness-making, electrical engineering, laundering, machinery, mattress-making, millinery, nurse training, painting, shoe-making, tailoring, tinning and wheelwrighting.

"We have made progress in the matter of training young women in outdoor occupations. Beginning with this school year, we are now giving a number of girls training in poultry-raising, bee culture, dairying, gardening, fruit-growing, etc. A large hennery is now being built, and it will be almost wholly under the supervision of our girls.

"Notwithstanding the stress put upon industrial training, we are not in any degree neglecting normal training for those who are to teach in the public schools. The number of graduates this year from all the departments is fifty-one. In addition to religious and academic training, each one of these graduates has had training at some trade or industry.

In considering the number that go out each year, account should be taken of those who are well trained, but who are unable to remain long enough to graduate. Our graduates and former students are now scattered all over the South; and, wherever they can, they not only help the colored people, but use their influence in cultivating friendly relations between the races.

"While our work is not sectarian, it is thoroughly Christian; and the growth in the religious tone of the school is most

NURSE-TRAINING CLASS, TUSKEGEE INSTITUTE.

gratifying. We have had more visits this year than ever from Southern white people, who are more and more showing their interest in our effort.

"In closing this report I would say that my feeling grows stronger each year that the main thing that we want to be sure of is that the Negro is making progress day by day. With constant, tangible, visible, indisputable progress being made evident, all the minor details regarding the adjustment of our position in the body politic will, in a natural way, settle themselves."

II. SUMMARY OF THE WORK DONE.

The following account of what has been accomplished by the Tuskegee School and of the character of Booker T. Washington is from the pen of Maj. W. W. Screws, editor of the *Montgomery* (Ala.) *Advertiser:*

"In the early part of the year 1881 there came to Tuskegee a very quiet, unassuming colored man, for the purpose of establishing an institution for the education of colored boys and girls. From the day of his arrival, when he had only modest surroundings, until the present, when his name and that of the institution over which he presides is known over the entire continent, Booker T. Washington has had the absolute confidence of the white people of that community. There is never a word of harsh criticism of him or his methods. He has been singularly imbued with a desire to cultivate good relations between the two races, and to be of lasting benefit to his own people. He is succeeding in both undertakings. There is nothing of the agitator about him. His ways are those of pleasantness and peace, and as far as his voice and example prevail, there will always be the best of feeling between the white and black people of this country. Fred Douglass and some other colored men have figured as orators and office-holders, but it is no exaggeration to say that Booker T. Washington far surpasses any of them who have at all figured in a public way. He does something for his people and his country, while the others have done mostly for themselves. The modest colored man of Tuskegee deserves to be classed as the foremost man of his race in the world. Evidence of his earnestness and sincerity of purpose is furnished by an incident that occurred not long ago. His salary is fixed by the Board of Trustees, several of whom are prominent citizens of Tuskegee. In view of the immense amount of work he was doing, it was thought proper to increase his salary. When informed of this action he promptly declined it, saying that the amount he was receiving was ample compensation, and that he did not desire any more.

"The people of the late slave States have to contend with the race question, and whoever pursues a course and policy calculated to remove difficulties, and to establish kind relations, is a public benefactor. No free people will remain in ignorance, and it has long since been demonstrated that the Negroes will receive such education as opportunity offers. Alabama makes no discrimination in the distribution of school money, for it is paid out per capita, and every school child, whether white or black, gets the benefit of the sum to which it is entitled. It is a blessing for the control of the colored schools to fall into the hands of such men as Booker T. Washington. It can be said to his credit that colored teachers are found all over Alabama who were educated at his institution, and, in every instance, the white people commend them for instilling correct notions into their pupils and for impressing upon them the fact that they cannot prosper unless their white neighbors prosper, and unless a proper understanding exists between them. It is infinitely better to have teachers who have such notions than those who would seek to create prejudice, which would inevitably lead to trouble.

"As stated at the outset, this institution began operations in 1881, and with only one small frame building. The *Advertiser* has published a great deal about it in the last few years, and its readers are fairly well acquainted with its object and scope. In a brief way, a presentation is here made of what is now being done at this institution.

"The Tuskegee Normal and Industrial Institute has, up to date, enrolled 987 students. This does not include the Primary Department, known as the Model School, which has an enrollment of 235. The work carried on at the institution is a high English course, combined with the industrial training, so arranged and correlated that one department does not interfere with the other, but aims to assist the other in every feature. The institution now has eighty-six officers and teachers in the various academic and industrial departments.

There are over 800 boarders in the institution, about three-fifths males and two-fifths females.

"The property consists of 2,300 acres of land and forty-five buildings, large and small. The large buildings are Phelps Hall, the Bible Training Department, Porter Hall, Science Hall, Cassedy Hall, Alabama Hall, the Seniors' Home, Willow Cottage, the Annex and Agricultural Hall. All of the largest buildings are built of brick manufactured by the students on the school grounds, and all the work done in constructing buildings on the grounds—both large and small—is done by the students, under their different instructors.

"From the beginning, the industrial work has been emphasized, to prepare tradesmen, who have been elevated to a very high point among their different trades. The government of the institution has felt that in order to put the Negro race on its proper footing in the South, and in order that they may hold their own, that they must be well educated in industrial pursuits, and that they should be carried as fast as their ability would allow them, in order that they might become leaders in the various sections of the South. The industries taught at the institution for the male pupils are as follows:

"Tailoring, where all the uniforms are made for the students, citizens' suits for teachers and a great number of the people in the town of Tuskegee.

"Harness-making in all of its branches, from the common farm harness to the highest grade of coach and express harness.

"The shoe-making department receives more orders than it can fill, from teachers, students and citizens.

"The tinning department is where all of the tinware for the institution is made; also there is a great demand from both the people in the town and the surrounding country for tinware manufactured in it. This department also does all the tin roofing for the institution.

BOOKER T. WASHINGTON.

"The painting department is kept busy painting buggies and carriages manufactured at the institution for sale, keeps up all the repair work and paints all of the new buildings as fast as they are constructed on the grounds. There is a great demand on it from the citizens of the town to paint buggies, carriages, etc.

"The wheelwright department turns out a large number of wagons, buggies, phaetons, dump-carts, wheelbarrows, hand-carts and other work in that line, besides doing a great deal of repairing for the country people. ·

"The blacksmith department is where all of the carriages, buggies, wagons, wheelbarrows and other new work from the wheelwright department is ironed off. It also does extensive horseshoeing for people in town. In fact, it is the only shop in this locality where first-class horseshoeing is done. The students are not only taught the principles of how to make and put on a shoe, but are taught the anatomy of a horse's foot.

"The foundry makes all of the small castings used in the institution, such as andirons, window-weights, etc. Castings for six small three-horse-power engines and two pumps have been made in this department.

"The machine shop has a good outfit for turning out machinery, such as engines, pumps, etc., and does a great deal of repair work on engines, pumps and other kinds of machines for the surrounding country.

"The carpentry department, which is, perhaps, the largest department connected with the institution, gives instruction in the line of house-building and making furniture of different kinds. It furnishes all the furniture for the students' dormitories, and tables and seats for the various recitation rooms. All of the wood-work done on the different buildings, from the beginning of the institution, has been done by this department.

"The institution owns a well-equipped saw mill. It cuts its own timber and hauls it to the mill to be sawed up and used in the construction of the various buildings and furniture for the institution.

"At the brickyard, all of the brick used in the various buildings on the grounds are made, and on an average ten thousand are sold to the people every month in various sections of the county. The machinery at the brickyard is of the latest improved, and has the capacity of making twenty-five thousand bricks daily. It is said by competent judges that visit the institution, that they have never seen better brick anywhere than those made in this department. All of the bricks are made and burned by the students.

"In the brickmason department the students lay all of the bricks put in the different buildings, build all the chimneys and do all the plastering, etc., of the various buildings. It is safe to say that no department on the place does better work than this department.

"The institution's dairy herd furnishes the institution and the people who live in this immediate section with all the milk and butter they use. It has three separators of different makes, and a large number of churns of different varieties. The dairy is run on scientific principles, both as to feeding and caring for the stock, and separating the milk and making the butter and cheese. Its aim is to turn out persons who are able to go out and take charge of a first-class dairy.

"Truck gardening is taught very extensively, also horticulture. The institution aims, as near as possible, to supply itself with vegetables, fruits, etc., raised on its own farm. From two to three crops are raised on all of its land. Besides the plats that are used for truck gardening, the institution owns an eight-hundred-acre farm about three miles from the school site, where large grain for feeding stock, sweet potatoes, peas and sugar-cane are raised on a very large scale. In fact, nearly all the syrup used in the institution this year was raised on this farm. Hog-raising is made a specialty, and is very successfully done.

20

"The agricultural building, which was given by the John F. Slater fund, and opened on the 30th of last November, makes a new feature in the institution in the line of teaching agriculture, dairying, horticulture and other branches of industry along that line. This building has been well equipped and good work is being done in it.

"All of the pupils who enter the institution are compelled to take some line of industry in some of the different trades: agriculture, office-work, or something that will put them in a position to earn an honest living after leaving the institution. All of the industries for both men and women are so arranged that they do not interfere with their literary course of study. On an average, they are instructed four days out of the week in the literary line of class-room work, and one half day in the shop or whatever industry they may pursue.

"The work for young women is laundering, domestic science in the line of housekeeping, cooking, nurse-training, dressmaking, plain sewing in all its forms and millinery.

"The object of all the industries is to make them educational in every feature, and to add dignity to labor.

"The institution has a very large, well-fitted printing office. Some of the machinery in this office is one large newspaper cylinder press, one large and three smaller job presses, wire stitching machine, paper cutter, perforating machine, and the necessary type to turn out work of a very high class very quickly. The presses are run by two small upright engines, made by the students in the machine shop.

"For eight years the institution has had on hand a small canning outfit. The amount of fruit and vegetables put up in this department has increased every year. The outfit is not a costly one, and could be attached to any steam boiler and operated by a man and a few small boys and girls. The institution has put out within the last few years, on an average, one thousand peach and other fruit trees every year, which are beginning to yield fruit to a greater extent than the present outfit can put up. All of the cans used in this department are made by the students, and the work of cooking the fruit and filling the cans is done by them. The institution has quite a number of young men and women who have served an apprenticeship in this department, and can go out in any section of the country and can fruit on a large or small scale, or give instructions in this line.

"It might be supposed that with so large a collection of colored people, about twelve hundred, in a town of this size, there would be trouble between the races. There has never been an instance of this kind, and there is not likely to be as long as the influence of President Washington prevails. The white citizens, without exception, say that you would scarcely know of so many colored pupils being here, as they are under the very best of discipline, and good behavior is the rule with all the students. It is really a pleasure to the citizens of Tuskegee to bear testimony to the excellence of this institution and its management."

III. BOOKER T. WASHINGTON EXPLAINS TO A NORTHERN AUDIENCE HIS CONNECTION WITH THE SCHOOL, AND NOTICES THE RELATIONS OF THE RACES IN THE SOUTH.*

Mr. President, Ladies and Gentlemen:

"My words to you tonight will be based upon an humble effort during the last fourteen years to better the condition of my people in the 'Black Belt' of the South. It was my privilege to start life at the point now occupied by most of my people—in a small, one-room log cabin on a slave plantation in Virginia. After slavery, while working in the coal mines of West Virginia for the support of my mother, I heard in some way of the Hampton Institute, General Armstrong's school in Virginia; heard that it was an institution where a poor boy could enter and have the privilege of working for a portion of his expenses. Almost without money or friends, by walking and begging rides, I reached Rich-

* Speech in Carnegie Hall, New York.

mond, Virginia, without a penny; and there, by sleeping
under the sidewalk by night and working on a vessel by day,
I earned money enough to enable me to reach the Hampton
Institute. At Hampton I found the opportunity, in the way
of buildings, teachers and industries, for me to remain there
and get training in the class-room; and by practical touch
with industrial life, thrift, economy, push, to be surrounded
by an atmosphere of business, Christian influences, and a
spirit of self-help that seemed to have awakened every faculty in me, and caused me for the first time to realize what
it meant to be a man instead of a piece of property.

"While at Hampton I resolved that I would go into the
far South and give my life to providing this same kind of
opportunity for self-awakening and self-help that I found
provided for me at the Hampton Institute; and so starting
at Tuskegee, Alabama, in 1881, in a small shanty with one
teacher and thirty students, without a dollar's worth of
property, this spirit of self-help and industrial thrift, coupled
with aid from the State and generosity from the North, has
resulted in our building, at Tuskegee, an institution of 800
students, gathered from nineteen States; seventy instructors,
1,400 acres of land and thirty-eight buildings, twenty-three
industries, in all, property valued at $225,000, all carried on
at a cost of $75,000 a year.

"This is kept uppermost: To train men and women in
head, heart and hand; to meet conditions that exist right
about them rather than conditions that existed centuries ago,
or that exist in communities a thousand miles away. And
so, in connection with our literary and religious training, we
have students cultivate, by the improved methods in farming,
650 acres of land, then we teach them dairying, horticulture,
cooking, sewing, millinery, and have them make the brick,
do the brickmasonry, plastering, sawing of the lumber and
do the carpenter work, and have them help draw the plans in
connection with thirty buildings. We are not saying that
education in the classics, of ministers, lawyers and doctors,

is not necessary and important, but we are saying, with every atom of our being, that since 90 per cent. of the black race depend at present upon the common occupations, and that since 85 per cent. of our people live by agriculture and are in the country districts of the South, it is of the utmost importance that we supply them as fast as possible with educated leaders with the highest training in agriculture, dairying, horticulture and the mechanical arts. With us as a race this is a question of growth or decay, life or death. Within the next two decades it will be decided whether the Negro, by discarding ante-bellum ideas and methods of labor, by putting brains and skill into the common occupations that lie at his door, will be able to lift up labor out of toil, drudgery and degradation into that which is dignified, beautiful and glorified. Further, it will be decided within this time whether he is to be replaced, crushed out as a helpful industrial factor by the fast-spreading trades unions and thousands of foreign skilled laborers that even now tread fast and hard upon his heels and begin to press him unto death. This question is for your Christian Church to help decide. And in deciding remember that you are deciding not alone for the Negro, but whether you will have 8,000,000 of our people in this country, or a race nearly as large as the population of Mexico, a nation within a nation, that will be a burden, a menace to your civilization; that will be continually threatening and degrading your institutions, or whether you will make him a potent, emphatic factor in your civilization and commercial life.

"What was three hundred years in doing cannot be undone in thirty years. You cannot graft a fifteenth century civilization into a twentieth century civilization by the mere performance of mental gymnastics. An educated man on the streets with his hands in his pockets is not one whit more benefit to society than an ignorant man on the streets with his hands in his pockets.

"What are some of the conditions in the South that need your urgent help and attention? Eighty-five per cent of my people in the Gulf States are on the plantations in the country districts, where a large majority are still in ignorance, without habits of thrift or economy; are in debt, mortgaging their crops to secure food; paying, or attempting to pay, a rate of interest that ranges between twenty and forty per cent.; living in one-room cabins on rented lands, where schools are in session (in these country districts) from three to four months in the year; taught in places, as a rule, that have little resemblance to school-houses. What state of morality or practical Christianity you may expect when as many as six, eight and even ten, cook, eat, sleep, get sick and die in one room, I need not explain. During slavery my people reasoned thus: my body belongs to my master, and taking master's chickens to feed master's body is not stealing; or, as one old colored man said whose master got too close to him: 'Now, massa, while youse got a few less chickens, youse got a good deal more nigger.' You must not be surprised if our people use something of this kind of logic in reference to the present mortgage system.

"If in the providence of God the Negro got any good out of slavery he got the habit of work. As is true of any race, we have a class about bar-rooms and street corners, but the rank and file of the Negro race works from year to year. Whether the call for labor comes from the cotton fields of Mississippi, the rice swamps of the Carolinas, or the sugar bottoms of Louisiana, the Negro answers that call. Yes, toil is the badge of all his tribe, but the trouble centers here: by reason of his ignorance and want of training he does not know how to utilize the results of his labor. His earnings go for high rents, in mortgages, whiskey, snuff, cheap jewelry; clocks are often bought on the installment plan for twelve and fourteen dollars, when everything else in the cabin is not worth that much money, and in five cases out of ten not a single member of the family can tell nine o'clock from twelve o'clock.

"Ten years ago there went out from one of the institutions

in the South, fostered and helped by your generosity, a young man into one of these plantation districts, where he found conditions such as I have described. He took three months' public school course as a nucleus for his work. Then he organized the older people into a club that came together every week. In these meetings, in a plain, common-sense manner, he taught the people thrift, how to economize, how to stop mortgaging their crops, how to live on bread and potatoes, if need be, till they could get out of debt; showed them how to take the money that they had hitherto scattered to the wind and concentrate it in the direction of their industrial, educational and religious uplifting. Go with me to that community today and I will show you a people full of hope and delight. I will show you a people almost wholly free from debt, living on well-cultivated farms of their own, in cottages with two and three rooms, schools lasting eight months, taught in a nice, comfortable, frame school-house. Go with me into their church and Sunday-school, through the model farm and house of this teacher, and I will show you a community that has been redeemed, revolutionized in industry, education and religion by reason of the fact that they had this leader, this guide, this object-lesson to show them how to direct their own efforts.

"It is to this kind of work we must look for the solution of the race problem. My people do not need charity, neither do they ask that charity be scattered among them; very seldom in any part of this country you see a black hand reached out for charity; but they do ask that, through Lincoln and Biddle and Scotia and Hampton and Tuskegee you send them leaders to guide and stimulate them till they are able to walk. Such institutions need reinforcement and strengthening many fold.

"The greatest injury that my people suffered in slavery was to be deprived of the exercise of that executive power, that sense of self-dependence, which are the glory and the distinction of the Anglo-Saxon race. For three centuries we

20

were taught to depend upon some one else for food, clothing, shelter, and for every move in life, and you cannot expect a race to renounce at once the teaching of centuries without guidance and leadership.

"Coupled with literary and religious training must go a force that will result in the improvement of the material and industrial condition. In Alabama we find it a pretty hard thing to make a good Christian of a hungry man. It is only as the Negro is taught to mix in with his religious fervor and emotion habits of industry, economy, land, houses with two or three rooms, and a little bank account, just as the white man does, that he will have a Christianity that will be worthy of the name.

"What of your white brethren in the South? Those who suffered and are still suffering the consequences of American slavery for which you and they were responsible, what is the task you ask them to perform? You of the great and prosperous North still owe to your less fortunate Caucasian brethren of the South, not less than to yourselves, a serious and uncompleted duty. Returning to their destitute homes after years of war, to face blasted hopes, devastation, a shattered industrial system, you asked them to add to their burdens that of preparing in education, politics and economics, in a few short years, for citizenship, four or five millions of former slaves. That the South, staggering under the burden, made blunders; that in some measure there has been disappointment, no one need be surprised.

"The American church has never yet comprehended its duty to the millions of poor whites in the South who were buffeted for two hundred years between slavery and freedom, between civilization and degradation, who were disregarded by both the master and the slave. It needs no prophet to tell the character of our future civilization when the poor white boy in the country districts of the South is in school three months, and your boy in school ten months; when the poor white boy receives one dollar's worth of education, and your boy twenty dollars' worth; when one never enters a library or reading-room, and the other has libraries and reading-rooms in every ward and town; when one hears lectures or sermons once in two months, and the other can hear a lecture or sermon every day. My friends, there is no escape; you must help us raise our civilization or yours will be lowered. When the South is poor, you are poor; when the South is ignorant, you are ignorant; when the South commits crime, you commit crime. When you help the South, you help yourselves. Mere abuse will not bring the remedy. The time has come, it seems to me, when in this matter we should rise above party, or race, or color, or sectionalism, into the region of duty of man to man, citizen to citizen, Christian to Christian; and if the Negro can help you, North and South, to rise, can be the medium of your rising into the atmosphere of generous Christian brotherhood and self-forgetfulness, he will see in it a recompense for all that he has suffered in the past. When you help the poor whites, you help the Negro.

"In considering the relation of the races in the South, I thank God that I have grown to the point where I can sympathize with a white man as much as I can with a black man; where I can sympathize with a Southern white man as much as I can with a Northern white man. To me a man is but a man 'for a' that and a' that.' I propose that no man shall drag me down by making me hate him. No race can hate another race without itself being narrowed and hated. The race problem will work itself out in proportion as the black man, by reason of his skill, intelligence and character, can produce something that the white man wants or respects. One race respects another in proportion as it contributes to the markets of the world, hence the value of industrial training. The black man that has mortgages on a dozen white men's houses will have no trouble in voting. The black man that spends ten thousand dollars a year in freight charges can select his own seat in a railroad car, else a Pullman palace car will be put on for him. When the black man, by reason of his knowledge of the chemistry of the soil and improved methods of agriculture, can produce forty bushels of corn on an acre of land, while his white brother produces only twenty bushels, the white man will come to the black man to learn, and they will be good friends. The black man that has fifty thousand dollars to lend will never want for friends and customers among his white neighbors. It is right and important that all the privileges granted to us by the constitution be ours; but it is vastly more important to us that we be prepared for the exercise of those privileges.

"Those who died and suffered on the battlefield performed their duty heroically and well; but a duty remains for you and me. The mere fiat of law could not make a dependent man an independent man; could not make an ignorant voter an intelligent voter; could not make one man respect another. These results come to the Negro, as to all races, by beginning at the bottom and gradually working toward the highest civilization and accomplishments. Unfortunately, for lack of leadership and guidance, my race, on the threshold of freedom, began at the top instead of the bottom; we have spent time and money attending political conventions, in attempting to go to Congress, that could have better been spent in becoming a real estate dealer or carpenter, or in starting a dairy farm, and thus having laid the foundation of the highest citizenship.

"In conclusion, my countrymen, I make no selfish plea; it is a plea to save yourselves. Let us do our duty and the keeper of us all will perform His. The Negro can afford to be wronged; the white man cannot afford to wrong him.

"Never since the day that we left Africa's shores have we lost faith in you or in God. We are a patient, humble people; there is plenty in this country for us to do. We can afford to work and wait. The workers up in the atmosphere of goodness, long suffering, and forbearance and forgiveness are not many or overcrowded. If others choose to be mean, we can be good; if others push us down, we can help push them up. No harm can come to the black man that does not harm the white man.

"Think, under God's help and yours, from whence we have come, spurred and cheered on in the darkest hour by our midnight groans, our songs, and before-day prayers and an inherent faith in the justice of our cause. We went into slavery property, we came out citizens; we went into slavery pagans, we came out Christians; we went into slavery without a language, we came out speaking the proud Aglo-Saxon tongue; we went into slavery with the slave chains clanking about our wrists, we came out with the American ballot in our hands. This, this is our past. I ask the church to say what shall be the future."

DEAN'S RESIDENCE, VIRGINIA UNION UNIVERSITY.

PICKFORD HALL, VIRGINIA UNION UNIVERSITY.

CHAPTER XII.

The College-Bred Negro.

I. Scope of the Inquiry, Colleges by Groups, etc.

ATLANTA UNIVERSITY is an institution for the higher education of Negro youth. It seeks, by maintaining a high standard of scholarship and deportment, to sift out and train thoroughly talented members of this race to be leaders of thought and missionaries of culture among the masses.

Furthermore, it recognizes that it is its duty as a seat of learning to throw as much light as possible upon the intricate social problems affecting these masses, for the enlightenment of its graduates and of the general public. It has, therefore, for the last five years (1896–1900) sought to unite its own graduates, the graduates of similar institutions, and educated Negroes in general throughout the South, in an effort to study carefully and thoroughly certain definite aspects of the Negro problem.

Graduates of Fisk University, Berea College, Lincoln University, Spelman Seminary, Clark University, Wilberforce University, Howard University, the Maharry Medical College, Hampton and Tuskegee Institutes, and several other institutions have joined in this movement and added their efforts to those of the graduates of Atlanta, and have, in the last five years, helped to conduct five investigations: One in 1896 into the "Mortality of Negroes in Cities;" another in 1897 into the "General Social and Physical Condition" of 5,000 Negroes living in selected parts of certain Southern cities; a third in 1898 on "Some Efforts of American Negroes For Their Own Social Betterment;" a fourth in 1899 into the number of Negroes in business and their success. Finally in 1900 inquiry has been made into the number, distribution, occupations and success of college-bred Negroes.

The results of this last investigation are presented in the following pages, as taken from the published reports and adapted to this work.

The general idea of the Atlanta Conference is to select among the various and intricate questions arising from the presence of the Negro in the South, certain lines of investigation which will be at once simple enough to be pursued by voluntary effort, and valuable enough to add to our scientific knowledge. At the same time the different subjects studied each year have had a logical connection, and will in time form a comprehensive whole. The starting-point was the large death-rate of the Negroes; this led to a study of their condition of life, and the efforts they were making to better that condition. These efforts, when studied, brought clearly to light the hard economic struggle through which the emancipated slave is today passing, and the Conference, therefore, took up one phase of this last year. This year the relation of educated Negroes to these problems and especially to the economic crisis was studied.

The general method of making these inquiries is to distribute among a number of selected persons throughout the South, carefully prepared schedules. Care is taken to make the questions few in number, simple and direct, and so far as possible, incapable of misapprehension. The investigators to whom these blanks are sent are usually well-educated Negroes, long resident in the communities; by calling on the same persons for aid year after year, a body of experienced correspondents has been gradually formed, numbering now about fifty.

In the investigation of 1900 the first task was to collect a reliable list of the Negro graduates of the colleges of the land, with their present whereabouts. There were many preliminary difficulties in this work, the chief of which were, first, what was to be considered a college, and next, how were the Negro graduates of mixed institutions to be distinguished? It was finally decided to call any institution a college which had a course amounting to at least one year in addition to the course of the ordinary New England high school; and to count the graduates of all such courses and longer courses as college graduates, provided they received the degree of Bachelor of Arts or of Science at graduation. Having selected the institutions, the Conference then sent to them for lists and addresses of their graduates, which were for the most part printed in their catalogues. In the case of other colleges, letters were sent asking if the college had ever had any Negro graduates. Most of these letters brought prompt and courteous replies. In some cases the replies were delayed. The returns thus collected represent probably over ninety per cent. of the truth. In some few cases, no records of color being kept, the authorities were not sure as to the exact number of Negro graduates. Usually, however, the presence of Negroes is so exceptional that they were remembered.

In this way the names of nearly 2,500 persons were collected. The matter of getting the exact addresses of these graduates was of course much more difficult and in many cases impossible. Returns were gathered from a little over half (1252) of those named, and not all these were complete. The following twenty-six questions were asked all whose addresses were obtained:

1. Name. 2. Address. 3. Sex. 4. Graduate of. 5. Class of. 6. Single, married, widowed or separated. 7. Birthplace. 8. Year of birth. 9. Year of your wife's (or husband's) birth. 10. Year of marriage. 11. Children. 12. Some account of your early life. 13. Occupation since graduation, with dates. 14. Present occupation (with length of service). 15. If you have taught school at any time, kindly estimate carefully: The total number of pupils you have instructed in primary grades; in secondary and preparatory grades; in col-

lege studies. How many of these have taught school? How many pupils do you suppose they have taught? What careers have your pupils followed mostly? Give any individual instances of success among them. 16. What bound books have you published? 17. What other literary work have you done? 18. What philanthropic, commercial or other useful work, not already mentioned, have you engaged in? 19. What public offices have you held and where? 20. Do you usually vote? 21. Do you belong to any learned societies? 22. From what institutions have you received academic degrees since graduation? 23. What is the assessed value of the real estate which you own? 24. Has your college training benefited you? Would some other kind of training have been of more service? 25. Will you not add here any additional facts which illustrate the kind of work you are doing, and the degree of success you have had? 26. Are you hopeful for the future of the Negro in this country? Have you any suggestions?

These questions were framed with the view of obtaining the largest possible number of actual facts. The chief defect of the method is of course that the persons are giving information about themselves; still there is little chance for unconscious exaggeration or bias, and the number of willful misrepresentations among such a class is small enough to ignore. Some correspondence was also had with the presidents of colleges and others on the general aspects of the question.

Omitting all institutions which have not actually graduated students from a college course, there are today in the United States thirty-four institutions giving collegiate training to Negroes and designed especially for this race.* These institutions fall into five main groups:

GROUP I. *Ante-Bellum Schools*, 3.—Lincoln University, Chester county, Pennsylvania; Wilberforce University, Greene county, Ohio; (Berea College, Berea, Kentucky).

* This includes Berea, where the majority of students are white, but which was designed for Negroes as well, and still has colored students.

GROUP II. *Freedman's Bureau Schools*, 13. — Howard University, Washington, D. C.; Fisk University, Nashville, Tennessee; Atlanta University, Atlanta, Georgia; Biddle University, Charlotte, North Carolina; Southland College, Helena, Arkansas; Central Tennessee College, Nashville, Tennessee; Rust University, Holly Springs, Mississippi; Straight University, New Orleans, Louisiana; Claflin University, Orangeburg, South Carolina; Talladega College,

ATHLETIC FIELD, ROGER WILLIAMS UNIVERSITY, NASHVILLE, TENNESSEE.

Talladega, Alabama; Lincoln Institute, Jefferson City, Missouri; Atlanta Baptist College, Atlanta, Georgia; Roger Williams University, Nashville, Tennessee.

GROUP III. *Church Schools*, 9.—Leland University, New Orleans, Louisiana; New Orleans University, New Orleans, Louisiana; Shaw University, Raleigh, North Carolina; Knoxville College, Knoxville, Tennessee; Clark University, Atlanta, Georgia; Wiley University, Marshall, Texas; Paine Institute, Augusta, Georgia: Philander Smith College, Little

Rock, Arkansas; Benedict College, Columbia, South Carolina.

GROUP IV. *Schools of Negro Church Bodies*, 5.—Allen University, Columbia, South Carolina; Livingstone College, Salisbury, North Carolina; Morris Brown College, Atlanta, Georgia; Arkansas Baptist College, Little Rock, Arkansas; Paul Quinn College, Waco, Texas.

GROUP V. *State Colleges*, 4.—Branch Normal College, etc., Pine Bluff, Arkansas; Virginia N. & C. Institute, Petersburg, Virginia; Georgia State Industrial College, Savannah, Georgia; Delaware State College, etc., Dover, Delaware.

The number of graduates from the foregoing list of colleges is as follows:

Lincoln University, 615; Wilberforce University, 130; Howard University, 96; (Berea College, 29;) Leland University, 16; Benedict College, 3; Fisk University, 180; Atlanta University, 85; Biddle University, 140; Southland College, 19; Roger Williams University, 76; Central Tennessee College, 46; New Orleans University, 30; Shaw University, 101; Rust University, 30; Straight University, 11; Branch College, Arkansas, 9; Claflin University, 46; Knoxville College, 44; Clark University, 21; Alcorn University† 98, Wiley University, 9; Paine Institute, 11; Allen University, 24; Livingstone College, 38; Philander Smith College, 29; Talladega College, 5; Virginia Normal and Collegiate Institute, 27; Paul Quinn College, 18; Lincoln Institute, 6; Morris Brown College, 6; Atlanta Baptist College, 7; Georgia State Industrial College, 1; Delaware State College, 2.

In most cases the college departments of these institutions are but adjuncts, and sometimes unimportant adjuncts, to other departments devoted to secondary and primary work. A comparison of colleges for this purpose will be of interest.

† This State institution confers the degree of B. S., but is rather an agricultural high school than a college.

In the single school year 1898–1899 we find 726 Negro collegians in the colleges specially designed for them; or adding the few others not counted here, we have possibly 750 such students.   If these students are of college grade according to a fair standard, we have here apparently work for perhaps ten Negro colleges, now being done by thirty or more institutions.   It is not, however, by any means certain that all these students are really of college grade.   A study of the curricula will throw some light on this question.

Curricula in Negro Colleges.—If, for convenience, we take only those colleges that have twenty or more students and consider them as representative, we find that for admission to the Freshman class the course of study they require ranges from one to three years behind the smaller New England colleges, while a large proportion are but little in advance of the ordinary New England high school.   So that of the 750 students, probably not more than 350 are of college rank according to New England standards.

After admission the course of study as laid down in the catalogues of eleven colleges is about as follows:

Freshman Year.—English, Latin, Greek, Mathematics, the Bible.*

Sophomore Year.—English, Latin, Greek, Mathematics, the Bible, History, Physical Geography, Physics, Philosophy.†

Junior Year.—English, Latin, Greek, Mathematics, the Bible, Physics, Chemistry, Physiology, Philosophy.

Senior Year.—English, Latin, Greek, Mathematics, the Bible, Geology, History, Modern Languages.

Of course, the studies vary somewhat in the different institutions, but the above is a fair average.

If we combine these studies and assume that fifteen to seventeen hours per week of recitations represent the work of an average student, we get the following average hours of recitation per week for the year for each study:

* Some colleges add a course in Rhetoric.
† Some colleges add Botany and Modern Languages.

Freshmen.—Latin, 4½; Greek, 4½; mathematics, 4¾; English, 1¾; other studies, 2.

Sophomores.—Latin, 4; Greek, 4; mathematics, 3¾; English, 1; history, 2; natural science, 3; civics, 1½; modern languages, 4½; other studies, 1¼.

*Juniors.** —Latin, 3¼; Greek, 3¾; mathematics, 3; English, 2½; history, 2; natural science, 4¾; political science, 4; modern languages, 4; psychology and philosophy, 2; other studies, 1¾.

*Seniors.** —Latin, 3; Greek, 2½; mathematics, 3; English, 2; history, 2; natural science, 4; political science, 2½; modern languages, 2¼; psychology, etc., 4¾; other studies, 1¼.

In the case of schools which do not publish the exact proportion in which their time is divided among the subjects catalogued, the most probable division according to school customs has been assumed by the editor, so that the above is only approximately correct. The errors, however, are probably small and unimportant.

Of the equipment of these colleges there are few data for comparison. Some, like Howard, Fisk, Atlanta and Lincoln, are very well housed, and nearly all have fairly comfortable quarters. Few, if any, have teachers who devote themselves to college work exclusively; some have laboratories for natural science work. The library facilities are reported as follows: Lincoln, 15,750 volumes; Howard, 13,000 volumes; Atlanta, 11,000 volumes; Biddle, 10,500 volumes; Fisk, 6,632 volumes; Wilberforce, 5,500 volumes; Paul Quinn, 1,000 volumes.

Negroes have attended Northern colleges for many years. As early as 1826 one was graduated from Bowdoin College, and from that time till today nearly every year has seen other such graduates. Oberlin has more Negro graduates by far than any other Northern college. The colleges in the order of the number of Negroes graduated are as follows:

Among the Larger Universities.—Harvard, 11; Yale, 10;

* The average is given for those taking the studies named, only.

University of Michigan, 10; Cornell, 8; Columbia, 4; University of Pennsylvania, 4; Catholic University, 3; University of Chicago, 2; Leland Stanford, 2. Total, 54.

Among Colleges of Second Rank—Oberlin, 128; University of Kansas, 16; Bates College, 15; Colgate University, 9; Brown, 8; Dartmouth, 7; Amherst, 7; Ohio State University, 7; Bucknell University, 7; Williams, 4; Boston University, 3; University of Minnesota, 3; Indiana University, 3; Adelbert College, 3; Beloit College, 3; Colby University, 3; State University of Iowa, 2; University of Nebraska, 2; Wesleyan University (Connecticut), 2; Radcliffe College, 2; Wellesley College, 2; Northwestern University, 1; Rutgers College, 1; Bowdoin College, 1; Hamilton College, 1; New York University, 1; University of Rochester, 1; University of Denver, 1; De Pauw University, 1; Mount Holyoke College, 1; Vassar College, 1. Total, 246.

Among Other Colleges.—University of South Carolina, 10; Geneva College, 9; Hillsdale College, 7; LaFayette College, 6; Iowa Wesleyan, 4; Dennison University, 4; Baldwin University, 4; Western University of Pennsylvania, 3; Hiram College, 3; Wittenberg College, 3; Butler's College, 3; Westminster College, 3; St. Stephen's College, 3; Antioch College, 3; Tabor College, 2; Knox College, 2; Washburn College, 2; Adrian College, 2; Washington and Jefferson College, 2; Ohio Wesleyan University, 2; Lombard College, 1; Otterbein College, 1; S. W. Kansas College, 1; Alleghany College, 1; Olivet College, 1; Albion College, 1; University of Idaho, 1; Iowa College, 1; Upper Iowa University, 1; University of Omaha, 1; McKendree College, 1; Illinois College, 1; Ohio University, 1. Total, 90. Grand Total, 390.

If we divide these graduates among the sections of the country, we have: Middle West, 250; New England, 78; Middle Atlantic States, 44; South, 10; Border States, 3; Pacific States, 5.

Most of the colleges addressed confined themselves in

answering to a simple list of graduates; some, however, added information as to the character of black students which is of considerable value, being unsolicited.   From the University of Kansas we learn (January, 1900):

"I am pleased to state that this year we have twice as many colored students in attendance at the university as ever before.   In all, twenty-eight.   The rule is that no student shall be allowed to take more than three studies.   If

LIBRARY, ROGER WILLIAMS UNIVERSITY, NASHVILLE, TENNESSEE.

he fails in one of the three, it is a 'single failure;' in two of the three, a 'double failure.'   The latter severs the student's connection with the university.   There are one thousand and ninety students in attendance at the present time.   The semi-annual examination was held last week, and as a result there are two hundred 'single failures' and eighty 'double failures.'   The gratifying part of it is that *not one* of the twenty-eight colored students is in either number."

From Bates College, Scranton, Maine, President Chase writes (February, 1900): "We have had about a dozen colored people who have taken the full course for the degree of A. B. at Bates College, one of them a young woman. They have all of them been students of good character and worthy purpose." One was a "remarkably fine scholar, excelling in mathematics and philosophy;" he was "one of the editors of the *Bates Student* while in college." Another was "an honest, industrious man of good ability, but of slight intellectual ambition." A third "was a good scholar, especially in mathematics." A fourth graduated "with excellent standing. He was a good, all-round scholar, but excellent in the classics." A fifth "acquired knowledge with difficulty." A sixth did work "of a very high order," etc. The secretary of Oberlin writes (February, 1900), in sending his list: "It is a list containing men and women of whom we are proud." Colgate University, New York, writes of a graduate of '74 as "a very brilliant student who was graduated second best in his class. It was believed by many that he was actually the leader." A graduate of Colby College, Maine, is said by the librarian to have been "universally respected as a student, being chosen class orator." Wittenberg College, Ohio, has two colored graduates; "they were both bright girls and stood well up in their respective classes." A Negro graduate of Washburn College, Kansas, is said by the chairman of the faculty to be "one of the graduates of the college in whom we take pride." The dean of the faculty of Knox College, Illinois, writes of two Negro students, Senator Bruce, of Mississippi, and another, who graduated and was remembered because of "his distinguished scholarship." A black student of Adrian College, Michigan, "was one of the best mathematicians I ever had in class," writes a professor. Adelbert College, of the Western Reserve University, Ohio, has a Negro graduate as acting librarian, who is characterized as "one of the most able men we know;" while of another it is said, "we expect

21

the best." Lombard University, Illinois, has "heard favorable reports" of its single Negro graduate. The dean of the State University of Iowa writes (December, 1899) of a graduate of '98: "He distinguished himself for good scholarship; and on that ground was admitted to membership in the Phi Beta Kappa Society. He is a man of most excellent character and good sense, and I expect for him a very honorable future. He won the respect of all his classmates and of the faculty. As president of the Phi Beta Kappa Society, I received him into membership with very great pleasure as in every way worthy of this honor. We have three colored people in the university at present, two in the college department, and one in law. You are aware that we have but a small colored population in Iowa."

II. FIRST NEGRO GRADUATE; NUMBER OF NEGRO GRADUATES, ETC.

The first American Negro to graduate from an American college, as far as we have been able to learn, was John Brown Russwurm, of Bowdoin College, Maine, class of 1826. His career is so interesting that we present his whole life here, as found in the History of Bowdoin College, pp. 352–354:

"He was born in 1799, at Port Antonio, in the Island of Jamaica, of a Creole mother. When eight years old he was put to school in Quebec. His father, meanwhile, came to the United States, and married in the District of Maine. Mrs. Russwurm, true wife that she was, on learning the relationship, insisted that John Brown (as hitherto he had been called), should be sent for and should thenceforth be one of the family. The father soon died, but his widow proved herself a faithful mother to the tawny youth. She sent him to school, though in consequence of existing prejudice it was not always easy to do so. She procured friends for him.

Marrying again, she was careful to stipulate that John

should not lose his home. Through his own exertions, with some help from others, he was at length enabled to enter college and to complete the usual course. From college he went to New York and edited an abolition paper. This did not last long. He soon became interested in the colonization cause and engaged in the service of the society. In 1829 he went to Africa as superintendent of public schools in Liberia, and engaged in mercantile pursuits at Monrovia. From 1830 to 1834 he acted as colonial secretary, superintending at the same time and editing with decided ability the *Liberia Herald*. In 1836 he was appointed governor of the Maryland colony at Cape Palmas, and so continued until his death in 1851. With what fidelity and ability he discharged the duties of this responsible post may be gathered from the following remarks of Mr. Latrobe, at the time president of the Maryland Colonization Society. He was addressing the board of managers: "None knew better," he said, "or so well as the board under what daily responsibilities Gov. Russwurm's life in Africa was passed, and how conscientiously he discharged them; how, at periods when the very existence of the then infant colony depended upon its relations with surrounding tribes of excited natives, his coolness and admirable judgment obviated or averted impending perils; how, when the authority and dignity of the colonial government were at stake in lamentable controversies with civilized and angry white men, the calm decorum of his conduct brought even his opponents over to his side; how, when popular clamor among the colonists called upon him as a judge to disregard the forms of law and sacrifice an offending individual in the absence of legal proof, he rebuked the angry multitude by the stern integrity of his conduct; and how, when on his visit to Baltimore in 1848 he was thanked personally by the members of the board, he deprecated the praise bestowed upon him for the performance of his duty, and impressed all who saw him with the modest manliness of his

character and his most excellent and courteous bearing.''
Resolutions expressing similar sentiments, and the highest
approval of his administration were passed by the board.
Dr. James Hall, a graduate of the Bowdoin Medical School,
the friend of Russwurm, and his predecessor in the chief
magistracy of African Maryland, has delineated him with
apparent candor.   A man of erect and more than ordinary
stature, with a good head and face and large, keen eye.   In
deportment always gentlemanly.   Of sound intellect, a great
reader, with a special fondness for history and politics.   Naturally sagacious in regard to men and things, and though
somewhat indolent himself, exceedingly skillful in making
others work.   A man of strict integrity, a good husband,
father, master and friend, and in later life a devoted member
of the Protestant Episcopal Church.   He married a daughter
of Lieut.-Gov. McGill, of Monrovia, and was succeeded in his
office at Cape Palmas by his brother-in-law, Dr. McGill.   He
left three sons and a daughter.''

Boston University writes of one graduate as ''a fine fellow.''
He is now doing post-graduate work at Yale, and the agent
of the Capon Springs Negro Conference writes (November,
1900) that ''I continually hear him mentioned in a complimentary way.   On the other hand, two Negro boys were in
the Freshman class not long ago and were both conspicu-
ously poor scholars.''   Otterbein University, Ohio, has a
graduate who ''was a most faithful and capable student.''
The dean of Dartmouth College, New Hampshire, writes (December, 1899) of their graduates: ''The last two or three are
hardly established in business yet, but the others are doing
remarkably well.   These men have been in each case fully
equal to if not above the average of their class.   We have been
very much pleased with the work of the colored men who have
come to us.   They have been a credit to themselves and
their race while here and to the college since graduation.   I
wish we had more such.''   The president of Tabor College,
Ohio, says of two colored graduates: ''They are brainy fel-

lows who have done very much good in the world." A graduate of Southwest Kansas College "was one of the truest, most faithful and hard-working students that we have ever had." One of the most prominent Methodist ministers in Philadelphia said to the president of Alleghany College, Pennsylvania, speaking of a colored graduate: "Any college may be proud to have graduated a man like him." The university of Idaho graduated in '98 a young colored woman of "exceptional ability." Westminster College, Pennsylvania, has graduated two Negroes; "both were excellent students and ranked high in the estimation of all who knew them." Of a graduate of Hamilton College, New York, the secretary says: "He was one of the finest young men we have ever had in our institution. He was an earnest and consistent Christian, and had great influence for good with his fellow-students. On leaving college, he spent three years in Auburn Theological Seminary—was licensed to preach by one of our Northern Presbyteries, and then went to Virginia—near Norfolk, where he built a church and gave promise of great usefulness, when, about two years ago, he suddenly sickened and died. He had many friends in Clinton outside of the college. He prepared for college in the Clinton Grammar School. On leaving the school for college the wife of the principal of the school made to me the remark, that it seemed as if the Spirit of the Lord had departed from the school. I received him into the church and was his pastor for a number of years. Everybody was his friend. Members of the Presbyterian Church of Clinton contributed to the erection of his church in Virginia, and the Sunday-school has educated his sister."

At the larger colleges the record of Negro students has, on the whole, been good; at Harvard several have held scholarships, and one a fellowship; there has been one Phi Beta Kappa man, one class orator, two commencement speakers, three masters of arts and one doctor in philosophy. In scholarship the eleven graduates have stood: Four good;

three fair; two ordinary, and two poor. At Brown one of the most brilliant students of recent years was a Negro; he was among the junior eight elected to the Phi Beta Kappa. At Amherst the record of colored men has been very good, both in scholarship and athletics. A colored man captained the Amherst football team one year and he is now one of the chief Harvard football coaches. At Yale and Cornell colored men have held scholarships, and some have made good records.

Among the women's colleges the color prejudice is much stronger and more unyielding.

They have one Negro graduate from Smith College, we learn: "Our first colored student graduated last year with the degree of A. B. . . . We also have two students of Negro descent in our present senior class."

Wellesley has had quite a number of colored students, of whom two graduated. "Both these young women had more than average ability and one did brilliant work." Radcliffe College, the Harvard "annex," has two colored graduates who are well spoken of.

Beside the Negroes who have graduated from these colleges there have been a large number who have pursued a partial course but taken no degree. They have dropped out for lack of funds, poor scholarship and various reasons. Then, too, many institutions having no graduates have promising candidates at present. The registrar of the University of Illinois informs us "that so far no Negro has ever been graduated from the University of Illinois. One member of our present senior class is a Negro, and he will doubtless be graduated next June. He is a good scholar and is very much respected in the university. He is this year the editor of the students' paper."

Wabash College, Indiana, "has had frequently colored students enrolled in her classes, but none have completed their course. We have at present two colored students in attendance at college."

Dickinson College, Pennsylvania, "has never conferred a degree upon a Negro. We have two, at the present time, in attendance at the college: one a member of the freshmen class, and the other a member of the junior class and one of the brightest scholars and most highly esteemed gentlemen in attendance at our institution."

The universities of Wyoming, Montana and California have all had at one time or another colored students. Syracuse University has three Negro students now, "especially bright and promising;" the University of Vermont dropped two colored members of the class of '97 "on account of inability to do the work." Wheaton College, Illinois, has "had many colored students and some good ones, but no one of them has gained the degree of A. B."

To sum up then: Negroes have graduated from Northern institutions. In most of the larger universities they have on the whole made good records. In the Western colleges they have done well in some cases, and poorly in others. The summer schools at Harvard, Clark and the University of Chicago have several Negro students.

According to the best information the Conference has been able to gather, the total number of Negro graduates has been as follows:

NEGRO COLLEGE GRADUATES:

1826—1	1855—1	1864— 2	1873—29	1882— 39	1891— 99
1828—1	1856—5	1865— 5	1874—27	1883— 74	1892— 70
1844—1	1857—1	1866— 1	1875—25	1884— 64	1893—137
1845—1	1858—1	1867— 4	1876—37	1885—100	1894—130
1847—1	1859—1	1868— 9	1877—43	1886— 94	1895—130
1849—1	1860—6	1869—11	1878—37	1887— 90	1896—104
1850—1	1861—3	1870—26	1879—48	1888— 87	1897—128
1851—1	1862—3	1871—15	1880—50	1889— 85	1898—144
1853—3	1863—1	1872—26	1881—54	1890— 95	1899—*57

TOTAL, - - - - -	2,209
Class not given, - - - -	122
GRAND TOTAL, - - -	2,331

*Partial report.

One hundred graduates of colleges of doubtful rank are not included here; these and unknown omissions may bring the true total up to 2,500.

It is plain that there is a steady increase of college-bred Negroes from decade to decade, but not a large increase. There is today about one college-trained person in every 3,600 Negroes. Since 1876, 1,941 Negroes have been graduated from Negro colleges and 390 from white colleges.

We now come to consider the personnel of this group of persons with regard to birthplace, age, sex, etc. The returns for these particulars are only partial, and fuller for later years than for earlier. They seem, however, to be fairly typical. First as to birthplace of 650 college-bred Negroes: South Carolina, 95; North Carolina, 80; Tennessee, 73; Virginia, 60; Georgia, 55; Mississippi, 48; Alabama, 34; Ohio, 34; Kentucky, 25; Maryland, 17; Indiana, 4; Massachusetts, 3; West Virginia, 3; Iowa, 3; New Jersey, 2; Michigan, 2; Rhode Island, 1; Connecticut, 1; Vermont, 1; Colorado, 1; Pennsylvania, 17; Missouri, 12; Louisiana, 12; Illinois, 11; District of Columbia, 10; Texas, 9; Kansas, 9; New York, 5; Arkansas, 4; Florida, 4; Delaware, 1. In foreign lands: Hayti, 4; West Indies, 3; West Africa, 2; Ontario, 1. 542 out of 650 having been born south of Mason and Dixon's line.

The most interesting question connected with birthplace is that of the migration of colored graduates—that is, where these men finally settle and work. If we arrange these 650 graduates according to sections where they were born and where they now live, it appears that of 254 college-bred Negroes born in the border states (*i. e.*, Delaware, Maryland, Virginia, Kentucky, Tennessee, North Carolina, Missouri and District of Columbia), 148, or 58 per cent., stayed and worked there; 39, or 15 per cent., went further south; 26, or 10 per cent., went southwest; 12, or 5 per cent., went to the middle west, etc. Or, again:

Of 73 college graduates born north, 35 stayed there and 38 went south.

Of 507 college graduates born south, 443 stayed there and 62 went north.

OWEN W. L. SMITH

Late U. S. Minister to the Republic of Liberia.

These statistics cover only about one-fourth of the total number of graduates, but they represent pretty accurately the general tendencies, so far as our observation has gone. It is therefore probably quite within the truth to say that 50 per cent. of northern-born college men come south to work among the masses of their people, at a personal sacrifice which few people realize; that nearly 90 per cent. of the southern-born graduates, instead of seeking that personal freedom and broader intellectual atmosphere which their training has led them in some degree to conceive, stay and labor in the midst of their black neighbors and relatives.

There is little in the matter of early training that lends itself to statistical statement, but there is much of human interest. A number of typical lives are therefore appended, which show in a general way the sort of childhood and youth through which these college-bred Negroes have passed. First as to the men:

MEN.

"I attended the public schools in Augusta, Georgia, and sold papers, brushed boots and worked in tobacco factories. While in college I taught school in summer time."

———

"Born in Springfield, Massachusetts, where I attended the public schools and acted as driver and hotel waiter. I attended Fisk University, and during vacations taught school, worked in a saw mill, waited on table and acted as Pullman porter."

———

"My parents were old and poor, and I worked my way through school and helped to support them by manual labor."

———

"I came to Texas with my parents about 1876, and attended the Galveston public schools. I then went to college, assisted in part by my parents and in part by my own efforts. The expenses of the last two years were paid by a scholarship which I won by examination."

"I spent most of my youth with my uncle, a merchant in Florence, South Carolina, where I attended the public school, which was poor. I afterwards worked five years on my father's farm, and finally went to college."

———

"I attended public schools in Virginia, working in white families morning and night for my board. I then worked my way through a normal course, and finally through Hillsdale College."

———

"I was a farmer before going to school. My church conference sent me to school. My parents were poor, and my mother died when I was but four years old."

———

"I came to Kansas when nine years old and lived on a farm until I was twenty, neither seeing nor hearing from any of my relations during that time. In 1871 I went to Oberlin and began work in Ray's Third Part Arithmetic."

———

"I was born a slave in Prince Edward county, Virginia. I worked as a farmer and waiter, and then went to Hampton Institute. After leaving Hampton I helped my parents a few years and then entered Shaw."

———

"I sold papers and went to school when a boy; I learned the brickmason trade of my father. After graduating from the high school I worked in the printing office of a colored paper, thus earning enough to go to college."

———

"I was born in Calvert county, Maryland, being one of seven children. We lived at first in the log cabin which my father had built in slavery times. Soon we moved away from there and settled on a farm which my father commenced buying on shares. I went to school, worked on the farm and taught school until I was twenty-two, when I entered Lincoln."

22

"I went to a private school at Thibodaux, Louisiana, about a year, and also to the Freedmen's school under the United States government in 1864–5. Finally I entered New Orleans University."

———

"I was born in Crawford county, Georgia. My father moved to Macon, then to Jones county, then back to Crawford county, then to the town of Forsyth, and finally to the State of Mississippi. I finally left home at the age of sixteen and roamed about for two and a half years. I saved some money by work on a railroad and started to school."

———

"I was born in Tennessee and lived there on a farm until I was thirteen. Then we went to Kansas, and finally to Arkansas, where I went to Philander Smith College."

———

"My parents, having been slaves, were poor. I was the fifth of ten children, and the task of educating all of us was a serious one for the family. My parents made every sacrifice, and at nine years of age I was helping by selling papers on the streets of Pittsburg, and colored papers among the Negroes on Saturday. After completing the common schools I worked as elevator boy and bootblack, and finally at the age of fifteen was enabled to enter the engineering course of the Western University of Pennsylvania."

———

"I was born in Greene county, Georgia, and lived on the farm until I was seventeen. My parents were poor and there were nine other children. I worked hard, saved my money, went to school, and finally entered Atlanta University."

———

"I was born in a stable; my father died when I was two years old. I blacked boots and sold sulphur water to educate myself until I was eighteen."

———

"My mother and father took me from Alabama to Mississippi, where my father joined the Union army at Corinth, leaving me with my mother, brother and sister. We went to Cairo, Illinois, and then to Island No. 10. There mother and brother died and my sister sent me to Helena, Arkansas, in charge of an aunt. My father died during the siege of Vicksburg, and I was sent to the orphanage in Helena, which afterward became Southland College.''

————

''My father died when I was five, and my mother when I was twelve, leaving me an orphan in the West Indies. At fourteen I left home with a white man from Massachusetts. I went to school one year in Massachusetts, then shipped as a sailor and stayed on the sea ten years, and finally returning started to school again.''

————

''I was one of the two sons of a Methodist preacher, and had to struggle pretty hard to get an education; I left school at the age of thirteen and could not return again until I was nineteen.''

————

''My father was a lumber dealer, and when he died I went into partnership with my uncle in the same business in Carroll county, Maryland. Later I left home, worked five years on a farm in Michigan, and finally entered Baldwin University.''

————

''I was born in Alton, Illinois, in 1864. In 1871 we moved to Mississippi, and happening to visit my grandfather at Wilberforce, Ohio, I begged him to let me stay there and enter school. He consented; and by housework, taking care of horses and his help I got through school.''

————

''I was born of slave parents who could neither read nor write. I had but five months' regular schooling until I was seventeen years of age. Then I worked my way through a normal school in South Carolina, and thus gained a certificate to teach and helped myself on further in school.''

"I was the son of a slave mother and her master. After emancipation a maternal uncle started me to school in Salisbury, North Carolina, which an army officer had organized. Afterward I entered Biddle and supported myself by teaching."

———

"Father died about my ninth birthday, so I attended the public schools and worked on the farm to assist mother earn a livelihood for herself and the four children. Late in my 'teens, after three months' day labor upon the farm, railroad, wood-chopping, etc., I entered Alcorn, with the sum of $20.50. By working there I was enabled to remain in school six years, during the last five of which I secured work as a teacher in Wilkerson county. The money I obtained was used by myself, my two brothers and a sister in common, as from time to time each joined me in college. Mother would accept very little of our earnings for herself, lest we might be deprived of an education."

———

"I was born and reared on my aged mother's farm near Thomastown, Mississippi. I began going to a country school at twelve years of age, having learned my A B C's under Uncle York Moss, at his Sunday-school, where we used Webster's 'Blue-back.' My chances for attending even a country school were meager, for I had to help on the farm. Attending two and four months in the year, I got far enough advanced by the time I was sixteen to teach a little and use my earnings in entering, first, Tougaloo, and then Alcorn."

———

"I was reared on a farm and was sixteen before I knew my letters, and twenty-one before I spent a month in school."

———

"In early life I lived with my parents, who were ex-slaves and took great pride in working hard to educate their children. I attended the first Yankee schools established in Sa-

E. E. COOPER.

Editor "The Colored American." Founder of First Illustrated Negro
Newspaper.

vannah. As soon as I could read, write and figure a little, I started a private afternoon school at my home which I taught."

———

"I was born a slave. Soon after the fall of Port Royal, South Carolina, in 1861, three of us escaped from Charleston to Beaufort, and joined the Union forces. We were taken on the U. S. gunboat *Unadilla*. There I was attached to a lieutenant in the Forty-eighth New York Regiment of Volunteers, and remained with him until he was wounded before Fort Wagner. I then went north, attended night school in Portland, Maine, and finally entered Howard University."

———

"I was the fifth child in a family of eleven. My father was a poor farmer and did not believe in education, so my training was neglected until I was able to work and help myself."

———

"I was born a slave and taken north to an orphanage by Quakers after the war, both my parents being dead. Afterward I was sent to New Jersey, and then worked on a Pennsylvania farm until I went to Lincoln."

———

"My father was set free prior to the war and purchased my mother. He died when I was eight, leaving a little home and $300 in gold. My mother was an invalid and I had to work at whatever came to hand, going to school from three to five months a year. At the age of fifteen I stopped school and labored and taught a three months' school at $25 a month. Finally I entered Roger Williams University, working my way through and helping mother."

———

"Twelve years of my life were spent as a slave. I worked at driving cows, carrying dinner to the field-hands and running rabbits. My master owned three hundred Negroes, so that boys were not put in the field until they were eighteen.. When I was freed I did not know a letter, but I worked my way through Webster's 'Blue-back' speller."

"I was born the slave of Jefferson Davis' brother and attended contraband schools before the close of the war."

WOMEN.

"I was born on a farm in Ohio and lived there until I was sixteen. My father died when I was twelve and I had to provide for myself. At the age of sixteen I taught a country school and saved one hundred dollars. With this I went to Oberlin and went through by teaching and working."

"Was born and schooled in Philadelphia during the dark days of slavery. Was intimately associated with the work of the Underground Railroad and the Anti-Slavery Society. I was sent to Oberlin in 1864."

'My early life was spent at my home at Shoreham, Vermont, where I attended Newton Academy. In the fall of '91 I entered Mr. Moody's school at Northfield, Massachusetts, graduating as president of my class. I then entered Middlebury College, Vermont."

"At a very early age I assumed the responsibility of housekeeper, as my mother died and I was the oldest of a family of five; hence I labored under many disadvantages in attending school, but nevertheless I performed my household duties, persevered with my studies, and now I feel that I have been rewarded."

"My mother and I 'took in' washing for our support and to enable me to get an education. After finishing the public schools of Jacksonville, Illinois, I was supported four years in college by a scholarship."

22

"My early life was spent in Darlington, South Carolina; I did not attend the public school until I was a large girl, but was taught at home, first by my mother, then by a private teacher. When the public school was graded, in 1889, I entered the high school course."

———

"While a school-girl I taught persons living out in service, going into the premises of some of the most prominent white people in New Orleans. I always kept a large class of night pupils at the same time. I paid my tuition out of these earnings."

———

"I was born in the State of Ohio, near the town of Delaware, on a picturesque farm purchased by my grandparents in 1836. My parents on both sides were Virginians. At this quiet homestead, sandwiched between the Scioto river on the east and maple groves on the west, I lived the life of a dreamy, yet restless child—one of a very large family with an angelically-disposed mother and an extremely eccentric and well-educated father. Our father early told us of Dante, Milton and similar literature, simplifying to suit our youthfulness. Mother repeated the story of 'Pilgrim's Progress,' and she also delighted in the book of Job, which her life so beautifully represented—patience personified. Our home being so near the Ohio White Sulphur Springs, where the wealthy leisure class spent much time, I saw much of cultured people, old and young, especially the latter. Indeed, when quite young I saw little else, for during the remainder of the year my brothers, sisters, birds, trees and nature in general were my only companions."

———

From the first the institutions of higher training founded in the South were, with few exceptions, open to girls as well as boys. Naturally fewer girls entered, but nevertheless a considerable number—over 250—throughout the country have finished a college course. Of the larger Negro colleges

JUDSON W. LYONS.

Register United States Treasury, Washington, D. C.

only Lincoln and Biddle do not admit girls.   The women graduates are as follows:

Women Graduates from Colleges.—Oberlin, 55; Shaw, 21; Paul Quinn, 13; Atlanta, 8; Southland, 8; Rust, 7; Claflin, 6; Philander Smith, 5; Iowa Wesleyan, 4; University of Kansas, 3; Cornell, 3; Geneva, 2; Leland, 1; University of Iowa, 1; Idaho, 1; Bates, 1; Clarke, 1; Straight, 1; Branch, Arkansas, 1; Mt. Holyoke, 1; Fisk, 31; Wilberforce, 19; Knoxville, 10; Howard, 8; Central Tennessee, 7; Livingstone, 6; New Orleans, 5; Roger Williams, 5; Berea, 4; University of Michigan, 3; Wittenberg, 2; Wellesley, 2; Butler 1; Adrian, 1; McKendree, 1; Virginia Normal and Collegiate, 1; Allen, 1; Paine Institute, 1; Vassar, 1. Total women, 252. Total men, 2,272.

If we arrange them according to years of graduation, we have from 1861 to 1869, 36; from 1880 to 1889, 76; 1890 to 1898, 119.

The rapid increase of college-bred women in later years is noticeable, and the present tendency is toward a still larger proportion of women.   Twenty-three per cent. of the college students of Howard, Atlanta, Fisk and Shaw Universities were women in the school year of 1898–'99.   The economic stress will probably force more of the young men into work before they get through college and leave a larger chance for the training of daughters.   A tendency in this direction is noticeable in all the colleges, and if it results in more highly trained mothers it will result in great good.   Of one hundred college-bred women reporting their conjugal condition, one-half had been married, against nearly seventy per cent. of the men.

The family is the latest of the social institutions developed by the Negro on American soil and as yet the weakest. He learned to labor, he organized for religious purposes, he started germs of other social organizations before the system of slavery allowed the independent monogamic Negro home. Consequently we look most anxiously to the establishment and strengthening of the home among members of the race, because it is the surest indication of real progress.

The Negro was brought originally from a polygamic home-life in Africa where women and children were strongly guarded, although subject to the practically unrestrained tyranny of the husband. On the West Indian plantations all the law and custom of marriage was rudely broken up and polygamy, polyandry and promiscuity were practiced. On the plantations of the United States some regularity was established, which, on the Virginia plantations, approached as near the monogamic ideal as the slave trade and concubinage would allow. With emancipation came the independent Negro home. Naturally the poor training of Negro women, the lack of respect or chivalry toward them, and the fact that the field-hand never had the responsibility of family life, all tended to make pure homes difficult to establish and maintain. Without doubt the greatest social problem of the American Negro at present is sexual purity, and the solving of this problem lies peculiarly upon the homes established among them. Great and marked progress has been made in thirty years, but there is still great work ahead.

Among a picked class of leaders like these we are studying, statistics of marriage and family life are consequently of peculiar interest. First, then, let us consider the age at which college-bred persons marry, compared with the age of graduation:

Of College-bred Men there Marry: Under 20 years of age, 1.4 per cent.; 20 to 24 years of age, 15.1 per cent.; 25 to 29 years of age, 39.3 per cent.; 30 to 34 years of age, 30.2 per cent.; 35 to 39 years of age, 8.6 per cent.; 40 years of age or over, 5.4 per cent.

The bulk of college men, it would seem, marry between the ages of twenty-five and thirty-five, a period nearly ten years later than was the case with their fathers and mothers. This indicates a great social revolution. The average age of marriage, compared with age of graduation is as follows:

MEN:

Graduating at age of	Average age of marriage	Graduating at age of	Average age of marriage	Graduating at age of	Average age of marriage
16	25	23	28	30	32
17	29	24	29	31	32
18	24	25	27	32	33
19	26	26	29	33	33
20	28	27	30	34	31
21	26	28	30	35	30
22	29	29	32	36 and over	35

The meager returns received made it very difficult to determine the truth as to the marriages of women graduates; the average age of marriage of those women reported was 62.8 years; compared with age of graduates it was:

WOMEN:

Graduating at age of	Married at age of	Graduating at age of	Married at age of	Graduating at age of	Married at age of
18	20	21	27	25	28
19	22	22	24	27	28
20	22	23	25	31	43

Out of 665 male graduates, 68 per cent. have married, and out of 99 female graduates, 51 per cent. have married. Of 19 graduates previous to 1870, 18 have married; of 97 from 1870 to 1879, 85 have married; of 251 from 1880 to 1889, 219 have married; of 393 from 1890 to 1899, 180 have married. Out of this total there has been but one divorce.

III. OCCUPATIONS, OWNERSHIP OF PROPERTY, ETC.

THE most interesting question, and in many respects the crucial question, to be asked concerning college-bred Negroes is: Do they earn a living? It has been intimated more than once that the higher training of Negroes has resulted in sending into the world of work men who can find nothing to do suitable to their talents. Now and then there comes a rumor of a colored college man working at menial service, etc. Fortunately the returns as to occupations of college-bred Negroes are quite full—nearly 60 per cent. of the total number of graduates.

This enables us to reach fairly probable conclusions as to the occupations of college-bred Negroes. Of 1,312 persons reporting there were: Teachers, 53.4 per cent.; clergymen, 16.8 per cent.; physicians, etc., 6.3 per cent.; students, 5.6 per cent.; lawyers, 4.7 per cent.; in government service, 4 per cent.; in business, 3.6 per cent.; farmers and artisans, 2.7 per cent.; editors, secretaries and clerks, 2.4 per cent.; miscellaneous, 5 per cent.

Over half are teachers, a sixth are preachers, another sixth are students and professional men; over 6 per cent. are farmers, artisans and merchants, and 4 per cent. are in government service. In detail, the occupations are as follows:

Occupations of College-Bred Men.—Presidents and deans, 19; teachers of music, 7; professors, principals and teachers, 675. Total, 701. Bishop, 1; chaplains United States army, 2; missionaries, 9; presiding elders, 12; preachers, 197. Total, 221. Doctors of medicine, 76; druggists, 4; dentists,

3. Total, 83. Students, 74; lawyers, 62. United States minister plenipotentiary, 1; United States consul, 1; United States deputy collector, 1; United States gauger, 1; United States postmasters, 2; United States clerks, 44; State civil service, 2; city civil service, 1. Total, 53. Merchants, etc., 30; managers, 13; real estate dealers, 4. Total, 47. Farmers, 26. Secretaries of national societies, 7; clerks, etc., 15. Total, 22. Artisans, 9; editors, 9; miscellaneous, 5.

These figures illustrate vividly the function of the college-bred Negro. He is, as he ought to be, the group leader, the man who sets the ideals of the community where he lives, directs its thought and heads its social movements. It need hardly be argued that the Negro people need social leadership more than most groups; they have no traditions to fall back upon, no long-established customs, no strong family ties, no well-defined social classes. All these things must be slowly and painfully evolved. The preacher was even before the war the group leader of the Negroes, and the church their greatest social institution. Naturally, this preacher was ignorant and often immoral, and the problem of replacing the older type by better educated men has been a difficult one. Both by direct work and by indirect influence on other preachers and on congregations, the college-bred preacher has an opportunity for reformatory work and moral inspiration, the value of which cannot be overestimated.

It has, however, been in the furnishing of teachers that the Negro college has found its peculiar function. Few persons realize how vast a work, how mighty a revolution has thus been accomplished. To furnish five millions and more of ignorant people with teachers of their own race and blood, in one generation, was not only a very difficult undertaking, but a very important one, in that it placed before the eyes of almost every Negro child an attainable ideal. It brought the masses of the blacks in contact with modern civilization, made black men the leaders of their communities and trainers of the new generation. In this work college-bred Negroes were first teachers and then teachers of teachers. And here it is that the broad culture of college work has been of peculiar value. Knowledge of life and its wider meaning has been the point of the Negro's deepest ignorance, and the sending out of teachers whose training has not been merely for bread-winning, but also for human culture, has been of inestimable value in the training of these men.

In earlier years the two occupations of preacher and teacher were practically the only ones open to the black college graduate. Of later years a larger diversity of life among his people has opened new avenues of employment.

We find that the profession of teaching is a stepping-stone to other work. Eighty-seven persons were at first teachers, and then changed, eleven becoming lawyers, seven going into business, twenty-six entering the ministry, twelve entering the United States civil service, etc. Seven have at various times engaged in menial work, usually as porters, waiters and the like, but all but one man working in a hotel have done this only temporarily. It is quite possible that others who are engaged in such work have on this account sent in no reports. We see in this way that of seven hundred college-bred men over five hundred have immediately on graduation found work at which they are still employed. Less than two hundred have turned from a first occupation to a second before finding apparently permanent employment.

There are still others who have tried two and three employments. The reports of these are naturally not as full as the others, through forgetfulness and the natural desire not to advertise past failures. One college man is known to have tried nine different occupations in ten years—but this is very exceptional.

It seems fair to conclude that the majority of college-bred men find work quickly, make few changes, and stick to their undertakings. That there are many exceptions to this rule is probable, but the testimony of observers together with these figures makes the above statement approximately true.

It might be well here to turn from the more general figures to the graduates of a single representative institution. A graduate of Dartmouth College who has been in the work of educating Negro youth for over thirty years writes as follows in a small publication which gives the record of Atlanta University graduates, including the class of 1899:

"This leaflet covers an experience of about a quarter of a century of graduating classes. It will tell of the work of only the *graduates* of Atlanta University, all of whom have been kept under the watchful eye of their *alma mater*. It would be difficult to trace the careers of the thousands of others who did not graduate but who have attended the institution for a longer or shorter period, although many of them are known to have made good use of their meager attainments and some are occupying prominent positions. If it were asked why no larger percentage of the students have obtained diplomas or certificates of graduation, a sufficient answer would be found in the one word, poverty. Their parents have been too poor to spare them from home or to pay their expenses at school, and they themselves have been utterly unable to find any employment sufficiently remunerative to permit them to keep on and graduate within a reasonable limit in time. Probably the world cannot show instances of greater sacrifices by parents or greater pluck, persistency and self-denial of students than are to be found among the patrons and pupils of Atlanta University.

"While the ninety-four graduates from the college department represent only a small portion of the work done by the university, they represent a very important part of that work, as will be evident from a statement of the positions they occupy and the work they are doing.

"Of these ninety-four graduates, twelve have died. . . . Of the eighty-two now living, eleven are ministers, four are physicians, two are lawyers, one is a dentist, forty-three are teachers, one is a theological student, one is studying at Harvard University and another at the University of Pennsylvania, ten are in the service of the United States, six in other kinds of business, and two are unemployed.

"One of these graduates has rendered a most conspicuous service to the Negro farmers of his State through the organization of a farmers' improvement society, with many branches, whose members are pledged to become land owners, to diversify their crops, to improve and beautify their homes, to fight the credit system by buying only for cash on a co-operative plan, and to raise their own supplies so far as possible. The fact that he can report today eighty-six branches of his society scattered over the State of Texas with 2,340 members who have bought and largely paid for 46,000 acres of land, worth nearly half a million dollars, is a valuable illustration of what one Negro with high ideals and an earnest purpose can accomplish for the economic and material advancement of his race.

"Several graduates have done considerable newspaper work and many sermons and addresses delivered by them have been published. At least two publications have been highly commended by the press. Of President Richard R. Wright's 'Historical Sketch of Negro Education in Georgia,' the *Journal of Education* says: 'And it is just this that makes his story so valuable and forces one to read it straight through from beginning to end, which is not the way books and pamphlets are usually read in newspaper offices.' And of Professor William H. Crogman's 'Talks for the Times,' the *New York Independent* says: 'The author speaks for his race and speaks in strong, polished English, full of nerve and rich in the music of good English prose.'

"And these graduates are not fickle and unstable, but retain their positions year after year, doing faithful, earnest and patient service. The length of the pastorates of the ministers has been far above the average, and one of the teachers is completing his twenty-fourth year in the same institution.

"Do not these simple statements impress their own les-

23

sons? Could less than a college course have fitted most of these men and women so well for the responsible positions they are occupying, and the work they are doing as pastors, professors, principals, physicians, editors, teachers, Sunday-school superintendents, home-builders and leaders of their people? If half of them had failed to fill the place for which their education ought to have prepared them, even then their teachers and friends would not have been disheartened. But

DINING HALL, ROGER WILLIAMS UNIVERSITY, NASHVILLE, TENNESSEE.

almost none have failed to meet reasonable expectations. This record of the college graduates is full of encouragement and inspiration.''

A glance at the work done by Negro college graduates in different fields can be but casual and yet of some value. The teachers we asked to estimate roughly the pupils they had taught. Some answered frankly that they could not, while others made a statement which they said was simply a careful guess. From these estimates we find that 550 teachers reporting think they have taught about 300,000 children in primary grades and 200,000 in secondary grades. From this we get some faint idea of the enormous influence of these 700 teachers and the many other college men who have taught for longer or shorter periods. Some of the teachers reported briefly the success in after life of some of the pupils they had taught:

"They farm mostly—a multitude preach, some act as men of commerce, and they are engaged in every pursuit. One is a successful practitioner of medicine."

———

"Several are successful as mail clerks, several are doctors, some are successful farmers."

———

"Eleven became doctors. The most of these are living and they are succeeding finely. Four are practicing law, and they are making passably good headway. Two are college presidents, four professors, one cashier of a bank."

———

"One taught successfully in the Louisville High School, one in an Alabama high school, one is a minister and one a grocer."

———

"Three are principals of large schools, five are clerks in United States service, several are lawyers, three are doctors."

———

"Several are successful physicians, lawyers, teachers and preachers, and one a bishop in the A. M. E. Z. church. Three are presidents of institutions of learning and two are successful pharmacists."

———

"Several of my pupils have been and are now successful ministers. One is quite an eminent physician, and one a lawyer, now an assistant in the district attorney's office of New York City."

"Several have secured first-grade licenses and are making successful teachers. Some are buying their own farms and not a few are owning their own lots."

———

"One is now professor of agriculture at the A. & M. College, West Virginia. Another has charge of the machine shops at High Point Normal and Industrial School, High Point, North Carolina; another is practicing law at some point in Florida. Quite a number are doing well."

———

"One is a first-class sign painter at Wilmington, North Carolina, another is one of the leading colored physicians of Atlanta."

———

"Two are successful teachers and one is principal of the largest public school in Birmingham, Alabama."

———

"One of the most notable and one over whom I may have exercised considerable influence, before and since his graduation, is the principal of Snow Hill Industrial School, at Snow Hill, Alabama."

———

"There were no individual instances of success among them so far as I know. Several of the young men went to farming, some of the young ladies married farmers. One young man became a miner for a while."

———

"I mention the following instances of success with which I am best acquainted at present in this State: A dentist at Houston, Texas; a practicing physician and surgeon at Washington, Texas; the deputy United States Revenue Collector at the port of Galveston; and the superintendent of the Deaf and Dumb Asylum, Austin, Texas."

———

"Several students of my tuition have made excellent teachers; all, with few exceptions, have made good citizens and proved worthy examples of honesty, trustworthiness and Christianity.''

————

''Among those graduated under me are four clerks in the civil service, three principals of schools, two chaplains in the United States army, one captain and two lieutenants in the United States volunteer service, eleven teachers in high schools and one postmaster.''

————

''Among my graduates are two high school teachers, one professor of agriculture, one principal of city schools, one founder of an industrial school and village.''

————

''Some have purchased farms, others are teaching, while a goodly number, young women and young men, are pursuing college education.''

————

''One is a graduate from medicine and one from law, and a large number have taken higher courses in other schools and are holding important positions as principals of schools.''

————

''There are many bright and promising ones among them, but as yet they have not fully shouldered the responsibilities of life, and therefore cannot be termed successful individuals, but rather promising.''

————

''Two of our last year graduates (a class of seven) are teaching music; one teaches in the schools of Crawford county, Arkansas; one is clerk and book-keeper in a store; the others are farming and housekeeping in their homes. Several of the undergraduates are or have been teaching. General satisfaction with their work is reported.''

————

''One young man won a prize at the University of Chicago; several have won prizes in other schools of the North. Two or three are now physicians; several are successful business men and farmers.''

"One of my pupils in the year 1867 is today the head of one of the leading Negro colleges in the Southwest. One of my pupils from this institution, a person of physical deformity, who worked his way through by means derived from labor, is vice-president of the largest colored public school in this State. In about eighteen months after leaving school he saved sufficient means from his limited salary as a teacher to purchase a lot, plan a house and help to construct it; the property is worth about one thousand dollars. The majority of graduates of the institution have either their own homes or improved property."

Some of the pupils referred to have afterward graduated from college and are included elsewhere in this study. Most teachers have picked out the cases of success and said nothing of the failures, of which there must have been many. Still, the record is interesting and shows something of the work of the college-bred teacher.

Outside the work of teachers, the chief professions followed are the ministry, law and medicine. In most cases a regular professional course is pursued after the college course is finished, in order to prepare for the profession. The chief theological schools are Biddle, at Charlotte, North Carolina; Howard, at Washington, District of Columbia; Gammon, at Atlanta, Georgia; Straight, at New Orleans, Louisiana; Payne, at Wilberforce, Ohio; Lincoln, in Pennsylvania, and Union, at Richmond, Virginia. These institutions, and others, have turned out large numbers of ministers, until the supply today is rather more than the demand, and the number of students is falling off. The work of replacing the ordinary Negro preachers by college-bred men will go on slowly, but it will require many years and much advance in other lines before this work is finished. Some colored men have gone to Northern theological schools, usually to the Hartford Theological School, Newton Seminary and Yale University. The leading Negro ministers today are not usually college-bred men; still a large number of the rising ministers are such, and the influence of the younger set is wide-spread.

There are comparatively few Negro law schools, those at Shaw University and Howard being practically the only ones. There has been a good deal of contempt thrown on the Negro lawyer, and he has been regarded as superfluous. Without doubt, today lawyers are not demanded as much as merchants and artisans, and they have often degenerated into ward politicians of the most annoying type. At the same time there has been a demand for Negro lawyers of the better type. The Negroes are ignorant of the forms of law, careless of little matters of procedure, and have lost thousands of dollars of hard-earned property by not consulting lawyers. There is, therefore, a distinct place for the black lawyer, but one hard to fill, with small and uncertain income in most cases. Here and there are exceptions, especially in the North. In Boston, for instance, there are four or five colored lawyers who make fair incomes, largely from white practice—foreigners, Jews, Italians and some few Americans. In Chicago there are two or three colored lawyers with large incomes and a host who make a living. Even in a city like Minneapolis, with only a handful of black folks, the *Journal*, in a review of the more prominent members of the bench and bar, February 10, 1898, speaks of a black man as:

"One of the few members of the Negro race who have succeeded in the practice of law. He was born near Flemingsburg, Kentucky, on February 22, 1859. His father died when he was two years old, and after the war his mother moved to Ohio, where he attended the public schools of New Richmond and Cincinnati. Later he went to school in Chicago, and afterwards entered the Fisk University at Nashville, Tennessee. In 1887 he received the degree of M. A. from Fisk University, and in the same year was admitted to the bar in Illinois, being one of a class of twenty-seven and one out of three who received the highest markings. He

23

was admitted to practice in Tennessee, and practiced to some extent at Nashville and Chicago. In 1889 he resigned his position at Fisk University and came to Minneapolis, where he was the first Afro-American lawyer to appear before the courts of Hennepin county. In the course of his practice here he has handled a number of important cases. One of his notable cases was that of the defense of Thomas Lyons in the famous Harris murder trial. Lyons was discharged. In addition to his activity in his profession, Mr. Morris has been identified prominently with all the affairs of his race in the city and State. He has also been prominent in politics.''

Some of the reports from other lawyers are of interest. A Memphis lawyer who has practiced for twenty-five years says: ''I cannot complain of the treatment I have received at the hands of both bench and bar.'' A lawyer of Vicksburg, Mississippi, says: ''There are two colored lawyers here in bar of about fifty. I do not enjoy any considerable white practice, but get my share from my race.'' A Kentucky lawyer writes: ''In my profession I am succeeding fairly well.''

A Nashville lawyer writes: ''I know of no special success attending my practice. I am making a living out of it.'' A North Carolina practitioner says: ''I handle real estate for both white and colored. I have a paying practice in all State courts. My clients are all colored.''

From the North the character of the replies differs somewhat: ''My practice is largely amongst the whites,'' says a Minnesota lawyer. From Chicago come several reports: ''As a lawyer of six years' practice here I have no reason to complain. My clients are about evenly divided between the two races.'' ''In my practice as a lawyer for the past seven years, I have done general law practice; nine-tenths of my patronage, from point of emolument, has been and is from white clientage. I do considerable business for Irish people, a few Germans, many Poles and Bohemians, and many of English descent.'' From Buffalo, New York, a lawyer writes: ''My practice has not yet assumed proportions sufficiently ex-

RT. REV. GEO. W. CLINTON.
Bishop A. M. E. Zion Church.

tensive or varied to warrant me in making deductions upon present success. I can see no reason, however, why a colored man of high character and the requisite qualifications, should not succeed in the practice of law." Another writes: "My experience as a lawyer in Buffalo has been pleasant, and in my intercourse with the lawyers, almost exclusively white, I have had no cause for complaint, being apparently respected by bench and bar." A Minnesota lawyer graduated in law in 1894, "was appointed clerk of criminal court, and resigned December 21, 1898, to serve as a member of the Minnesota House of Representatives; am still a member and have been practicing law. The district I represent, the forty-second, is an entirely white district. I led the Republican ticket by six hundred and ninety votes." A Cleveland, Ohio, lawyer says: "My practice is increasing." An Omaha, Nebraska, lawyer says: "My practice has been mixed both as to kind of cases and classes of people." A Boston lawyer who is common councilman of Cambridge, from a white ward, reports "fair success." Another Boston lawyer has been alderman of Cambridge for several years. A Philadelphia lawyer says: "My practice is largely confined to Jews. The better class of Negroes is not so likely to patronize me as the whites are."

The chief Negro medical schools are Meharry, at Nashville, Tennessee; Leonard, at Raleigh, North Carolina; Howard, at Washington, District of Columbia; Knoxville, at Knoxville, Tennessee, and New Orleans, at New Orleans, Louisiana. These institutions have done remarkable work in sending out colored physicians. Their standard is lower than the great Northern schools, but in most cases the work seems honestly done and the graduates successful. Negroes have also graduated at the Harvard Medical School, the Medical School of the University of Pennsylvania and other Northern institutions. The rise of the Negro physician has been sudden and significant. Ten years ago few Negro families thought of employing a Negro as a physician.

Today few employ any other kind. By pluck and desert black men have cleared here a large field of usefulness. Moreover, in this profession far more than in the ministry and the law, the professional standard has been kept high. The college-bred physician has had quacks and root doctors to contend with, but to no such extent did they hold and dominate the field as was the case in the churches and criminal courts. The result is today that there is scarcely a city of any size in the United States where it is not possible to secure the services of a well-trained Negro physician of skill and experience. The Freedmen's Hospital, of Washington, has made an extremely good record in the difficult operations performed, general efficiency and training of nurses. Hospitals have grown up in various cities under colored medical men, notably in Chicago, Charleston and Philadelphia. There are State medical associations in Georgia, South Carolina, Tennessee and several other States.

The testimony of physicians themselves is usually hopeful. From the North, a report from Newark, New Jersey, says: "I am and have been medical representative on our grand jury. Two-thirds of my practice is among whites. I run a drug store in connection with my practice." From New York City: "At first I found the whites very backward in dealing with me, but success in several emergency cases gave me some reputation. Now my practice is about equally divided among black and white." Another from New York City says his practice amounts to about $10,000 a year, and he actually collects about half of that. About a third of his patients are white. From Philadelphia one reports a large practice, chiefly among blacks and the colored hospital. One colored physician is connected with a large white hospital. A lady physician from the same city reports "marked courtesy and respect on the part of all." From the West a Chicago physician says: "I have been quite successful in the short time I have been practicing. About one-half of my patients are white." Another Chicago physician repre-

sented the State of Illinois at the Association of Military
Surgeons of the United States. From Minnesota, one
writes: "I am succeeding in the practice of medicine in a
city whose Negro population is very small." From Denver
it is reported that a Negro was the first chief medical inspector of the Denver health office, and he was also State
sanitary officer. He has a large practice. From the border
States a Tennessee doctor reports: "I have succeeded in
building up a good practice here among my own people. No
missionary ever had a better field for useful labor." A man
who ranked his class at the Harvard Medical School reports a
practice between $3,000 and $4,000 a year and says: "I am
fully successful as a practitioner and surgeon, and I believe
I enjoy the confidence of a large number of people." From
Missouri a report says: "I meet with most of the best white
physicians in consultation and they treat me with courtesy."
From Kentucky a young physician reports: "I am located
in a town of twelve thousand inhabitants, one-third of whom
are colored, and am thoroughly convinced that there is a
great field here in the South for the educated young colored
man. As a physician I am well received by my white pro-
professional brother." A report from Baltimore, Maryland, reads: "As a physician I find my practice a paying one." From the heart of the South come many interesting reports. A North Carolina man says: "I have
a fair practice for the length of time I have been at work.
My intercourse with the white members of my profession
is cordial along professional lines. I seek no others."
Another North Carolina physician "has treated more than
forty thousand patients with reasonable success." He is
now conducting a sanitarium for consumptives. A colored
man of Savannah, Georgia, has been one of the city physicians for more than five years. "I have treated no less than
twenty-five thousand patients, including several hundred
whites." A Columbia, South Carolina, practitioner is often
"called upon by white physicians to consult with them in

medical cases and assist in surgical cases in their practice. I have an extensive and paying practice among my own people, and a considerable practice among the poorer classes of the white people." An Arkansas man reports that he "has had a half-interest in some of the important surgical operations done in this city. I have a large field and am often called to see patients at a distance of twenty and thirty miles." In Macon Mississippi, an unusually successful doctor says: "My practice here is very large and among both colored and white. Before I settled here no one had heard of a 'colored doctor.' The history of my parents, who had always lived here, helped to establish me. I have had white people come here from a distance and board here to get my treatment."

No thoughtful man can deny that the work of Negro professional men, as thus indicated, has been and still is of immense advantage in the social uplift of the Negro. There have of course been numerous failures, and there has been a tendency to oversupply the demand for ministers and lawyers. This is natural and is not a racial peculiarity, nor indeed is it chargeable to the higher education of the Negro. It was the natural and inevitable rebound of a race of menials granted now for the first time some freedom of economic choice. In the ministry this natural attraction was made doubly strong by the social prominence of the Negro church and by the undue ease with which theological students can get their training all over the land. Nevertheless, granting all the evils arising from some overcrowding of the professions, the good accomplished by well-trained ministers, business-like lawyers and skilled physicians, has far outbalanced it.

Beside the regular occupations indicated above, college-bred Negroes have been active in literary and philanthropic work of various kinds. The following cases are especially reported:

Active work in religious societies, 101; investing in

business enterprises conducted by Negroes, 48; contributing to Negro and other newspapers, 105; editing and publishing newspapers, 40; lecturers, 21; college and student aid, 20; benevolent club work, 9; farming and truck gardening, 10; nurseries, orphanages and homes, 12; slum, prison and temperance work, 16; organized charity, 15; kindergartens and mothers' meetings, 7; building associations, 7; hospitals, 10; savings banks, 4; contributing to magazines, 11; papers before learned societies, 9.

The above represent the principal activities of 450 persons in philanthropic and social lines outside of their regular occupations. Much of the work thus done has been of great benefit, especially in the establishment of refuges and hospitals and business enterprises of various sorts. The character of the work done may be gained from some of the following reports of social and benevolent activities:

"One of the founders of the Provident Hospital, Chicago."

———

"Member of the advisory board of the St. Louis Orphans' Home."

———

"Member of the board of managers of the Home for Aged and Infirm Colored Persons, Philadelphia."

———

"Member of the board of managers of the Educational and Charitable Association of Baltimore, Maryland."

———

"One of the founders of McKane Hospital, Savannah, Georgia."

———

"Organizer of the S. C. Association of Colored Physicians."

———

"Helping out in a joint stock grocery company."

"Assisting in the movement to secure a Home for Colored Orphans and also to establish a Day Nursery for Poor Children in St. Louis."

———

"Helped establish the St. Louis Colored Orphans' Home."

———

"Was chief commissioner for the State of Georgia for Negroes at the time of the Cotton States Exposition."

———

"Have charge of a Sunday-school, night school and choir, besides instrumental and vocal music in my church."

———

"We have organized a savings society to loan small amounts to members on personal security."

———

"I am superintendent of the Anti-Saloon League work among the colored people of Arkansas."

———

"I have assisted in establishing a drug store, a grocery and a cigar factory in Durham, North Carolina."

———

"Beside my teaching, I am president and manager of the Orangeburg, South Carolina, Mercantile Association."

———

"Am a director of the Capitol Savings Bank and former president of the Industrial Building and Loan Association, Washington, D. C."

———

"I established and, under the management of a partner, ran the first store in Brownsville, Tennessee."

———

"I am a director of the Home for Orphans and Aged Colored People in San Antonio, Texas."

———

"For the last eight years I have taught gratuitously children of the neighboring farms, in Arkansas, in my house in winter, and under the trees in summer."

"I was one of the chief promoters of the Colored Orphan Asylum at Oxford, North Carolina, to which the State now contributes $5,000 annually."

———

"For fifteen years I have been president of the lady managers of the Colored Orphan Asylum of Cincinnati, Ohio."

———

"I am interested in relief societies and the Capitol Savings Bank."

———

"I am president of the McDonough Memorial Hospital of New York City, and have invested in mercantile ventures."

———

"I am one of the editors of African Methodist Sunday-school literature."

———

"I have raised in all $3,800 toward purchasing school property and building school-houses."

———

"I have aided forty-three students through college."

———

"I am manager of a teachers' summer home and normal school Chautauqua in Alabama."

———

"I was instrumental in establishing a savings bank at Birmingham, Alabama."

———

"I have organized a citizens union in South Atlanta, Georgia, for the purpose of caring for the streets and sanitary condition of said place."

———

"I have helped conduct mothers' meetings and helped in charitable work of various kinds."

———

Important Public Offices Held at Various Times by College-Bred Negroes.—United States minister to Hayti; six members of the legislature—North Carolina, Illinois, Georgia, Tennessee, Mississippi, Minnesota; engrossing clerk, general assembly; four tax assessors—Illinois, Arkansas,

Mississippi, North Carolina; deputy collector of customs—Louisiana; seven members city council—Kentucky, North Carolina, Pennsylvania, Massachusetts; eight members board of education—North Carolina, Ohio, Tennessee, District of Columbia, Georgia, Kansas; five officials in custom houses—Louisiana, Tennessee, Georgia, Virginia; two State superintendents of public instruction—Louisiana, Alabama; two assistant district attorneys—New York; two district county clerks—Kansas; deputy circuit clerk—Arkansas; prosecuting attorney—Illinois; secretary of Haytian legation; tax collector—Pennsylvania; mayor—South Carolina; chaplain house of representatives—South Carolina; two medical inspectors—Pennsylvania, Colorado; registrar of births and deaths—West Indies; registrar of deposits, United States mint—Louisiana; warden of town—South Carolina.

It is very difficult to collect reliable statistics of property which are not based on actual records. It was not advisable, therefore, to ask those to whom reports were sent the amount of property they were worth, for with the best of motives on the part of those answering, the resulting figures would be largely estimates and personal opinion. One kind of property, however, is least of all liable to be unknown to persons, or to be exaggerated in honest reports, and that is real estate. Each college-bred Negro was asked, therefore, to state the assessed value of the real estate owned by him; the following table was the result of five hundred and fifty-seven answers:

ASSESSED VALUATION OF REAL ESTATE.

	Number.	Actual Amt.		Number.	Actual Amt.
Under $100	3	$ 150.50	$ 5,000–6,000	36	$182,275.
$ 100–200	3	410.	6,000–7,000	13	75,540.
200–300	15	2,035.	7,000–8,000	7	56,500.
300–400	10	4,810.	8,000–10,000	9	79,375.
400–500	5	1,625.	10,000–15,000	17	161,000.
500–750	58	31,400.	15,000–20,000	5	71,550.
750–1,000	28	23,375.	20,000–25,000	1	21,700.
1,000–2,000	129	162,230.	Own no real estate	85	
2,000–3,000	73	158,400.			
3,000–4,000	42	239,887.		557	$1,342,862.50
4,000–5,000	18	82,600.	Average per individual,		2,411.00

24

There is no way of knowing, of course, how far these five hundred and fifty-seven persons are representative of the 2,331 Negro graduates. All things considered, however, this is probably an understatement of the property held, for while many of those not reporting held no property, yet most of those who did report represent the more recent graduates who have just begun to accumulate, while numbers of the other graduates with considerable property could not be reached. Some who are known to own property did not report it. It is therefore a conservative statement to say that college-bred Negroes in the United States own on an average $2,400 worth of real estate, assessed value. If the assessed value is two-thirds of the real value in most cases, this represents $3,600 worth of property, market value. To this must be added the worth of all personal property, so that the average accumulations of this class may average $5,000 each, or $10,000,000 for the group. Such figures are, of course, mere estimates, but in the light of the testimony they are plausible.

Among the most interesting of the answers received were those given to the questions: "Are you hopeful for the future of the Negro in this country?" "Have you any suggestions.

Following are some of the answers received:

"The Negro must know that he must rid himself of obnoxious characteristics, save money, acquire property, learn trades and become moral. The leading men among us must have sense enough to denounce the rapist as well as the lynchers."

———

"Guard well the sanctity of the home. Make a home, beautify it, make it pure, protect it, defend it, die by it. If the youths of our race were sent out from pure, happy, well-regulated homes, half the battle would be fought to begin with."

———

"In spite of conditions, apparently inauspicious, I am sufficiently optimistic to be hopeful of the future of the

American Negro. I consider the ostracism, political, social, industrial, etc., to which he is subjected, to be a training school out of which he will emerge a united race, and, as a necessary concomitant, invincible. The key to the situation is the fostering of the spirit of race pride and the formation of ideals, necessary to be realized and possible of realization.''

"I think the strong caste prejudice in certain sections will lessen as those sections become less provincial and more cosmopolitan.''

"I suggest that one-tenth of his religious energy be applied to the accumulation of homes and desirable lands.''

"The future of the Negro depends upon him making himself felt as a race. Not by force, but by intelligence and wealth.''

"The Negro should engage in business, have his own stores, dry goods, drugs, groceries, banks, his own professional men; and make morality and education the basis of worth.''

"I would suggest that we accumulate more property, get homes, and that those who have homes invest their money in Negro enterprises.''

"I am indeed hopeful for our future. Daily I ride through thousands of acres of land owned by Negroes in Mississippi. They are happy and prospering. Let us fear God, treat our white neighbor with courtesy, save money and educate our children, and the close of the twentieth century will find us a great and prosperous people.''

"I have an abiding faith in the triumph of the right, based on merit, virtue and capacity.''

"I am hopeful of the Negro in this country, and, moreover, hopeful of him in Africa. 'Behold, He that keepeth Israel shall neither slumber nor sleep.'"

———

"Education, refinement, character and money will settle the Negro problem everywhere."

———

"I am hopeful of the future of the race. As we become better educated, we shall then be better prepared for our protection."

———

"I believe that the success of the Negro is assured if he pursues and is allowed to pursue the different employments that have led to the success of other citizens in this country. We must have intelligent laborers, farmers and mechanics among colored men. We must have also men learned in law, medicine and theology; in time, men eminent in science and literature."

———

"For a long time it will be the task of the intelligent Negro kindly to point out deficiencies of the race and make helpful suggestions. Our country demands a better Negro. To produce him will require better homes, better schools and better churches."

———

"Get everything that the white man gets, and that he wants. Protect the virtue of deserving females of any race. Have principle and dare defend it. These done and clouds will clear away."

———

"I would suggest that our leading men do less talking on the Negro question as such. Much talking means much concession, and much concession means less opportunity."

———

"More should turn their attention to business and fewer enter the professions of teaching or preaching."

"Those of us who are getting out of the wilderness and mire of ignorance and degradation must help those who will not or cannot help themselves."

"Why should I not be hopeful? The abandonment of the priesthood of a race has always been attended with disasters. Let the Negro stick to his church in the service of God. Be honest, honorable, peaceable, make and save money, educate his children as highly as he can afford to."

"I suggest that religious and educational work should be done on the missionary plan in the lanes and quarters where the lowest and most vicious Negroes live. Negro churches are not practical enough in their work. Religion is too often mistaken for piety. Our educated young people are too high above the masses to help them. Let them personally help in the moral uplift of the criminal classes and especially their children. Industrial training should be advocated for the masses, but higher education should not be discouraged when the means and ability are sufficient."

"I am optimistic in spite of the lowering clouds. We have but recently burst from the storm and are not far enough away from it to become settled. I believe this to be the *Sturm und Drang* period of the Negro's existence. I am aware of the strong arguments against such a position, but in the light of the teaching of history there must be, there is, a turning-point down near the gates of despair, where once the opposing currents are mastered, brighter and better conditions must arise. A better understanding and the practical application of the laws of chastity, morality, Christianity; an ever-increasing acquisition of wealth and practical intelligence; the adoption of principles of courageous manhood; the wholesale banishment of buffoonery and instability; a closer study of those elements that have made the Anglo-Saxon great, and a strong pull, a long pull and a pull individually and collectively towards the acquisition of the same traits, seem to me to be a few of the essential things that may possibly level our barriers.''

———

''As the conditions of American life demand that the Negro shall take an active part in bringing about a change for the better in his situation, there are some things which should engage his most earnest endeavor. I venture to suggest those that now occur to me:

''1. To try and make himself a necessity. Whatsoever his hands find to do, he must do it so well that his services will be indispensable. And he should strive to be a producer as well as a consumer. In order to gain this position let him follow the example of his prosperous Anglo-Saxon brother, namely, of cultivating and applying the resources of his intellect. To this end an opportunity could be afforded by means of the University Extension system, adapted to the peculiar needs and circumstances of the race. The plan should provide for night schools, in which professional men and women can, in their own communities, give their services freely or for a small remuneration.

''2. The practice of thrift and frugality.

''3. The establishing of *real* unity and co-operation of the race.

''4. The making the best use of the opportunities which are *at hand.*''

The literary activity of the college-bred Negro has not been great, but some of it has had considerable importance. Nearly all the larger magazines and reviews have published articles by them, as, for instance, the *Atlantic*, the *Forum*, the *North American Review*, the *Century* and others. They have published a large number of pamphlets, notably those issued by the American Negro Academy, and many religious publications. The *African M. E. Church Review*, a quarterly, has usually been under the management of college

men, and is now. Of the larger publications in book form
these may be noted:

Matthew Anderson: "Presbyterianism and Its Relation
to the Negro."

J. W. E. Bowen: "Africa and the American Negro."

A. O. Coffin: "A Land Without Chimneys."

A. J. Cooper: "A Voice from the South."

W. E. B. Du Bois: "Suppression of Slave Trade." "The
Philadelphia Negro."

F. J. Grimke: "The Negro, His Rights and Wrongs."

A. Grimke: "William L. Garrison" (American Reformers Series). "Charles Sumner" (American Reformers
Series).

J. M. Gregory: "Frederick Douglass."

W. H. Lewis: "A Primer of College Football."

G. W. McClellan: "Poems."

C. W. Mossell: "Toussaint L'Ouverture."

B. F. Ousley: "Gospels and Acts Translated Into African Tongues."

J. H. Paynter: "Joining the Navy."

W. H. Crogman: "Talks for the Times."

A. W. Pegues: "Our Baptist Ministers and Schools."

W. S. Scarborough: "First Greek Lessons." "Birds
of Aristophanes."

L. A. Scruggs: "Afro-American Women of Distinction."

Alexander Crummell: "Africa and America."

J. M. Langston: "From the Virginia Plantation."

D. A. Payne: "History of the A. M. E. Church."

Let us now gather up the scattered threads of this social
study and seek the lesson which the accumulated facts have
to teach. We have learned that there are in the United
States thirty-four institutions designed especially for Negroes, which give collegiate instruction leading to the
bachelor's degree. Besides these, seventy-three other colleges of the land have Negro graduates, so that in all we
have a record of 2,331 Negro graduates of college courses.

24

We have studied these graduates carefully so far as the reports submitted have enabled us to. They are mostly freedmen's sons and grandsons who have gained this training by self-denial and striving. They usually marry between the ages of twenty-five and thirty-five, go to work in the South at teaching, preaching, practicing the professions, or in the civil service or business life. They have accumulated property and usually made good citizens and leaders.

Several questions may now be asked: First—Is the college training of Negroes necessary? Second—If so, how large a proportion of the total expenditure for education ought to be devoted to this training? Third—What curriculum of studies is best suited to young Negroes?

A. Is the college training of Negroes necessary? A few opinions of prominent men in answer to this query are subjoined. They are partly in answer to a circular letter sent to a few college presidents:

I believe not only in common school and industrial education for the Negroes of the South, but also in their higher education. The higher education is necessary to maintain the standards of the lower. Yours truly,

GEORGE E. MacLEAN,

President of the State University of Iowa.

December 11, 1900.

———

I believe fully in the higher education of every man and woman whose character and ability is such as to make such training possible. There are relatively fewer of such persons among the Negroes than among Anglo-Saxons, but for all of these the higher training is just as necessary and just as effective as for anyone else.

For the great body of the Negroes the industrial and moral training already so well given in certain schools seems to me to offer the greatest hope for the future.

Very truly yours,   DAVID S. JORDAN,

President of Leland Stanford Junior University.

December 14, 1900.

Your circular of December 8th comes duly to hand. In response I would say that in my judgment no race or color is entitled to monopolize the benefits of the higher education. If any race is entitled to be specially favored in this respect, I should say it is the one that has by the agency of others been longest deprived thereof.

Yours cordially, WM. F. WARREN,
December 13, 1900. President of Boston University.

In reply to your request of December 5th, I would say that it seems to me that the collegiate or higher education is not a special favor to be granted to men on the ground of race, family, or any such minor consideration. The only condition for the receiving of a college education should be the ability to appreciate and to use it. Human nature is substantially the same everywhere. It should be the glory of our country to afford to all her young men and women who crave the broadest culture and who have the spirit and ability to acquire it, the amplest opportunity for development. Looking at it more specifically, I can see that the general uplifting of our Negro population requires a proper percentage of college-bred Negro leaders.

Yours sincerely, GEORGE C. CHASE,
December 17, 1900 President of Bates College.

You ask for my opinion in regard to the desirableness of higher training for the Negroes. Let me begin my statement by saying that I have the utmost faith in the management of the Atlanta University and several other institutions for the training of Negroes in the South. I will, however, candidly say that in my judgment there are a great many of the Negroes whom it is not worth while to guide through a course of university training. I think that is true also of the white race, but in the present condition it is peculiarly true with regard to colored people. My idea would be that all the training that the colored man is capable of thoroughly mastering should be given him, but that in the higher departments of learning, like political economy and history, the ancient classics and the natural sciences, only selected men should be given the fullest opportunities. I have the strongest confidence that such training as is given at Hampton and at Tuskegee, largely manual and industrial, is of the greatest importance for the Negroes, and is to be the means of fitting the race a generation or two hence, to enter more fully into the more abstract and philosophical studies. I do not know that I have made myself perfectly clear, but in a general way I should say the multiplication of universities of the higher sort is not desirable in comparison with the multiplication of training schools for all the trades and manual activities.

With best wishes, very sincerely yours,

FRANKLIN CARTER,

December 12, 1900. President of Williams College.

———

I believe in the Southern Negro college and the higher education of Negroes. . . . . .

Very truly yours, JOSEPH SWAIN,

President University of Indiana.

December 10, 1900.

———

I am, like many others, greatly interested in the question of education of the Negroes. There seems to me to be a place for the college properly so-called which shall teach a certain number, who may be leaders of their race in the South, as preachers and advanced teachers. At the same time I have much sympathy with Mr. Booker T. Washington's idea, that a large proportion of them should be educated for industrial pursuits. Yours truly,

JAMES B. ANGELL,

December 10, 1900. President University of Michigan.

———

President Charles W. Eliot, of Harvard College, in an address at Trinity Church, Boston, said:

"How, then, are the teachers, the preachers, the physicians for the colored race of the South to be provided, unless the South has institutions of the higher education, serving the Negro, fitting him for these higher positions? We know very well that the Negro, as he rises in the social scale, will live in better houses and follow better trades, and, in general, be industrially and financially elevated.

"But there is another essential thing—namely, that the teachers, preachers, physicians, lawyers, engineers, and superior mechanics, the leaders of industry, throughout the Negro communities of the South, should be trained in superior institutions. If any expect that the Negro teachers of the South can be adequately educated in primary schools or grammar schools or industrial schools pure and simple, I can only say in reply that that is more than we can do at the North with the white race. The only way to have good primary schools and grammar schools in Massachusetts is to have high and normal schools and colleges, in which the higher teachers are trained. It must be so throughout the South: the Negro race needs absolutely these higher facilities of education."

———

President William D. Hyde, of Bowdoin College, in an address at Trinity Church, Boston, said:

"The higher education is the last thing that the individual pupil reaches; it is what he looks toward as the end. But from the point of view of the teachers, from the point of view of the educational system, the higher education is the very source and center and beginning of it all; and if this is wanting the whole must collapse. Take away the higher education and you cannot maintain the level of the lower; it degenerates, it becomes corrupt, and you get nothing but pretentiousness and superficialty as the residuum. In order to maintain the lower education which must be given to the South, you must have a few well-equipped institutions of higher learning."

William T. Harris, United States Commissioner of Education in an address to the students of Atlanta University, said:

"It gives me great pleasure to meet you. I have heard of the great work that this school has done in the higher education of the colored people. I am glad to see you, and congratulate you on the fact of getting higher education. It is good for you to get lower education, and then still better to get higher education. Your people have lived for two or three hundred years in this country, and have learned the methods of white people, and, as I said in Washington, while speaking on this subject, you have the same mind that the white people have. Now, as it is very necessary for white people to study Latin and Greek, so it is very necessary for you. If you lived in Egypt, Abyssinia, or Arabia, it would not be so necessary to study Latin and Greek, but people who live in the United States, France, England, Italy, or Germany, are greatly helped by these studies.

"There are a great many people who think colored people should not have the higher education. Now, I would not discourage the study of mechanics and industrial education, but it is very important to study Greek and Latin. Some people say it is better to know how to work than to study Greek and Latin, because work is practical; but nothing is more practical than getting an insight into the civilization of which we form a part, and into the motives of the people among whom we live.

.   .   .   .

"Now, it is a very necessary thing that the higher education should be opened to every part of the whole community. For the colored people to be self-directing, they must have higher education. They will be appreciated for the good they can do, and will be respected because they are helping the common civilization. We should understand also the art of invention. That is what this Atlanta Exposition is showing. The colored man is not always going to be the

DORMITORY.

CHAPEL.

DINING HALL.

PRESIDENT'S RESIDENCE.

V'RGINIA UNION UNIVERSITY, RICHMOND, VIRGINIA.

person who draws water and cuts wood; he is going to help on with civilization. He is going to be up on all the difficult questions. He is going to study mathematics, sciences and the languages.

.   .   .   .

"And you must not be misled by the opposition to the higher education. But you should uphold it in your homes and among your people until many more are seeking it."

It seems fair to assume, from these and other letters, that the conservative public opinion of the best classes in America believe that there is a distinct place for the Negro college designed to give higher training to the more gifted members of the race; that leaders thus trained are a great necessity in any community and in any group. On the other hand, there is considerable difference of opinion probably as to how large this "Talented Tenth" is—some speaking as though it were a negligible quantity, others as though it might be a very large and important body.

The opinions of some other persons ought perhaps be added to the above. First, there is the almost unbroken line of testimony of the heads of Negro colleges; this is, of course, interested testimony, and yet it is of some value as evidence. A man who left a chair in the University of Michigan to go South and teach Negroes before the war ended, wrote after twenty-five years' experience in college work:

"By this experiment certainly one thing has been settled: the ability of a goodly number of those of the colored race to receive what is called a liberal education.

"The entire work of instruction in the colored public schools of the South is done by colored teachers. These teachers cannot be prepared in the white schools and colleges of the South. Where, then, shall they be prepared, if not in special higher institutions of learning open to them? What is to become of the millions of colored people in the United States? Who are to be their leaders? Doubtless persons of their own race. Do they need less preparation for their calling than do members of the white race for theirs? Is not their task even more difficult? Have they not questions of greater intricacy to solve? Did not Moses, when leading ex-slaves out of Egypt, need special wisdom? Are not the colored people of today 'perishing for lack of knowledge?'

"But the objector will say, Why have these long courses, these colleges for colored people? Would not shorter courses be as well, or even better? The following is my belief on this point, after twenty-five years of thought and experience: If the Negro is equal to the white man in heredity and environment, he needs an equal chance in education; if he is superior, he can get on with less; if he is inferior, he needs more. The education required is not simply that of books, but of life in Christian homes, such as are supplied in nearly all our missionary schools for that people, and of religion through the Christian Church and its influences."

The president of another Negro college said:

"To imagine that the Negro can safely do without any of the institutions or instrumentalities which were essential to our own advancement, is to assume that the Negro is superior to the white man in mental capacity. To deprive him of any of these advantages, which he is capable of using, would be to defraud ourselves, as a nation and a Christian Church, of all the added power which his developed manhood should bring to us. It does not seem to be necessary in this audience to discuss the proposition that intelligence is power, and that the only road to intelligence is through mental discipline conducted under moral influences."

These two extracts sufficiently represent the almost unanimous opinion of the presidents and teachers in Negro colleges, that this training is a success and necessity.

From a careful consideration of the facts, and of such testimony as has been given, the following propositions seem clear:

1. The great mass of the Negroes needs common school and manual training.

2. There is a large and growing demand for industrial and technical training, and trade schools.

3. There is a distinct demand for the higher training of persons selected for talent and character to be leaders of thought and missionaries of culture among the masses.

4. To supply this demand for a higher training there ought to be maintained several Negro colleges in the South.

5. The aim of these colleges should be to supply thoroughly trained teachers, preachers, professional men and captains of industry.

Finally we come to the query:

What curriculum of college studies is best suited to young Negroes?

Little careful work has been done in the direction of ascertaining what improvements in the Negro college course are needed. Nor is this strange; so much time and energy is consumed in collecting funds and defending principles that there is little leisure left presidents for internal adjustment and development. The exposition and comparison of college courses made elsewhere in this book, show obvious faults. The older New England college curriculum of forty years ago still holds in the Southern institutions with little change. This should be remedied. A large place should be made for English, history and natural science in most curricula at the expense of some other studies. Various other changes might obviously be made. All this work can easily be done when the existence problem of these struggling institutions is nearer solution.

The central truth which this study teaches to the candid mind is the success of higher education under the limitations and difficulties of the past. To be sure, that training can be criticised justly on many points. Its curriculum was not the best; many persons of slight ability were urged to study algebra before they had mastered arithmetic, or German before they knew English; quantity rather than quality was in some cases sought in the graduates, and, above all, there was a tendency to urge men into the professions, particularly the ministry, and to overlook business and the mechanical trades. All these charges brought against the higher training of Negroes in the past, have much of truth in them. The defects lay in the application of the principle, not in the principle; in poor teaching and studying rather than in lack of need for college-trained men. Courses need to be changed and improved, teachers need to be better equipped, students need more careful sifting. With such reform there can be no reasonable doubt of the continued and growing need for a training of Negro youth, the chief aim of which is culture rather than bread-winning. Nor does this plain demand have anything in it of opposition or antagonism to industrial training—to those schools which aim directly at teaching the Negro to work with his own hands. Quite the contrary is the case, and it is indeed unfortunate that the often intemperate and exaggerated utterances of some advocates of Negro education have led the public mind to conceive of the two kinds of education as opposed to each other. They are rather supplementary and mutually helpful in the great end of solving the Negro problem. We need thrift and skill among the masses, we need thought and culture among the leaders. As the editor has had occasion to say before:

"In a scheme such as I have outlined, providing the rudiments of an education for all, industrial training for the many and a college course for the talented few, I fail to see anything contradictory or antagonistic. I yield to no one in advocacy of the recently popularized notion of Negro industrial training, nor in admiration for the earnest men who emphasize it. At the same time, I insist that its widest realization will but increase the demand for college-bred men —for thinkers to guide the workers. Indeed, all who are working for the uplifting of the American Negro have little need of disagreement if they but remember this fundamental and unchangeable truth: *The object of all true education is not to make men carpenters—it is to make carpenters men.*"

25

M. W. GIBBS.
Ex-United States Consul to Tamatave, Madagascar.

CHAPTER XIV.

HISTORY OF SOME NEGRO UNIVERSITIES.

THERE are now in the United States nearly forty institutions designed especially for the higher education of the Negro race—giving them college and university training. We give the history of three old and prominent ones, to indicate how promptly the country acted after the close of the war to provide facilities for the thorough education of a generation of colored people who were now to take upon themselves, for the first time in the history of their race, the duties and responsibilities of citizenship. How promptly they availed themselves of the opportunities offered them may be gathered by a study of the book of which this chapter forms a part.

I. SHAW UNIVERSITY.

President Charles F. Meserve gives the following account of the rise, progress and work of this school:

Shaw University—named in honor of the late Elijah Shaw, of Wales, Massachusetts, is situated in Raleigh, the capital city of North Carolina. It has a beautiful location, within the city limits, and is only a few minutes' walk from the Union Station, the Capitol, and the United States Government Building.

Although within the city limits, it has an entire square to itself, and is as quiet and secluded as if it were situated miles away in the country. This quiet and seclusion, together with a bountiful supply of pure water, perfect sanitation and sewerage and other city advantages, make Shaw well-nigh an ideal place for study. Its grounds are spacious and well kept, and its principal buildings large, imposing brick structures. Its buildings (eleven in number) and grounds are the most attractive feature in the southern part of the city.

This institution was started in a very humble way in a
Negro cabin on the outskirts of the city in the year 1865, by
Rev. Henry Martin Tupper, an ex-Union soldier and a native
of Monson, Massachusetts. The enterprise grew on his
hands, and a larger building became necessary, but there was
little money either for carrying on or extending the work.
Accordingly, with a few faithful helpers, day after day, he
shouldered his axe and went out of the city into the woods,
and together they felled huge yellow pines and hewed the
logs into timber. After many weeks of struggling, and after
receiving a little help from the North, the actual work of
building began. A large two-story structure, to be used both
for a church and a school, was finally erected on Blount
street, a block north of the present location of the university.

The work continued to grow, and again larger quarters
were required. At this juncture the mansion and grounds
of the late General Barringer, ex-minister to Spain, were for
sale. This property, comprising several buildings and twelve
acres of land, and occupying an entire square, was purchased,
and then began the great expansion that has made the institution what it is today. Shaw was incorporated in 1875.
At that time the work was more elementary than now, but
such as was adapted to the needs of the people. The management, however, has kept pace constantly with the progress of the race and the demands of the times, until there are
today, in addition to normal, college, missionary training,
and industrial departments, schools of law, medicine and
pharmacy.

The blessing that Shaw has been to the colored race can
hardly be estimated. Thousands of young men and women
have gone forth from her walls into positions of usefulness
and influence. They are found in nearly every State and
Territory of the Union, though naturally the largest numbers
are found in the South. They are making their way in
every walk in life, and the majority of them are the substantial, influential leaders of the race. In the teaching pro-

JOHN R. LYNCH.
Paymaster in United States Army.

fession they have made themselves particularly felt. At one time five of the seven colored normal schools of the State were presided over by principals who received their education at Shaw University. Dr. J. O. Crosby, for some years president of the State Agricultural and Mechanical College for Colored Young Men and Women; Dr. E. E. Smith, ex-minister to Liberia; Hon. H. P. Cheatham, for several years a member of Congress, and at present recorder of deeds of the District of Columbia, as well as several of the professors at Shaw, are Shaw men.

The Third North Carolina Regiment of United States Infantry is composed of colored men, and Shaw figures prominently in this regiment. Col. James H. Young, Adjutant E. E. Smith, Chief Surgeon J. E. Dellinger, Assistant Surgeons M. T. Pope and M. W. Alston, Captains J. J. Hood and J. T. York, and other officers and many in the ranks are graduates or former students of Shaw. The chief surgeon and his assistants and Captain Hood are graduates of the medical department.

Graduates of the law department go into court and plead their cases with the same courteous treatment from judge and jury as is accorded to white members of the bar.

Success has also been won by the graduates in medicine and pharmacy, and they are found very generally throughout the Southland. A graduate in pharmacy, A. W. Benson, of Atlanta, class of '95, was the first colored man to obtain a license from the Virginia Board of Examiners. His standing in examination was slightly in excess of 95 per cent. The first man of any race to receive 100 per cent. in an examination before the Virginia Board of Medical Examiners was C. R. Alexander, of Lynchburg, class of 1891, who practiced medicine for several years in Petersburg, Virginia, and had the respect and confidence of the community. He is at present chief surgeon of the Sixth Regiment of United States Infantry from Virginia.

A goodly number of our young men, as has been the case

from the founding of the institution, are studying for the ministry. Shaw has furnished nearly all of the denominational leaders in North Carolina and many in other States. In the gospel ministry her greatest influence has been exerted, for her theological department has always been well attended, and the minister is still the influential factor in directing the life of the great masses of colored people in every community.

Many of her former students are thrifty farmers, successful business men, and occupy positions of honor and trust in their respective counties. The aim of the institution, from the very beginning, has been to turn out well-equipped Christian men and women who shall be leaders in the best sense of the term, and thus, indirectly, but effectually, reach the masses of the people. This has been done with signal and gratifying success.

Shaw believes in co-education. Men and women meet in the class-room, in the chapel and around the family board, on terms of equality. The women's department is known as Estey Seminary. Estey Hall, the gift of the late Deacon Estey, of Brattleboro, Vermont, is said to be the first building ever erected for the education of colored women. It was predicted that co-education would be a dismal and disgusting failure, but it should be said to the great credit of the race that there never has been a scandal connected with the institution.

The influence exerted by Shaw is well-nigh world-wide. At the present time she has students from the West Indies and Africa, and has enrolled them from Central and South America. Although a Home Mission School, her spirit reaches out to other lands. Missionary Hayes, the well-known African missionary, was a Shaw student. Dr. Lulu C. Fleming and four others from Shaw are in missionary work on the Congo.

It is worthy of note that Shaw men and women do **not** become criminals, and seldom, if ever, do educated colored

25

young men and women belong to the criminal or lawless
classes.   Rather are they conservators of law and order and
preservers of the peace.   Our students and graduates are, as
a rule, Christian men and women of clean lives, and some of
them are earnest workers in the cause of temperance and social
purity.

N. F. ROBERTS, D. D.

N. F. Roberts, D. D., was born in Seaboard, North Carolina, October 13, 1849.   He spent his early years upon a

N. F. ROBERTS, D. D.
Vice-President Shaw University.

farm.   He evinced very early an eager desire for knowledge,
and showed especial liking for mathematics, being considered
a genius in his neighborhood.   In October, 1871, he entered
Shaw University, graduating in 1878.   On graduation he
was made professor of mathematics in the university, a position which he still holds.   He is also vice-president of the
institution.   He has served as pastor of different churches;
for many years has been president of the Baptist State

Sunday-school Convention; has been corresponding secretary and the president of the Baptist State Convention, and has done considerable editorial work. He is business manager of the *Baptist Sentinel*

A. W. PEGUES, PH. D.

A. W. Pegues, Ph. D., was born of slave parents in 1859, near Cheraw, South Carolina. During the winter of 1866–7, he spent a few months in the school-room, but on the death

A. W. PEGUES, PH. D.

of his father was obliged to return to work on the farm. At the age of eleven years he was thrown upon his own resources. For four months in each of the years of 1871–2–3 he walked three miles to attend night school. In 1876 he entered Benedict Institute at Columbia, South Carolina. In 1879 he entered Richmond Theological Seminary, from which he graduated as class valedictorian in 1882. He then spent two years in Bucknell University, meanwhile supplying the church at Williamsport, Pennsylvania. Three years later he received from the university the degree of Ph. D. In 1894 and 1895 he was Sunday-school missionary for North Carolina; he then served for three years as supervisor of the Colored Institution for the Deaf, Dumb and Blind. In 1897 he accepted the position of dean of the theological department of Shaw University.

GRACE J. THOMPSON

Grace J. Thompson says of herself: "I was born in Darlington, South Carolina, January 25, 1875. My parents were not educated, and lived in an humble way all through

GRACE J. THOMPSON.

my early years; my mother, assisted by the smaller children, gave her time to sewing and laundry work as means of support, and my three older brothers, who took the responsibilities of a father, devoted theirs to trades. My father died in my twelfth year. Because of these things, and because of the poor school system of Darlington, the educational advantages offered were poor until 1889, at which time the system was revised.

"From the Mayo graded school I graduated in 1894. Having finished from this school, I attempted to teach; but as I lacked the training which I did not get from the public school, my attempt was a complete failure. The following fall I went to Shaw University, where I remained four years, graduating in 1897. In September, 1898, I came to Little Rock, Arkansas, as a teacher in the Arkansas Baptist College."

II. ROGER WILLIAMS UNIVERSITY.

Roger Williams University was founded in the city of Nashville, in 1864, by Rev. D. W. Phillips, D. D., a Baptist minister who came here from New England. Its beginning was small. At first Doctor Phillips taught a class of colored men at his own home. Later he secured a room in the basement of the Spruce Street Colored Baptist Church. In 1865 he had formulated his plan for a school, so he went north and raised money enough among the philanthropic white people to purchase a site and erect a wooden building. This building is now the Thirteenth District Colored School, of Nashville. In it Dr. Phillips maintained the school until 1873, when, by the munificent bequest of Nathan Bishop, of New York, the Baptist Home Missionary Society was enabled to purchase the present beautiful plot of thirty acres of land on the Hillsboro pike, opposite Garland avenue, and erect a building costing fifty thousand dollars, now used for dormitory, recitation rooms and chapel. When the property was bought there was a residence on it. This has been enlarged and is the dormitory for young ladies. Since the purchase of the present site two more buildings have been added—Hayward Hall and the president's mansion. All these buildings are of brick. The property is valued at $150,000. The faculty numbers fourteen persons—eleven white and three colored.

The purpose of this institution of learning at first was to train colored people in the rudiments of an education and to fit them to become teachers and ministers of the gospel.

This purpose has not been departed from, but along with that have developed normal, academic and collegiate courses, and a large number of students have been graduated with the degree of B. S. and A. B. The courses are being broadened and strengthened each year. The English branches are being taught with as much care and skill as formerly, and the Bible has the same place of importance, but collegiate training and instruction in music are receiving increased emphasis. In addition to this instruction, special care is

PRESIDENT'S HOUSE, ROGER WILLIAMS UNIVERSITY, NASHVILLE, TENNESSEE.

given to teaching the young ladies to improve along domestic lines. To this end, dressmaking is taught by a professional dressmaker, and constant instruction in deportment, hygiene and general household economy is given.

Although this institution is under the control of the Baptist Home Missionary Society, and is, therefore, classed among sectarian institutions of learning, the most liberal spirit prevails, and nothing is said or done to alter the denominational views of any student. With this in view, it

MAIN BUILDING ROGER WILLIAMS UNIVERSITY, NASHVILLE, TENNESSEE.

has been the policy of the school to have no college church, but to allow and urge every student to attend a city church of his or her own denomination.

The general policy of the institution may be gathered from the following extract:

"In supplying educated men for the pulpits and trained teachers for the public schools, this institution claims to be contributing in the largest possible way to the general up-

HAYWARD HALL, ROGER WILLIAMS UNIVERSITY, NASHVILLE, TENNESSEE.

lifting of the people; and in sending into the various communities of this and adjoining States educated lawyers, doctors, farmers and business men, and into the homes of such communities intelligent and consecrated wives and mothers, it claims to be inspiring in the young and the less fortunate portions of the community that respect for education and that desire to possess it without which even the common school cannot be largely influential or successful."

NATIONAL BAPTIST PUBLISHING BOARD.

Probably the most complete publishing plant carried on and controlled by Negroes in the United States is the National Baptist Publishing Board. This institution was created by a resolution passed by the National Baptist Convention in 1896. Its growth has been phenomenal and has increased each succeeding year, as the following figures will show: The grand total of periodicals published in 1897 was 746,500; in 1899, 4,695,950. In 1897 total orders filled were 5,764; in 1899, 22,245. In 1897 the total amount of money collected was $5,864.29; in 1899, $31,683.22. This house publishes not only Sunday-school magazines and pamphlets, but carries on regular book making, such as Bibles, song books and other hard cloth and morocco bindings, and besides does regular book and job printing.

Seventy skilled laborers are kept regularly employed in this institution. The machinery, appliances, etc., are of the best.

The institution is under the control of the National Baptist Convention.

Nine grades of periodicals and eleven books are published regularly as denominational literature for the benefit of Baptist Sunday-schools.

MEHARRY MEDICAL COLLEGE.

The Meharry Medical College was organized in 1876 as the medical department of Central Tennessee College, Nashville, Tennessee, and was the first medical school opened in the Southern States for the education of colored physicians. It takes its name from the generous and philanthropic family who so liberally contributed toward its establishment and support.

Since its organization in 1876, several hundred students have completed their medical course of study and received the degree of M. D. The greater portion of this number are now practicing their profession in the Southern and

Southwestern States. They have uniformly been treated with kindness and consideration by the white physicians of the South, who have consulted with them in dangerous cases and assisted in difficult operations in surgery.

Nearly 90 per cent. of the graduates have been members of some Christian Church, and over 10 per cent. had received a collegiate education before taking the study of medicine. They have made a good record in passing the required county, district and State examining boards, and very few failures have occurred.

Five of the alumni have served on the United States pension examining boards. A large proportion of the alumni have purchased homes of their own, and their professional income is probably greater than that of any other class of colored citizens.

CHARLES SPENCER DINKINS, D. D.

Charles Spencer Dinkins, D. D., was born September 15, 1856, at Canton, Mississippi. He was converted in 1868. In June, 1870, he entered Roger Williams University at Nashville, Tennessee, graduating therefrom in 1877 as valedictorian of his class. His pastor, Rev. Jordan Williams, and the church at Canton gave him financial aid. During his period of study he taught public school during vacations. After pursuing a post-graduate course of one year at Roger Williams he entered Newton Theological Institution in 1878, and graduated in 1881. He received the degree of D. D. from the State University at Louisville, Kentucky, in 1890. After serving as pastor and teacher in Alabama for about fifteen years, he became (1893) president of the Alabama Baptist Colored University at Selma

MRS. DAISY MILLER HARVEY.

Mrs. Harvey was born in Mississippi, but reared in Memphis, Tennessee, where she attended the public schools and later Le Mayne Institute. In September, 1877, she entered the Roger Williams University, and was graduated from the normal course in 1879. She began at once to teach, and, with the exception of one year, has been engaged in educational work continuously for the past nineteen years. In 1885, she was appointed by the Women's Baptist Educational Society as their missionary. She says: "I traveled throughout the State of Kentucky from east to west and from north to south, visiting churches, organizing mission-

MRS. DAISY MILLER HARVEY.

ary bands, making special talks to the young people, visiting the homes, and helping when I could to encourage the women to live pure, clean lives, and to make their homes all they ought to be—types of the heavenly home." In 1884, Mrs. Harvey began a movement which has resulted in the establishment of the Colored Orphans' and Old Ladies' Home. Since 1896 Mrs. Harvey has been matron in Bishop College, Marshall, Texas.

JOHN HOPE.

John Hope was born in Augusta, Georgia, June, 1868. Losing his father at the early age of eight years he was thrown chiefly upon his own resources. After leaving the public schools of Augusta at thirteen years of age, he spent five or six years in work. After his conversion at eighteen, in 1886, he entered the Academy of Worcester, Massachusetts, where he spent four years, graduating in 1890—the last two years

JOHN HOPE.

supporting himself entirely by his own labor. While at the academy he had valuable experience as business manager, associate editor and editor-in-chief of the school paper. He was the historian of his class.

In 1890 he entered Brown University, graduating with the honor of class orator in 1894. He supported himself while in college by doing chores and by newspaper work, being the university correspondent for the New York

Tribune. After teaching four years in Roger Williams University he was transferred to Atlanta Baptist College. Since graduating at Brown he has spent two summer seasons in post-graduate study in the University of Chicago.

JOSEPH A. BOOKER, D. D.

President Booker was born in Ashley county, Arkansas, December 26, 1859. His parents having died while he was

JOSEPH A. BOOKER, D. D.
President of Arkansas Baptist College.

yet a child, his guardian gave him the opportunity of irregularly attending country schools for a number of years; after having spent three years in the Normal School at Pine Bluff, he entered Roger Williams University in 1881 and graduated in 1886. Having served as State missionary, in association with Rev. Harry Woodsmall, he became, in 1887, principal of the Negro school at Little Rock. He says: "I am a firm believer in the self-exertion of the Negro, for it is to this end that he is being educated. But I am just as firm a believer in co-operation between the Negroes and the white people."

Mrs. Maria Talley Kenney was born in Shelbyville, Tennessee. Her parents, though not "educated," were industrious, ambitious Christian people, who took the keenest interest in the education and general advancement of their children. Maria entered Roger Williams University at a

MRS. MARIA T. KENNEY.

somewhat early age, and graduated from the college department in 1887. She taught school during vacations. When teaching near her home she very often did the family washing and sewing, taught music and sewed at night for friends to make "extra" money. While teaching she boarded with a woman who took in washing, and Maria ironed evenings, and thus secured money enough to buy all her clothing. The money she received for teaching went to make the first payment on the little farm her father had bought.

Since her graduation Mrs. Kenney has taught in the public schools of Tennessee; on the faculty of Natchez College, Natchez, Mississippi; Roger Williams University, Nashville, Tennessee; Howe Institute, Memphis, and Arkansas Baptist College, Little Rock, Arkansas.

III. HOWARD UNIVERSITY.

Howard University was established at Washington, District of Columbia, just after the close of the war, when the interest excited in philanthropists and statesmen by the abolition of slavery was at its height.

During and immediately after the war many thousands of freedmen made their way to Washington. Since that time the Negro has composed one-third of the population of that city. This influx of Negro population made it necessary that steps be immediately taken to provide for the education of both children and adults. Day schools were promptly provided by the aid of the various freedmen's organizations. After this was done, and it was reasonably certain that primary education would be provided, thoughtful men began to look toward measures for securing also a higher education for a portion of the colored people. The First Congregational church in Washington had been recently organized, and on November 20, 1866, Mr. Henry A. Brewster, one of the members of that church, gathered eight or ten friends at his house to take steps in this direction. The enterprise rapidly took shape, a board of trustees was elected, and on January 18, 1867, the title of Howard University was given to the new institution in honor of Major-General Oliver O. Howard, who was at that time commissioner of the Freedmen's Bureau.

Application was made to Congress for a charter under which to organize the university, which was promptly granted. This act of incorporation expressly provided that the university should make no distinction between whites and blacks as it was not intended to make it a distinctively colored institu-

tion. The university was, therefore, formed on broad lines,
the promoters believing that the idea of color should not enter
at all into the question of education.

The charter did not contain the word "Negro," or "black,"
or "colored," or "African," but simply provided for the establishment of a university for the education of youth in the liberal arts and sciences. While, however, the direct intention
was to make provision for the higher education of the Negro
race, it was not intended to shut out any race or color. As
a matter of fact, the institution has had, besides Negro students, Indians, Chinese, Japanese, various European nationalities, and white stu-
dents from both the
Northern and Southern
States. These students
have been found in all
departments of the uni-
versity, but especially in
the medical school.
Among these there was a
white student who had
carried off the valedictory
honors at Harvard, and

HOWARD UNIVERSITY.

afterward entered the theological department at Howard.
The university is open to students from all parts of the
United States or the world, and to all races of men; also to
both sexes.

In religion the university is undenominational and no discrimination has been made in the interest of any of the great
religious bodies. The men who first started the work were,
for the most part, Congregationalists and Presbyterians, but
the board of trustees has embraced Methodists, Baptists,
Episcopalians and Unitarians, and all of these denominations
have had representatives among the teachers and professors,
as have also the Lutherans, Roman Catholics and the Re-
formed Church.

The university is located in a commanding position on the line of hills in the northern part of the city of Washington, overlooking the city and much of the surrounding country, with a splendid view of the two branches of the Potomac, as well as the main river. The site originally contained one hundred and fifty acres of what was known as "Effingham." The purchase price was $140,500 and the money was obtained mainly from the Freedmen's Bureau, and later repaid by the university from the proceeds of the sales of land not needed for university purposes.

After the site had been selected it became a serious question as to how the necessary buildings were to be secured. The founders were mostly poor men, but they were enthusiastic and had faith in the accomplishment of the objects for which they were working. The way was opened as follows: General Howard as the head of the Bureau of Refugees, Freedmen and Abandoned Lands had disbursed in various ways large sums of money for the establishment and maintenance of all grades of schools throughout the Southern States, and had offered to erect buildings for a certain denominational colored institution in the District of Columbia, on condition that it should become undenominational, but the offer was declined. The trustees of Howard University, learning of this fact, made application, as an undenominational institution, to receive this aid. In this way there was secured something more than $500,000, which went principally into lands and buildings. With this money there were erected, according to plans drawn up by Henry R. Searle, architect, four large edifices, viz.: the main University Building, Miner Hall, Clark Hall, and the Medical College, also several houses for the professors.

For three or four years all seemed to go well. Grounds and buildings had been furnished and leading philanthropists had contributed liberally to the maintenance of the institution. Such men as Hon. Gerritt Smith, of New York; John Taylor, of London and David Clarke, of Hartford, Connect-

26

icut, made liberal donations; the British Freedmen's Aid
Commission also contributed; and the generous public, when
appealed to, responded favorably.

Encouraged by the success of their plans the trustees
began to open the numerous departments in rapid succession,
paid high salaries, and made lavish expenditures in every

WM. H. H. HART.
Instructor in Agriculture, Howard University.

direction. In the early seventies, however, it was found
necessary to retrench, and the efforts in this direction were
so successful that while the expenses in 1872 amounted to
$87,000, in 1877 they amounted to only $16,000. This re-
duction in expenses was not accomplished, however, without
considerable loss to the institution in the way of professors,

students and prestige. Since 1877 the condition of the institution has steadily improved. In 1879 Congress appropriated $10,000 for current expenses, and since that time an annual appropriation has been made, which has increased to more than double that for 1879. At the present time the university holds improved real estate from which rents are derived, and various unimproved land which can be made to produce revenue. The present holdings of the university are upwards of $1,000,000.

Among the various departments of the university are the Normal and Preparatory departments, College department, Theological department, Medical department, Law department, Musical department and the Industrial department. Of these the Medical department deserves especial notice. It has three divisions, namely, Medicine, Pharmacy and Dentistry, with an able faculty in each. This department is always full, and white and Negro students are about equally divided.

The Industrial department has a shop 75x40 feet in which there is a Carpenter shop, Printing office, and Shoemaking and Tailoring rooms, and an Iron and Tin shop in the basement. There are also sewing rooms for the girls in Miner Hall, and type-writing is taught in the main building. All students in the Normal and Preparatory departments are required to attend, at certain hours, in the Industrial department for three years, and all other students are encouraged to attend. In this department the carpenters work from plans drawn in the school, and the *University Record* is set up and printed on the premises. The carpenter shop is equipped with the most modern appliances, the printing office with a good outfit of newspaper and job type and one Gordon press. The tin shop is also well fitted with machinery and tools. The sewing class is taught plain sewing both by hand and by machine, also dress cutting and fitting. There is a cooking class and a book-bindery.

The professors have usually been white, although quite a

large number of colored instructors have been employed from time to time. The first dean of the theological department was a Negro, and there is also a Negro in the faculty of that department at the present time. There are also Negro instructors in the law and medical departments, and in the college and normal courses the majority of instructors are colored.

The university has also a well-furnished chemical laboratory, and also a laboratory for work in biology, botany and every branch of natural science, which is connected with the museum, and contains a valuable mineralogical cabinet and botanical collection.

About three thousand students have been graduated from the various departments. While some of them have proved failures, as could only be expected, most of them have done creditable work and stand high among their people. Among the graduates has been a United States minister to Liberia, a district attorney of Norfolk, Virginia, and a member of Congress.

It is, of course, impossible in the space at our disposal to give a review of the work of the university. The work done has been in the direction of training Negro youths in the ways in which they most need training. While some people have contended that higher education of the Negro is a mistake, it is quite evident that in the case of the Negro, as in the case of other races, the lower education of the masses depends upon the higher.

The race needs preachers and teachers—leaders who can show them the way to better methods of living and lead their thoughts in the way of modern ideas, elevate their ideals and improve them morally, intellectually and industrially. The leaders of the past have been ignorant, and often immoral. They have gained a hold on their people and left their impressions upon them; but in many cases their influence has not been altogether good. Even men like the Rev. John Jasper, who were morally above reproach, led the thoughts of those who followed them towards the prejudices of ignorance rather than that broad-minded view of life which is the best thing in our modern civilization. It is important that these old leaders should be replaced by a new class—preachers who practice as well as preach, and teachers who can instill into their pupils, not only the ordinary information usually imparted in primary and grammar schools, but also those ideals and ambitions for a better life which the race must have in order to make the most of itself. The importance of replacing the old-time leaders with the new will be readily appreciated, and it has been the aim of Howard University to supply such leaders.

J. WESLEY HOFFMAN.

George R. Smith College, Sedalia, Missouri,

CHAPTER XV.

SOME NOTABLE EDUCATORS OTHER THAN THOSE AL-
READY NAMED, WITH NOTICE OF THE SCHOOLS
WITH WHICH THEY HAVE BEEN
CONNECTED.

JOHN WESLEY HOFFMAN.

A MONG the many colored men of America who have won a prominent place in the field of science, no one has achieved greater fame than the subject of this sketch—John Wesley Hoffman, Ph. D. An honor to himself and to his race, it is with special pride that the Afro-Americans of the United States can point to him as one of their own race, and pay homage to him in recognition of the honors that have been given him. Formerly professor of agriculture in the State College of Florida, he now occupies the chair of chemistry, biology and agriculture in the Geo. R. Smith College, Sedalia, Missouri.

His special work along the line of chemistry and agricultural biology has placed him in the very front rank of science, and today he is the leading Negro scientist of the world.

He was born in Charleston, South Carolina, receiving his early education in his native city. He went north and pursued his studies at Howard University, Washingto District of Columbia; Michigan Agricultural College, Lansing, Michigan and Albion College, Albion, Michigan. He has also pursued special studies at Harvard University and Sumner Scientific School in organic chemistry; Cornell University summer course in biology and nature study; Marine School of Biology at Wood's Hole, Massachusetts, in embryology and bacteriology. At the Agassiz Scientific Institute at Cottage,

Massachusetts, a few years ago, he attracted the attention of the most noted men of science in America and Europe, by his thorough knowledge of the marine plants known as the Algæ. He has made a special study of butter and cheese-making and dairy bacteriology at the well-known Ontario Agricultural College at Guelph, Ontario, Canada.

He has occupied chairs in some of the leading colored colleges of the country—State University, of Louisville, Kentucky; Tuskegee Institute, of Alabama; State Colored College of South Carolina, and Florida State Industrial College. In all these institutions he has won fame for himself. As an instructor, he imparts his knowledge to his pupils with enthusiasm and ease. He is blessed with a kind, magnetic, sympathetic and charming disposition, a most striking and pleasing personality, that endears him to his pupils and renders him a most admirable companion and friend and popular instructor. Quiet and unassuming in manners, chaste and cautious in speech, he at once becomes much admired by all with whom he comes in contact. He is highly respected for his counsel, and is popular with his associates in the faculty.

Since coming to Geo. R. Smith College, Professor Hoffman has awakened a new and lively interest in the department of science, has organized a scientific club (The Pasteur), of which he is the president. The students are manifesting a decided interest in the department, which is indeed gratifying to him, and is another proof that even his beginnings are brilliant and his success limitless. He is by no means a mere recluse, but is eminently practical in his work, and uses his great scientific information to effect immediate results in ameliorating the condition of his people. Among some of his many achievements may be mentioned the fact that he was the first Negro to introduce the science of dairying and the latest scientific butter making among his people in the South. He travels extensively, visiting dairy factories and scientific schools in the United States, Canada and

Europe; is constantly on the lookout for new and improved methods, thus opening up a new industry to the colored youths and assisting them in a practical way to better their condition. Among the young people of the South he has been an inspiration, and has caused them to take a new interest in dairying and agriculture.

The "Hoffman improved seedling strawberry" is the name of a new variety of strawberry that he contributed to the science of agriculture a few years ago. The *St. Louis Journal of Agriculture* mentions it as "one of the finest in the South." It is cultivated from New Jersey to Florida and on the Pacific Coast.

He is a member of the Massachusetts Horticultural Society, having been elected a member of that body in recognition of the great work he is doing for the practical scientific culture of the Negro race, and for being the producer of the new variety of strawberry. He was appointed by the United States Department of Agriculture to make a dietary study of the kind, quality and quantity of food used by the Negroes of the "Black Belt" of Alabama, while a professor at Tuskegee Institute. Much scientific labor was expended in performing this arduous task, but the work was accomplished in such a very creditable manner that his investigations were published by the Department of Agriculture, and are considered invaluable in the dietetic study of the different races of the world. It is very gratifying to know that physiologists have the use of that report, as it has been translated into many languages.

Professor Hoffman has had occasion to deliver addresses before many scientific societies both in the United States and Canada. He is honored by membership in more scientific associations than any other living Negro. Among them, in this country and abroad, the following may be mentioned: American Society of Naturalists, Boston Society of Natural History, Torrey Botanical Club of Columbia University, New York City, American Association for the Advancement of Science, Boston Mycological Society, American Geographical Society, Royal Society of Biology of Berlin, Societè Royale de Zoologique of Antwerp, Fellow of the Royal Agricultural Society of England.

He is a member of the New York Zoological Society, of which Hon. Levi P. Morton is president, and such men as Andrew Carnegie, Morris K. Jessup, the railroad magnate, and Hon. Seth Low are members. He is also a member of the New York Botanical Garden at Bronx Park, New York City, of which Hon. J. Pierpont Morgan is the honored president. A few years ago the presidency of the Monrovia College, West Coast of Africa, was offered to him.

It is very evident that his work is being more appreciated by his own people, for continually he receives many fine inducements to accept a chair in the faculty of the leading Negro colleges of the South. He has chosen the South for his field of labor because of the magnificent opportunity to develop the agricultural resources of that section, if the science of agriculture is properly taught to those whose life-work it will be to make that country what it is possible to make it. He comes in direct touch with the farmers of the South, for a part of each vacation is spent in holding farmers' institutes in different parts of the South, giving them such practical and helpful advice that he has inspired them to do better work.

Farmers' clubs have been organized; they subscribe to agricultural journals; they are buying their lands, doing more extensive and diversified farming, and they are putting forth greater efforts for their improvement, due to his labors. Appreciation of the work that Professor Hoffman is doing among his people is not confined to his own race, but North and South he has been favorably commended by the American press for the efforts he has made and is still making for the elevation of his people. His talks on practical agriculture are published in the leading daily papers of the South, and the white and colored people alike read his sound advice. Among others in late years he has conducted a very interesting experiment in Florida. He has grown at Talla-hassee, Florida, from tea seed imported from Japan and India, a very excellent plant. He has therefore demonstrated that tea can be grown in the South, and especially in Florida.

He is anxious to get his people interested in this new agricultural industry. A grade of tea could be grown in the South that would be superior in every way to the tea imported from China and Japan, and a better price would be obtained for it. He is anxious to have every farmer's wife and daughter grow a little plat of tea in which event a small curing house could be established for drying and curing the tea at some central point in each county, just as cotton gins are established in the South for cleaning the cotton. By this plan tea growers could pay the curing houses so much for curing the tea or could sell them the tea leaves in bulk.

Appreciation of Professor Hoffman's great work will grow with the enlightenment of the race and with the growth of liberal sentiment among the people of other races. He has proved himself equal to the most exacting demands upon his intellectual resources, and has demonstrated that he is no dreamer. No opportunity for advancement will pass him unnoticed.

The youth who falters by the wayside to complain of "no chance" will look to this brilliant young scientist and find a light and an inspiration that cannot but restore his courage and bring to his soul the conquering power of Professor Hoffman's practical philosophy. The place that the professor occupies in the educational and scientific world plainly proves that color is no bar to success. His life should be an incentive to every young Negro, who by emulating his example may lift himself and his race to better things.

J. D. COLEMAN.

J. D. Coleman was born in Halifax county, Virginia, April 24, 1863. He spent the first fourteen years of his life upon the farm, attending school meanwhile for the period of seven months. At twenty-one years of age, having enjoyed ten months' schooling, and with a few dollars saved from labor at $10 a month, he entered Wayland Seminary, and completed the normal course. After teaching in the public schools of Virginia two years, he was appointed to his present position as teacher in Wayland College.

C. S. BROWN, D. D.

C. S. Brown was born of slave parents, March 23, 1859, in Salisbury, North Carolina. For a number of years he at-

C. S. BROWN, D. D.

tended the Freedmen's School in his native town, but at sixteen years of age, on the death of his father, he was forced to work on the farm and in the brick-yard to assist his mother in the support of the family. In 1880 he entered Shaw University, completing the course in 1886, as valedictorian of his class,

Mr. Brown has served for several years as president of the North Carolina Baptist State Convention, and also as secretary of the convention; was the first general missionary for the State under the plan of co-operation; has been president of the Lott Carey Foreign Mission Convention. Since 1890 he has been principal of the Waters Institute at Winton, North Carolina, which he administers with rare intelligence and vigor.

ENOS L. SCRUGGS, B. D.

Enos L. Scruggs was born of slave parents in Cole county, Missouri, February 23, 1858. His father became a soldier

ENOS L. SCRUGGS, B. D.

in the Union army. He spent his boyhood days on a farm near Jefferson City, attending the public school as opportunity permitted. At fourteen he became an orphan, and thereafter had to depend upon his own efforts for a livelihood. After serving as a porter in a store in St. Louis for five years, he entered Lincoln Institute in 1880, from which he graduated in 1885. In 1886 he entered the Theological Department of the University of Chicago, graduating in 1890. After serving as pastor of the Second Baptist Church of Ann Arbor, Michigan, for twenty-eight months, he became principal of the Western College, at Macon, Missouri, a position which he still occupies. In addition to his duties as administrator of the college, he is the chief editor of the *Missouri Messenger*

MRS. RACHEL E. REEVES ROBINSON.

Mrs. Robinson was born in Anderson, South Carolina, December 1, 1866—one of nine children. At the age of five she entered the public schools and continued eleven years. She entered Benedict College when sixteen years of age. After four years of study she was compelled, for lack of means, to be absent from school one year, teaching. In 1888 she returned to the college, and graduated in 1889. After leaving the college she taught until her marriage, in 1890, to Rev. A. R. Robinson, one of the best and most influential pastors of the State. For two years she and her husband taught in the Piedmont High School of Greenville. Afterward she was elected principal of the graded school at Pendleton. Here she labored until 1896, when she and her husband returned to Greenville, South Carolina, to live in the beautiful house which they purchased. She was at once elected president of the Woman's Missionary Society.

MISS JUDITH L. CHAMBERS.

Miss Judith L. Chambers was born March 15, 1876, the fourth child of James and Terriza Chambers, formerly slaves, of Spartanburg county, South Carolina. Her childhood was spent on a farm, with but one or two months of country school per year until fifteen years of age. She began attending school when but four years of age, having already learned the alphabet. In her public school days she aspired to be a poetess and wrote considerable school-girl poetry. She taught her first school when but fifteen. In 1892 she entered Benedict College and remained two years, paying nearly all

MRS. RACHEL E. R. ROBINSON.   MISS JUDITH L. CHAMBERS.

her expenses by work. The next year she served as assistant in a private colored school in Spartanburg. The following year she served as clerk in a store. In 1897 she returned to college and graduated in 1898, working her way through college. Since graduation she has been teaching in the public schools. She is a great power for good in church, school and society, and in inciting and helping others to intellectual and moral culture.

JOSHUA B. SIMPSON.

Joshua B. Simpson was born July 23, 1861, in Washington, Mason county, Kentucky. After preliminary instruction at home and in the inferior schools of his native village, he attended public school in Maysville, walking more than six miles a day for that purpose. In September, 1882, he entered Wayland Seminary, Washington, D. C., and graduated in May, 1886. He largely supported himself by labor during his period of study. Applying for entrance to Colby College, Waterville, Maine, he received from the president this encouragement: "If you have the three Ps—Push, Pluck and Perseverance—you need not hesitate to come on account of lack of money." He entered in 1886, and graduated in 1890, supporting himself by his labor. He was

JOSHUA B. SIMPSON.

absent from but two recitations during the four years. He thus proved his possession of the president's three Ps. After pursuing a partial course in Newton Theological Institution he received an appointment as teacher in Wayland College, which he still holds.

JOHN H. JACKSON.

John H. Jackson was born at Lexington, Kentucky, October 31, 1850; graduated at Berea College, Kentucky, June, 1874; first colored man to graduate in Kentucky; was elected as delegate-at-large to the Republican National Convention of 1880, being the first colored man so elected from Kentucky; was one of the "306" who cast their votes for thirty-six ballots for U. S. Grant at Chicago; moved to Kansas in 1881; became principal of Lincoln High School, Kansas City, Missouri;

also clerk of the Jury Commission, and also clerk of the Police Board of Kansas City, Kansas, receiving both appointments from the governor; was a member of the Board of Examiners for Kansas City, Kansas, being the first colored man in Kansas to be so honored; was prominently mentioned for auditor of State to succeed Hon. E. P. McCabe; returned to Kentucky in 1887 and took charge as president of the State Normal School for Colored Persons, at Frankfort, which position he held until 1896, when he was elected president of the Lincoln Institute in Jefferson City, Missouri.

He was the first man to raise his voice against the separate coach bill when it was known that it would be brought up in the Kentucky legislature of 1891–2–3. This he did at a public gathering in the Corinthian Baptist Church at Frankfort; and thenceforth he was persistent in his efforts to arouse a sentiment that would defeat the measure. He was the first man to speak before the railroad committee, urging the passage of a law based upon condition rather than upon color. Until very recently he devoted his life to the education of his race. At present he is engaged in business at Colorado Springs, Colorado. Wherever he goes, or however occupied, he has the confidence of both races and of all political parties in Kentucky.

MRS. HANNAH HOWELL REDDICK.

Hannah A. Howell was born in 1872, near Midville, Burke county, Georgia, of slave parents, the seventh daughter of a large family. Before she was large enough to attend school her older sisters taught her to read. She attended the district school three months each year until twelve years old, when she entered Haven Normal School at Waynesboro, Georgia. In her fifteenth year she began teaching. She entered Spelman Seminary in 1887. Her parents were greatly pleased with her progress, but were unable to pay her expenses. By teaching and going to school alternately she continued her studies till she graduated from the academic department in

27

1892. In 1894 she returned and completed the teachers' professional course, and was appointed teacher at Spelman Seminary. In the same year she was appointed by the State School Commissioner to assist in conducting Peabody Insti-

MRS. HANNAH HOWELL REDDICK.

tute, in Georgia. In May, 1899, she resigned her position to become the wife of Mr. M. W. Reddick, principal of the institute, Americus, Georgia. Since her marriage she has been a member of the faculty of that institution.

M. W. REDDICK, A. M.

M. W. Reddick was born in Randolph county, Georgia, March 2, 1868. The first twenty years of his life were spent in the country, working as a farm laborer from eight to seventeen, and then for four years he was engaged in cutting cross-ties for the railroad. During these years he spent, in all, about five months in school. On becoming of age, in 1888, and having been converted, he entered the Baptist Seminary, Atlanta, Georgia, and graduated from that institution in

1897. He had a hard struggle to maintain himself in the institution. On graduation he became principal of a new

M. W. REDDICK, A. M.

school called Americus Institute, which has steadily grown under his skillful administration.

JAMES R. L. DIGGS.

James R. L. Diggs was born in 1865, at Upper Marlboro, Maryland, of Roman Catholic parents. He was confirmed by Cardinal Gibbons at ten years of age, and retained his membership in the Catholic Church for five years. In 1883 he entered Wayland Seminary, graduating in 1886. He was converted in 1885, and united with the Nineteenth Street Baptist Church, Washington, District of Columbia. After teaching four years, 1886–90, in the public schools of Maryland, he returned to Wayland Seminary, where he taught four classes, and prepared himself for college, entering Bucknell University in 1894, and graduating in 1898 with the degree of B. A.   In 1899, after an examination on a year's extra work, he received from his Alma Mater the degree of

JAMES R. L. DIGGS.

M. A.   After graduation he became a teacher in Wayland College, which position he still holds.

JAMES SHELTON HATHAWAY.

The subject of this sketch was born at Mt. Sterling, Montgomery county, Kentucky, March 29, 1859.

His early education was received in the schools of that place. At the age of seventeen he went to Berea College, Kentucky, where he remained until he graduated from the classical course in the year 1884, receiving the degree of Bachelor of Arts.

The day after his graduation he was elected tutor in Latin and mathematics in his Alma Mater by its trustees. Three years later he married Miss Celia Anderson, of Clyde, Ohio, who was then a teacher in the schools of Kentucky.

He remained with Berea College nine years, during which

JAMES S. HATHAWAY.

President Kentucky State Normal and Industrial School, Frankfort, Kentucky.

time he received the honorary degree of Master of Arts; and
when in 1893 he resigned, to accept a professorship at the
Kentucky State Normal School, the faculty notified him that
they had appointed a committee to express to him in fitting
terms their appreciation of him and of his work in that college.

For four years he served as professor in the State Normal
School, when, failing of a re-election, he accepted the principalship of the Maysville High School. After a service in
this capacity of nearly three years he was called to the presidency of the Kentucky State Normal School, where he had
previously labored.

As president of the institution his administration is marked
by energy and development. Although only in the second
year of his administration, the driveways have been put in
good condition; the buildings have been remodeled and improved; the course of study broadened; new industries added;
attendance largely increased; additional grounds and buildings have been purchased and the legislature has been induced to increase the State's annual appropriation by
$5,000, besides giving $15,000 for a new dormitory for girls.
His administration has been highly satisfactory and the following editorial mention from a newspaper which knows
whereof it speaks will sufficiently indicate the satisfactory
manner in which he has presided over the institution provided by the commonwealth of Kentucky for the education
of its colored citizens:

"The re-election of Prof. James S. Hathaway as president
of the State Normal School, by its board of trustees, meets
with general and hearty approval. It is a merited compliment to this able educator. It is an emphatic endorsement
of his worth and work during the school year now rapidly
approaching its close. The enrollment of the school at the
present time is far in excess of that of any previous year of
its existence, being nearly, if not quite, two hundred. The
work of the present year has been of a high standard, and
such as to give general satisfaction to both students and

patrons. President Hathaway's administration of affairs has been up to date, efficient, praiseworthy, above and beyond criticism.

"We congratulate President Hathaway on his re-election, the board on its good judgment, and the school on its good fortune."

MISS MARY KIMBLE.

Miss Mary Kimble was born in Austin, Texas, 1876. Her parents had been slaves and lived in Austin at the time of their emancipation. Mary attended the Austin public schools. She graduated from the normal course in Bishop

MISS MARY KIMBLE.
Assistant Principal at Houston.

College, at Marshall, Texas, 1894. She has taught school several years since graduation, and is at present teacher of mathematics in Houston Academy. She is first assistant to the principal of the academy. She has the reputation of being an earnest student, a successful teacher and a faithful Christian worker.

CHARLES L. PURCE, D. D.

Charles L. Purce, D. D., was born July 4, 1856, in Charleston, South Carolina. He received his early education in private and public schools of his native city. After a course of study at Benedict College, Columbia, South Carolina, he entered the Richmond Theological Seminary, whence he graduated with honor in 1883. After graduation he pursued a correspondence course in Greek and Hebrew under Doctor Harper, of the University of Chicago. After serving as

CHARLES L. PURCE, D D.
President of State University, Louisville, Kentucky.

pastor for one year of a church of eleven hundred members, at Society Hill, South Carolina, he became (1884) teacher of Latin and Greek in Selma University. From 1886 to 1893 he served as president of the institution. He received from Shaw University the degree of A. B., and from the State University at Louisville, of which he is now president, the degree of D. D. During his seventeen years of service as teacher, he has instructed about five thousand different students.

ECKSTEIN NORTON UNIVERSITY.

The *Courier-Journal* of May 18, 1902, noticed the above-named institution as follows:

"Kentucky has not been behind other Southern States in noble efforts to give colored students the benefit of a most thorough industrial training One notable example of this is in the well-known Berea College, where colored and white students are equally welcome and where both sexes have equal chances.

"There is, however, an institution for the aid of colored youth by industrial training much nearer Louisville, and one which deserves the heartiest encouragement and interest of all well-wishers of the colored race. This institution is located at Cane Spring, Bullitt county, Kentucky, only twenty-nine miles from Louisville and on the line of the Louisville and Nashville railroad. It is ambitiously called the Eckstein Norton University, and its history shows that indomitable pluck and never-failing courage have been behind it thus far.

"Eleven years ago a great industrial school for the colored race was proposed by the Rev. William J. Simmons and the Rev. C. H. Parrish, who is now the president of the university. The plans were feasible and practical, but these men had no money with which to carry out their plans. They applied to Messrs. Eckstein Norton and Milton H. Smith for aid, and were cordially received by them. These gentlemen said that they had long desired to do something for the education of the colored people, and were ready to act. A few days later $3,050 was deposited in the Fidelity Trust and Safety Vault Company for the construction of a main building. This splendid gift enabled Dr. Simmons and the Rev. Mr. Parrish to open the doors of the school in October, 1890.

"The most unique railway station building between Bardstown Junction and Springfield was built at Cane Spring, the site of the university.

"In January, 1892, the main building was destroyed by fire. Appeals through the daily papers and through Mr. Smith resulted in a sum of $1,700. Another start was made, and, in the years since, upwards of 1200 students from sixteen States and foreign countries have received instruction. One hundred and thirty-one have graduated from the different departments, the majority of whom are doing creditable work among the people.

"The main building is a substantial brick structure with twenty-five rooms. There are also five frame buildings with twenty rooms for dormitories and assembly halls, the printing office, laundry and blacksmith shop. The accommodations are not adequate to the demands upon them.

"The principle of the school is that all must work. Students must do as well as know. It is designed to give here a Christian education, a trade and college advantages to those who show any special fitness for the highest training. Classes are conducted in laundry work, cooking, sewing, shoemaking, farming, carpentering, waiting on table, printing and blacksmithing.

"The school is undenominational, and is, of course, without denominational aid. Nor does it have State or general government assistance, but is simply a brave effort dependent entirely upon voluntary aid. Here is, indeed, an endeavor to better the condition of the Negro race along lines which, in the case of Tuskegee and other similar institutions, are receiving substantial support and much praise from Northern philanthropists."

EDWARD L. BLACKSHEAR, B. A.

Edward L. Blackshear is a native of the State of Alabama. He was born in Montgomery, September 28, 1862, of slave parents. His father, Abram Blackshear, and his mother, Adeline Pollard, instilled into their son at an early age the principles of honesty, perseverance and self-reliance, which have developed into the now useful and honorable educator

REV. C, H. PARRISH.
President Eckstein Norton University.

of his people. He is one of the leading characters in shaping the destiny of the Negro race in the Lone Star State, and directing them to a higher life of usefulness and prosperity.

Professor Blackshear was one of a large family of children, of whom only three reached maturity and are still living; one graduated in medicine and pharmacy, and is now in the government employ at Washington; another graduated at Roger Williams University, is an ordained Baptist minister and teacher of theology at Guadalupe College, Seguin, Texas.

EDWARD L. BLACKSHEAR.
President Prairie View, Texas, State Normal and Industrial College.

The education of the subject of this sketch was begun in the common school, where he made rapid progress and won distinction in all his classes, until he completed all the curriculum of Swayne's College of his native city. It was now manifest that he was a boy of unusual intellect, and a Northern man became interested in him and made it possible for him to enter a college in Iowa, where he completed with credit a classical course, and received the degree of B. A. in June, 1881. While here, being surrounded by the Christian influences of the home of the professor (McPherron), he became a Christian, and began—to use his own words—"to realize the possibilities of Christian manhood."

Later he returned to the old home in Alabama, and entered upon a life of active usefulness to his own people of the South. From Alabama he came to Texas in 1882, located

PRAIRIE VIEW, TEXAS, STATE NORMAL AND INDUSTRIAL COLLEGE.

first in Ellis and then in Bastrop county, in both of which counties he taught school.

In a competitive examination at Austin he made the highest average, and was elected principal of one of the city schools (colored), from which he was promoted several times without his solicitation. He taught school in Austin for thirteen years, where his faithful and effective service gained for him the confidence and esteem of the leading educators of the State to such an extent that he was appointed to the principalship of the Prairie View State Normal Institute, where his present occupancy is the very best evidence of his executive ability and pre-eminent worth as an educator.

He has a true and noble wife, who has contributed largely to the unprecedented usefulness of her husband and shared his honors.

B. F. ALLEN, A. B., A. M.

Prof. B. F. Allen, vice-president of the Lincoln Institute, was born in Savannah, Georgia, and received his early education in the public schools of his native city. He completed the course of study at the University of Atlanta, graduating with high honors. In languages he became very proficient, and served as a student teacher—an honor much envied. He was afterward elected principal of the Monticello High School, which position he filled most creditably, and later as principal of Risley High School of Brunswick, Georgia. Soon afterward he was elected principal of the Florida Baptist College at Jacksonville, Florida, but before accepting the offer he was notified of his election to the chair of natural and physical science in the State University at Louisville, Kentucky. While both these were under consideration he received a telegram from Prof. I. E. Page, president of Lincoln Institute, asking him to accept the chair of Latin and Greek in that school, which he accepted, with little time to notify the other institutions of his inability to accept their offers, and has filled the position with honor to the institution. He is professor of modern languages, history and

B. F. ALLEN,
Vice-President Lincoln Institute.

pedagogy, and has been prominently connected with all movements of the work for the past five years, and specially interested in the collegiate department, which department he has done more to build up than any one else connected with the school.

Few men so young have been so useful in life and can accomplish so much with apparent ease. He is a fearless speaker, a born teacher, and those who have been under his instructions say they cannot fail to get the essence of the subject he is teaching. He has a reading knowledge of four of the modern languages, which, together with his well-stored mind, makes his work especially advantageous to the students under his instruction. Very few men of the Negro race have been so favored by nature or enjoyed such educational advantages as he.

W. H. COUNCILL.

The Normal and Industrial School at Normal, Alabama, is one of the South's great schools for the education of the Negro. Not that its endowment fund has been sufficient to develop it into a much-embracing, well-appointed university, but that under the presidency of Professor Councill it has been doing admirable work, and has won the confidence and the warm, good wishes of all thoughtful white people, who insist that the young people of the former slave race must be not merely educated but rightly educated. If, as one has affirmed, the process of true education is "nine parts inspiration, one part drill," the Normal is peculiarly fortunate in its presiding officer. Occupying a high plane of thought and aspiration, and having just views of the relation of the races and of the Negro's power to achieve, his example, his daily walk and conversation, and his public addresses awaken laudable ambition, arouse to exertion and lead in the direction of all that is best in the life of any race.

Instead of a labored sketch of his life and works we can give the reader a just and sufficient view of him by presenting in brief what some have said of him, what he says of himself, and what he urges in vindication of his people's claim to the generous consideration of mankind.

Referring in one of his speeches to his origin and his early life, he said: "I came through the Richmond slave-pen to this platform. I do not regret the hard struggles of my life and the bitter experiences necessary to my growth, for, after all, adversity tests and develops man. Let all who toil and struggle take heart and labor on. Let us be concerned about only one thing—that is, how to be a useful and helpful man in the world."

Ben P. Hunt, of Huntsville, Alabama, wrote of him: "Councill came up from slavery, and his history is as thrilling and interesting as the Arabian Nights. . . . He has traveled much and received many large honors, but his heart is still true to the South and devoted to his white people. He has never on either side of the Ohio, or on either side of the ocean, said one unkind word about the South. . . . He has had the courage and the manhood to defend the white people of the South at home and abroad, before foes as well as friends. He seems to have bent all his energies in the South to establish peace and good-will among the races, and to have all the outside world recognize the mutual helpfulness between the races in the South. He has held up these ideas everywhere. . . . He has also claimed that the Negro got more out of slavery than the white man did. . . . He never presents his work to an audience except in an incidental way; but Normal has quietly and steadily grown from one teacher, one school-room cabin and nineteen local pupils, to two hundred acres of land, a score of buildings (some stately and spacious), forty teachers, five hundred students, more than a score of well-equipped industries, sending out trained teachers, domestics and mechanics to fifteen States of the Union, to Africa and to the West Indies. . . . The young people from this school are a

28

credit to the country. They are polite and competent. The domestics from Normal honor any home.''

The *Clarinda* (Iowa) *Herald*, noticing Councill's speech before the Chautauqua there, in 1891, said: "His speech was a clean, dispassionate statement of conditions, and an earnest, eloquent plea for sympathy, not charity; for justice, not assistance; for equality before the law, not social recognition. He asks only that his race be given a chance to prove itself; he petitions that his race be set free from the shackles of prejudice and discrimination that bind its development in tighter and more galling chains than ever fettered the limbs of a slave; he pleads that the lash of ignorant censure, which is more brutal than was the whip of the overseer, may be suspended till the actual facts as to his race are known.''

In a speech before the Southern Industrial Association at Huntsville, Alabama, October 12, 1899, he said: "The Negro is true to his trust. Has he ever deceived you? As badly as he wanted freedom he would today be in slavery had his freedom depended on his betraying your confidence in those dark days when you could not protect your wives and children. That Negro character is still here. Cultivate it.''

We close the sketch with the eloquent peroration of his address before the Carlisle Indian School:

"It is said we have no history. Take Egypt from us, if you please. We give up Hannibal. We will not remember noble Attucks. Wipe from history's page great Toussaint L'Ouverture and grand Douglass, and still the Negro has done enough in the last forty years to give him creditable standing in the society of races, and to place his name in letters of gold across the azure blue above. Although we may be considered the baby-race in civilization, we have answered every test which your highest civilization has applied. In science, in art, in literature, your best critics give us good standing. In invention your own records give us credit. In music and song you say we lead the world. In oratory you place us with your best. In industrial walks we

PROF. W. H. COUNCILL.

President State Normal and Industrial School, Normal, Alabama.

have piled up a billion dollars for ourselves and billions for you in thirty-nine years. In the military your government records place us first. In Christian fervor and generosity we have taught the world lessons of self-denial, patience and love transcendently beautiful and glorious. And it doth not yet appear what we shall be. We will light up our wonderful imagination and emotion by the lamp of culture, turn our imagination into mechanical and philosophical invention, turn our deep emotion into music and poetry, turn our constant stream of feeling into painting and sculptuary. We will send wonder and amazement through the scientific and literary world. There are more inventions to be thought out, higher classes of forces yet undiscovered to be harnessed to appliances; more worlds to be discovered and dissected— more of God to be brought down to man. If the Negro is true to himself he may be God's instrument to bring it all about. God does not pay large prices for small things. Four millions of men did not meet forty years ago upon the battlefield, bankrupt the nation and redden the earth with their blood for nothing. God is helping the Negro to rise in the world."

WILLIAM S. SCARBOROUGH.

William S. Scarborough, now vice-president of Wilberforce University (Wilberforce, Ohio) and professor of Greek and Latin in the same, was born in Macon, Georgia, February 16, 1852. He received his early education in his native city before and during the war. In 1869 he entered Atlanta University, where he remained two years in preparation for Yale University, but instead entered Oberlin College, Oberlin, Ohio, in 1871, and was graduated from the department of Philosophy and the Arts with the degree of A. B. in 1875. He spent a part of the following year in Oberlin Theological Seminary in special study of the Semitic languages and Hellenistic Greek.

In 1877 Professor Scarborough was elected as head of the Classical Department in Wilberforce University. In 1881 he published, through A. S. Barnes & Co., a Greek text-book—"First Lessons in Greek"—the first and only Greek book ever written by a Negro. This book was widely used in both the white and colored schools of the country, especially in the North. Professor Scarborough has also written a treatise entitled, "The Birds of Aristophanes: a Theory of Interpretation," besides numerous tracts and pamphlets, covering a variety of subjects—classical, archæological, sociological and racial. He has written many papers for the various societies to which he belongs. In 1891 he was transferred to the chair of Hellenistic Greek in Payne Theological Seminary, Wilberforce, Ohio. He has been one of the editors of the A. M. E. Sunday-school publications since 1893, and its exegetical editor since 1895. He again accepted the chair of Greek and Latin in 1896, and still holds this position.

Professor Scarborough is a member of various associations: American Philological, American Dialect, American Social Science, Archæological Institute of America, American Spelling Reform, American Folk-Lore, American Modern Language, American Negro Academy, of which he is first vice-president, American Academy of Political and Social Science and the Egyptian Exploration Fund.

Aside from the degrees of A. B. and A. M. received from Oberlin, his Alma Mater, he has also been honored with those of LL. D. and Ph. D. He has written many papers for the societies to which he belongs, and is also a frequent contributor to the magazines and periodicals of the day. He has several times been chosen one of the orators of the Lincoln League Banquet of the State of Ohio. At a conference of the leaders of the race held in the city of Columbus, Ohio, he was elected president of the Afro-American State League, designed to further the interests of the Negro throughout the country. As a delegate to the Methodist Ecumenical Conference he met that body in London, England, September, 1901. He has traveled extensively on the continent of Europe and in Great Britain.

H. E. ARCHER.

Prof. H. E. Archer is a young colored man who has worked his way up in the world, and has succeeded through perseverance and study, having worked his way through  Olivet College, Olivet, Michigan, and took the degree of B. S. with honors. He later took postgraduate work at his Alma Mater and received the degree of M. S. Not satisfied, he then took a special course at the University of Chicago.

He is one of the promising young Negroes in the scientific field, and is to be praised especially because so few of the race enter this field.

He is in charge of the science department at the A. and M. College, Normal, Alabama, and assistant to the principal of the school.

H. E. ARCHER.

Though not noticed at length elsewhere in this volume, the following men and women are distinguished in their several departments of educational work:

One of the best known of those men of the race who stand prominently at the head of State educational institutions is Richard R. Wright, president of the State Normal College, at College, Georgia.

Miss Anna Jones, a graduate of the University of Michigan, is a brilliant linguist and a successful teacher in the Kansas City High School for colored persons.

Miss Sarah A. Blocker is principal of the Normal Department of Florida Baptist College, Jacksonville, Florida.

Miss Lulu Love is a prominent teacher of physical culture in the public schools of Washington, District of Columbia.

Mary C. Jackson is assistant principal in Haines' Normal and Industrial School in Augusta, Georgia.

Mrs. Henrietta M. Archer is principal of the Department of Latin and Music in the Agricultural and Mechanical College at Normal, Alabama, and is connected with the National Colored Woman's Association.

Mrs. John R. Francis is a member of the Board of Trustees of Public Schools, Washington, District of Columbia.

Mrs. Haydee Campbell is kindergarten directress in St. Louis, Missouri.

Miss Helen Abbott is a noted kindergarten teacher in St. Louis, Missouri.

Mrs. Anna J. Cooper, author of "The Voice from the South," is a teacher of Latin in Washington High School.

Mrs. Booker T. Washington is, of course, closely identified with her husband in his great work.

William H. Mayo is distinguished for long and continuous service as principal of a city school for colored persons, which, of course, implies character, scholarship, executive ability and efficiency. He has had charge of the Frankfort (Kentucky) public school twenty years, and has been elected for the twenty-first time. In 1885 he was chairman of the State convention of colored persons to discuss educational needs and to memorialize the legislature to provide for the present State Normal and Industrial School. After the passage of the act to establish this, he was chairman of a delegation of colored citizens who petitioned the city council to donate such a site for the institution as would insure its location at Frankfort—in which they were successful. He and Professor Jackson (alluded to elsewhere) were the first men in the State to agitate the question of a training school for colored teachers.

S. W. BENNETT.　　REV. N. B. STERRETT, D. D.　　W. J. PARKER.

WILLIAM INGLISS.　　THOS. J. JACKSON.　　DR. THOS. E. MILLER.

REV. J. L. DART.　　W. D. CRUM, M. D.　　E. A. LAWRENCE.

EXECUTIVE OFFICERS OF THE NEGRO DEPARTMENT OF SOUTH
CAROLINA INTERSTATE AND WEST INDIAN EXPOSITION,
CHARLESTON, SOUTH CAROLINA, 1901-1902.

[NOTE.—Booker T. Washington was also a member of the Board, but his portrait appears
elsewhere in this book.]

CHAPTER XVI.

MISCELLANEOUS MATTERS.

I. BOOKER T. WASHINGTON ON THE NEGRO AND HIS ECONOMIC VALUE.

I HAVE had letters from the Sandwich Islands, Cuba and South America, all asking that the American Negro be induced to go to those places as laborers. In each case there would seem to be abundant labor already in the places named. It is there, but it seems not to be of the quality and value of that of the Negro in the United States.

These letters have led me to think a good deal about the Negro as an industrial factor in our country.

To begin with, we must bear in mind that when the first twenty slaves were landed at Jamestown, Virginia, in 1619, it was this economic value which caused them to be brought to this country. At the same time that these slaves were being brought to the shores of Virginia from their native land, Africa, the woods of Virginia were swarming with thousands of another dark-skinned race. The question naturally arises: Why did the importers of Negro slaves go to the trouble and expense to go thousands of miles for a dark-skinned people to hew wood and draw water for the whites, when they had right about them a people of another race who could have answered this purpose? The answer is, that the Indian was tried and found wanting in the commercial qualities which the Negro seemed to possess. The Indian would not submit to slavery as a race, and in those instances where he was tried as a slave, his labor was not profitable and he was found unable to stand the physical strain of slavery. As slaves the Indians died in large numbers. This was true in San Domingo and in other parts of the American continent.

The two races, the Indian and the Negro, have been often compared, to the disadvantage of the Negro. It has been more than once stated that the Indian proved himself the superior race in not submitting to slavery. We shall see about this. In this respect it may be that the Indian secured a temporary advantage in so far as race feeling or prejudice is concerned; I mean by this that he escaped the badge of servitude which has fastened itself upon the Negro, and not only upon the Negro in America, for the known commercial value of the Negro has made him a subject of traffic in other portions of the globe during many centuries. Even to this day portions of Africa continue to be the stamping-ground of the slave-trader.

The Indian refused to submit to bondage and to learn the white man's ways. The result is that the greater portion of the American Indians have disappeared, and the greater portion of those who remain are not civilized.

The Negro, wiser and more enduring than the Indian, patiently endured slavery; and the contact with the white man has given the Negro in America a civilization vastly superior to that of the Indian.

The Indian and the Negro met on the American continent for the first time at Jamestown, in 1619. Both were in the darkest barbarism. There were twenty Negroes and thousands of Indians. At the present time there are between nine and ten millions of Negroes and fifty-eight thousand eight hundred and six Indians. Not only has the Indian decreased in numbers, but he is an annual tax upon the government for food and clothing to the extent of $12,784,676 (1899), to say nothing of the large amount that is annually spent in policing him. The one in this case not only decreased in numbers and failed to add anything to the economic value of his country, but has actually proven a charge upon the State.

Let us see how it is with the other. For a long time our national laws bearing upon immigration have been framed

J. B. PARKER.

The Colored Man Who Captured Czolgosz, the Assassin of President McKinley.

so as to prevent the influx into this country of any classes or races that might prove a burden upon the tax-payers, because of their poverty and inability to sustain themselves, as well as their low standard of life which would enable them to underbid the American laborer. The effect has been, then, to keep out certain races and classes. For two centuries and more it was the policy of the United States to bring in the Negro at great cost. All others who have come to this country have paid their own passage. The Negro was of such tremendous economic value that his passage was paid for him. Not only was his passage paid, but agents were sent to force him to come. This country had two hundred and fifty years in which to judge of the economic value of the black man, and the verdict at the end was that he was constantly increasing in value, especially in the southern part of the United States.

Would any individuals, or a country, have gone to the expense during so many years to import a race of people that had no economic value?

The Negro seems to be about the only race that has been able to look the white man in the face during the long period of years and live—not only live, but multiply. The Negro has not only done this, but he has had the good sense to get something from the white man at every point he has touched him; something that has made him a stronger and a better race.

As compared with the Malay race, the Negro has proven his superiority as an economic factor in civilization. Take for example the Malays in the Sandwich Islands. Before the Sandwich Islanders came into contact with the white race, they had a civilization that was about equal to that of the twenty Negroes who came to Jamestown in 1619. Since their contact with the white man they have constantly decreased in numbers, and have so utterly failed to prove of economic value that practically the industries of the islands are now kept in motion by other races, and a strong effort has recently been made to induce a large number of black Americans to go to these islands as laborers.

The industries that gave the South its power, prominence and wealth prior to the Civil War, were mainly cotton, sugar-cane, rice and tobacco. Before the way could be prepared for the proper growing and marketing of these crops, forests had to be cleared, houses built and public roads and railroads constructed. In all of this no one will deny that the Negro was the chief dependence.

The Negro was not only valuable as a common workman, but reached a degree of skill and intelligence in mechanics that added a large per cent. to his money value. Indeed, many of the most complicated structures of the South today stand as monuments to the skill and ability of the Negro mechanic of ante-bellum days.

In the planting, cultivation and marketing of the cotton, rice, sugar-cane and tobacco, the black man was about the sole dependence, especially in the lower tier of the Southern States. In the manufacture of tobacco, he became a skilled and proficient workman, and at the present time, in the South, holds the lead in this respect in the large tobacco manufactories.

Not only did the black American prove his worth in the way of skilled and common labor, but there were thousands of Negroes who demonstrated that they possessed executive ability of a high order. Many of the large plantations had Negro overseers, to whom the whole financial interests of the masters were very largely intrusted. To be able to plan months ahead for planting and harvesting of the crop, to reckon upon the influence of weather conditions, and to map out profitable work for scores of men, women and children, required an executive ability of no mean order. In very few instances did the black manager prove false to his trust.

Without the part which the Negro played in the physical development of the South, it is safe to say that it would be as undeveloped as much of the territory in the Far West.

The most valuable testimony that I have seen upon the subject that this article covers is from the pen of Prof. N. S. Shaler, dean of the Scientific School of Harvard University. My readers, I am sure, will forgive me for using a rather long quotation from Professor Shaler's article. I do it for the reason that Professor Shaler is not only a recognized scientist, but for the further reason that he is a Southern man and has had abundant opportunity to secure valuable testimony. Professor Shaler says:

"The Negroes who came to North America had to undergo as complete a transition as ever fell to the lot of man, without the least chance to undergo an acclimatizing process. They were brought from the hottest part of the earth to the region where the winter's cold is of almost arctic severity; from an exceedingly humid to a very dry air. They came to service under alien taskmasters, strange to them in speech and in purpose. They had to betake themselves to unaccustomed food and to clothing such as they had never worn before. Rarely could one of the creatures find about him a familiar face, or friend, parent, or child, or an object that recalled his past life to him. It was an appalling change. Only those who know how the Negro cleaves to all the dear, familiar things of life, how fond he is of warmth and friendliness, can conceive the physical and mental shock that this introduction to new conditions meant to him. To people of our own race it would have meant death. But these wonderful folk appear to have withstood the trials of their deportation in a marvelous way. They showed no peculiar liability for disease. Their longevity or period of usefulness was not diminished, or their fecundity obviously impaired. So far as I have been able to learn, nostalgia was not a source of mortality, as it would have been with any Aryan population. The price they brought in the market, and the satisfaction of their purchasers with their qualities, show that they were from the first almost ideal laborers.

"If we compare the Algonquin Indian, in appearance a

A. M. CUSTIS, A. M., M. D.
Surgeon-in-Chief Freedmen's Hospital.

sturdy fellow, with these Negroes, we see of what stuff the
blacks are made. A touch of housework and of honest toil
took the breath of the aborigines away, but these tropical exotics fell to their tasks and trials far better than the men of
our own kind could have done. . . . . Moreover, the
production of good tobacco requires much care, which extends
over about a year from the time the seed is planted. Some
parts of the work demand a measure of judgment such as intelligent Negroes readily acquire. They are, indeed, better
fitted for the task than white men, for they are commonly
more interested in their task than whites of the laboring
class. The result was that before the period of the Revolutionary War slavery was firmly established in the tobacco
planting colonies of Maryland, Virginia and North Carolina;
it was already the foundation of their only considerable industry. . . . . This industry (cotton), even more
than that of raising tobacco, called for abundant labor, which
could be absolutely commanded and severely tasked in the
season of extreme heat. For this work the Negro proved
to be the only fit man, for while the whites can do this work,
they prefer other employment. Thus it came about that the
power of slavery in the country became rooted in its soil.
The facts show that, based on an ample foundation of experience, the judgment of the Southern people was to the effect
that this creature of the tropics was a better laborer in their
fields than the men of their own race.

"Much has been said about the dislike of the white man
for work in association with Negroes. The failure of the
whites to have a larger share in the agriculture of the South
has been attributed to this cause. This seems to be clearly
an error. The dislike to the association of races in labor is,
in the slave-holding States, less than in the North. There
can be no question that if the Southern folk could have made
white laborers profitable, they would have preferred to employ
them, for the reason that they would have required less fixed
capital for their operation. The fact was and is that the

Negro is there a better laboring man in the field than the white. Under the conditions he is more enduring, more contented and more trustworthy than the men of our own race.''

So much for the Negro as a financial factor in American life before the Civil War. What about his value as a free man?

There were not a few who predicted that as soon as the Negro became a free man he would not only cease to support himself and others, but he would become a tax upon the community.

Few people in any part of our country have ever seen a black hand reached out from a street corner asking for charity. In our Northern communities a large amount of money is spent by individuals and municipalities in caring for the sick, the poor, and other classes of unfortunates. In the South, with very few exceptions, the Negro takes care of himself and of the unfortunate members of his race. This is usually done by a combination of individual members of the race, or through the churches or fraternal organizations. Not only is this true, but I want to make a story illustrate the condition that prevails in some parts of the South. The white people in a certain "Black Belt" county in the South had been holding a convention, the object of which was to encourage white people to emigrate into the county. After the adjournment of the convention, an old colored man met the president of the meeting on the street and asked the object of the convention. When told, the old colored man replied: '' 'Fore God, boss, don't you know that we Niggers got just as many white people now in this county as we can support?''

The fact is often referred to that the Negro pays a very small proportion of the taxes that support his own schools. As to whether or not this is true depends a good deal on the theory of political economy that we follow. Some of the highest authorities on political economy contend that it is the man who rents the house that pays the taxes on it, rather than the man who simply holds the title to it. Certain it is that without the Negro to produce the raw material in the

29

South, from which a large proportion of taxes are paid, there would not be a very large tax paid by any one.

Reliable statistics concerning the economic progress of the Negro are difficult to obtain, owing to the fact that few of the States keep a record separating the property owned by Negroes from that owned by white people. The State of Virginia and one or two other Southern States do keep such a record. Taking the matter of taxes as a basis for indicating the Negro's value, Professor J. W. Cromwell, of Washington, District of Columbia, gave the following statistics bearing upon the colored people of the State of Virginia, at a recent conference at the Hampton Institute:

"The colored people contributed in 1898 directly to the expenses of the State government the sum of $9,576.76, and for schools $3,239.41, from their personal property, a total of $12,816.17; while from their real estate for the purposes of the commonwealth there was paid by them $34,303.53, and for schools $11,357.22, or a total of $45,760.75; a grand total of $58,576.92.

"The report for the same year shows them to own 978,118 acres of land, valued at $3,800,459, improved by buildings valued at $2,056,490, a total of $5,856,949. In the towns and cities they own lots assessed at $2,154,331, improved by buildings valued at $3,400,636, a total of $5,554,967 for town property, and a grand total of $11,411,916 of their property of all kinds in the commonwealth. A comparative statement for different years would doubtless show a general upward tendency.

"The counties of Accomac, Essex, King and Queen, Middlesex, Mathews, Northampton, Northumberland, Richmond, Westmoreland, Gloucester, Princess Anne and Lancaster, all agricultural, show an aggregate of 114,197 acres held by Negroes in 1897, the last year accounted for in official reports, against 108,824 acres held the previous year, an increase of 5,379, or nearly five per cent. The total valuation of lands owned by Negroes in the same counties for 1897 is $547,800,

W. F. POWELL.

Minister to Hayti.

against $496,385 for the year next preceding, a gain of
$51,150, or more than ten per cent. Their personal property,
as assessed in 1897, was $517,560; in 1896, $527,688, a loss
of $10,128. Combining the real and personal property for
1897, we have $1,409,059, against $1,320,504 for 1896, a net
gain of $88,555, an increase of six and a half per cent.''

The greatest excitement and anxiety has been recently
created among the white people in two counties of Georgia,
because of the fact that a large proportion of the colored
people decided to leave. No stone has been left unturned to
induce the colored people to remain in the counties and prevent financial ruin to many white farmers.

Any one who has followed the testimony given recently
before the United States Industrial Commission, will see that
several white men from the South have stated, in the most
emphatic language, that the Negro is the best laborer that
the South has ever had, and is the best that the South is
likely to get in the future. Not the least part of the Negro's
worth at the present time (and this is going to be more apparent in the future than now) is that he presents a conservative,
reliable factor in relation to "strikes" and "lockouts." The
Negro is not given to "strikes." His policy is to leave each
individual free to work when, where and for whom he pleases.

The cotton crop of the South has increased many fold since
the beginning of freedom. Of course the Negro is not the
only labor element to be considered in the production of cotton, but all will agree that the black man is the chief dependence in this country for that purpose. In order to be more
specific, I give some figures that will indicate the difference
between the number of bales of cotton produced by slave and
free labor:

SLAVE LABOR.		FREE LABOR.	
YEAR.	BALES.	YEAR.	BALES.
1845	2,394,503	1890	8,652,597
1850	2,233,781	1899	8,900,000

While there are several factors, among them increase in population, entering into these figures, still I think they show clearly that freedom has not destroyed the economic value of the Negro.

What I have thus far stated relates mainly to the common Negro laborer before and since the war. But what about the educated Negro?

Reference is often made to the large proportion of criminal and idle colored men in the large cities. I admit that this class is much larger than it should be, and in some cities it is beginning to present a rather serious problem. Two things, however, should be kept in mind when considering the younger generation of colored people: First, that the transition from slavery to freedom was a tremendous one; that the Negro's idea of freedom for generations had been that it meant freedom from restraint and work; that the Negro mother and father had little opportunity during slavery to learn how to train children; and that family life was practically unknown to the Negro until about thirty years ago. Secondly, the figures relating to criminality among all races in all countries show that it is the younger people, those between the ages of sixteen and thirty-five, that are given to crime and idleness.

Notwithstanding these facts, I want to present some testimony showing that the young, educated Negro is not failing to prove his worth.

Some time ago I sent letters to about four hundred white men, scattered throughout the Southern states, in which these three questions were asked:

1. Has education made the Negro a more useful citizen?

2. Has it made him more economical and more inclined to acquire wealth?

3. Has it made him a more valuable workman, especially where thought and skill are required?

Answers came from three hundred of my correspondents, and nine-tenths of them answered the three questions emphatically in the affirmative. A few expressed doubts, but only one answered the questions with an unmodified ''No.''

In each case I was careful to ask my correspondents to base their replies upon the conditions existing in their own neighborhood.

The Negro is branching out into nearly all lines of business. For an illustration of this remark the reader is referred to Chapter VII, of this work, where he will find the results of the inquiries as to many cities.

From all the foregoing facts I think we may safely find ground for the greatest hopefulness, not only for the Negro himself, but for the white man in his treatment of the Negro. In the South, especially, the prosperity of the one race enriches the other.

The greatest thing that can be done for the Negro at the present time is to make him the most useful and indispensable man in his community. This can be done by thorough education of the hand, head and heart, and especially by constantly distilling into every fiber of his being the thought that labor is ennobling and that idleness is a disgrace.

II. ADDRESS OF BOOKER T. WASHINGTON ON RECEIVING THE HONORARY DEGREE OF MASTER OF ARTS FROM HARVARD UNIVERSITY.

This speech was made at the alumni dinner of the university. Respecting the conferring of the degree by this eminent institution, Thomas J. Calloway wrote, in the *Washington Colored American*, as follows:

''First in the history of America, a leading American university confers an honorary degree upon a colored man. Harvard has been always to the front in ideas of liberty, freedom and political equality. When other colleges of the North were accepting the Negro as a tolerance, Harvard had been awarding him honors, as in the case of Clement G. Morgan of recent date. Her present action, therefore, in placing an honorary crown upon the worthy head of Mr.

GEO. W. WILLIAMS.
The Colored Historian.

Washington, is but a step further in her magnanimity in recognizing merit under whatever color of skin.

"The mere announcement of this event is a great testimony to the standing of Mr. Washington, but to any black person who, as I did, saw and heard the enthusiasm and applause with which the audience cheered the announcement by President Eliot, the degree itself was insignificant. The Boston Lancers had conducted Governor Wolcott to Cambridge, and five hundred Harvard graduates had double filed the march to Sander's Theater. It was a great day. Latin orations, disquisitions, dissertations and essays in English were delivered by selected graduates, clad in stately and classic cap and gown. Bishops, generals, commodores, statesmen, authors, poets, explorers, millionaires and noted men of every calling sat as earnest listeners. President Eliot had issued five hundred diplomas by handing them to the representatives of the graduates in bundles of twenty to twenty-five. Then came the awarding of honorary degrees. Thirteen were issued. Bishop Vincent and General Nelson A. Miles, commander of the United States Army, being among the recipients. When the name of Booker T. Washington was called, and he arose to acknowledge and accept, there was such an outburst of applause as greeted no other name, except that of the popular soldier patriot, General Miles. The applause was not studied and stiff, sympathetic and condoling; it was enthusiasm and admiration. Every part of the audience from pit to gallery joined in, and a glow covered the cheeks of those around me, proving that it proceeded from sincere appreciation of the rising struggle of an ex-slave and the work he has accomplished for his race.

"But the event of the day was the alumni dinner, when speeches formed the most enjoyable bill of fare. Two hundred Harvard alumni and their invited guests partook of their annual dinner. Four or five speeches were made, among them one from Mr. Washington.

"At the close of the speaking, notwithstanding Senator

Henry Cabot Lodge, Dr. Minot J. Savage and others had spoken, President Eliot warmly grasped Mr. Washington by the hand, and told him that his was the best speech of the day.

"Anent the conferring of the degree and the toasts, the papers have been unusual in favorable comment. Says the *Boston Post:*

" 'In conferring the honorary degree of master of arts upon the principal of Tuskegee Institute, Harvard University has honored itself, as well as the object of this distinction. The work which Prof. Booker T. Washington has accomplished for the education, good citizenship and popular enlightenment in his chosen field of labor in the South, entitles him to rank with our national benefactors. The university which can claim him on its list of sons, whether in regular course or *honoris causa*, may be proud.

" 'It has been mentioned that Mr. Washington is the first of his race to receive an honorary degree from a New England university. This, in itself, is a distinction. But the degree was not conferred because Mr. Washington is a colored man, or because he was born in slavery, but because he has shown, by his work for the elevation of the people of the 'Black Belt' of the South, a genius and a broad humanity which count for greatness in any man, whether his skin be white or black.'

"The *Boston Globe* adds: 'It is Harvard, which, first among New England colleges, confers an honorary degree upon a black man. No one who has followed the history of Tuskegee and its work, can fail to admire the courage, persistence and splendid common sense of Booker T. Washington. Well may Harvard honor the ex-slave, the value of whose services, alike to his race and country, only the future can estimate.'

"The correspondent of the *New York Times* kindly remarks: 'All the speeches were enthusiastically received, but the colored man carried off the oratorical honors and the applause which broke out when he had finished was vociferous and long-continued.'

"Most of the papers have printed his portrait, and congratulations have come from every source.

"The grandest feature of the whole thing is that the fame and honor that are coming thus to Mr. Washington do not spoil him. Twelve months in the year, night and day, he works for Tuskegee—his heart and love. No vacation, no rest; his life is one unceasing struggle for his school. This is the secret of his power. Here is the lesson to be learned."

MR. WASHINGTON'S ADDRESS.

Mr. President and Gentlemen:

"It would in some measure relieve my embarrassment if I could, even in a slight degree, feel myself worthy of the great honor which you do me today. Why you have called me from the 'Black Belt' of the South, from among my humble people, to share in the honors of this occasion, is not for me to explain; and yet it may not be inappropriate for me to suggest that it seems to me that one of the most vital questions that touch our American life is how to bring the strong, wealthy and learned into helpful touch with the poorest, most ignorant and humble and at the same time make the one appreciate the vitalizing, strengthening influence of the other. How shall we make the mansions on yon Beacon street feel and see the need of the spirits in the lowliest cabin in Alabama cotton fields or Louisiana sugar bottoms? This problem Harvard University is solving, not by bringing itself down, but by bringing the masses up.

"If through me, an humble representative, seven millions of my people in the South might be permitted to send a message to Harvard—Harvard that offered up on death's altar young Shaw, and Russell, and Lowell and scores of others, that we might have a free and united country, that message would be: 'Tell them that the sacrifice was not in vain. Tell them that by the way of the shop, the field, the

CLASS IN DOMESTIC SCIENCE, SUMNER HIGH SCHOOL, ST. LOUIS, MISSOURI.

skilled hand, habits of thrift and economy, by way of industrial school and college, we are coming. We are crawling up, working up—yea, bursting up; often through oppression, unjust discrimination and prejudice, but through them all we are coming up; and with proper habits, intelligence and property there is no power on earth that can permanently stay our progress.'

"If my life in the past has meant anything in the lifting up of my people and the bringing about of better relations between your race and mine, I assure you from this day it will mean doubly more. In the economy of God there is but one standard by which an individual can succeed—there is but one for a race. This country demands that every race measure itself by the American standard. By it a race must rise or fall, succeed or fail; and in the last analysis mere sentiment counts for little. During the next half century and more my race must continue passing through the severe American crucible. We are to be tested in our patience, our forbearance, our perseverance, our power to endure wrong, to withstand temptations, to economize, to acquire and use skill; our ability to compete, to succeed in commerce, to disregard the superficial for the real, the appearance for the substance, to be great and yet small, learned and yet simple, high and yet the servant of all. This, this is the passport to all that is best in the life of our republic, and the Negro must possess it or be debarred.

"While we are thus being tested, I beg of you to remember that wherever our life touches yours, we help or hinder; wherever your life touches ours, you make us stronger or weaker. No member of your race in any part of our country can harm the meanest member of mine without the proudest and bluest blood in Massachusetts being degraded. When Mississippi commits crime, New England commits crime, and in so much lowers the standard of your civilization. There is no escape. Man drags man down or man lifts man up.

"In working out our destiny, while the main burden and center of activity must be with us, we shall need, in a large measure in the years that are to come, as we have in the past, the help, the encouragement, the guidance that the strong can give the weak. Thus helped, we of both races in the South soon shall throw off the shackles of racial and sectional prejudice and rise, as Harvard University has risen and as we all should rise, above the clouds of ignorance, narrowness and selfishness, into that atmosphere, that pure sunshine, where it will be our highest ambition to serve MAN, our brother, regardless of race or previous condition."

III. WOMEN WHO LABOR FOR THE SOCIAL ADVANCEMENT OF THE RACE.

Mrs. Fannie Barrier Williams, a member of the Chicago Woman's Club, and prominent among those who are seeking to organize for more effective work in promoting social advancement, says that: "Among colored women the club is the effort of the few competent in behalf of the many incompetent. The club is one of many means for the social uplift of the race. . . . . The emancipation of the mind and spirit of the race could not be accomplished by legislation. More time, more patience, more suffering and more charity are needed to complete the work of emancipation."

The first national conference of colored women to consider the work of organization was held in Boston, July, 1895, but there were clubs previously, in certain of the larger cities. Since the movement to nationalize took shape in the organization of the National Association of Colored Women, the interest has increased annually, and local clubs have multiplied till there are at least three hundred of such bodies in the United States. The object of these clubs is not merely social and sisterly intercourse, but they have well-defined aims which they seek to attain by thoughtful discussion and active work for the improvement of individual and home life. Mrs. Williams says of them: "These club women are students of their own social condition, and the clubs themselves are schools in which are taught and learned, more or less thoroughly, the near lessons of living. All these clubs have a programme for study. In some of the more ambitious ones literature, music and art are studied, ... and in all of them race problems and sociological questions directly related to the condition of the Negro race in America are the principal subjects for study and discussion. . . . The lessons learned in the organizations all have a direct bearing on the social conditions of the Negro race. They are such lessons as are not taught in the schools or preached from the pulpits. Home-making has been new business to the great majority of the women whom the women's clubs aim to reach and influence. For this reason the principal object of club studies is to teach that homes are something better and dearer than rooms, furniture, comforts and food. How to make the homes of the race the shrines of all the domestic virtues rather than mere shelters, is the important thing that colored women are trying to learn and teach through their club organizations."

To attempt such work is an emphatic declaration to mankind that a host of the colored women of America have worthy ambitions and lofty ideals, and as representatives of the women of their race they make manifest the fact that there are possibilities open to all that are higher and better than mere menial service and that state of poverty which is known as "living from hand-to-mouth." The degree of success attained in extending the organization to cover such a wide field, and awakening an interest that is finding its way to a class of women that have been sadly in need of some regenerating, quickening and elevating influence, is proof that the longings and strivings of these club women are by no means disproportioned to their powers of achievement.

Among the women of the race who are prominent in club work and are otherwise actively engaged in something de-

N. W. CUNER.

signed to promote the honor and welfare of their people, we have the names of the following:

Mrs. Josephine St. Piérre Ruffin, of Boston, leader of the club movement among the colored women.

Miss Mattie B. Davis, president of the Woman's Club, Athens, Georgia.

Mrs. C. S. Smith, of Nashville, Tennessee, late secretary of the National Association of Colored Women.

Mrs. Mary L. Davenport, president of the Chicago Woman's Conference.

Mrs. Mary Church Terrell, president of the National Association of Colored Women.

Mrs. Helen Clark, president of the Washington (D. C.) Woman's League.

Mrs. Hart, of Jacksonville, Florida, promoter of a movement to erect monuments to commemorate the deeds of the black soldiers in the Spanish War.

S. J. Evans is the chief stenographer in one of the largest mercantile houses in Chicago, and furnishes a striking example to the young of what may be achieved by application and good conduct.

IV. INVENTIVE GENIUS, MECHANICAL SKILL, ETC.

The constructive genius of the race cannot as yet number many illustrative names, but there have been occasional notable manifestations. In March, 1902, the *Woodford* (Kentucky) *Sun* published the following account:

"Lewis Harvey, an uneducated eighteen-year-old Negro boy, living on Mr. Emelius Morancy's farm near the river, has shown remarkable mechanical genius by constructing, without assistance, and with the crudest material, a miniature stationary steam engine that runs perfectly. A piece of old pipe, which he inclosed in Babbitt metal, forms the cylinder; the boiler is a large tin can and the governor is made of a brass link cuff button. He built the engine after seeing several engines in operation. It is certainly a wonderful machine. He is now preparing to build a larger engine, that will have power enough to operate a sewing machine.

"He also possesses remarkable talent as a wood carver, and recently completed a very interesting walking stick, which is a mass of portraits of public men, animals, snakes and lizards carved in bold relief.

"Lewis Harvey's younger brother, Will Harvey, aged

SUMNER HIGH SCHOOL, ST. LOUIS, MISSOURI.

fifteen, is gifted with his pencil and can sketch crayon portraits and landscape views with rare fidelity. There are two other brothers, and all four of them are talented musicians, performing upon a variety of instruments. They are sons of James Harvey. Their mother is a Mexican."

James Harvey, the father, was for a long time the engineer in a large distillery near Frankfort, and was regarded as a natural mechanic. He was accustomed to making neces-

30

sary repairs on any machinery which he might have in charge.

Benjamin Danneker, born in Maryland in 1831, was another man of his race—he was the son of a native African—who was remarkable for diversified talent. He was a mathematical and mechanical genius, and had a wide acquaintance with general literature. With imperfect tools and a watch for a model he constructed a clock; amused himself by stating mathematical problems and their solution in rhyme; devoted himself to astronomical studies till he could calculate an eclipse; and for ten or twelve years he prepared and published annually an almanac; accompanied the commissioners to run the lines of the District of Columbia, on their invitation; kept himself acquainted with everything of importance that was passing in the United States, and was a pleasing conversationalist. He lived a somewhat retired life, and was always modest in deportment, but so striking were his talents and in general so usefully employed that he came to be known in Europe, as well as in America, as a most intellectual and distinguished man.

One of the prodigies of the eighteenth century was a native African, Thomas Fuller, brought to Virginia and sold into slavery—an untaught mathematician of the most extraordinary powers. A Boston paper, noticing his death in December, 1790, said of him: "Had his opportunities of improvement been equal to those of thousands of his fellow-men, neither the Royal Society of London, the Academy of Science at Paris, nor even a Newton himself need have been ashamed to acknowledge him a brother in science."

V. HOW MELBOURN AND OTHERS REGARDED COLONIZATION
IN LIBERIA, AND WHAT TIME HAS DISCLOSED
AS TO THAT SCHEME.

Discussing the question as to the difficulties then in the way of freeing the slaves (about eighty years ago), Melbourn says: "It is worthy of remark that neither Thornton nor

JOHN M. LANGSTON.
Ex-Minister to Hayti.

Lundy (two scholarly and philanthropic gentlemen who were his friends), noticed the Colonization Society as a scheme which promised any benefit to the black man of America. Hence I inferred that they did not anticipate any good from that project, and I afterward ascertained that that inference was correct; in which opinion I now entirely concur. That the society can ever effect the emancipation of the Negro race is so obviously absurd that no man who has any brains can fail of perceiving it. As a means of extending Christianity and the arts of civilization in Western Africa it may be beneficial; but in my judgment it will retard, as by many it was intended to retard, the liberation of the slaves in the United States. . . . The project is universally unpopular with the colored people of America. They regard transportation to Africa as a banishment from their native land to an unhealthy, savage country. The idea is to many more terrible than death itself.

"In the year 1816, a few days after the Colonization Society was organized in Washington, I went in the stage from that city to Richmond, Virginia. The weather was pleasant, and for the sake of viewing the country I rode a part of the way on the box with the driver, who was a Negro. . . . Though a very sensible man this driver was a slave, but he had heard of the Colonization Society and its objects. He soon began to make some inquiries of me about it. In turn, I asked him what he thought of the plan. He said he did not like it. I expressed surprise at his answer, for at that time I really thought favorably of the project. I suggested to my companion that if all the colored people in this country were set free, such was the prejudice against color that they could never acquire equal standing with the whites; that in all the free States they were treated as an inferior race of beings; that they were excluded from all offices of honor and profit; and that the most worthy colored man was not permitted to come to the table and eat with the meanest white man; that in Liberia it would be entirely different; that competition for wealth, promotion and honor would be as open to the black man as to the white man.

"He answered that he had reason to believe Africa was a barren country—that he knew it was a savage country, with a most unhealthy climate, entirely unsuited to the constitution of Americans; . . . and that the Negro loved the soil on which he was born as well as the white man, and that he could not endure the idea of banishment for life from his native country."

Helpless as the prospect of liberation seemed to all men then, it was but little more than forty years till the slaves were freed, and the American people were confronted with a great problem—that of adjusting the relations of two distinct and diverse races of freemen intermingled, and involved in some antagonisms created by the great war and the legislation which followed it. Various schemes for settling the race problem by separating the races have been suggested— one of which is the removal of the colored people to another clime, there to form them into a distinct and homogeneous commonwealth. One great and sufficient objection to this project, though it has been advocated by good and able men, is found in the words quoted above: "The Negro loves the soil on which he was born as well as the white man, and he could not endure the idea of banishment for life from his native country. The thought would be to many more terrible than death itself."

All schemes looking to removal and the formation of distinct colored communities, whether in a foreign land or in any particular State or Territory of the Union, have come to be regarded as impracticable, if not utterly chimerical. The race, as it exists among us, has risen from barbarism through contact with the whites, which thoughtful Negroes themselves regard as some compensation for two hundred and forty years of slavery; and those who have given existing conditions the most careful study, conclude that if the race is to continue to advance it must maintain its present relations with the ever-dominant Anglo-Saxon. That wholesale emigration and a separate and independent existence as a people would be a serious interruption to their progress, intellectual, moral and material, seems to be borne out by the result made in Liberia.

Without entering into the details of the history of that commonwealth, we may note some facts from which the intelligent reader will reach the conclusion that American Negroes have a better future on American soil than would be possible to them as a separate race on the west coast of Africa—or, indeed, anywhere else. The government of Liberia is modeled on that of the United States. Its executive head is a president elected by the people; its Congress consists of a Senate and a Lower House—eight senators elected for four years and thirteen representatives elected for three years; it has a Supreme Court, and the president has a cabinet of the American type.

It was founded in 1822, the territory allotted to the freedmen of America being in extent about the size of the two states New Hampshire and New Jersey, and twenty-five years afterward it was declared an independent republic. Fifty-eight years after its founding the population of civilized Negroes was about 18,000, with about 1,000,000 half-wild natives. Some of the latter were adopting a settled life and conforming to the habits of their civilized countrymen. One writer (who is in the main corroborated by various others) says that "socially and politically the State cannot be pronounced a marked success. The Negroes of America display little desire to throw in their fortunes with it, now they are free to go whither they list, nor do the barbarous tribes on the border of the republic seem to admire this imitation of a white man's government which for eighty years has been presented to them. There is now and again a small immigration from the United States, but Liberian civilization, cut off from the benefit of intercourse with a higher and broader culture, is apt to deteriorate, while neither the climate nor

H. A. RUCKER.

Collector Internal Revenue, Atlanta, Georgia.

the laws and social surroundings are ever likely to attract many white men to its shores. Its finances are badly managed, so that it is hardly able to meet the interest on a public debt contracted long ago, to say nothing of lessening the principal; and internal disorder is too often the rule. It shows an appreciation, however, of education and religion, and a keen desire to stand well in the opinion of the powers with which it has relations by accredited representatives.''

VI. HIGH TRIBUTES TO THE MANHOOD OF SOME NEGRO SLAVES.

When Henry Clay, December 9, 1844, freed one of his Negro men he said in the article of manumission: ''For and in consideration of the fidelity, attachment and services of Charles Dupey, and my esteem and regard for him, I do hereby liberate,'' etc.

The Hon. Abel P. Upshur, of Virginia, for a while Secretary of the Navy, and afterward Secretary of State under President Tyler (1841–5), left, in an article of manumission, a remarkable tribute to the intelligence and character of the Negro slave whom he freed. ''I emancipate and set free,'' says the document, ''my servant, David Rich, and direct my executors to give him one hundred dollars. I recommend him in the strongest manner to the respect, esteem and confidence of any community in which he may happen to live. He has been my slave for twenty-four years, during all of which time he has been trusted to every extent and in every respect. My confidence in him has been unbounded. His relation to myself and family has been such as to afford him daily opportunities to deceive and injure us, and yet he has never been detected in any serious fault, nor even in an intentional breach of the decorums of his station. His intelligence is of a high order, his integrity above all suspicion, and his sense of right and propriety correct and even refined. I feel that he is justly entitled to carry this certificate from me in the new relations which he must now form. It is due

BLANCHE K. BRUCE.

Ex-United States Senator from Mississippi.

to his long and faithful services, and to the sincere and steady friendship which I bear him. In the uninterrupted and confidential intercourse of twenty-four years I have never given him, nor had occasion to give him, an unpleasant word. I know no man who has fewer faults or more excellences than he.''

REV. MOSES DICKSON.

Rev. Moses Dickson was born in the city of Cincinnati, Ohio, April 5, 1824. He was the son of Robert and Hannah Dickson, natives of Virginia. His father died in 1832, and his mother in 1838. He learned the barber's trade while he was a young man and at the same time attended school and mastered all the branches of study that were taught at that early day. At the age of sixteen he secured employment on a steamboat and for three years traveled in various boats upon the different Southern rivers and bayous. In these travels through the South he saw slavery in all its aspects, and what he saw in these three years of travel made a lasting impression on him and determined him to devote his best efforts to secure freedom for his race. He had made the acquaintance of a few true and trusty young men, who were ready to join with him in any plan that seemed feasible and likely to assure freedom to the slaves. Eleven of these young men met with him and agreed to form an organization for that purpose. Knowing that the work was one of great magnitude and would require time, courage and patience, they took two years to study over it and planned to meet again in St. Louis on the 12th of August, 1846.

Mr. Dickson embarked on the steamer *Oronoco* at New Orleans in May, 1844, and made a trip to St. Louis, where he remained during the summer. He then traveled for two years through Iowa, Illinois, Wisconsin and other Northern States, and in August, 1846, was in St. Louis prepared to meet his friends with an outline of the plan to be submitted to them. The twelve met on the second Tuesday in August and Mr. Dickson unfolded to them his plan which was

REV. MOSES DICKSON.

Founder of the International Order of Twelve.

adopted. This meeting resulted in the formation of the "Knights of Liberty." The twelve organizers went actively to work and formed local organizations in every slave State except Missouri and Texas. Mr. Dickson remained the head of the Order with headquarters at St. Louis. The Knights of Liberty were not to commence active operation for ten years from the time of organization, the intervening time to be used in making preparations. When the ten years were ended, in 1856, the trend of events was such that it was not thought advisable to carry out the plans of the organization, inasmuch as it seemed probable at that time that freedom would come in the natural course of events.

During the ten years of preparation and up to the breaking out of the war, the Knights of Liberty, in connection with their other work, were actively interested in the "Under Ground Railroad," and in ten years transported more than 70,000 slaves from bondage to freedom. The organization was so compact and its affairs so secretly conducted that for years nobody knew the names of the original twelve organizers, or that such an organization existed. The methods by which the Knights of Liberty expected to accomplish their object will probably never be known, but the extent of the movement and the secrecy maintained proves Mr. Dickson to have been a past master in the art of organization.

Mr. Dickson was actively engaged in the field during the war, and was in thirteen hard-fought battles, returning home in 1864 without a scratch from the enemy's bullets.

After the war he turned his energies and efforts to the education of the freedmen and their children. He led a powerful lobby to Jefferson City, Missouri, and worked hard for the establishment of schools for colored children. His efforts were successful, and, under the administration of Governor McClurg, the present school laws of Missouri were adopted. This being achieved, the next movement was to procure colored teachers for colored schools, and after a hard fight he was successful in that also.

He took an active part in the founding of Lincoln Institute, at Jefferson City, Missouri, and was trustee and vice-president of the board for several years until the success of the institution was assured. He has given his time largely since the war to educational movements for the benefit of the colored race.

In 1878 he became president of the Refugee Relief Board in St. Louis, and the board under his management cared for about sixteen thousand people. These refugees were comfortably clothed, given provisions to last them several months, and forwarded to Kansas, Nebraska, Colorado and other Northern States, where they settled and became good citizens. More than ten thousand of these refugees settled in Kansas.

Mr. Dickson was prominent in politics in his State. He was a delegate to every Republican State Convention of Missouri from 1864 to 1878, and during several campaigns stumped the State in the interest of his party. He was elector at large on the Grant ticket in 1872.

He was converted and joined the A. M. E. Church in 1866, and in 1867 was licensed to preach. He has held a number of large and small charges, and was well known as a successful manager of churches, and particularly as a church builder, a debt payer and a revivalist. During his several pastorates about fourteen hundred persons have been converted by him.

After the war, when the work of the "Knights of Liberty" was ended, he decided to institute a beneficial order in memory of the twelve original organizers of that society. After three years of preparation he organized, in 1871, the first Temple and Tabernacle of the "Order of Twelve of the Knights and Daughters of Tabor," which has for its object the encouragement of Christianity, education, morality and temperance among the colored people. Its object is to teach the art of governing, self-reliance and true manhood and womanhood. Part of its work is to encourage home-building and the acquiring of wealth. The Order, in twenty-seven years, has taken its place with the greatest organizations of the world. It now has more than sixty thousand members, and wields a powerful influence for good among the colored people.

Mr. Dickson was married on the 5th of October, 1848, to Mrs. Mary Elizabeth Peters. She died in 1891. The couple had one child, Mrs. Mamie Augusta Robinson, and one grand-child, who was adopted by the Knights of Tabor, and bears the title of "Princess of the Knights and Daughters of Tabor."

After a long life spent in the service of his race, Mr. Dickson died in the early part of 1902.

INDEX.

	PAGE.
Abbott, Miss Helen,	445
African Zion Methodist Episcopal Church,	89
Alexander, Lieut. John H.,	51
Allen, Bishop Richard,	103
Allen, B. F., Sketch of,	436
Ames, Alexander,	43
Anderson, Duke W.,	86
Anderson, Louis B.,	81
Answers to Question: "Has Your College Training Benefited You?"	376
Antoine, C. C.,	62
Archer, Hiram E.,	444
Archer, Mrs. Henrietta M.,	445
Arnett, Bishop B. W.,	103
Asbury, Bishop,	103
Assessed Value of Real Estate Held by 557 College-bred Negroes,	369
Attucks, Crispus,	42
Babcock, Primus,	43
Ball, J. P.,	199
Barnett, Ferdinand L.,	81
Bassett, E. D.,	62
Birthplace of 650 College-bred Negroes,	334
Blackshear, Edward L., Sketch of,	432
Blackwell, William,	57
Blind Tom,	116
Blocker, Mrs. Sarah A.,	444
Booker, Rev. Dr. Joseph A., Sketch of,	403
Bouey, Rev. H. N., Sketch of,	114
Bowen, Capt. P. J., Sketch of,	53
Bowles, Charles,	43
Boyd, Henry,	199
Brown, Bishop Morris,	103
Brown, Bishop John M.,	103
Brown, Rev. Dr. C. S., Sketch of,	418
Bruce, Blanche K.,	59
Bruce, Roscoe Conkling,	59
Burns, Bishop Francis, Notice of,	95
Burr, Seymour,	43
Business, Kinds of, According to Capital,	159
Business, Kinds of, According to Number of Years Engaged,	159

485

PAGE.

Cain, Richard H., ... 62, 103
Calloway, Thomas J., on the Bestowing of a Harvard Degree on Booker
    Washington, ... 460
Campbell, Bishop Jabez Pitt, ... 103
Campbell, Mrs. Haydee, ... 445
Camper, Miss Julia A , ... 107
Candler, Gov. Allan D., Speech of, ... 133
Carmouche, Lieut. P. L., ... 54
Carroll, Rev. Richard, ... 51
Cassagnac de, Paul Granier, ... 117
Chambers, Miss Judith L., Sketch of, ... 420
Chesnutt, Charles W., Sketch of, ... 122
Chiles, Nick, Sketch of, ... 67
Clark, Mrs. Helen, ... 470
Clark, Private, ... 52
Clark, Daniel, Act to Pension, ... 263
Cleveland, President, Letter from, ... 207
Coburn, Titus, ... 43
Coker, Rev. Daniel, ... 104
Coleman, J. D., Sketch of, ... 417
College-bred Negroes, Important Offices Held by, ... 317
College-bred Negroes, Literary Activity of, ... 375
College Graduates, Migration of, ... 334
College Graduates, Age at which Married, ... 347
College-bred Women Graduates, ... 346
Colored Women, National Conference of, ... 467
Colored Militia, States in which Organized, ... 50
Colored Methodist Episcopal Church, The 108
Conjugal Condition of College-bred Negroes, ... 348
Cooper, E. E., ... 62
Cooper, Mrs. Anna J., ... 445
Corrothers, James D., ... 121
Cotton, Increased Production Under Free Labor, ... 458
Councill, Prof. W. H., Speech in Philadelphia, ... 276
Councill, Prof. W. H., mentioned, ... 438
Crime and Illiteracy, Whites and Blacks Compared, ... 280
Cromwell, Oliver, ... 43
Curricula of Various Negro Colleges and Universities, . . . 323

Danneker, Benjamin, ... 472
Davenport, Mrs. Mary L., ... 470
Davis, John, ... 48
Davis, Alexander, ... 62
Davis, Miss Mattie B., ... 470
Deas, Edmund H., Sketch of, ... 59
Declarations Adopted at Tuskegee Conference, ... 199
De Grasse, John V., ... 82
Delaney, Miss Emma B., Sketch of, ... 106
De Large, Robert C., ... 63
Derham, James, ... 82
Dickerson, Bishop Wm. F., ... 103

PAGE.

Dickson, Rev. Moses, ... 480
Diggs, James R. L., ... 425
Dinkins, Rev. Dr. C. S., Sketch of, ... 400
Disney, Bishop Richard R., ... 103
Dorsey, Rev. J. Harry, ... 64
Douglass, Frederick, ... 77
Dumas, Gen. Alexandre de la Pailleterie, ... 39
Dumas, Alexandre Davy de la Pailleterie, *pere*, . . . 117
Dumas, Alexandre, *fils*, ... 117
Dunbar, Paul Laurence, Sketch of, ... 119
Dunn, Oscar J., ... 62
Dupey, Charles, Henry Clay's Tribute to, ... 478
Durham, John Stephens, ... 116

Eckstein Norton University, ... 431
Elliott, Robert B., ... 63
Escridge, Miss Hattie G., on the Need of Negro Merchants, . . 147
Estill, Monk, ... 45
Evans, L. J., ... 470

Farms Owned by Negroes, in 1890, ... 278
Fearn, C. H., on Negro Co-operative Foundry, ... 154
Francis, Dr. John R., ... 82
Francis, Mrs. John R., ... 445
Freeman, Jordan, ... 43
Fuller, Thomas, ... 472
Future of the Negro, Suggestions and Answers to Questions, . 370

Gaines, Bishop Wesley J., Sketch of, ... 106
Gannett, Deborah, ... 43
Garnet, Belle, ... 82
Garnett, Henry W., ... 62
Gleaves, Richard H., ... 62
Grady, Henry W., Speech in New York, Extracts from, . . 215
Grady, Henry W., Speech in Boston, Extracts from, . . 216
Grant, Bishop Abraham, Sketch of, ... 106
Green, Col. Christopher, ... 42
Griggs, Rev. Dr. A., Sketch of, ... 113
Grove, Jack, ... 44

Ham, Descendants of, ... 33
Hamet, Revolutionary Pensioner, ... 43
Haralson, Jere, ... 63
Hart, Mrs., ... 470
Harvey, Mrs. Daisy Miller, Sketch of, ... 400
Harvey, James, ... 471
Harvey, Lewis, ... 470
Harvey, Will, ... 471
Hathaway, James Shelton, Sketch of, ... 426
Heredia, Jose Maria, ... 116
Hoffman, John Wesley, Sketch of, ... 413

31

PAGE.

Hoke, Rev. Dr. J. H., Sketch of, ... 110
"Honey Chile," a Poem by Miss Inez C. Parker, ... 128
"Hope," a Poem by Miss Inez C. Parker, ... 127
Hope, John, on the Meaning of Business, ... 140
Hope, John, Sketch of, ... 403
Howard, Rev. W. J., Sketch of, ... 96
Howard University, ... 405
Howe, Cato, ... 43
Howell, Hon. Clark, Letter to *New York World*, ... 208
Humphrey, Col. David, ... 42

Jackson, Mary C., ... 445
Jackson, John H., ... 422
Jasper, Rev. John, Sketch of, ... 89
Jefferson, Thomas, and Julius Melbourn, ... 201
Jenkins, Samuel, ... 42
Johnson, John, ... 48
Johnson, Rev. E. P., Sketch of, ... 101
Jonah, Jeremy, ... 43
Jones, Rev. Absalom, ... 104
Jones, Rev. Dr. Joseph E., Sketch of, ... 105
Jones, Miss Anna, ... 444

Kealing, H. T., ... 62
Kenney, Mrs. Maria T., Sketch of, ... 404
Kentucky State Normal and Industrial School, ... 428
Kimble, Miss Mary C., Sketch of, ... 429
Kirby, Rev. Dr. J. W., ... 98

Langston, John M., ... 62
Latham, Lambo, ... 43
Lee, Rev. Dr. James W., Speech Before Current Topics Club, . . . 228
Lee, Rev. Dr. James W., Speech Before St. Louis Evangelical Alliance, . 240
Lethierre, Guillaume Guillen, ... 115
Lew, Barzillai, ... 48
Lewis, Edmonia, ... 115
Liberia, Melbourn's Views of, ... 474
Lindsay, H. E., on Negro Business Men in Columbia, South Carolina, . 148
L'Ouverture, Dominique Francois Toussaint, ... 39
Love, Miss Lulu, ... 444
Lynch, John R., ... 51, 63
Lyons, Judson W., ... 65, 280
Lytle, Miss Lutie A., ... 82

McKee, Col. John, ... 196
McKinley, Dr. J. Frank, ... 82
Maceo, Antonio, ... 51
Maceo, Jose, ... 51
Marshall, Col. J. R., ... 51
Martin, W. L., ... 62
Mayo, Wm. H., ... 445
Meharry Medical College, ... 399

PAGE.

Melbourn, Julius, ... 48–201–472
Miles, Rev. W. H., ... 108
Miles, Alexander, ... 198
Mitchell, John G., ... 62
Morris, Robert, ... 81
Murphy, W. O., on the Negro Grocer, ... 151

Nash, Charles E., ... 49
National Baptist Publishing Board, ... 399
Nazery, Bishop Willis, ... 103
Nelson, Ida Gray, ... 83
Negroes in Northern and Other Colleges, ... 327
Negro Soldiers, Number of, During Revolutionary War, . . . 42
" " Number of, in Civil War, ... 49
" " Enlistments and Service in Spanish War, ... 50
" Lawyer in Paris, France, ... 81
" Divine in London, England, ... 87
" Churches, Church Membership, etc., ... 87
" Business Men in Atlanta, Georgia, ... 158
" Business Men by States, ... 164
" Business Men According to Occupations, ... 166
" Merchants, Twenty Cities Having Twenty or More, . . . 182
" Merchants, Class of Business of, in Twenty-four Cities, . . 182
" Beneficiaries of Schools in Georgia, ... 288
" Population and Wealth, Increase of, . . , . . . 299
" Problems, Annual Conferences Provided to Consider, . . 317
" College Graduates, Number of, ... 328
" " " According to Years and Institutions, . . 333
" Graduates from White Colleges, ... 330
" College Graduates, Childhood and Youth of, ... 336
" " " Occupations of, ... 349

Olsson, Jessie Macaulay, ... 116

Paine, Moses U., ... 109
Parker, Miss Inez C., Sketch of, ... 125
Parrish, Rev. C. H., ... 433
Payne, Bishop D. Alexander, ... 101
Pegues, Albert W., Sketch of, ... 393
Penn, Dr. Wm. F., Sketch of, ... 83
Periodicals Published by Negroes, ... 70
Philippines, Negro Troops Serving in, ... 53
Phillips, Rev. D. W., ... 395
Pinchback, P. B. S., ... 62
Placidio, ... 116
Poor, Salem, ... 43
Poushkin, Alexander, ... 116
Prince, a Soldier, ... 43
Pierce, Rev. Dr. Charles L., ... 430

Quinn, Bishop Wm. Paul, ... 103

  PAGE

Rainey, Joseph H., ... 64
Rausier, Alonzo J., ... 62, 66
Rapier, James T., ... 66
Ray, Miss Charlotte E., ... 81
Reddick, Mrs. Hannah Howell, Sketch of, ... 423
Reddick, M. W., ... 424
Revels, Hiram R., ... 62
Rich, David, Upshur's Tribute to, ... 478
Richards, Prince, ... 43
Richardson, Mrs., ... 79
Roberts, Bishop John Wright, ... 95
Roberts, Robert R., ... 103
Roberts, Rev. Dr. N. F., Sketch of, ... 392
Robinson, Mrs. Rachel E. R. Sketch of, ... 420
Rock, John R., ... 82
Roger Williams University, ... 395
Rucker, H. A., ... 62
Ruffin, Mrs. Josephine St. Pierre, ... 470
Russwurm, John Brown, ... 328

Salem, Peter, ... 43
Scarborough, W. S., ... 442
Scott, I. B., ... 62
Scott, Bishop Levi, ... 95
Screws, Maj. W. W., on Work Done by the Tuskegee School, . . . 300
Scruggs, Enos L., Sketch of, ... 419
Shaw University, ... 387
Shorter, Bishop James A., ... 103
Shurtliff, Robert, ... 43
Siboney, Reminiscence of, ... 52
Simpson, Joshua B., Sketch of, ... 421
Smalls, Robert, ... 49
Smith, John H., ... 62
Smith, Mrs. C. S., ... 470
Stewart, McCants, Sketch of, ... 85
Stillwell, Rev. W. M., ... 89
Stockton, Ben, ... 44
Sweetsa Language, Bible Translated Into, ... 86

Tanner, Bishop Benjamin T., Sketch of, ... 104
Tanner, Henry Ossawa, ... 115
Taylor, Samuel Coleridge, ... 116
Tenney, E. P., Quoted, ... 86
Terrell, Mrs. Mary Church, ... 470
"The Bucks," 44
Thomas, Wm. Hannibal, ... 49
Thomas, A. S., ... 199
Thompson, Grace J., Sketch of, ... 394
Titus, Israel, ... 42
Totten, Rev. Father, ... 65
Truth, Sojourner, ... 76

PAGE.

Turner, Bishop Henry M., Sketch of, ... 98
Turner, J. Milton, ... 62
Turner, Benjamin S., ... ' . . 63
Tuskegee Normal and Industrial Institute, ... 291
Uncles, Rev. C. R., ... 65

Vanderhorst, R. H., ... 108
Vass, Rev. Dr. S. N., Sketch of, ... 100

Walker, E. G., ... 81
Walker, Rev. C. T., ... 51
Waller, Capt. John L., ... 51
Waller, Miss Effie, Sketch of, ... 131
Waller, Rev. Garnett Russell, Sketch of, ... 110
Walls, John T., ... 63
Ward, Bishop Thomas M. D., ... 103
Washington, Booker T., ... 210
    "   " on the Negro and Signs of Civilization, . . 252
    "   " on the Negro's Part in the South's Upbuilding, . 255
    "   " on the Negro and His Relation to the South, . 260
    "   " on Industrial Training, ... 265
    "   " on Tuskegee Normal and Industrial Institute, . 291
    "   " Address in Carnegie Hall, New York, . . . 307
    "   " on the Negro's Economic Value, , . . . 447
    "   " Address on Receiving Harvard Diploma, . . 464
Washington, Mrs. Booker T., ... 445
Waters, Bishop Edward, ... , . 103
Wayman, Bishop Alexander W., ... 103
West, Narcissa, Sketch of, ... 85
Wheatley, Phillis, ... 118
Wheaton, J. Frank, ... 82
"When Daddy Plays de Banjo," Dialect Poem, Miss Parker, . . . 129
White, Rev. C. P. T. 69
Whitted, Rev. Dr. John A., Sketch of, ... 97
Wilcox, Samuel T., ... 199
Williams, George W., Quoted, ... 42, 117
Williams, S. Laing, ... 81
Williams, Dr. Daniel H., ... 82
Williams, Mrs. Fannie Barrier, ... 116, 467
Wilson, Edward, ... 82
Wood, Rev. N. B., ... 62
Wright, Richard R., ... 51, 444

Young, Col. James H., ... 51
Young, Maj. Charles E., ... 51

1000095552

WILKES COLLEGE LIBRARY